The First Negro League Champion:
The 1920 Chicago American GIANTS

Edited by Frederick C. Bush and Bill Nowlin

Associate Editors Carl Riechers and Len Levin

Society for American Baseball Research, Inc.
Phoenix, AZ

The First Negro League Champion: The 1920 Chicago American Giants
Edited by Frederick C. Bush and Bill Nowlin
Associate editors Carl Riechers and Len Levin
Copyright © 2022 Society for American Baseball Research, Inc.
All rights reserved. Reproduction in whole or in part without permission is prohibited.
ISBN 978-1-970159-79-0 Ebook
ISBN 978-1-970159-80-6 1920 Paper
Library of Congress Control Number: 2022908381

Cover images: Bingo DeMoss, Rube Foster, Dave Malacher, Jelly Gardner, and Dave Brown –
all by Graig Kreindler.
5" x 7" Oils on linen mounted to panel
From the collection of Jay Caldwell.
L to R: Front row: Jim Brown, Otis Starks, George Dixon, Dave Malarcher, Dave Brown, unidentified,
Jim Reese, unidentified. Back row: Cristobal Torriente, Tom Johnson, unidentified, unidentified, Rube Foster,
Bingo DeMoss, Leroy Grant, Tom Williams, Jack Marshall. Courtesy of NoirTech Research, Inc.
Book design: Rachael E. Sullivan

Society for American Baseball Research, Inc.
Cronkite School at ASU
555 N. Central Ave. #416
Phoenix, AZ 85004
Phone: (602) 496-1460
Web: www.sabr.org
Facebook: Society for American Baseball Research
Twitter: @SABR

CONTENTS

PREFACE AND ACKNOWLEDGMENTS

On December 16, 2020, Major League Baseball announced that seven Negro Leagues, from various seasons spanning the years 1920 to 1948, were being recognized as major leagues and that all statistics from those leagues and seasons would henceforth be considered part of the major league record books. The earliest league to be included is the first iteration of the Negro National League (NNL), founded by Rube Foster, which extended from 1920 through the end of 1931. Foster, as owner and manager, led his 1920 Chicago American Giants squad to the NNL1's inaugural championship.

That first Black major-league title-winning squad is featured here in the fifth volume of a SABR series on great teams from Negro Leagues history. Rube Foster and John Schorling, Foster's White business partner, are featured. Biographies of every player on the team include Cristóbal Torriente, a member of both the National Baseball Hall of Fame and the Cuban Baseball Hall of Fame, as well as early Blackball stalwarts Dave "Lefty" Brown, Bingo DeMoss, Judy Gans, Dave Malarcher, Frank Warfield, and Frank Wickware. The American Giants' home field, Schorling Park, is also chronicled. A comprehensive timeline of the 1920 season, a history of the founding of the Negro National League in 1920, and the complete story of Foster's franchise, both during his ownership and beyond, round out the narrative of the American Giants franchise. A generous number of historical photographs are also included to illustrate the players and events recounted here and to commemorate this landmark team.

As has been the case with other teams profiled in this series, several players are listed in various sources as members of the 1920 Chicago American Giants but turned out not to have played for the team or were so obscure that no information about them could be discovered. In a couple of instances, the players in question played only the briefest of roles with the team and there was not enough information about them for a full biography. The following players fall into one of these three categories:

1) ? Gerhart. SABR researchers Rich Bogovich and Margaret "Peggy" Gripshover corresponded and collaborated on the effort to locate information about this mysterious player for whom no first name is available and who is credited with only one plate appearance for the American Giants on the Seamheads.com Negro Leagues database. Although the two researchers uncovered some intriguing possibilities, none of them bore the fruit of certainty. Thus, Gerhart's identity currently remains unknown.

2) Ralph "Squire" Moore. *The Biographical Encyclopedia of the Negro Baseball Leagues* (1994) and *The Negro Leagues Book* (1994) both list this player as a pitcher for the American Giants. Seamheads.com lists a pitcher named Square (also "Squire") Moore, who played for many of the teams listed under the entry for "Moore, Ralph Thomas (Squire)" in *The Negro Leagues Book, Volume 2* (2020). However, Square Moore was born in Little Rock, Arkansas, in 1900, and Seamheads.com does not list him as having played for any professional Negro League team until 1923. A player named Ralph Thomas Moore, who was born in Mooresburg, Tennessee, in 1897, and his brother, Roy Moore, who was born in the same town in 1893, both played for the Cleveland Tate Stars in 1921, but no news articles or box scores were found to indicate that Ralph Thomas Moore was a member of the 1920 American Giants.

3) Otis "Lefty" Starks. *The Negro Leagues Book* lists Starks as a pitcher for the 1920 American Giants. However, a game recap in the April 25, 1921, edition of the *Chicago Tribune* referred to "Lefty Starks, Rube Foster's new hurler," indicating that the 1921 season marked the first time that Starks had pitched for the Chicago squad. Additionally, Seamheads.com lists

Lefty Otis Starks is sometimes listed on the roster of the 1920 American Giants; however, he did not join the team until 1921 when he had a 4-2 record for Chicago's second NNL championship squad.

(*Courtesy Noir-Tech Research, Inc.*)

1921 as the only season in which he pitched for the American Giants.

4) John "Red" Taylor. *The Negro Leagues Book* and *The Negro Leagues Book, Volume 2* both list John "Red" Taylor as a pitcher for the 1920 Chicago American Giants. However, news articles and box scores, as well as the Seamheads.com database, indicate that Taylor played for the similarly named Chicago Giants, an intracity and intraleague rival of Foster's American Giants, and pitched to a 2-11 record on the season for that team. The lone exception occurs in the May 1 edition of the *Chicago Defender*, which published a recap of an April 25 exhibition game headlined "Leaguers Rout the Giants" in which it wrote that "Big Taylor, the pitcher recruit was put on trial for his baseball life with the American Giants." John "Red" Taylor was also known by the nickname "Big" at times; thus, given the *Defender's* wording, he may have pitched this single preseason game as a tryout for the American Giants in 1920. There remains the remote possibility that the "Big" Taylor in question here was a different pitcher altogether.

5) ? Taylor. A player named Taylor, whose first name is unknown, is listed on Seamheads.com as having had a 0-for-4 day at the plate while manning third base for the American Giants in one game. No new information has been discovered to shed light on the identity of this player.

6) ? Wiggins. Both *The Biographical Encyclopedia of the Negro Leagues* and *The Negro Leagues Book* list Maurice Wiggins as a shortstop for Foster's 1920 squad. *The Negro Leagues Book, Volume 2* lists a shortstop named Wiggins, first name unknown, as a member of the 1920 American Giants and lists a shortstop named Maurice Caldwell Wiggins as having been a member of the Gilkerson's Union Giants in 1932 and the Chicago Palmer House Stars in 1939, but it does not indicate that these two individuals are the same player. Oddly, Seamheads.com has no listing at all for a player named Maurice Wiggins, or for any player by that last name who played for the American Giants at any time.

Our research uncovered articles and box scores for three games that listed a shortstop-third baseman named Wiggins, without any mention of his first name, as playing for the American Giants. Evidently Wiggins made his debut in an April 11 game against the Rogers Park team at Schorling Park. The April 17 edition of the *Chicago Defender* ran a game recap headlined "Foster's Crew are Trounced" in which it stated, "Wiggins, the recruit infielder, was given an opportunity to display his goods, and the fans voiced their approval of his form and ability." Wiggins garnered his only hit in his second game, an April 25 exhibition contest at Schorling Park in which the *Chicago Defender's* May 1 recap (headlined "Leaguers Rout the Giants") noted, "Wrriggins [*sic*] was not at home on the hot corner." The misspelling of Wiggins's last name leads to the question whether the player in question might have been Arvell Riggins. The box score in the April 26 edition of the *Chicago Tribune* had "Wiggins" at third base for Chicago, which supports the idea of a player named Wiggins. However, Arvell Riggins was also a shortstop at the outset of his career and, in the *Defender's* words, "was not at home on the hot corner" either. Thus, it is entirely possible that there never was a player named Wiggins who played for the American Giants in 1920; it may have been Riggins all along, and the press simply had the incorrect name.

Wiggins was listed in the box score for one final game against the Dayton Marcos on May 16 at Schorling Park. It was the only league game in which he played, likely because he made three errors in the contest. Foster reassigned Arvell Riggins to the Detroit Stars early in the season; if the player in question truly was Riggins, then this three-error game may have been what prompted Foster to reassign Riggins. The *Chicago Defender's* May 22 recap, which is headlined "American Giants Walloped by the Dayton Marcos," creates additional confusion by listing "Wiggins" in the box score but then erroneously referring to him as "Wingfield" in the article about the game. This error is easily cleared up: David Wingfield did play in this game, but he manned second base for Dayton.

7) **David Wingfield.** A May 27 article in the *Atlanta Constitution*, headlined "Black Crackers Sell Star Center Fielder," reported that the Atlanta Black Crackers had sold Wingfield to the American Giants. However, Wingfield did not play a single game for Chicago as league president Rube Foster assigned him to the Dayton Marcos, for whom he played in the outfield and at second base (as mentioned above in the final paragraph about Wiggins).

We would, of course, welcome more information on any of the above.

This book is the result of the collaborative efforts of more than 20 SABR members, each of whom has been dedicated to uncovering as much information as possible about their subjects. Our thanks go to the efforts of all the authors as well as our fact-checker, Carl Riechers, and our final copy editor, Len Levin. Numerous other individuals contributed to this book, and most of these persons have been acknowledged by the authors at the end of their articles. Special thanks go to Graig Kreindler, who generously contributed his Negro League baseball card art for our front cover, and to SABR's Negro Leagues Research Committee Chair Larry Lester and his company Noir-Tech Research, Inc., for providing many of the photographs found herein. As always, if we have neglected to mention anyone who has given assistance, we offer our apologies now.

It is our hope that readers will learn much about this landmark team from *The First Negro League Champion: The 1920 Chicago American Giants*. We are already looking forward to presenting the next volume in this series, which will feature the 1934 Philadelphia Stars, champions of the second iteration of the Negro National League.

Frederick C. Bush
Bill Nowlin
February 2022

RUDOLPH ASH

BY FREDERICK C. BUSH

Rudolph Ash played in eight league games for the 1920 NNL champion Chicago American Giants, though he also may have participated in a few exhibition games. Subsequently, it took another three years before

Rudolph Ash, who batted .208 in a brief stint with Chicago in 1920, is pictured here in his University of Michigan uniform. He batted .405 for Michigan's 1923 Big 10 championship squad.

Ash's name again was mentioned in association with baseball in the press. At that time, he was enrolled in the University of Michigan in Ann Arbor, where he was – in one sense – a college precursor to Jackie Robinson. As it turned out, Ash's collegiate baseball career lasted only slightly longer than his stint with the American Giants. After he moved from his native state of Indiana to New York City in 1926, Ash had one last cup of coffee in the Eastern Colored League. Ed Bolden signed Ash to his Hilldale club,[1] but he played in only one league game before being released. He caught on with the Newark Stars in June and played in three games before an unexpected circumstance ended his season and his pursuit of a career as a professional baseball player.

After Ash married in 1927, he found employment off the diamond, although he also played semipro ball for a few more years. In 1942, Ash's coach at Michigan, Ray Fisher, named him as a member of his all-time Michigan baseball team.[2] Fisher had pitched to a career 100-94 record with a 2.82 ERA for the New York Yankees (1910-17) and Cincinnati Reds (1919-20). As of 2021, he was still Michigan's winningest head coach, having led his teams to a 636-295-9 record and one national championship between 1921 and 1958.[3] The fact that Fisher bestowed such high praise on an athlete who had participated in his program for only one year was remarkable, but it also poses the question why Ash did not have a successful professional career. Perhaps Rube Foster, the American Giants' Hall of Fame owner, was correct when, upon firing drunken former college pitcher Tom Williams in 1918, he asserted that "in all his experience in baseball this sort of players [college players] are the hardest kind to keep straight in the world."[4] Considering why Ash left Michigan, it is entirely possible that Foster's comment could be applied to him as well.

Ash's family background and college years are perhaps of more historical interest than his stunted professional baseball career. Regarding his ancestry, he was descended from one of the first Black families to settle in South Bend, Indiana. Ash's maternal great-grandfather, Pharaoh Powell, was a freed slave from South Carolina who brought his wife, Rebecca, and their children to the Hoosier State circa 1853.[5] The fact that Powell settled in Indiana at that time put his family and the residents of South Bend who allowed him to stay there in violation of Article 13 of Indiana's 1851 state constitution, which read:

"Section 1: No negro or mulatto shall come into or settle in the State, after the adoption of this Constitution.

Section 2: All contracts made with any Negro or Mulatto coming into the State, contrary to the provisions of the foregoing section, shall be void; and any person who shall employ such Negro or Mulatto, or otherwise encourage him to remain in the State, shall be fined in any sum not less than ten dollars, nor more than five hundred dollars."[6]

The law also stipulated that all fines collected for violations of Article 13 would be set aside to send the "negro or mulatto" in question to Liberia, if said person(s) were willing to emigrate there.

Despite Indiana's official hard-line stance against Black settlers, the city of South Bend proved to be a hospitable location, and no one is known to have been fined under Article 13. According to a local historian, "Beginning in 1858, Pharaoh Powell bought several acres of land to the southwest of downtown South Bend, in Union Township, along Main Street and elsewhere in the county."[7] In addition to becoming a prominent family in the area, three of the Powells' sons enlisted in the Union Army to fight in the Civil War.[8]

Pharaoh and Rebecca's daughter, Nancy Powell, married William Henderson on August 5, 1879. Henderson was from La Porte County, Indiana, and had also served in the Civil War. At a banquet given in his honor in October 1934, he recollected, "My ancestors were freed slaves. When about 13 years of age,

I entered the civil war [sic] near its close as a handy boy to Colonel Milroy, of the Ninth Indiana Infantry. Peace was declared before I saw a battle."[9] William later moved to South Bend, where he met Nancy.

William and Nancy Henderson had one child, a daughter named Cora Bell, who was born on January 8, 1881. On February 21, 1899, Cora Bell Henderson married Thaddeus Ash, who was from Michigan, and the couple resided with the Hendersons. Rudolph Thaddeus Ash, the future baseball player, was born on November 2, 1899, in South Bend.

Although William Henderson provided a roof over his daughter and son-in-law's heads, he was not so well off that he could support them financially. Henderson worked as a waiter at the Grand Central Hotel while Thaddeus Ash held a job as a porter and Cora found work at the local YMCA. The family's hardscrabble existence is hinted at by how young Rudolph Ash referred to himself in his 1906 letter to Santa Claus, which was printed in the *South Bend Tribune* on December 15. Seven-year-old Rudolph wrote (with all misspellings and grammar errors left intact by the newspaper):

"Dear Santa Clause – I want a new suit and a cap and a pair shoes and lagerns. Please send also a large engine with 5 cars and a coal car. I want a Xmas book with nice Xmas pieces in it. I would like to have all these things hung on a tree in my parlor good by Santa Clause please make some little poor boy happy thanks for every thing I am Rudolph Ash 422 S Main St South Bend Ind."[10]

His childhood interest in railroads cars must have had a lifelong appeal for Ash, since he eventually found a career with the Pennsylvania Railroad and worked for the company long enough to receive a pension.

Less than a year after Christmas 1906, life became harsher for Ash's family due to his father's excessive drinking. On July 11, 1907, Thaddeus Ash pleaded guilty to charges of assault and battery upon his wife and father-in-law. He was ordered to pay $20 (a $5 fine and $15 for court costs) and received a 30-day jail sentence. However, "upon his promise to the court as well as his father-in-law to refrain from drinking in the future, he was released upon suspended sentence by paying the fine and costs."[11]

Thaddeus soon reneged on his promise and he and Cora separated on August 9, 1907. Thaddeus moved back to Kalamazoo, Michigan, and young Rudolph continued to live with his mother and his grandparents in South Bend. Thaddeus kept in touch with Rudolph and even listed him as his contact on his World War I draft registration card in 1918. It appears that Cora wanted to give her husband every chance to make good; however, on February 23, 1917, she finally sued for divorce, "making a general charge of cruel and inhuman treatment."[12]

According to the US Census, South Bend had seen a 49.1 percent population growth between 1900 and 1910, and the crime that often accompanies such growth affected the Henderson-Ash household in 1911. A thief who had become known as a "gentleman burglar" had been working the neighborhood and continually eluded the police. On October 9 he targeted the Henderson house, but he picked the wrong time as its occupants were still awake. Cora "screamed while her father stood by the rear window with a club in hand to receive the midnight visitor, but he was frightened away."[13]

Although Ash and his family had their struggles, he also experienced some benefits of growing up in South Bend. At a time when most schools throughout America were still segregated, Ash was able to attend South Bend High School, the only high school in town, and graduated in 1918.[14] In September Ash registered for the draft and indicated that he was working at Notre Dame University and was preparing to attend college.

As the United States continued to ramp up its war efforts since having become involved in World War I the previous year, Ash joined the Student Army Training Corps at Indiana University in Bloomington. The Corps existed on many campuses and had been "created to keep students in college while preparing to fight the war."[15] At Indiana University it "included four companies and well over 1,000 men. Members wore uniforms, were paid $30 a month and lived in barracks that were converted fraternity houses."[16]

Ash was one of "only a handful" of Black men at Indiana University, who "drill[ed] with white classmates and liv[ed] separately in Barracks No. 7."[17] All branches of the US military maintained racially segregated units at that time; thus, the separate living quarters at IU were no surprise. However, by drilling with their White classmates, Ash and his Black classmates had become trailblazers. John Summerlot, the director of the university's Veterans Support Services, asserted, "I would argue the first racially integrated Army unit was the SATC. And it may have been just

at IU. I've yet to find any other integrated SATC units during World War I."[18]

When the 1918 flu pandemic reached Bloomington, Indiana's State Board of Health closed the IU campus from October 10 until November 4. As a result, "SATC members were confined to their barracks, and other students were sent home. ... By the end of December 1918, the SATC members had been discharged from the military."[19] Ash returned home to South Bend in time for Christmas. Before the next academic year, he visited his father in Kalamazoo and then announced that he was going to attend the University of Michigan.[20]

Surprisingly, since Ash had not spent any time in the limelight, his life had been well documented to this point. South Bend directories and the 1920 US Census list Ash as a university student, presumably at the University of Michigan, although he was not yet a member of the Wolverines' baseball team. He did, however, have a brief stint with Chicago American Giants in the summer of 1920.

Ash must have played baseball somewhere to be discovered and signed by Foster, but when and where are unknown. Ash was so unfamiliar to the Chicago press that he was listed in box scores as "Rudolph" more often than by his surname, Ash. Professional baseball may have been just a summer diversion for Ash as he received most of his playing time in July. He manned left field in a series against the St. Louis Giants from July 11 to 13 at Schorling Park in Chicago; the American Giants triumphed by scores of 5-2, 4-2, and 7-6. Ash, listed as "Rudolph" for all three contests, contributed two hits in the middle game and scored a run in the July 13 contest.[21]

On July 19 Ash – now listed in the box score by his surname – played right field in a 3-1 triumph over the Dayton Marcos at Schorling Park.[22] He had one hit but did not score a run. Ash participated only in games in Chicago, a city that he and his family often visited. He did not distinguish himself during his brief time with the American Giants; he batted .208 (5-for-24), scored three runs, and had two RBIs in eight NNL games.

In October, it was reported that Ash had "returned to Ann Arbor, Mich., where he [was to] resume his law studies at the University of Michigan."[23] At this point in his life, Ash did not yet combine academic and baseball pursuits. In late May of 1921, after the spring semester ended, it was reported that "Jess Elster and his new gang of Colored Athletics" from Grand Rapids, Michigan, had "obtained Rudolph Ash of Ann Arbor, an infielder, who should be a big attraction during the season."[24] No further mention of Ash is found in articles about the Colored Athletics' games; he may not have reported to Elster's team after all.

After a one-year baseball hiatus, Ash popped up again in 1923. The *Chicago Defender* claimed, "Rudolph Ash of South Bend, Ind., is the first student of Color to ever play on the Michigan university baseball team."[25] Since the *Defender* had not been founded until 1905, perhaps it can be forgiven for its error. However, the fact is that Moses Fleetwood Walker had enrolled at Michigan in 1881 and had become the first Black player on the university's baseball team in 1882.[26] Ash held the distinction of being Michigan's first Black baseball player in the twentieth century. As such, he was a precursor to Jackie Robinson. In 1946 Robinson – at the outset of his Hall of Fame career – became the first Black player in the International League since Walker in 1889 (Syracuse) and, in 1947, the first Black player in the White major leagues since Walker in 1884 (Toledo).

Ash made the most out of his on-field opportunities for Michigan. On May 5, against Notre Dame – his former employer – Ash "clouted a home run in the tenth after the score stood 10 all in the ninth and won the game."[27] Two days later, in a victory over Iowa, "Ash's rap sent in two runs in the early part of the game ... [and] in the tenth he again aided in pushing his teammate to third from where he scored on the next play."[28]

Ash continued to excel as Michigan went 10-0 in Big Ten Conference play in 1923. In a 6-3 win over the University of Illinois on May 12 in Urbana, Illinois, Ash and catcher Jack Blott were "responsible for the Michigan victory" in front of "[a] crowd estimated at 10,000."[29] Ash was 3-for-5 at the plate and scored a run. Against Ohio State on May 28, he hit an RBI triple in the top of the first inning and scored on an error as Michigan prevailed, 5-2. He went 2-for-4, scored two runs, and stole second base in the seventh inning (which led to his second run scored).[30]

Ash batted .405 for the season for Michigan's Big Ten championship squad and made a name for himself in baseball circles.[31] He spent the summer back home in South Bend, and, in July he agreed to be co-director of a YMCA camp "for the colored boys of the city" that was "the first camp of its kind to be directed in the state of Indiana."[32] Ash was hailed by his hometown press as the "foremost athlete in the city and Michigan university outfielder extraordinary [sic]."[33]

Ash had certainly turned heads on the baseball diamond for Michigan in 1923. However, he had failed to distinguish himself in the classroom. In a report about how Michigan's athletes had fared on their June exams, the *Grand Rapids Press* noted, "Very few athletes met with reverses during the past term although Rudolph Ash, star Negro outfielder and leading hitter on the Michigan baseball team, failed in his studies and it is doubtful if he will return next season."[34]

The *Press*'s prediction was accurate, and Ash's collegiate baseball career was at an end. More than a year later, in December 1924, it was reported that "Rudolph Ash, who is attending the University of Chicago, is spending his vacation with his mother, Mrs. Cora B. Hill, 428 South Main Street."[35] Six years after her divorce, Cora had married Henry Hill on July 24, 1923.

The cause for Ash's failure at the University of Michigan is unknown. The stereotype about college students who like to drink and have a good time, rather than to study and earn a degree, is an old one but is right on the mark for some individuals. Rube Foster implied as much about college students' drinking and behavior in his 1918 comment after he fired Tom Williams. Whether Ash exhibited some of his father's fondness for alcohol while in college is a matter of speculation, and unsubstantiated conclusions on the matter would wrongfully impugn an otherwise respectable reputation. One thing is certain, however, and that is the fact that Ash never graduated from the University of Chicago either; the 1940 census lists his highest grade completed in school as "College, 3rd year."

In 1926, sans college diploma, Ash moved to New York City, though he apparently spent some amount of time in Philadelphia as well. Ed Bolden signed him for his Hilldale (Darby, Pennsylvania) Daisies, a member club of the Eastern Colored League, and gave him only the briefest tryout: one game in which he did not even make a plate appearance. Ash then signed with the ECL's Newark Stars and was in the lineup for both games of a June 20 doubleheader against the New York Lincoln Giants at the Catholic Protectory Oval in the Bronx. Ash manned right field in both contests and was 1-for-4 at the plate in each game as well. He scored one run in Newark's 7-6 loss in the opener but did not score in the Stars' 9-2 victory in the nightcap. The Game Two triumph was the first win in nine ECL games for Newark.[36]

Ash batted .200 (2-for-10) in three games for Newark, but his stint with the team was not cut short due to his performance. On July 10, the *New York Age* reported, "The Newark Stars, organized at the beginning of this season by Andy Harris, have 'given up the ghost,' at least for the remainder of this season. ...

Lack of money to pay salaries is said to have caused several members of the team to quit even before the project was finally abandoned."[37]

After the Newark franchise folded in 1926, Ash turned his attention to Anna Perdita Sanford, his bride-to-be. The couple was married on June 9, 1927, in Brooklyn. Perdita gave birth to their only child, Rudolph Thaddeus Ash Jr., on November 17, 1928. Ash found steady work to support his new family, but he continued to indulge his love for baseball by playing for various semipro squads for a time, including occasional stints with Ed Bolden's Darby Phantoms.[38] However, baseball was now an avocation and, by the time of the 1940 census, Ash's occupation was listed as "red cap,"[39] and on his 1942 World War II draft registration card he listed the Pennsylvania Railroad as his employer. Ash worked for the railroad until his retirement.

Ash's father, Thaddeus, had died in May 1928, six months before Rudolph Jr.'s birth, and his mother, Cora, died in 1931. His grandfather, William Henderson, long outlived his wife – Nancy Powell Henderson, who had died in 1922 – and was, in 1940, the last family member from Ash's childhood home to pass away. Rudolph Thaddeus Ash Sr. died on February 16, 1977, in New York City "after a two-week illness" of an unspecified nature.[40] Upon Ash's death, his body was returned to South Bend for burial.

Rudolph Jr. served in the Army during the Korean War and later worked for the General Motors Corporation. He died on September 26, 1980, in the Veterans Administration Hospital in New Rochelle, New York, at the youthful age of 51.[41] As had been the case with his father, no cause of death was given, and his body was interred in South Bend.

After the deaths of her husband and son, Perdita Ash – who was originally from Macon, Georgia – moved from New York City to South Bend. Members of her husband's extended family, the Powells from his maternal grandmother's side, still lived there and she connected with them. Perdita died on February 17, 1985, at the Fountainview Place nursing home in Mishawaka, Indiana, which is a few miles west of South Bend.[42]

Rudolph Sr., Perdita, and Rudolph Jr. are buried in South Bend's Highland Cemetery. They were the last of the Ash family in South Bend, but other descendants of Pharoah and Rebecca Powell still live in the city.

SOURCES

All Negro League player statistics and team records were taken from Seamheads.com, except where otherwise indicated.

Ancestry.com was consulted for US Census information; military records; as well as birth, marriage, and death records.

NOTES

1   Neil Lanctot, *Fair Dealing & Clean Playing: The Hilldale Club and the Development of Black Professional Baseball, 1919-1932* (Syracuse: Syracuse University Press, 1994), 146.

2   "Johnny Gee Starts Fast/Long Michigan Pitcher Does Well for Toronto in Opener; Saginaw Honors Top Bowler, *Grand Rapids Press*, May 20, 1942: 19.

3   "Michigan Baseball Coaching History," https://mgoblue.com/news/2009/6/5/michigan_baseball_coaching_history.aspx, accessed June 6, 2021.

4   "Rube Fires Tom Williams Outright: Latter Is Accused of Being Under Influence of Liquor on Training Trip," *Chicago Defender*, April 6, 1918: 9. Williams had attended Morris Brown College in Atlanta.

5   Jeanne Derbeck, "Plan Powell House Benefit," *South Bend Tribune*, February 24, 1975: 17.

6   "Article 13 – Negroes and Mulattoes," Indiana Constitution of 1851 as originally written, https://www.in.gov/history/about-in-diana-history-and-trivia/explore-indiana-history-by-topic/indiana-documents-leading-to-statehood/constitution-of-1851-as-origi-nally-written/article-13-negroes-and-mulattoes/, accessed June 6, 2021.

7   Travis Childs, "Blacks Settled in the Area Around Potato Creek State Park in 1830s, 1840s," *South Bend Tribune*, January 29, 2006: B7.

8   Childs.

9   "'Handy Boy' in Civil War Dies at South Bend," *Indianapolis Recorder*, February 3, 1940: 8.

10   "South Bend, Ind., Dec. 5, 1906," *South Bend Tribune*, December 15, 1906: 30.

11   "Promises to Be Good," *South Bend Tribune*, July 11, 1907: 5.

12   "Wife Asks Divorce," *South Bend Tribune*, February 23, 1917: 9.

13   "Bold Thief Still Defies Detectives," *South Bend Tribune*, October 10, 1911: 5.

14   "In Colored Circles," *South Bend News-Times*, June 6, 1918: 6.

15   "World War I Transformed Campus, Opened Indiana University to the World," IU and World War I, https://news.iu.edu/stories/features/world-war-i-anniversary/iu-during-wartime.html, accessed June 7, 2021.

16   "World War I Transformed Campus."

17   "World War I Transformed Campus."

18   "World War I Transformed Campus."

19   "World War I Transformed Campus."

20   Ellis S. Bell, "South Bend Ind.," *Chicago Whip*, October 4, 1919: 9.

21   "Fosters Upset St. Louis Giants," *Chicago Tribune*, July 12, 1920: 15; "Foster's Giants Win Again, 4-2," *Chicago Tribune*, July 13, 1920: 13; "Fosters, 7; St. Louis, 6," *Chicago Tribune*, July 14, 1920: 15.

22   "American Giants Trim Dayton Nine Again, 3-1," *Chicago Tribune*, July 20, 1920: 14.

23   "Society," *South Bend Tribune*, October 9, 1920: 5.

24   "Elster and Reuben Will Clash Again on Ramona Field," *Grand Rapids Press*, May 25, 1921: 18. Ash normally played the outfield, both in college

THE 1920 CHICAGO AMERICAN GIANTS

and as a professional; however, he did play one game at second base for the American Giants in 1920, so he could play certain infield positions as well.

25   "Rudolph Ash Makes Good at Michigan 'U,'"
      Chicago Defender, May 12, 1923: 10.

26   "Moses Fleetwood Walker," Go Blue: Competition, Controversy,
      and Community in Michigan Athletics, http://michiganinthe-
      world.history.lsa.umich.edu/michiganathletics/exhibits/show/
      key-players/fleetwood-walker, accessed June 7, 2021.

27   "Rudolph Ash Makes Good at Michigan 'U.'"

28   "Rudolph Ash Makes Good at Michigan 'U.'"

29   "Michigan in Great Rally Beat Illini," *Rockford*
      (Illinois) *Republic*, May 14, 1923: 8.

30   "Ohio State Fails to Grasp Chance/Michigan Keeps Its
      Conference Slate Clean by Defeating Our Boys, 5-2,"
      Columbus (Ohio) *Dispatch*, May 29, 1923: 14.

31   James Tobin, "The Belford Lawson Mystery: A Family Story and Racism's
      Long Shadow, *Ann Arbor Observer*, https://annarborobserver.com/articles/
      the_belford_lawson_mystery.html#.YL5NPvlKjIU, accessed June 7, 2021.

32   "Will Open Camp Lincoln," *South Bend Tribune*, July 22, 1923: 17.

33   "Will Open Camp Lincoln."

34   "Michigan Grid Heroes Pass June Exams," *Grand
      Rapids Press*, June 28, 1923: 23.

35   "In Colored Circles," *South Bend Tribune*, December 22, 1924: 10.

36   "Newark Stars at Last Win Game in Eastern Colored
      League Race," *New York Age*, June 26, 1926: 6.

37   "Newark Stars Disbanded," *New York Age*, July 10, 1926: 6.

38   "Corley Cashes In," *Philadelphia Inquirer*, May 1, 1929: 23; "Phantoms
      Win First from Rival Foes," *Philadelphia Inquirer*, July 10, 1929: 18;
      "Darby Phantoms Win," *Philadelphia Inquirer*, August 3, 1930: 42. The
      January 31, 1986, edition of the *South Bend Tribune* contained a photo of
      a jersey worn by Ash that had the name Tigers across the front ("Museum
      Exhibit to Mark Black Experience in Area," *South Bend Tribune*, January
      31, 1986: 15). Inquiries to the History Museum in South Bend, where the
      exhibit containing the jersey was housed, yielded no information due to
      the change of museum personnel in the interval between 1986 and 2021.
      In a July 13, 2021, email to this author, Negro League researcher Gary
      Ashwill wrote, "To my knowledge Ash didn't play for the Philadelphia
      Tigers, but there were semipro teams in the Philadelphia area in the late
      1920s called Tigers – most notably the Main Line Tigers, but also the
      Norwood Tigers." No newspaper articles were found to indicate which
      Tigers team Ash played for, and efforts to locate any surviving mem-
      bers of Ash's extended family proved unfruitful. Currently, it appears
      that the year 1930 may have marked Ash's last attempt to play baseball
      (whether as a semipro or professional) as the final mention of his name
      is found in that year's August 3 edition of the *Philadelphia Inquirer*.

39   Red caps – so-called because they wore red caps in the early
      twentieth century – were porters at train stations.

40   "Rudolph T. Ash," *South Bend Tribune*, February 20, 1977: 49.

41   "Rudolph T. Ashe," *South Bend Tribune*, September 27, 1980: 6. Either
      Rudolph Jr. added an "e" to his last name, perhaps to distinguish himself
      from his father, or the *Tribune* inadvertently added the letter to the name.

42   "Anna Perdita Ash," *South Bend Tribune*, February 18, 1985: 20.

EDDIE BOYD

BY FREDERICK C. BUSH

Eddie Boyd was a little-known player who had brief stints with the Detroit Stars and Chicago American Giants in 1920, the first year of the Negro National League's existence. After his time with those two franchises, Boyd became a jack of all trades for the barnstorming Winnipeg Giants team that served as a developmental squad for the entire NNL. In 1921 he continued to travel throughout the Upper Midwest – Wisconsin, Minnesota, North Dakota – and Canada with essentially the same team, which now called itself the Calgary Black Sox. Amazingly, during his two barnstorming seasons, Boyd is known to have played every position except first base and second base, displaying a versatility not often seen that should have made him a prized commodity. However, after the 1921 season, Boyd retreated into the anonymity whence he had come, and there is no further public record of his whereabouts until his death in 1962.

On his June 5, 1917, World War I draft registration card, Henderson Edward Boyd listed his date of birth as January 23, 1893,[1] and his place of birth as St. Louis. Boyd lived in Kansas City, Missouri, at the time, recorded his marital status as single, and attempted to claim an exemption from the draft by stating that his father and a brother were his dependents.[2] The 1920 US Census indicates that Boyd's mother and father both had been born in Arkansas; however, no further records of the family in Arkansas or Missouri have been discovered, and it is unknown whether his mother was deceased or whether his parents were separated or divorced.

Although Boyd's exact origins appear to have been lost to history, two events that occurred after he registered for the draft are certainties. The first is that he did not receive an exemption. Instead, he was drafted into the Army and served in Company D of the 806th Pioneer Infantry Regiment. The second is that he married his wife, Lottie, before being drafted since she is listed as his contact person in wartime military records.[3]

Boyd's military service began in July 1918; the 806th was organized that month at Camp Funston, Kansas. All branches of the US military were still segregated at this time, and Boyd's regiment was one of 20 African American regiments, out of a total of 37, in the Pioneer Infantry. After two months of training, Private Henderson E. Boyd and the 806th shipped out from Hoboken, New Jersey, aboard the *USS Mercury* on September 8, 1918, and arrived in Brest, France, on September 21.

Colonel Joseph L. Gilbreth of the 51st Pioneer Infantry described the Pioneer regiments' responsibilities for the public in 1919. Regarding the infantry portion of their duties, he wrote that they "are not primarily fighting troops, but are trained as Infantry, simply in so far as to be able to protect their working parties."[4] Their work consisted of "semi-technical" combat engineering that included building "temporary roads, railroads, bridges, trenches and all kinds of shelter both in active operations and in rest areas. They make demolitions and destroy enemy obstacles so as to prepare the ground for the advance of our attacking troops."[5] An unknown Pioneer Infantry officer described their assignment more succinctly, asserting, "They did everything the Infantry was too proud to do, and the Engineers too lazy to do."[6] In sum, these troops had to work with a shovel in one hand, a rifle in the other, and their heads on swivels.

The Pioneer Infantry regiments were "attached to armies or corps on an as-needed basis,"[7] but not all of them saw combat. Boyd's regiment was attached to the US First Army and was involved in combat during the Meuse-Argonne Offensive in France from October 3 to October 9, 1918. Boyd served honorably and well, as is evidenced by the fact that by the time the 806th returned to the United States in June 1919, he had attained the rank of corporal. Boyd's regiment was briefly stationed at Camp Upton, New York, and then the troops were discharged from service at Camp Shelby, Mississippi, in July.

After his military service, Boyd returned to his wife in Kansas City. In 1920 he was working as a laborer in one of K.C.'s many meat-packing houses. There is little doubt that Boyd played baseball on his company's team in the city's Packers' League because he came to the attention of Detroit Stars owner Tenny Blount. On February 13, 1920, Blount was in Kansas City to attend the meeting at which the first Negro National League was founded. During that time, he also may have scouted players and signed Boyd; the *Chicago Defender* reported on March 13 that Boyd was to be a member of Detroit's outfield and, in a March 27 article, indicated that Boyd had come from Kansas City.[8] On April 11 the *Detroit Free Press* noted that Blount "has signed players from as far West as Kansas City and as far South as Texas in an effort to make his 1920 club the best in the land."[9]

Although each NNL member franchise signed players for its team, Rube Foster, the league president and the Chicago American Giants owner, wanted competitive balance in the hope that it would ensure the survival of the new league. The *Defender* asserted, "The wisest move made by Foster was in distributing the stars in various clubs, equalizing the playing strength, and each series will be better attended. ... The fans in the cities opposed losing their idols, but as the plan was explained, they warmed up to it."[10] Not only were star players reassigned, but other players who did not make the team for which they tried out were to be "traded to the other clubs in the circuit."[11]

Once all team rosters were filled, the best of the rest were assigned to the Winnipeg Giants (sometimes called the Winnipeg Colored Giants). After the Valley

City, North Dakota, nine had played its first game against Winnipeg, the local newspaper described the team thusly:

> "The Giants are composed of colored ball players, consisting of some of the overflow from the new colored league now in operation in the east. ... The Colored Giants are made up of young players that are not quite old enough and well enough seasoned to make these teams so are 'farmed out' to this traveling organization where they will finish their base ball education."[12]

Although Boyd did not fall into the "not quite old enough" category at 27 years of age, he was assigned to the Winnipeg Giants at the beginning of June.

Before joining the traveling Giants squad, Boyd started in center field for the Stars as the "Detroit 'Semi-pro' baseball season was mustered in for 1920 at Mack Park" on Sunday, April 11.[13] The Stars "wielded the old willow" well as they clobbered the Denby Motors team, 12-0.[14] One week later, on April 18, Boyd – showing the versatility that became his calling card – manned third base as the Stars defeated the Delray All-Stars by a 7-2 score; Boyd had one hit, stole a base, and scored a run in the game.[15]

Exactly when or why Boyd was transferred from the Stars to the Chicago American Giants is unknown. However, in May he played three games in the outfield for Foster's team. He was 1-for-4 with one hit, three walks, and three runs scored. His most important contribution to the American Giants' season took place at Schorling Park in Chicago on May 23. That day,

(Grand Forks Herald, June 7, 1920)

Eddie Boyd and catcher Buck Ewing both had a cup of coffee with the 1920 American Giants but spent most of the year with the Winnipeg Giants, who served as the NNL's developmental squad.

"[m]ore than 7,000 persons witnessed the hand-to-hand battle between the K.C. Monarchs and American Giants."[16] Chicago pitcher Tom Williams, who had relieved starter Dave Brown at the top of the fifth inning, smashed a single to right field in the bottom of the 11th inning that drove home Boyd from second base for a 6-5 victory. The *Chicago Whip*'s game report indicated that there had been some controversy over Boyd's winning run, stating that he "was called safe, then out[,] then safe again."[17] However, neither the *Whip* nor the *Defender* provided any details about the dispute. As mysterious as the circumstances surrounding Boyd's game-winning tally is the reason why he was reassigned to the Winnipeg Giants within about a week after this game.

Whatever transpired, on June 1 Boyd started in center field for Winnipeg in a game against Valley City that the Giants won, 6-5. As had been the case in Chicago on May 23, there was excitement at the very end of the game. In the bottom of the ninth, "with three on and none out[,] Valley City was not allowed to score – two men being caught at the plate in two hair raising plays."[18] This likely was Boyd's first game with Winnipeg, and it was not a memorable affair for him personally. He was hitless and, when he did reach base safely on an error, he was thrown out at second on a steal attempt. Soon, however, Boyd began to flash his versatility and value to the Giants.

Four days later, Boyd started at shortstop in Grand Forks, North Dakota, in a game that Winnipeg lost, 9-6. The local press enthused that "[s]everal sensational catches by the outfielders of both teams added greatly to the interest of the game" and raved that an unassisted double play by Boyd was "nothing short of sensational."[19]

The next day, the same two squads clashed again at Grand Forks' Dacotah Park, and Winnipeg fell by a 6-1 score. It was noted that "[t]he playing field was too heavy to allow any sensational plays because of the heavy rains early Sunday morning."[20] Nonetheless, there was excitement aplenty and Boyd was involved in two key plays for the Giants:

"The visitors' lone run came in the first frame when Boyd, the lead-off man, singled and stole second. Sacrifice hits by Reed and Singer scored him. The 'clouds' nearly scored again in the third when Boyd was up again with two men out. He singled and stole second and third. Two strikes were called on the batter and when Bird started to deliver the ball again[,]

Boyd made a pretty steal to home but the umpire called the pitched ball a strike, retiring the side[,] and the run did not count."[21]

Boyd had started the game in center field but at some point traded positions with catcher William "Buck" Ewing, who also had played one game with the 1920 Chicago American Giants.

Before the third and final game of the series, there were rumblings about bad blood between the two teams. The local newspaper reported, "The colored warriors are peeved about having their perfect record broken and have been saying terrible things during the day about what they are going to do to the locals tonight."[22] The *Daily Herald* failed to recount any of the "terrible things" the Giants players were alleged to have said, but it did print Grand Forks manager Fadden's threat that "there would be dead 'chocolate drops' lying around the field tonight after the game."[23]

As it turned out, the only violence committed in the June 7 game was by the Grand Forks batters against the baseball. Boyd played the entire game at catcher as the locals "gave the Winnipeg Colored Giants a terrible drubbing" by an 11-1 score.[24] Winnipeg manager Sam Gordon tried to smooth over relations between the squads by conceding about the Grand Forks nine, "They are a well organized bunch ... and they play ball like big league clubs."[25]

After the debacle in Grand Forks, the Giants continued to barnstorm through the Upper Midwest while also venturing into and out of Canada. On September 11 Boyd was the starting pitcher in both games of a doubleheader against an amateur team from Saskatoon, Saskatchewan. Boyd scored Winnipeg's first run in the first inning of the opener that became an 8-6 victory; at some point in the game, he ceded the mound to a reliever and moved to center field. In the nightcap, "Boyd, who was on the mound for the descendants of Ham[,] was in fine form and had the better of the pitchers' argument, striking out four[,] walking one and allowing but five hits" in a complete-game 5-1 triumph.[26] At the plate, he was 1-for-4, stole a base, and scored a run.

On October 10, in what was the final game of the season for the DeKalb, Illinois, team – and likely for the Winnipeg Giants as well – Boyd started at shortstop but took the mound in the eighth inning after the locals had scored four runs to take a 10-3 lead. Boyd went hitless in what ended as a 10-5 game, and then he went home for the offseason. The *Defender* later noted that the Winnipeg Giants had traveled over 22,000 miles in 1920 and made the dubious claim that the team had lost only five games in three months.[27]

In 1921 Sam Gordon was named manager of the Calgary Black Sox, a team owned by Calgary businessman Charlie Ross that took on the role of the Winnipeg Giants minus the identity as the NNL's developmental squad. The club was scheduled to "train in Chicago starting after the first of April,"[28] and its roster was populated by many of the same players from the 1920 Winnipeg team, including Boyd and Ewing.

Available game recaps show that Boyd played one or the other corner outfield spot in most games. Speed was Boyd's forte as an outfielder and on the basepaths. In a game against the Appleton, Wisconsin, team on May 8, Boyd registered three hits, reached base once on an error, stole two bases, and scored four runs as Calgary notched a 7-2 victory.[29] After the Black Sox vanquished the Minot, North Dakota, team, 7-3, on June 4, the *Defender* maintained that "[t]he Sox have one of the best teams in the country and up to date have won all their games with the exception of two."[30]

Box scores reveal that Boyd was a more consistent player in 1921, likely because he was able to focus on playing in the outfield most of the year and because the Black Sox played some home games in Calgary rather than barnstorming exclusively.[31] He became a true batting threat and continued to wreak havoc as a base stealer. Late in the season, Boyd did take the mound as the starting pitcher in the second game of a doubleheader against a team from Red Deer, Alberta. He was 3-for-5 with the bat, stole a base, and scored two runs to support his complete-game pitching effort in a 5-4 win.[32] At 28 years of age, Boyd was still in his prime as an athlete, but he never again played for a team of major-league caliber in the Negro Leagues.

In fact, the 1921 season appears to have been Boyd's final campaign as a professional baseball player at any level; his name is not found in any further articles or box scores. In 1922 the Cream City Giants, a team "made up of many of last year's Calgary Black Sox,"[33] debuted in Milwaukee on May 28. The team received far less coverage than either the Winnipeg Giants or the Calgary Black Sox and did not last long. Boyd's name was never mentioned in association with the Cream City Giants.

From this point forward, Boyd's life became like that of most people who are not in the spotlight – anonymous to all but those who knew him. Perhaps his wife, Lottie, had encouraged him to give up the rigors of barnstorming and settle down with her; however,

it is not known whether the couple remained married or had any children. Boyd's choice of a post-baseball career also remains a mystery.

The only certainty about Boyd's life after the 1921 baseball season – found in the records of the US Veterans Administration – is that he died in Devils Lake, North Dakota, on August 2, 1962.[34] Boyd had played in Devils Lake as a member of the Winnipeg and Calgary teams. Whatever his later life's experiences may have held, perhaps he found contentment by settling in a place he had visited and enjoyed while he was a young baseball player with great potential and a significant amount of time still before him.

SOURCES

Ancestry.com was consulted for public records such as census information; birth and death records; military draft registration cards; and ships' passenger logs.

Although data specific to Boyd's military service was gathered from Ancestry.com, the information about the Pioneer Infantry Regiments was taken from the following source:

McMahon, Margaret M., Ph.D. *A Guide to the U.S. Pioneer Infantry Regiments in WWI* (No city listed: Margaret M. McMahon Teaching & Training Co., LLC, 2018).

Direct quotes taken from McMahon's book are cited in the endnotes.

Unless otherwise indicated, Negro League player statistics and manager/team records were taken from Seamheads.com.

NOTES

1   All military records show January 23, 1893, as Boyd's date of birth since that is what he wrote on his draft registration card. The 1920 Census – the only census in which Boyd currently can be located – lists his birth year as "abt 1895," while the Social Security Death Index has the date as January 23, 1889. The conundrum surrounding a player's exact birthdate is not unique to Boyd, but in this instance, it is impossible to determine which year is correct. Since this is the case, the author has decided to use the year that Boyd provided to the draft board.

2   Boyd did not provide his father's or brother's names.

3   The author was unable to locate marriage records for the couple; thus, Lottie Boyd's maiden name is unknown.

4   McMahon, 5.

5   McMahon, 5.

6   McMahon, 4.

7   McMahon, 4.

8   "Detroit Stars Will Report Last of March," *Chicago Defender*, March 13, 1920: 9; "Detroit Stars Are Ordered to Report," *Chicago Defender*, March 27, 1920: 11.

9   "Baseball Game Set for Sunday/Detroit Stars and Denby Motors Open Season with Elaborate Ceremony," *Detroit Free Press*, April 11, 1920: 24.

10   "'Rube' Assigns Players to Giants," *Chicago Defender*, March 20, 1920: 9.

11   "Detroit Stars Are Ordered to Report."

12   "Valley City Fans See Real Base Ball," *Valley City* (North Dakota) *Weekly Times-Record*, June 3, 1920: 5.

13   "Detroit Stars in an Easy Victory/Open Semi-Pro Season Here by Trimming Denby Motors," *Detroit Free Press*, April 12, 1920: 14.

14   Detroit Stars Win/Initial Event Is a Walkaway for Blunt's [*sic*] Boys," *Chicago Defender*, April 17, 1920: 9.

15   "Stars Trim Delrays/Overflow Crowd Sees the Victory of Blunt's Boys," *Chicago Defender*, April 24, 1920: 9.

16   Dave Wyatt, "American Giants Win in 11th/Plucky Fight of Visiting Pitcher Goes for Naught When Teammates Falter," *Chicago Defender*, May 29, 1920: 9.

17   "Giants Take Two Falls from K.C. Monarchs/Giants [*sic*] Wins Own Game for Giants in 11th," *Chicago Whip*, May 29, 1920: 6. The *Whip* erroneously named Tom Johnson as Chicago's pitcher in its game write-up; however, the box score in the *Whip* as well as the *Defender's* game article and box score show that it was Tom Williams.

18   "Valley City Fans See Real Base Ball."

19   "Grand Forks Won Opener from Giants/Locals Take Slug-fest from Winnipeg Colored Giants Saturday," *Grand Forks Daily Herald*, June 6, 1920: 17.

20   "Grand Forks Defeated the Winnipeg Colored Giants in the Second Game of Series," *Grand Forks Daily Herald and the Evening Times*, June 7, 1920: 18.

21   "Grand Forks Defeated the Winnipeg Colored Giants in the Second Game of Series."

22   "Grand Forks Defeated the Winnipeg Colored Giants in the Second Game of Series."

23   "Grand Forks Defeated the Winnipeg Colored Giants in the Second Game of Series."

24   "Locals Took Final Game of Series Monday," *Grand Forks Daily Herald*, June 8, 1920: 10.

25   "Locals to Play at Devils Lake," *Grand Forks Daily Herald*, June 8, 1920: 10.

26   "Local Team Falls Twice on Saturday/Colored Giants Prove Too Much for City League Amateurs," *Saskatoon Star-Phoenix*, September 13, 1920: 7.

27   "Calgary Black Sox Ready for Busy Season," *Chicago Defender*, April 9, 1921: 10. The Winnipeg Giants played from at least June into October, which is longer than three months. Additionally, recaps for many of the team's games are not available; however, the few recaps cited in the present article show the team to have lost four games, so it is doubtful that the Giants suffered only one additional loss in 4½ months of play.

28   "Calgary Black Sox Ready for Busy Season."

29   "Calgary Black Sox Trim Appleton, Wisconsin, Nine," *Chicago Defender*, May 14, 1921: 10.

30   "Calgary Black Sox Beats [*sic*] Minot (N.D.) 7 to 3," *Chicago Defender*, June 11, 1921: 10. In this instance, the *Defender's* claim that the Black Sox had lost only two games may have been accurate; the season was still young.

31   See, for instance, "Drumheller Drops Another Game to Black Sox, 4 to 3," *Calgary Herald*, August 6, 1921: 22, and "Calgary Black Sox/Take Two Games from Red Deer – First Game 9-0, Second Game 5-4," *Red Deer Advocate*, August 19, 1921: 3.

32   "Calgary Black Sox/Take Two Games from Red Deer – First Game 9-0, Second Game 5-4."

33   "Watching the Scoreboard/Cream City Giants Win," *Chicago Defender*, June 3, 1922: 10. See also, "Colored Nine to Play Here," *Milwaukee Journal*, May 26, 1922: 45. For an in-depth discussion of the Cream City Giants and Black baseball in Milwaukee, see: Ken Jon-Edward Bartelt, "Brew City Black Ball: Milwaukee as Microcosm of the Early-Twentieth Century Black Baseball Experience" (2020). Theses and Dissertations. 2454. https://dc.uwm.edu/etd/2454

34   Efforts to locate an obituary or death certificate that might shed more light on Boyd's life and the circumstances of his death proved unsuccessful.

DAVE "LEFTY" BROWN

BY FREDERICK C. BUSH

Baseball has always lent itself to mythmaking. The sport's very origin once was shrouded in the legend that Abner Doubleday had invented the game in Cooperstown, New York. Although this myth was debunked long ago, it still led to the Hall of Fame being built in that august little town in upstate New York. Fictional works also have added to baseball's mythos. One such work is Bernard Malamud's 1952 novel *The Natural*, which actor Robert Redford introduced to the masses via his 1984 film adaptation. The story involves a player, Roy Hobbs, who is shot by a crazed female fan but eventually makes a comeback that culminates in a championship. Hobbs's shooting likely was inspired by one or more real-life incidents, proving that sometimes fact can be as strange as fiction.[1]

In the case of pitcher Dave Brown, however, the true story is far odder than any fictional tale possibly could be. The southpaw became one of the early pitching stars in the Negro National League with Rube Foster's Chicago American Giants. Allegations that Brown had scrapes with the law in his native Texas before he joined Foster's squad are part of his story, but Foster may have fabricated the charges in 1923. What is fact is that Brown shot a man to death in New York City in 1925 and then went on the lam. In a time when communication was still limited, Brown was able to elude police and the FBI, of which famed director J. Edgar Hoover had taken control one year earlier. While on the run, Brown used the alias William "Lefty" Wilson as he pitched for numerous semipro aggregations throughout the Midwest. After Brown's

baseball-playing days ended, he settled in North Carolina, where his past caught up to him by most unusual circumstances before he disappeared for all time.

Dave K. Brown was born on June 9, 1897, in Marquez, Texas, a small town in Leon County

Dave "Lefty" Brown was one of the aces of the 1920 American Giants, pitching to a team-leading 13-3 record and 1.82 ERA in NNL games.

approximately 68 miles southeast of Waco.[2] His parents, Silas and Anna (Walton) Brown, were farm laborers, and Dave was their ninth and last child.[3] Mystery surrounds the story of Brown's life from birth. For reasons unknown – though it may have been as simple as the fact that his place of residence changed – Brown filled out two World War I draft registration cards that contained slightly different information. In June 1917 he gave his birthdate as June 9, 1895, and indicated that he was a "Ball Player" in the employ of Enos Whittaker, owner of the Texas Colored League's Dallas Black Giants team. However, in August 1918, he provided June 9, 1897, as his birthdate and stated that he was a warehouse worker in Dallas; this may have been a second (or offseason) job, since he was still pitching for the Black Giants that year. Documents, including official military service records, show that Dave's brother Felix was born on January 18, 1895, and the 1900 census listed June 1897 for Dave's birth; thus, the year 1897 appears to be the correct birth year for Dave.

Nothing is known about Brown's childhood or how he developed his baseball skills, but his pitching acumen garnered him a position on the Dallas team in 1917. On June 6, just three days before his 20th birthday, Brown pitched for the Black Giants in a 5-3 loss to the Hot Springs Bear Cats; his catcher that day was Jim Brown.[4] The two Texans gained renown as "the Brown Battery" and soon moved into the next stage of their careers together. Oliver Marcell, who went on to hit .306 over 13 seasons in the Negro major leagues, was also in the Dallas lineup in 1917.

One week after the game against Hot Springs, on June 14, Brown earned what may have been his first professional victory as he pitched all 12 innings in a 4-3 triumph over the same opponent. Hot Springs' starting pitcher was listed only by the nickname "Nacogdoches" – presumably, a nod to the hurler's hometown – and the press noted that "[t]he game was witnessed by a good crowd, about half the spectators being white persons."[5]

Brown returned to the Black Giants for the 1918 season. On May 24, he struck out 11 batters in a 7-0 whitewashing of an Army team from Camp Travis, Texas, in the first game of a doubleheader.[6] Brown had become a local star as was evidenced by the fact that news articles used his name to draw fans to coming games. For an August game against the Fort Worth Wonders, one newspaper noted, "Dave Brown has been nominated to pitch for the Giants" and "[m]usic will be furnished by a brass band."[7]

In the spring of 1919, fellow Texan Rube Foster signed the Brown Battery for his Chicago squad, which was in its final season as an independent team. Once again, though, mystery and rumors surround the circumstances by which Brown moved into the next phase of his career. In an April preview article about the American Giants, the *Chicago Defender* reported, "No one in the world knows better how to pick a player than 'Rube.' ... Brown and Brown of the Dallas, Tex., Giants are here. They were a whirlwind in Texas."[8] No mention was made of any special circumstances by which Dave Brown was obtained, either at that time or during any other point in Brown's tenure with the team.

However, in 1923, after Brown had jumped his contract with Foster and joined the New York Lincoln Giants of the Eastern Colored League, Rube related a different tale. Foster may have invented this new narrative out of anger, as no contemporary documentation has yet come to light to corroborate it. He asserted about Brown:

"He did not leave because he was not treated right nor because his salary was not remunerative enough for his services. He simply wished to compensate me for staking the reputation of the American Giants baseball club and my own when convicted and sentenced to the penitentiary for highway robbery by going into court and having him paroled to me; this being done by me giving bond for $20,000 for him.

"This was before Dave Brown showed any real pitching ability. It was when he had only pitched two games for me during the season. I promised his mother to take care of him if he came to Chicago and it was this promise that I was carrying out.

"Should I now get down off of that parole, he would have to serve his sentence."[9]

Foster asserted that he had dirt on numerous players, in addition to Brown, that "would shock the public beyond measure."[10] There is no question that some ballplayers – no matter the era, their race, or their league – have committed shocking acts, but this screed sounded more like the grievances of a spurned suitor.

Foster's claim about Brown seems dubious for numerous reasons. First and foremost is the question of whether Foster could finagle such a parole and whether he would have paid the large sum required for the bond.[11] Secondly, the lack of any press coverage during or after the alleged crime is unusual, especially since Brown had become well known for his pitching in the Dallas area. Whether or not Foster ever met Brown's mother so that he could promise her to take care of Dave is also questionable, but it is the one element of the story that might have a grain of truth considering what happened to one of Dave's older brothers, Webster.

According to one news account, Webster Brown, who was six years older than Dave, was "a bad man generally" and was "well-known in police circles in the southwest."[12] On January 31, 1919, Webster led Dallas police on a chase that ended with him being shot and killed. It was reported that the chase "resulted from a theft of clothing that occurred yesterday [January 30] afternoon."[13] Captain J.C. Gunning, chief of detectives, said that Webster "had been in jail several times and was an escaped convict from the county farm."[14]

If Foster did meet Anna Brown in 1919, after Webster's violent death, it is possible that she asked him to look after Dave in the hope that her youngest son would stay out of trouble. Perhaps in his fit of pique in 1923, Foster shifted one of Webster's crimes to Dave. Of course, there remains the possibility that Dave was already beginning to follow in Webster's footsteps, since he did become involved in future criminal activity himself. As is the case with many chapters in Dave Brown's life, the lack of sufficient evidence leads to speculation and makes him one of baseball history's great enigmas.

Although the exact manner by which Dave Brown joined Foster's squad remains uncertain, it is definite that he was used sparingly in 1919. Officially, he is credited with a 1-2 record and a 4.40 ERA in games pitched against other top-caliber Western Independent Clubs.[15] He also pitched against semipro aggregations and notched one of his earliest victories for Chicago against the Nash Motors team of Kenosha, Wisconsin, on May 11. Brown, who was identified in the press as "the new southpaw of the Giants," pitched Chicago's third consecutive shutout in a 5-0 complete-game effort; he scattered four hits while walking three batters and striking out three.[16] The Chicago American Giants finished the 1919 season with a 27-16 record that was second-best in the West to the 27-14 mark posted by the Detroit Stars, but there was no league and, therefore, no pennant to be won. However, that was no longer to be the case after Foster and his fellow team owners founded the first Negro National League

at the Paseo branch of the YMCA in Kansas City, Missouri, on February 13, 1920.[17]

Chicago dominated the early years of the NNL, claiming the first three league championships from 1920 through 1922 with Brown contributing a composite 43-8 record in league play during those seasons. Brown's first appearance in an official NNL game took place on May 9, 1920, against the similarly named Chicago Giants at Schorling Park, the American Giants' home field. According to the press account of the game, "while Dave Brown was on the rubber, [the Giants] simply could not see his offerings" as he hurled six shutout innings to earn the win.[18] He ceded the mound to Tom Williams with an 8-0 lead in what ended as an 8-3 triumph, but it was an auspicious debut that heralded 1920 as Brown's breakout season.

As the American Giants rolled to a 43-17-2 record (a .717 winning percentage) in NNL games to claim the pennant by eight games over the Detroit Stars, low-hit, low-run outings became the norm for Brown. In addition to capturing the ERA title with a 1.82 mark – albeit edging out teammate Tom Williams by only 0.01 – Brown paced his team in victories with a 13-3 record that also put him in a tie for fourth in the league – two wins behind Detroit's Bill Gatewood. Brown also tied for fourth in the league in strikeouts with 101, five behind the league-leading total of Kansas City's Sam Crawford. Perhaps the most remarkable statistic of all was Brown's 0.908 WHIP as he allowed only 84 hits and 51 walks in 148⅔ innings pitched.

At the conclusion of the 1920 NNL season, Foster took his squad on a swing through the South in late September and early October. The American Giants emerged victorious against all opponents and repeatedly clubbed the Negro Southern League's champion, the Knoxville Giants, into submission. Chicago defeated Knoxville at Birmingham's Rickwood Field on September 21, 22, 23, and 30. The two teams met again in Knoxville on October 2 as Brown opposed Steel Arm Dickey in a classic pitchers' duel. The game remained scoreless until the bottom of the eighth inning when Knoxville, which managed only three hits, broke through with the contest's first tally. Chicago came back with two runs in the top of the ninth, and Brown shut down Knoxville's lineup in the bottom of the frame to give the American Giants their 14th consecutive victory, a triumph that, according to Negro League historian James A. Riley, "sealed their status as the best black ball club in the country."[19]

It certainly seemed that Foster was bent on his team laying claim to being the best in the nation as next they traveled northeast to take on the Atlantic City Bacharach Giants in a series of games played at Philadelphia's Shibe Park and Brooklyn's Ebbets Field. This series was to serve as "a dress rehearsal for what Rube envisioned as the black World Series."[20] The Bacharach team proved to be a stiffer challenge than Knoxville had, but Chicago emerged with a 4-3-1 record in the series against the East's top independent club, and the American Giants reigned supreme in 1920.[21]

In 1921 Brown and the American Giants picked up where they had left off the previous season. Foster's team claimed its second straight NNL pennant as its 44-22-2 record resulted in the league's best winning percentage (.667); the Kansas City Monarchs won more games, posting a 54-41 (.568) league ledger, but finished 4½ games behind Chicago. Brown once again paced the American Giants' pitching staff and was among the NNL leaders in every major category. He tied for first in wins with 17, though his 17-2 mark was far superior to St. Louis hurler Bill Drake's 17-11 record; his 2.50 ERA was second only to Bullet Rogan's 1.72 mark for Kansas City; and his 126 strikeouts were tied for third, 14 behind league leader Bill Holland, a late-season addition to the American Giants who had spent the bulk of the season with Detroit. Brown's five shutouts put him in a tie for first place with Jim Jeffries of Indianapolis, and 1-0 games proved to be his forte.

On August 14, Brown faced Drake and the St. Louis Giants at Schorling Park in what the *Chicago Defender* raved was "one of the best games – if not THE best – played at this park this summer and a humdinger of a pitchers' battle."[22] Neither hurler surrendered a hit until the bottom of the seventh inning, when Bingo DeMoss singled off Drake, and the game remained scoreless until the bottom of the eighth. At that point Cristobal Torriente led off Chicago's half of the inning with a single, advanced to second on catcher George Dixon's sacrifice, and then stole third base. Floyd "Jelly" Gardner then beat out a bunt on a squeeze play, and Torriente crossed home plate with the game's only run. According to the *Defender*, "Hats were broken and every stunt possible was pulled off by the rabid fans," who now wanted to see Brown finish his no-hitter.[23] However, such history was not in the making that day as St. Louis catcher Sam Bennett led off the ninth with his team's first safety; Sidney Brooks ran for Bennett and was promptly erased when Drake grounded into a double play. Doc Dudley garnered the second hit against Brown, a single to right

field, but the game ended when Dixon threw Dudley out at second base on a steal attempt.

Slightly less than one month later, on September 11 at Schorling Park, Brown engaged in another duel against Steel Arm Dickey and the Negro Southern League's Montgomery Grey Sox. Although Dickey now plied his trade for a different team, the game was almost an exact replica of the previous year's matchup between the two aces. There was more traffic on the basepaths on this day, but neither team managed to score for the first eight innings. Prior to the bottom of the ninth, the most exciting event had occurred off-field in the bottom of the seventh inning. The *Defender's* Frank Young described the incident in a clipped style:

> "Someone over on Wentworth avenue [*sic*] shoots a gun out of a house window. A hundred fans on top of the house watching the game begin to scatter. Finally[,] a bluecoat goes over and all of a sudden we see the housetop empty. We also see the bluecoat take out a white handkerchief and wave to us. Means all is at peace."[24]

Everyone on the field and in the stands managed to calm themselves and the on-field action resumed.

With the game still scoreless, Brown led off the bottom of the ninth with a single but was forced at second on Jimmie Lyons' fielder's choice grounder. Lyons bolted to second on a wild pitch by Dickey. DeMoss attempted a sacrifice bunt and ended up safe at first on a throwing error, with Lyons advancing to third. DeMoss then attempted to steal second, and Lyons scored when the Grey Sox catcher's wild throw to second rolled into the outfield. Once more, the American Giants had clinched a 1-0 victory in the ninth with Dave Brown emerging as the winning pitcher.

At the conclusion of the NNL season, Foster again took his team east to play two series against the region's most powerful independent clubs, the Bacharach Giants and the Hilldale Club of Darby, Pennsylvania. As had been the case in 1920, Foster intended these clashes to be "a dry run for the planned future 'East-West World Series,'" and they were sometimes already billed as championship series in the press.[25] However, this time around, Chicago struggled to stay even against both squads, so much so that Foster entered into damage control mode and "reminded everyone that the American Giants had won the NNL pennant."[26]

Things went downhill from there for Foster as 1921 neared its end. He was arrested (and quickly bailed out) for alleged fraud in Atlanta, canceled the American Giants' planned trip to Cuba due to political turmoil on the island nation, and, most tragically, suffered the unexpected death of his five-year-old daughter, Sarah, on the train ride home to Chicago after an exhibition series in New Orleans. Despite his grief, Foster tended to the business of the NNL and wrote a series of blunt articles for the *Defender* in which he outlined the challenges for the league; the most controversial piece voiced Foster's opposition to hiring Black umpires as arbiters for NNL games.

Between Foster's misfortunes, his controversial columns, and the fact that Dave Brown was the American Giants' only pitcher to return from the 1921 championship team's staff, the outlook for the Chicago nine was not as positive as in previous years. The American Giants opened the regular season at Schorling Park in early May with a tough series against the powerful Monarchs, who soon would supplant Chicago as the dominant force in the NNL. The Monarchs captured the first game, 5-1, and Brown made his first start in the second tilt on May 7. The game did not bode well for Chicago's season.

The Sunday contest featured a matchup between two of Black baseball's premier pitchers in Dave Brown and Bullet Rogan. So many fans wanted to witness the proceedings that problems began before the game ever started. The *Defender* described the chaos:

> "Early in the afternoon, about two o'clock, the bleacher seat box office was closed. The fans in that section attempted to violate law and decency by jumping over the fence into the higher priced seats. Over 200 followed this course. The crowd surged into fair territory time and again during the game. The play was stopped and Rube Foster with two or three players pleaded with the populace to give the outfielders a chance to play."[27]

Initially, the game itself went as expected. While it was noted that "Brown was not in his usual cool form. He walked men and was in many tight holes," he and Rogan dueled to a 1-1 tie through seven innings.[28] The *Defender* observed, "The sixteen thousand that crowded the park got just what they came out to see," but the newspaper also had to add, "only they did not see the ending."[29] Kansas City scored to take a 2-1 lead in the top of the eighth inning. When Chicago came back to tie the game in the bottom half of the frame, the crowd went berserk. According to the game account, "The overflow broke loose. On the field they went. ... That was all. They just couldn't play. Folks wouldn't let them."[30]

The crowd became so unruly that play was called off and the game was declared a tie. In response, fans began to throw cushions and pop bottles at one another, and the outmanned police force at the field had trouble bringing the melee under control. The *Defender* declared that "[t]he most disgraceful scenes were enacted" and that "[i]n all Chicago's baseball history it cannot be recalled that such actions have ever taken place at any park."[31]

The American Giants won the last two games of the opening series, a sign that they would barely hold off the Monarchs and retain the NNL title for one more season. At the end of the 1922 NNL campaign, Chicago won the pennant by virtue of having an almost infinitesimally greater winning percentage than Kansas City: The American Giants' 37-24-1 record gave them a .607 winning percentage compared with the Monarchs' 47-31-2, .603 mark.

Brown certainly did not slump in 1922, posting a 13-3 record with 103 strikeouts and a 2.90 ERA in 155 innings pitched in NNL play. As usual, his numbers put him in the top five of most major pitching categories: He finished tied for third in wins (though considerably behind Jim Jeffries' 21 victories for Indianapolis), fourth in ERA, and fifth in strikeouts. As had also become typical for Brown, he was involved in a stellar 1-0 victory, this time against the Atlantic City Bacharach Giants.

Chicago did not sojourn east in 1922. Instead, the Bacharachs and the Hilldale Club visited Schorling Park for the first time. On August 16, "[a] bit of history was made ... when the American Giants were involved in one of the longest games ever in Negro League history" against the Bacharachs.[32] Ed "Huck" Rile started the game for Chicago, but Foster pulled him after four scoreless innings and sent Brown to the mound. Brown went 16 innings, an amazing feat but one that paled in comparison to that of his mound opponent, Harold Treadwell, who pitched all 20 frames for Pop Lloyd's Bacharach squad. Eventually, one of the two hurlers had to tire, and it turned out to be Treadwell in the bottom of the 20th inning. Torriente draw a leadoff walk from the exhausted Treadwell and advanced to second on Bobby Williams's sacrifice bunt. Dave Malarcher then banged out a single to drive in Torriente with the game's only run, giving Brown yet another 1-0 victory and allowing Treadwell to ice his rubber arm.[33]

At the conclusion of the 1922 season, Brown was one of several Negro League players who traveled to Cuba to play winter baseball. His first foray to the island was unremarkable as he played for Santa Clara, which finished in last place with a 14-40 record and withdrew from the league on January 14, 1923.[34] Brown distinguished himself via his 4-3 record, which tied teammate Eustaquio Pedroso (also 4-3) for the team lead in victories.[35]

By the time Brown returned from Cuba, Ed Bolden, owner of the Hilldale Club, had founded the Eastern Colored League to compete with Foster's Western circuit.[36] Soon thereafter, the *Defender* reported:

> "Baseball fans in Chicago were much surprised last week when Dave Brown, first string pitcher for the American Giants, caught a rattler for New York. ... It is strongly rumored that Brown will work for the Lincoln Giants this summer, making his exit from organized ball and jumping to the outlaws."[37]

Teammate Ed Rile was also heading east, and the *Defender* alleged, "According to well founded rumors, Rile has been acting as an agent for the Eastern association in their raid on players belonging to the Negro National league."[38] Foster responded one month later with his story – be it fact or fiction – that he was disappointed in Brown's disloyalty since he had bought him out of prison in Texas.[39]

Brown, who was leaving behind one former Dallas teammate, Jim Brown, was reunited with another old friend from his playing days in Texas, Oliver Marcell. He also appeared simply to shrug off Foster's allegations, but his first season in New York was not a rousing success. The Lincoln Giants finished in fifth place with a 17-23 league record (18-23 overall). Brown pitched to a 5-6 record with 47 strikeouts and a 3.28 ERA in 74 innings. His totals still placed him in the top 10 – but no longer the top five – of most statistical categories in the ECL, but he was not even the best pitcher on his team. Bill Holland had 48 strikeouts and a 3.13 ERA in 72 innings pitched but was a victim of hard luck as he finished the season at 0-7.

Brown, Marcell, and Holland were three of the numerous Negro League players who joined the Santa Clara squad for the 1923-24 Cuban winter season. The now talent-laden team managed a 180-degree turnaround from the previous season, finishing in first place with a 36-11 record. In fact, this Santa Clara squad came to be "[c]onsidered as the most dominant team ever in the history of Cuban baseball by amassing an 11½ game bulge over their nearest rival."[40] Bill Holland led the team and league in wins with a 10-2 record, Rube Currie contributed an 8-2 mark, and Brown finished with a 7-3 ledger.

The 1923-24 Cuban season was such a popular success that fans clamored for more baseball, and a special season, named Gran Premio, was quickly arranged. Santa Clara finished with a 13-12 record that enabled them to edge out Almendares by a slim half-game margin. Brown (4-2) and Holland (4-3) tied for the team lead in wins in this second season.[41]

When Brown returned stateside in 1924, he was riding high from his Cuban experience and rejoined the New York Lincoln Giants with an eye toward a better outcome in the ECL's second season. After Brown won the second game of a doubleheader against the Washington Potomacs, one of the ECL's two new squads, on May 18, the "rejuvenated Lincoln Giants" had run out to a 7-2 record.[42] One week later, the Lincoln Giants ran their win streak to eight by sweeping a doubleheader from the Bacharachs, and they led Hilldale by a half-game in the standings.[43]

The Lincoln Giants greatly improved their performance in 1924, but they could not sustain their quick start. The team and Brown faded down the stretch, a fact that was clearly in evidence by a late-September sweep suffered at the hands of the Cuban Stars. Brown lost the second game, 7-0, and the press noted that he "put his team at a disadvantage in the very first inning by walking two men and then allowing two hits, causing four runs to be made."[44]

Hilldale won the ECL title with a 47-26 record while the Lincoln Giants finished third, seven games back, with a 35-28-1 record. Foster had to be chagrined that two of his Chicago team's rivals, Bolden's Hilldale club and the NNL's Kansas City Monarchs, faced off in the first-ever Negro League World Series. The Monarchs captured the title in 10 games, with one game resulting in a tie.

As for Brown, he returned to the old form he had exhibited with Chicago. He led all ECL pitchers with a 2.00 ERA, and his 13-8 record and 107 strikeouts were second only to Hilldale's Nip Winters, who finished the year at 20-5 and struck out 114 batters. Brown would have been the darling of the modern sabermetric crowd, however, which would point out that he finished with an ERA+ of 241 compared with Winters' 142, thus denoting him as the far superior pitcher.

In the winter, Brown returned to Cuba, where he again toiled for Santa Clara. The team's fortunes went up and down like a yo-yo, and the 1924-25 campaign was a down time. The squad finished in third place with a 20-28 record and "attendance at the games in Santa Clara's Boulanger Park was so disappointing ... that in early January owner Abel Linares moved the franchise to Matanzas."[45] Brown's performance typified the moribund team's fortunes: His final foray to the island resulted in a 2-4 record.[46] At least he could look forward to competing for the ECL title with the Lincoln Giants in 1925.

Or so Brown and everyone else thought after an Opening Day doubleheader against the Bacharachs on Sunday, April 26, that kicked off the regular season for both teams. Brown, who started the first game, "was the master of the Atlantic City boys throughout the fray, allowing them seven scattered hits and only [being] scored upon once."[47] After winning the first game, 6-1, the New Yorkers also captured the nightcap, which turned into a 10-inning affair, by a 4-3 score. The sweep was a sweet start to the season.

Teammates Brown, Marcell, and Frank Wickware (who had played for the American Giants in 1920) apparently spent two days celebrating their early success. In the wee hours of the morning on Tuesday, April 28 – at 3:25 A.M., to be precise – a man named Benjamin Adair confronted the trio at 69 West 135th Street. According to eyewitnesses, Adair had a revolver and shouted at the players, "Now, I've got you."[48] As the men argued, Brown drew his own gun and shot Adair, who was taken to Harlem Hospital and declared dead on arrival. The three Lincoln Giants hailed a passing taxi, jumped in, and rode away from the scene.[49]

The Lincoln Giants canceled practice on April 28 because they were missing three players that day. Marcell and Wickware soon reappeared, were questioned by the police, and then were released. Brown was never seen in New York City again. Eyewitnesses had taken down the number of the taxi in which the trio had escaped, and police arrested the driver, William Holland (not to be confused with pitcher Bill Holland). Holland stated that "he took the men as he would have taken any other passengers. He denied having seen them before."[50] Upon checking out Holland's story, the police released him as well. After their investigation made no progress for a couple of months, the New York police released something else: the only known wanted poster in history with a photo of the perpetrator wearing a baseball uniform. The poster declared that Dave Brown was wanted for murder.

W. Rollo Wilson of the *Pittsburgh Courier* took the three players to task in his column, asserting, "Whatever the outcome of this matter these men must leave the game. The integrity of the pastime demands it." Of the New York team's fortunes, Wilson wrote, "The serious trouble in which Dave Brown, Wickware, and Marcelle are involved will just about wreck the Lincoln Giants."[51] That much was certainly true as the team finished the season in last place with a dismal 7-41 record. As for the three players, Marcell spent the rest of 1925 with the Bacharachs and played through the 1930 season; the 37-year-old Wickware's career ended after 1925; and Brown soon reappeared under an alias.

In the summer of 1926, newspapers in the Midwest began to report the exploits of a pitcher named Lefty Wilson, who played for various semipro teams throughout the region. As a member of Gilkerson's Union Giants, Wilson dominated local competition in Iowa. On June 20 he notched an 11-4 victory over Davenport's Knights of Columbus team, with the local newspaper noting that he "eased up slightly in the latter innings" to allow the Knights to score.[52] Wilson extended no such courtesy against the Spencer team – the state semipro champion – on July 10 in Mason City, Iowa. He struck out 17 batters while allowing

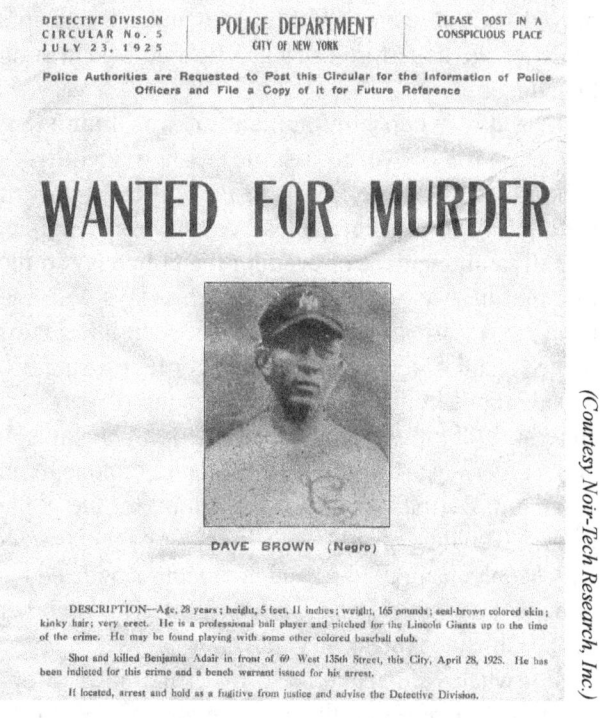

Pitcher Dave Brown, pictured in a New York Lincoln Giants uniform, was wanted for murder for killing Benjamin Adair less than two days after he had hurled an Opening Day victory in 1925.

(Courtesy Noir-Tech Research, Inc.)

only one hit, one walk, and a hit batsman in a 2-0 triumph.[53]

Shortly thereafter, Wilson pitched for the Pipestone (Minnesota) Black Sox. In a 7-2 victory over a team from LeMars, Iowa, the "well-known negro pitcher twirled for the visitors and held the home club under control at all times."[54] The player wanted for shooting a man with a real gun now became a figurative hired gun for any semipro team that wanted to pay him, though he played mostly for teams from Iowa and Minnesota.

In 1927 Wilson joined the team in Wanda, Minnesota, and helped lead them to the Tri-County League championship by defeating Comfrey in two games – 8-1 and 2-1 – while striking out 10 and 13 batters respectively. Wanda played the Franklin Creamery team from Minneapolis in the state tournament in St. Paul, but Wilson ended up on the losing end of a 6-0 game.[55]

Still, Wilson was ready to return to Wanda in 1928, but the Tri-County League had issued an edict aimed directly at him. The league decreed, "The rules under which the circuit operated last year were approved with the exception that the color line was drawn and the status of home players was defined."[56] With that ruling, Lefty Wilson's time in the Tri-County League came to an end. However, he stayed in Minnesota and played for the team in Bertha, becoming the team's ace after the departure of Negro League legend John Donaldson.[57]

In a day when communication was limited, it was easy for Brown to assume his new identity as William (Bill) "Lefty" Wilson in a different part of the country from where he had committed his crime. The difficult element of evading the police lay in the fact that he was well known from his days with the Chicago American Giants, and many semipro teams played against Negro League teams or fellow semipro squads that hired former Negro League players. On June 14, 1928, it was announced that John Donaldson and Lefty Wilson would be the mound opponents in a game in Bertha, with Wilson pitching for the home team.[58] Donaldson had been a member of the Kansas City Monarchs in 1920-21 and no doubt recognized his opponent as being Dave Brown, formerly a member of the Chicago American Giants.

For whatever reason, no former teammates or opponents ever revealed that ace semipro pitcher Lefty Wilson was the wanted criminal Dave Brown. Various players, including Hall of Fame shortstop Willie Wells and former House of David catcher/teammate L.J.

Favors, admitted in later years that they were aware of Wilson's true identity. Both players claimed that teams that employed Wilson always kept their bags packed in case someone – primarily the police – learned who he was and their team had to depart quickly in the middle of the night to avoid trouble.[59]

Wilson finished with a 14-8 record for Bertha in 1928, but the team's attendance was so low that the owner joined a new, small-town league for 1929 that allowed its teams to use only home talent on their rosters. The second loss of employment in Minnesota did not faze Brown, who took his Lefty Wilson act back to the state of Iowa in 1929.[60] By this time, obviously emboldened by the fact that no one had turned him over to the law, Brown, although he maintained his alias, did less and less to conceal his past and his identity.

On April 14, 1929, it was reported that Lefty Wilson would take the managerial reins for a Sioux City, Iowa, team sponsored by the Auto Kary-All Manufacturing Company. According to the local press, "'Lefty' Wilson, regarded as the greatest negro southpaw hurler in the game and formerly a member of the Chicago negro National league [sic] club, has been signed as manager and has secured a lineup of players from Scott's Giants, Gilkerson's Union Giants and negro league clubs."[61] The Chicago American Giants never had a pitcher named Wilson, but apparently Brown wanted to tout his past accomplishments and attributed them to his new alter ego without any concern for blowing his cover. Not only was Brown not lying low from people who might recognize him, he was now audacious enough to recruit players from Negro League teams.

The Kary-All nine did not receive extensive coverage. However, if the team's May 11 game against the Kari-Keen squad was representative of their efforts, the team and its pitcher-manager did not fare well. In what the press termed a 12-5 "drubbing," it was stated that "[t]he winners hammered 'Lefty' Wilson for 14 hits in six innings and had the game 'sacked up' before he was relieved by Truesdale."[62] By August, whether Kary-All's season had ended or not, Wilson was a member of the Cubans, John Donaldson's barnstorming team.

On August 29, in a game against the House of David team, "'Lefty' Wilson, the colored pitcher who had reached second base, started a chewing match [with the House of David shortstop] that ended in a real fistfight that took several of the players to separate." Home-plate umpire Bunny Clouton ejected both players, but the House of David shortstop refused to leave the field. Eventually, to get the player to depart, Clouton agreed to be replaced by fellow arbiter Scoop Hunter. The fistfight and dispute over who would umpire the game took so much time that the game had to be called on account of darkness in the seventh inning.[63]

In 1930 and 1931, Lefty Wilson pitched for the Colored House of David team with varying degrees of success. He had, however, made quite a name for himself in the Midwest. After he pitched the House of David to an 8-6 victory over the Cold Spring (Minnesota) team on June 21, 1930, the press noted, "'Lefty' Wilson, well known in this community, did the chucking for the Davids against Cold Spring on Saturday,"[64] Perhaps the last report of Lefty Wilson was in a preview article for a game between the Colored House of David and a team from La Crosse, Wisconsin, that was to take place on August 31, 1931. Wilson was mentioned as the possible starting pitcher for the Davids, who were "considered one of the outstanding negro teams in the country."[65]

After Lefty Wilson faded into history, Dave Brown resurfaced seven years later in North Carolina. How, or why, he came to live in the Tar Heel State is another of the many unknown circumstances in Brown's life. However, on July 15, 1938, "David Brown, 30-year-old negro, was taken into custody by Greensboro police and held for questioning ... following an incident in which Jess [sic] Wells, white man, was said to have been pushed from the porch of a residence. ... Wells, in an unconscious condition, was taken to Piedmont Memorial hospital around 3 o'clock. It is thought possible that he suffered a fractured skull."[66] Wells regained consciousness that night and identified Brown as his assailant. The next day a warrant was issued against Brown that charged him with robbery with deadly weapons since he had taken $4 from Wells in the assault.

When Brown was brought to the police station, he wore a "glossy green shirt" that "gave him an unusual appearance and he was questioned as to athletics."[67] Brown confessed that he had played baseball at one time but claimed that he had never been a professional ballplayer and that he had never been out of North Carolina. Upon Brown's admission that he had played ball, a detective "recalled the 13-year-old poster with the picture of a man wearing a baseball suit in the center thereof."[68] Police dug out the poster and noticed a striking resemblance between the photo and the man they had in custody. Brown was photographed and fingerprinted, and the information was forwarded to the authorities in New York.

On July 22 the Greensboro police received word that their prisoner was the same man on the wanted poster and were asked whether Brown would agree to waive extradition. Brown agreed, and awaited transport to New York, where he was to stand trial for murder. What happened next is best described by a one-word headline in the July 31, 1938, *Raleigh News and Observer*: "Lucky." The news article explained:

"Today a telegram came from the New York police saying that all witnesses had disappeared in the intervening 13 years, and

The Wanda, Minnesota, team won the 1927 Tri-County Championship with "Lefty" Wilson (formerly known as Dave Brown, fourth from left) striking out 10 and 13 batters respectively in their two-game triumph over Comfrey.

(Redwood Gazette, May 25, 1927)

that since Brown could not be convicted, the charge would be dropped. When the Greensboro police turned to the local offense, they found that Wells had left Greensboro. There was nothing to do with Brown except turn him loose."[69]

The Greensboro police did exactly that, and that is the last certainty in the life of Dave Brown, Negro League pitching ace of the early 1920s.

According to some articles about the Greensboro case, Brown claimed to live in Winston-Salem, North Carolina, but no evidence has been found to support that assertion. Greensboro telephone directories list a Black man named Dave Brown between the years 1938 and 1959. This Dave Brown was a taxi driver, first for the Harlem Cab Company and later for United Taxi, and he was married for a time to a woman named Estelle. Dave Brown the taxi driver is absent from many common public records, which invites speculation that the two individuals may have been one and the same person; however, his death certificate from 1967 shows that he was a different individual.

In fact, Dave Brown the ballplayer appears to have left North Carolina in the aftermath of the Greensboro episode. Legendary Negro League pitcher/catcher Ted "Double Duty" Radcliffe claimed, "I saw him in 1949 in Frisco. I think he was working at the post office."[70] Radcliffe was well known for spinning fanciful yarns, but there are "unconfirmed reports that Brown died in California."[71] James A. Riley wrote that "[u]nverified reports also persist that he [Brown] died in Denver, Colorado, under mysterious circumstances."[72] Oliver Marcell, Brown's longtime friend and former teammate, lived in Denver after he retired from baseball. Perhaps Brown went west to visit his old companion and became involved in an incident that resulted in his demise. Perhaps he became a postal worker in California and lived there until his death. Perhaps one day documentation will come to light that will explain how Brown's life continued after 1938 as well as where, when, and how he eventually died. Until such time, Brown will remain one of history's mysteries and the mythology about him and his final whereabouts can continue to grow.

ACKNOWLEDGMENT

Gratitude is extended to Negro League researcher Gary Ashwill, who maintains the Agate Type website about Negro and Latin baseball and compiles statistics and information for Seamheads.com's Negro League database. Gary's research led him to be the first person to discover and to write about Dave Brown's 1938 arrest in Greensboro, North Carolina. As he informed me in an email, he came across the first article about the incident quite by accident while researching another topic. As a fellow Negro League researcher, I know the excitement that comes with such a discovery as well as the serendipity that can be involved in unearthing such gems; such was the case as I discovered the information about Webster Brown's criminal history and how it may have morphed into Foster's 1923 tale about Dave. It is to be hoped that further discoveries about Dave Brown will one day be made.

SOURCES

All player statistics and team records were taken from Seamheads.com, except where otherwise indicated.

Ancestry.com was consulted for US Census information, military records, and birth and death records.

NOTES

1   Rob Edelman, "Eddie Waitkus and 'The Natural': What is Assumption? What is Fact?" https://sabr.org/journal/article/eddie-waitkus-and-the-natural-what-is-assumption-what-is-fact/, accessed January 10, 2021.

2   Multiple sources list Dave Brown's place of birth as San Marcos, Texas; however, that was the birthplace of catcher Jim Brown. There is no evidence that the two players were related; even if they were kin, they certainly were not members of the same immediate family.

3   Silas Brown is listed as "Cyrus" in the 1900 census, but this appears to be a census-taker's error that was typical of that time. Dave gave his father's name as "Silas" on his 1918 World War I draft registration card, and Felix Brown gave the initials "S.B." – with "S." presumably standing for "Silas" – when he provided family information for their brother Webster's death certificate.

4   "Arkansas Negroes Clean Up on Dallas," Fort Worth Record, June 7, 1917: 7. Since the two players had the same last name, their positions were sometimes listed incorrectly in newspaper lineups or line scores. The error is readily apparent because, while a catcher might pitch in an emergency if he were able to do so, it is extremely doubtful that any team in any era would risk an injury to a star pitcher by having him catch. (As Negro Leagues fans are likely already aware, there was one notable exception to this rule in the person of Ted "Double Duty" Radcliffe, who earned his nickname by sometimes pitching one game of a doubleheader and then catching the second game.)

5   "Dallas Black Giants Win Game in Twelfth," Fort Worth Record, June 15, 1917: 11.

6   J. Alba Austin, "Dallas Black Giants Take 2 from Camp Travis Nine," Chicago Defender (Big Weekend Edition), May 25, 1918: 9.

7   "Plenty of Baseball Provided for Fans of Dallas Today," Dallas Morning News, August 11, 1918.

8   "American Giants Open Sunday: 'Rube' Foster Will Present the Greatest Team of his Career," Chicago Defender, April 12, 1919: 11.

9   "League Moguls Here This Week; Baseball War Looms," Chicago Defender, March 17, 1923: 10. Foster's allegations became rumors that were widespread enough to be included in different works by noted Negro League historians James A. Riley and John B. Holway; however, no evidence has ever been offered to substantiate the story. In fact, Foster's initial tale took on additional uncertainty, with Riley even stating that the highway robbery incident involving Brown occurred in the year 1917; see James A. Riley, Of Monarchs and Black Barons: Essays on Baseball's Negro Leagues (Jefferson, North Carolina: McFarland & Company, Inc., 2012), 71. Riley's claim contradicts Foster's assertion that the incident occurred after Brown had first pitched for the Chicago American Giants in 1919 and demonstrates how the story took on a life of its own beyond the initial news article in the Defender.

10   "League Moguls Here This Week; Baseball War Looms."

11   Foster would not have had to pay $20,000 for the bond; however, even the standard 10 percent of that figure is $2,000, which would have been an exorbitant sum for Foster to pay for a pitcher he claimed had not yet proven himself. Another problem with Foster's story involves the terminology used. Foster claimed that he paid a bond to have Brown paroled to him; however, these two things do not go together. A bond is paid so that an accused person who is being released from jail will show up in court for his hearing and/or trial, whereas parole is granted to a person who has already been convicted and has been serving time in prison. Thus, if Foster truly paid money to have Brown released from prison – an action that seems highly doubtful – he may have managed to bribe Texas officials rather than to follow any legal procedures.

12   "Desperado Is Slain in Fight with Cops," *Tampa Bay Times*, March 14, 1919: 3.

13   "Negro Killed after Long Chase by Officers," *Dallas Morning News*, February 1, 1919: 5.

14   "Negro Killed after Long Chase by Officers."

15   The other major independent teams in the West in 1919 were the Detroit Stars, Cuban Stars West, St. Louis Giants, Dayton Marcos, Jewell's ABCs, and the Chicago Giants.

16   "Foster Giants, With Two Hits, Nip Kenosha, 5-0," *Chicago Tribune*, May 12, 1919: 19.

17   Except for the Jewell's ABCs, all the major Western Independent Clubs from 1919 became members of the NNL in 1920; two additional squads – the Indianapolis ABCs and the Kansas City Monarchs – also were founding members of the circuit.

18   Captain James H. Smith, "Foster's Crew Puts Kibosh on Chicago Giants," *Chicago Defender*, May 15, 1920: 9.

19   "American Giants, 2; Knoxville, 1," *Chicago Defender*, October 9, 1920: 6; Riley, *Of Monarchs and Black Barons*, 74.

20   Paul Debono, *The Chicago American Giants* (Jefferson, North Carolina: McFarland & Company, Inc., 2007), 80.

21   Chicago's 4-3-1 record against the Bacharach Giants was derived from the game accounts found in Bill Nowlin's timeline for the 1920 American Giants in the present volume.

22   "Pitchers' Battle Goes to Dave Brown, 1-0," *Chicago Defender*, August 20, 1921: 10.

23   "Pitchers' Battle Goes to Dave Brown, 1-0."

24   Frank Young, "It's All in the Game: The Montgomery Grey Sox-American Giants Game," *Chicago Defender*, September 17, 1921: 10.

25   Debono, 85; "Chicago American Giants Beat Hilldale Team 5-2," *Wilmington* (Delaware) *Morning News*, October 11, 1921: 7.

26   Debono, 85.

27   "Near-Riot Stops Baseball Game," *Chicago Defender*, May 13, 1922: 1.

28   Mister Fan, "American Giants Find K.C. Monarchs a Tough Bunch," *Chicago Defender*, May 13, 1922: 10.

29   "American Giants Find K.C. Monarchs a Tough Bunch."

30   "American Giants Find K.C. Monarchs a Tough Bunch."

31   "Near-Riot Stops Baseball Game."

32   Debono, 90.

33   "The Game Play by Play," *Chicago Defender*, August 26, 1922: 10.

34   Jorge S. Figueredo, *Cuban Baseball: A Statistical History, 1878-1961* (Jefferson, North Carolina: McFarland & Company, Inc., 2003), 143.

35   Figueredo, 147.

36   The founding teams of the Eastern Colored League were Hilldale, the Atlantic City Bacharach Giants, the Cuban Stars East, the Brooklyn Royal Giants, the New York Lincoln Giants, and the Baltimore Black Sox.

37   "Pitchers Brown and Rile Jump to the Outlaws," *Chicago Defender*, February 17, 1923: 10.

38   "Pitchers Brown and Rile Jump to the Outlaws."

39   "League Moguls Here This Week; Baseball War Looms."

40   Figueredo, 148.

41   Figueredo, 154.

42   "Lincoln Giants Grab Two Games from Washington," *Chicago Defender*, May 24, 1924: 9. The Harrisburg Giants were the other new addition to the ECL in 1924.

43   "Lincoln Giants Outclass Bacharach Giants in Two Games and Lead League," *Chicago Defender*, May 31, 1924: 9.

44   "Cubans Win Two Games from the Lincolns," *Chicago Defender*, October 4, 1924: 9.

45   Figueredo, 157.

46   Figueredo, 157-58, 160.

47   "Lincolns Win Two from Bacharach Giants," *Delaware County Times* (Chester, Pennsylvania), April 28, 1925: 8.

48   "Local Baseball Players Alleged to Be Mixed in Shooting of Benj. Adair," *New York Age*, May 2, 1925: 1.

49   "Local Baseball Players Alleged to Be Mixed in Shooting of Benj. Adair"; "Extra: Kill Man and Escape in Taxi," *New York Amsterdam News*, April 29, 1925: 1.

50   "Taxi Driver Freed in Adair Murder," *New York Amsterdam News*, May 6, 1925: 2.

51   W. Rollo Wilson, "Eastern Snapshots," *Pittsburgh Courier*, May 9, 1925: 13.

52   "Colored Boys Run Wild to Win, 11 to 4," *Davenport Daily Times*, June 21, 1926: 14.

53   "Union Giants Hurler Whiffs 17 at Spencer," *Cedar Rapids Gazette*, July 10, 1926: 9.

54   "LeMars Loses to Pipestone by 7-2 Score," *Sioux City Journal*, July 31, 1926: 15.

55   Peter W. Gorton, "The Mystery of Lefty Wilson" in Steven R. Hoffbeck (ed.), *Swinging for the Fences: Black Baseball in Minnesota* (St. Paul: Minnesota Historical Society Press, 2005), 108-111.

56   Gorton in Hoffbeck, 110.

57   Gorton in Hoffbeck, 110.

58   "Donaldson and Wilson to Be Opposing Pitchers," *Brainerd* (Minnesota) *Daily Dispatch*, June 14, 1928: 5.

59   Riley, *Of Monarchs and Black Barons*, 73-74; John Maher, "A Tale of Baseball, Murder, Mystery," *Austin American-Statesman*, August 25, 1997: 15, 22.

60   Gorton in Hoffbeck, 110-11.

61   "S.C. Firm Will Back Fast Club," *Sioux City Journal*, April 14, 1929: 21.

62   Joe Ryan, "Keri-Keen Wins from Kary-All," *Sioux City Journal*, May 12, 1929: 21.

63   "Cubans Drop Final Tilt 5-4," *Saskatoon* (Saskatchewan) *Star-Phoenix*, August 30, 1929: 21.

64   "Colored Davids Down Springers by 8 to 6 Count," *St. Cloud* (Minnesota) *Times*, June 23, 1930: 13.

65   "Bewhiskered Colored Team Invades Copeland Today," *La Crosse* (Wisconsin) *Tribune*, August 30, 1931: 9.

66 "Jess Wells Injured and Negro Is Held," *Greensboro* (North Carolina) *Daily News*, July 16, 1938: 4. Dave Brown previously had never used the name David, and his actual age by this time was 41; however, given Brown's prior alias and his continued need for cover-ups to dodge the law, as well as the information that next came to light, it appears that this David Brown was indeed Dave Brown the former Negro League pitcher. Subsequent articles in both Greensboro newspapers always gave the victim's first name as Jack, which appears to have been his correct name.

67 "Negro May Be Involved in 13-Year-Old Murder," *Greensboro Record*, July 23, 1938: 10. This article erroneously gave Brown's first name as George.

68 "Negro May Be Involved in 13-Year-Old Murder."

69 "Lucky," *Raleigh News and Observer*, July 31, 1938: 6.

70 Maher, "A Tale of Baseball, Murder, Mystery," 22.

71 Maher, 22.

72 James A. Riley, *The Biographical Encyclopedia of the Negro Baseball Leagues* (New York: Carroll & Graf Publishers, Inc., 1994), 118.

JIM BROWN

BY FREDERICK C. BUSH

When the name Jim Brown is mentioned, most sports fans call to mind the NFL's Hall of Fame running back who starred for the Cleveland Browns from 1957 to 1965. There was, however, an earlier Jim Brown – a catcher, first baseman, and, later, a manager – who played for Chicago American Giants squads that won five Negro National League pennants and two Negro League World Series in the 1920s. The worst thing reported about Brown was that a sheriff remembered him "as having kicked a dog a few years back and [that he] hasn't any particular love for the guardians of the law."[1] Whether Brown cared for legal authorities or not, he was never reported to have been arrested or accused of any crime. Nonetheless, he has been depicted as a miscreant to the point that a sensationalized story about how he died has become better known than reality.[2] The truth about Brown is that he put together a solid career as a player and manager that spanned the years 1914 to 1942, and the only troubles he was reported to have were occasional disciplinary actions due to vehement arguments with umpires.

James Rattles Brown was born on May 16, 1892, in San Marcos, Texas, to John and Emma Brown.[3] He was the couple's second child and had an older sister named Mary. In 1900 John worked as a press feeder at an oil mill and Emma was a laundress. James, or Jim as he was called, attended school, though the highest grade he completed is unknown. Also lost to history is how he attained his baseball skills and what type of work he did prior to becoming a professional ballplayer.

Whatever Brown did in his early years, in 1914, at the age of 22, he first appeared as a catcher for owner Enos Whittaker's Dallas Black Giants team.[4] Brown continued to grow into a top talent with Dallas in 1915 and 1916 as the Black Giants' everyday backstop and developed the switch-hitting skills that made him a desirable asset. Press coverage of the team was sparse, but one known highlight for Brown was a two-out, 12th-inning home run for a 6-5 victory over the Austin Black Senators in a game on July 3, 1915, at Gardner Park in Dallas.[5]

In 1917 pitcher Dave Brown (no relation) joined the Dallas team, and the two players became renowned as the "Brown Battery" during their tenure with the Black Giants in 1917 and 1918.[6] Rube Foster, owner of the Chicago American Giants, signed both Browns for his team in 1919. The *Chicago Defender* raved about Jim Brown after his arrival in the Windy City on April 6, declaring, "He has a whip of steel and a clouting eye. ... Brown looks like a winning type of ball player and room just had to be made for him."[7]

The 1919 season marked the American Giants' last campaign as an independent ballclub, and the team finished with a 27-16 record against rival Black teams in the West. George Dixon was Chicago's starting catcher, but Brown made the most of his opportunities and batted .310 with a .394 on-base percentage compared with Dixon's .261 BA and .344 OBP. The handwriting was on the wall for Dixon and the two catchers reversed roles in 1920.

Prior to the start of the 1920 season, Rube Foster and owners of most of the West's other major independent Black ballclubs formed the first Negro National League on February 13 at the Paseo Branch of the YMCA in Kansas City, Missouri.[8] Foster's American Giants dominated the league by winning the first three pennants (1920-1922).

Brown was the starting catcher in 1920 as the American Giants romped to a 43-17-2 league record that put them eight games ahead of the second-place Detroit Stars in the final standings. He had impressed Foster enough to become the first-string backstop, but the toll that catching takes on a player's body was evident when Dixon outperformed him at the plate over the course of the season with a .324 batting average and .391 on-base percentage compared with Brown's .235 and .330 marks.

Nonetheless, Brown was a key component in the team's success, and he once again formed the Brown Battery with his former Dallas teammate Dave Brown. On August 22 the Brown Battery worked its magic against the Kansas City Monarchs in a 5-1 victory at Schorling Park in Chicago. Dave hurled a complete game, and Jim scored one of Chicago's five runs. The American Giants embarrassed the Monarchs' battery of pitcher Sam Crawford and catcher Vicente Rodriguez by stealing bases at will. Jim Brown joined in the fun by stealing second base in the third inning (and later scoring) and adding a steal of third in the eighth, an inning in which Chicago swiped a total of five bases.[9]

At the conclusion of the NNL's inaugural season in 1920, Foster took his squad on a swing through the South in late September and early October. The American Giants defeated the Knoxville Giants for their 14th consecutive victory on October 2 that "sealed their status as the best black ball club in the country."[10] Next, they traveled northeast to take on the Atlantic City Bacharach Giants in a series of games played at Philadelphia's Shibe Park and Brooklyn's Ebbets Field. This series was to serve as "a dress rehearsal for what Rube envisioned as the black World Series."[11] The Bacharachs provided a stiff challenge, but the American Giants emerged with a 4-3-1 record in the series against the East's top independent club, and Foster's Chicago squad reigned supreme in 1920.[12]

In 1921 the American Giants held off the Kansas City Monarchs and St. Louis Giants to win a second consecutive NNL pennant. Dixon and Brown shared the catching duties to such an equitable extent that they appeared in the same number of games (53) and had the exact same number of plate appearances (186). Brown batted .289 and drove in 30 runs while Dixon hit .224 with 33 RBIs.

The following year, Chicago barely held off the Kansas City Monarchs to retain the NNL title. The American Giants won the pennant by virtue of having an almost infinitesimally greater winning percentage than Kansas City: The American Giants' 37-24-1 record gave them a .607 winning percentage compared with the Monarchs' 47-31-2, .603 mark. Brown recaptured the lion's share of the time behind the plate – playing in 62 games to Dixon's 28 – and batted .268 with 43 RBIs while Dixon hit .250 and drove in 14 runs. Brown also flashed a bit of speed by stealing 12 bases, an impressive number for a catcher.

The 1923 season marked a reversal of fortunes between the American Giants and the Monarchs. Ace pitcher Dave Brown defected to the New York Lincoln Giants of the new Eastern Colored League, which had been founded by Ed Bolden, owner of the Hilldale Club, to compete with the Western teams of the NNL. American Giants pitcher Ed "Huck" Rile was accused of luring players – such as Dave Brown – to teams in the new Eastern circuit and it was thought that he too would defect from Foster's team.[13] Instead, Rile emerged as the American Giants' new ace, going 15-7 with a 2.53 ERA in NNL play, but it was not enough to keep Chicago atop the league standings as the team finished 3½ games behind first-place Kansas City. Jim Brown was firmly entrenched as Chicago's starting catcher – Dixon was gone now – and, in 69 league games, he batted .238 with 45 RBIs.

Although the American Giants had finished second in the NNL, they were still a top-flight team, and they scheduled what was initially to be only a two-game series against the American League's Detroit Tigers at Schorling Park in late October.[14] Ty Cobb, the Tigers' legendary player-manager, did not participate in the series, but the Detroit team – which had also finished in second place in its league – was otherwise at full strength. The Tigers' roster included future Hall of Fame outfielders Harry Heilmann and Heinie Manush as well as 21-game winner George "Hooks" Dauss.

The first game took place on Saturday, October 20, and ended in a 5-5 tie when darkness forced the game to be halted at the end of the ninth inning.[15] Brown committed two costly errors in the game: The first miscue resulted in two Detroit runs that tied the game at 2-2 in the top of the fifth, and the second allowed Detroit to tally three more runs in the top of the sixth and take a 5-4 lead.[16] Chicago tied the game in the bottom of the eighth when Oscar Charleston crossed the plate, and the first game remained deadlocked.

The next day, 8,000 fans were in attendance as Detroit dominated the second game and won by a 7-1 score. The Tigers pounced on Rile for one run in the first inning and two more in the second and never looked back. For good measure, Detroit tacked on four more runs against Slim Branham, Chicago's third pitcher of the day (after Tom Williams), in the top of the ninth inning.[17]

Since the first game had ended tied, the two teams played again on October 22, and "[t]he American Giants rang the curtain down on their 1923 baseball season by winning an 8 to 6 game from the Detroit Tigers."[18] With the game tied, 3-3, Chicago erupted for five runs against Dauss (who pitched the entire game) in the bottom of the seventh inning and then held on for the victory. Brown went 2-for-3 at the plate and scored two runs in the finale, thus atoning for his gaffes behind the dish in the first game. In finishing the series at 1-1-1, the American Giants had shown themselves to be the equals of their White major-league counterparts.

During the offseason, Brown had another reason to celebrate as he married Hattie Mae Trymise in his hometown of San Marcos.[19] The joy, however, may have been short-lived as the couple was divorced by the time of Brown's death and they did not have any children.

The 1924 NNL season resulted in another second-place finish for Chicago, five games behind the Monarchs. The disappointment was even more palpable as the year 1924 marked the first Negro League World Series between representatives of the Negro National League and the Eastern Colored League. Foster had been preparing for such an event via his postseason tours to the East since 1920 and had been a key figure in bringing about this World Series. Now, all he could do was watch as the NNL rival Monarchs defeated Hilldale – owned by ECL founder Ed Bolden – in a 10-game classic (5-4-1).

Prior to the 1925 season, Foster cleaned house and released numerous aging stars in an effort to rebuild his team.[20] Although Brown turned 33 in May, he remained the American Giants' starting catcher. In a season preview article, the *Pittsburgh Courier* extolled Brown as having "[o]ne of the best throwing arms in the game [and being] fleet of foot and a dangerous left-hand batter."[21]

The *Chicago Defender* had high hopes for the American Giants at the 1925 season's outset after the team beat the city champion Chicago Blues, 5-3, at Schorling Park on Opening Day (Sunday, April 12). Columnist Frank A. Young declared, "With the weatherman dishing out sunshine and warmth of a June afternoon, 5,000 fans wended their way to the 39th St. grounds to get a glimpse of Foster's rejuvenated team, which from the brand of the national pastime they handed the assemblage Sunday, promises to bring to this city the National league championship."[22] By season's end, however, Chicago finished in third place, a full 10 games behind first-place Kansas City and 6½ games behind the second-place St. Louis Stars.

(Courtesy Noir-Tech Research, Inc.)

Starting catcher Jim Brown batted a solid .273 during his 17-year career, the vast majority of which was spent with the American Giants; he also managed the team in 1929 and 1930.

Despite the preseason accolades he had received, Brown's batting average dropped from .266 in 1924 to .232 in 1925 and reflected his team's temporary decline.

On top of Chicago's continued slide in the standings, Foster had almost died of asphyxiation due to a faulty gas heater at the team's boarding house in Indianapolis on May 26. Foster, who lived life at a frenetic pace, "brushed off the near-death experience and returned to Chicago with Mrs. Foster the next day."[23] Although he had survived the ordeal, Foster's behavior became more erratic from that time forward.

Nonetheless, Foster's baseball acumen was intact as the 1926 American Giants soared to new heights. Brown had his finest season for Chicago, batting .309 with a .395 on-base percentage and 46 RBIs in 75 league games. Age and the rigors of catching had begun to take their toll on him, and he played 50 of 74 regular-season games at first base, which helped to reinvigorate his bat. Pythias Russ was the primary catcher, and the two backstops caught a revamped pitching staff that posted a 2.74 team ERA, the best mark since the 1920 staff's 2.32 ERA. The ace of the 1926 staff was none other than Willie Foster, Rube's younger brother and a future Hall of Famer, who went 13-4 with a 1.80 ERA in NNL play.

Rube began the 1926 campaign in his familiar position as skipper. Chicago finished the first half of the NNL season with a 27-17-1 record under Foster as Kansas City again captured the title. However, Rube's behavior had become so bizarre that he was urged to take a two-week vacation to get some much-needed rest. Third baseman Dave Malarcher took over as player-manager in the season's second half and guided the team to a stellar 30-7-2 record to capture the second-half title. Malarcher's managerial position became permanent after Foster's vacation did not help to heal him. Eight days after a violent incident in August, during which he destroyed furniture in his apartment and threatened a friend with an ice pick, Foster "was declared mentally irresponsible and committed to the state hospital in Kankakee, Illinois. The event sent shock waves through the world of black baseball."[24]

Foster spent the last four years of his life in the asylum in Kankakee. It was a tragic end to the life and career of a stellar pitcher, manager, and entrepreneur. It also meant that he did not get to see his Chicago American Giants win their first World Series in 1926. First, Chicago defeated the Kansas City Monarchs in a tough nine-game NNL playoff series. In an equally challenging World Series, the American Giants defeated the ECL's Atlantic City Bacharach Giants in 11 games, with two of the contests ending in ties. Foster's rebuild had paid off and the American Giants were indisputably Black baseball's best team for the first time since 1920. Brown, for his part, struggled in the postseason, batting .250 against the Monarchs and only .158 against the Bacharachs while alternating between catcher and first base; however, by this time he had become an indispensable member of the team.

In 1927 the American Giants set to work to retain their status as kings of the baseball hill. Brown was now the longest-tenured player on the team. He again was Chicago's starting first baseman, although he did spell catcher James Bray occasionally. Brown's mid-30s batting renaissance continued apace as he batted .299 with a .360 on-base percentage and 35 RBIs during the NNL season.

John Schorling, Rube Foster's business partner, seized sole control of the American Giants from Rube's wife, Sarah Foster, in what can only be termed as a hostile takeover. Schorling retained Malarcher as the manager and held on to most of the players, so the 1927 squad was still equipped to mount a defense of its title. Chicago won the NNL's first-half championship, but again had to compete in a NNL playoff series when the Birmingham Black Barons captured the second-half flag.

Chicago had a composite 61-32-1 record in the NNL, but the team also excelled against outside competition. Over the Labor Day weekend, "the American Giants just had a gang of fun all to themselves at the expense of the Mills nine from the West side, the Hammond nine, with Buck Weaver, and the Duffy Florals, all white teams."[25] Brown's bat was quiet on Saturday, September 3, when the American Giants defeated the Mills team, 3-1, but he was the offensive hero of the next two contests. On Sunday the local fans celebrated Buck Weaver Day, and the disgraced former White Sox third baseman "received a warm welcome from the crowd."[26] Brown greeted Weaver's Hammond team with a 2-for-5 day in which he scored two runs and drove in the deciding run with an eighth-inning double as Chicago won, 5-3. The next day, Brown followed up with a 2-for-4 performance against the Duffy Florals and scored the game's only run after drawing a one-out walk in the 11th inning.[27]

On September 19, it was back to business in the NNL as Chicago faced Birmingham in the playoffs. After losing the opener, the American Giants won the next four games to return to the World Series, where they faced a familiar foe. The Atlantic City

Bacharach Giants had won both halves of the ECL's split season and had been able to rest while Chicago battled Birmingham. It did not matter, though, as "[t]he similarities between the World Series of 1926 and that of 1927 [were] startling. The American Giants again won, five games to three, Willie Foster again won the final game against Hubert Lockhart, and an obscure left-handed Atlantic City pitcher [again threw] a no-hitter."[28] The American Giants extended their reign over the Black baseball world, and Brown had been a major contributor on offense this time around, batting .314 and driving in six runs while playing in all nine World Series games (one game had ended in a tie). These were heady days for the American Giants, but all was not well with the franchise or the Negro Leagues.

During the second half of the 1927 season, Schorling had sold the team to William Trimble, a White businessman from Princeton, Illinois. In addition to the American Giants missing Rube Foster, who had been both the team's and the NNL's guiding light, the Negro Leagues in general began to wane. In his wisdom, Foster "had always been a stern disciplinarian," but now, "[w]ithout Foster, player behavior worsened and physical attacks on umpires weren't uncommon. Scheduling, always an issue, became even tougher, and attendance waned. Black journalists began criticizing Negro League players for lackadaisical play, consuming alcohol during games, and excessive umpire baiting."[29] As his career progressed, Brown had his share of run-ins with umpires on the diamond.

The 1928 season was filled with adversity for Brown and the American Giants. The St. Louis Stars took the first-half title while Chicago coped with injuries. Manager-third baseman Malarcher missed several weeks after breaking a bone in his shoulder, during which time pitcher George Harney skippered the team to an 18-19 record (they were 40-21-1 under Malarcher).

On July 7, the *Chicago Defender* reported that Brown had undergone "an operation ... Wednesday morning" – although the type of surgery was not mentioned – and he was expected to be hospitalized for "about 11 days."[30] Like Malarcher, Brown missed several weeks of playing time. He returned in time to take part in one of the ugly incidents with umpires that were plaguing the Negro Leagues. During an August 25 game against the Detroit Stars in Chicago, American Giants right fielder Walter "Steel Arm" Davis "lost his temper and hit [umpire] Moore in the

face," for which action he was suspended indefinitely by the league.[31] Brown and four Chicago teammates were fined $5 each for arguing with the umpire about the call that caused Davis to commit assault on the game's arbiter.[32] It was a nasty confrontation in an abbreviated season for Brown that saw him appear in a mere 37 games during which he batted .264 with only 12 RBIs.

The American Giants mounted one final charge to garner the NNL's second-half championship and earned the right to face St. Louis in the playoffs. The Stars routed the American Giants, 19-4, on October 4 in St. Louis to tie the series at four games apiece. The next day, the dispirited Chicagoans suffered a 9-2 defeat that put an end to their title hopes. St. Louis had to settle for the NNL championship since the ECL had folded early in the season, putting the Negro League World Series on hiatus for what turned out to be a 14-year period.

Prior to the 1929 season, Malarcher, who was unhappy with Trimble's ownership style, left the team. As a result, Brown "was appointed the 'captain,' and took up the field manager duties."[33] Unfortunately for Brown, numerous other stalwarts from the past two seasons were also displeased with Trimble and defected from the team, leaving him with a depleted roster. Future Hall of Famers Cool Papa Bell, Mule Suttles, and Willie Wells all played for Chicago in 1929 but only for four games. Willie Foster was the only Hall of Famer whom Brown was able to count on all season, and he managed only a 9-7 record due to a lack of run support.

At one point, as the American Giants struggled in NNL play, a known felon thought things were so bad that he might finagle a slot in Chicago's pitching rotation. Memphis Red Sox pitcher Robert Poindexter, upset over a 14-3 shellacking by the St. Louis Stars, had taken umbrage at teammate J.C. McHaskell's attempt to cheer him up, pulled a revolver, and shot McHaskell in the foot. After Poindexter was arrested, it was discovered that he was wanted in Atlanta "about a little matter of a violated parole."[34] Inexplicably, Poindexter was able to extricate himself from legal trouble on both counts and went about searching for new employment. After being rebuffed by the Detroit club, "[h]e failed also to convince Jim Brown that he should be hired or come to Chicago via trade."[35] Brown may well have remembered what had happened to his former Brown Battery mate from Texas, Dave Brown, after he left Chicago and decided that on-field success was not worth off-field crimes. Dave Brown was, at that very moment, playing semipro ball in the Midwest under the alias Lefty Wilson while being wanted for murder for an April 28, 1925, shooting in New York City.

In late June, it was reported that Brown and catcher Pythias Russ were facing suspensions for their roles in another dust-up with an umpire during a midmonth series with the Monarchs in Kansas City. According to the *Defender*, "the [NNL] president's office [was] simply awaiting a detailed report from the umpires in Kansas City where some serious trouble was narrowly averted."[36]

The next time Chicago and Kansas City faced off, in a late-June/early-July series, the two teams split six games, but the Monarchs claimed the NNL's first-half championship. To add insult to injury, Andy Cooper hurled a 2-0 no-hitter against the American Giants in the third game of the series on July 1 at Schorling Park.[37] The Monarchs also claimed the second-half title and were the undisputed champions of the NNL. Chicago finished 51-40 in NNL play, which put the team in third place in the composite standings, 17½ games behind Kansas City. Brown's first season at the helm was by no means an abject failure – the team finished 62-42 against all competition – but, compared with the three previous campaigns, it was a disappointment. As a player, Brown had inserted himself into the lineup wherever he was needed – infield, outfield, catcher, pinch-hitter – and had batted .248 with 21 RBIs.

Brown's second season as skipper started off promisingly, with Chicago taking four of five games from the Detroit Stars in their opening series and then splitting a four-game set with the New York Cubans. However, things quickly went downhill and Brown's frustration with his team began to show. In mid-June, the *Defender* noted, "He has tried benching Jelly Gardner, Walter Davis, Charlie Williams, Murray and Jeffries, but none of the substitutes he has put in the game have shown any better work."[38] Brown became so distressed by the American Giants' perceived lack of effort that he resigned as manager on July 1 – but stayed on as a player – and, on July 12, it was reported that Willie Foster would take the reins.[39]

The St. Louis Stars won the NNL's first-half title, but Chicago took five games against the Cubans early in the season's second half as they tried to right their ship. Brown, liberated from the pressures of managing, hit better than he had in some time and was the key player in the sweep. Once again, though, the good feelings did not last long.

In the second game of an August 17 doubleheader against Birmingham at Schorling Park, Satchel Paige threw three consecutive pitches that almost hit Chicago shortstop Eddie Miller. A riled-up Miller "left the box and went to the pitcher's box to hit Satchel in the head with his (Miller's) bat. Satchel ran. Miller chased him. Fans began to leave the park. Players intervened and two or three fights were narrowly averted."[40] The *Defender* blasted both teams and averred, "No such actions would be tolerated in either the [White] American or National league."[41] In the aftermath of this fiasco, Willie Foster decided to clean house. The *Defender* applauded Foster's effort to rebuild, stating, "There are many on the Windy City outfit that have been there just too long – have outlived their usefulness, not as ball players, perhaps, but as drawing cards."[42]

In the hope of recapturing a dwindling fan base, the American Giants also began to schedule series against top clubs outside of the NNL such as the independent Homestead Grays from Pittsburgh and the Houston Black Buffaloes, champions of the Texas-Louisiana League. Brown sparkled in both series as Chicago lost five of six to Homestead but won four of five against Houston. He had become a beloved elder statesman on the team, who was appreciated for his efforts, and "the folks [were] calling him good old Jim Brown."[43]

The Detroit Stars won the NNL's second-half title but lost the championship series to the St. Louis Stars. The American Giants finished 1930 in fourth place in the composite standings, 20 games behind St. Louis. A revitalized Brown batted .305 with 26 RBIs in 56 games during his last season as a full-time player with the American Giants.

Late in the 1930 season, the *Defender* had lamented, "The league in its 10th season is in worse shape than in its whole history. The efforts of Rube Foster, who lost his health because of his untiring work to build up the league, seems [sic] to have gone to waste. The league is like a drowning man – someone must save it."[44] Rube Foster died on December 9, 1930. Two months later, on February 7, Chicago found out that Willie Foster was not going to play the role of savior for his older brother's team or league. Foster announced that he was resigning as manager of the American Giants to focus on his pitching, and then he bolted Chicago to join the Homestead Grays for the 1931 season.[45] On top of all that, Trimble had sold ownership of the franchise to Charles Bidwell in the second half of the 1930 season and Bidwell now "treated the American

Giants like a pot he lucked upon in a poker game and was at a loss about what to do next."[46]

Many players followed in Willie Foster's footsteps and abandoned the American Giants. Brown and several teammates formed an independent team and went on a barnstorming tour. The Cleveland Cubs, a new entry in the NNL, opened their season on May 23 against Brown and company.[47] Meanwhile, Malarcher returned to Chicago and agreed to resume a leadership role as the American Giants were reformed and renamed the Chicago Columbia Giants; the team remained a member franchise of the NNL. The Columbia Giants opened their season with a two-game sweep of the Nashville Elite Giants over the Decoration Day (Memorial Day) weekend.[48] Brown was not yet back in the fold, but he returned in time for the next series against the St. Louis Stars and split his time between catching and first base.[49]

On July 4 it was reported that the Columbia Giants were departing for a five-game set in St. Louis, after which the team would return to Chicago and play the remainder of the season as an independent ballclub.[50] Chicago finished the NNL season with a 6-17-1 record that placed the squad last out of six teams; St. Louis played twice as many league games and won the championship with a 37-10-1 record. Brown, who was now 39 years old, batted .292 but that number was deceptive since he had played in only nine league games.

In late August Brown headed back to his home state of Texas as a member of the barnstorming Charles Wesley Giants. Wesley, who had played for several NNL squads in the 1920s had formed an all-star team and now combined seven members of his squad with eight former American Giants to form a new team.[51] After their tour through Texas, the team returned to the Midwest and played anywhere a game could be scheduled until winter arrived.[52]

Rube Foster's first iteration of the Negro National League collapsed after the 1931 season. In 1932 the American Giants joined the Negro Southern League while Brown formed a traveling squad named the Rube Foster Memorial Giants. The NSL's Nashville Elite Giants opened their season against Brown's team on April 10.[53] By the end of the month, it was announced that Brown's squad would replace the Cleveland Cubs and would become a member of the NSL.[54]

Although the *Defender* now used the moniker Jim Brown's Cleveland Cubs,[55] Brown and the team never represented Cleveland because the franchise could not secure a home ballpark. The team finished a brief tour of the South and had an abysmal 1-15 record when its

season and existence came to a merciful end. In mid-May, the mighty Monroe Monarchs swept a four-game series from Brown's squad, including a doubleheader in which Elbert Williams threw a 6-0, one-hit victory that Barney Morris followed with a 4-0 no-hitter.[56]

Two weeks after the debacle against the Monarchs, Brown signed to take over as the skipper of the NSL's Louisville Black Caps after that team started the season 0-8 (0-4 in the NSL) under ex-American Giants outfielder Jimmie Lyons.[57] The *Defender*, which never printed a harsh word about Brown, ran the headline "Louisville Eyes Flag" after the Black Caps swept a three-game series from the Montgomery Grey Sox.[58] That was wishful thinking, however, as the team disbanded in late July prior to a series against Monroe. It was reported that "[t]he Louisville club gave out no news of its plans to quit until Monroe had arrived on the scene Saturday [July 23] and then the sign was displayed, 'No game today.'"[59] A new semipro squad – the Red Birds, soon renamed the Red Sox – was cobbled together from the remnants of the Black Caps and another local team, and Brown finished the season in the same manager-catcher role that he had played for the Black Caps.[60]

After his itinerant 1932 season, Brown's whereabouts for most of 1933 are a mystery. The *Defender* reported in March that Brown would manage the Nashville team, which now belonged to the second iteration of the Negro National League (as did the Chicago American Giants).[61] On March 25 the *Defender* still claimed, "Dunn, an infielder, and Jim Brown, manager, who is now in Chicago, are expected to be on hand when the train pulls out of here."[62] However, on April 2 the *Nashville Banner* reported that "[Felton] Stratton, a local boy, will be the playing manager."[63] Stratton managed Nashville for the entire 1933 season, and Brown is known to have played in a mere two games at catcher for Chicago.

In 1934 Brown was back on the map and had steady employment throughout the year. He managed the barnstorming Van Dyke House of David team that had been founded by Harry Crump in Des Moines, Iowa.[64] The original (White) House of David team had belonged to a religious commune in Benton Harbor, Michigan, and its players were known for their long hair and beards. This was not the first Black team to take the House of David name and to wear fake beards, but rather was one of many such ballclubs. Brown's squad toured the entire Western half of the United States and even made a foray into Canada. After a grueling tour that lasted from May 18 into early

October, the team was scheduled to "head to Omaha, Nebr., where new headquarters will be opened up and then players will depart to Chicago for the winter."[65] The 42-year-old Brown not only managed the Van Dykes but also continued to play and "established quite a reputation as a slugger, pounding the ball at [a] .356 clip."[66]

Although Brown had excelled in 1934, the arduous tour had to have taken its toll on him, and in 1935 he returned to the Chicago American Giants. The team was alternately known as the Cole's American Giants, thus named after new owner Robert Cole, a Black undertaker who had bought the franchise prior to the 1932 season. The *Defender* hailed Brown's hire, noting, "[he] will serve as first assistant to [new manager] Larry Brown both in the catching department and running of the team. [Jim] Brown is one of the keenest judges of players and plays ever to don a uniform. He was acting captain of the Giants for years during the old regime."[67]

Brown was basically the bench coach for his new catcher-manager Larry Brown (no relation) and appeared in only 11 games as a player in 1935. When he did play, he contributed all he could with a .476 batting average and a .522 on-base percentage. The glory days for Chicago were long gone, however, and the team finished 24-31-1, which was only good enough for sixth place (out of eight teams) in the NNL2's composite standings.

After the 1935 campaign, Brown temporarily retired from baseball. He did not play or manage in 1936, made one appearance at catcher for the American Giants in 1937, and remained retired through 1939. Brown resided in Chicago and eventually responded to the siren call of baseball in 1940, when he emerged from retirement to manage the Palmer House All-Stars.[68] The team was sponsored by Chicago's Palmer House Hotel and was composed mostly of former Negro League players who worked for the hotel. Brown took over a squad that had "won the Illinois State Semi-pro championship and competed in the national tourney in Wichita" the previous year.[69]

Although Brown appeared to have enjoyed leading the Palmer House team, he retired again and sat out the 1941 season.[70] In 1942, however, he was lured out of retirement a second time to manage the Minneapolis-St. Paul Gophers of the new Negro Major Baseball League.[71] The circuit was the brainchild of promoter Abe Saperstein (of Harlem Globetrotters basketball renown), and top personnel were hired to run what was to be a first-rate operation. League President R.R.

Jackson of Chicago gave assurances that the league "plans to go its own way on a high-class plane, has no axes to grind and does not contemplate injurious measures in the other circuits of Negro baseball."[72]

The Gophers played their home games at St. Paul's Lexington Park, the home of the American Association's St. Paul Saints, and were set to open their home slate on June 21 against Brown's old team, the Chicago American Giants.[73] However, the honeymoon between the Gophers and the Twin Cities ended quickly.

On Sunday, June 28, the Gophers lost a 1-0 game to the Cincinnati Ethiopian Clowns that was called after six innings due to rain.[74] Three days later, the *Minneapolis Star* printed complaints from a disenchanted fan named Lyle Dowdal:

> "In order to keep the gate receipts, says Dowdel [sic], both teams swung at first balls offered them, no matter how bad they were. The players rushed into action as fast as they could UNTIL THE NECESSARY FOUR AND A HALF INNINGS WERE PLAYED AND THE MONEY BELONGED TO THE PROMOTERS. Then they just took things leisurely until the rain stopped proceedings for the afternoon.
>
> 'It was the worst case of cheating the spectators I have seen in baseball in all my life,' Dowdal relates."[75]

The *Star* contacted Saperstein, whom it named as "the Director, schedule maker, financier and publicity agent" of the league, to solicit his opinion on the matter. Saperstein replied with a written rebuttal in which he denied any wrongdoing on the part of either team or the league. In its July 10 edition, the *Star* asserted, "We are not backing down one bit on [the accusations], but call it a closed incident by printing the Saperstein rebuttal with the added warning that no one can successfully establish a new promotional enterprise in these parts by making customers mad."[76]

After the Gophers and Chicago Brown Bombers became the first Black baseball teams to play a game in Waterloo, Iowa, the local newspaper also was unimpressed. This time, however, the dissatisfaction was with the style of play between the two Negro Major Baseball League teams compared with that of White baseball nines. The *Waterloo Courier* remarked:

> "The Negro boys have their own systems of baseball. It was apparent Wednesday evening.

They bunted when orthodox baseball called for a full cut at the ball; they stole bases or attempted it when three runs behind and otherwise performed in a manner that bewildered old baseball heads who are accustomed to seeing Johnny Mostil and White Hawk baseball.

"... It was apparent from the very start that the White Hawks or any other team in the Three-I could handle both teams at one and the same time. A better match would be the East High nine and a combined team from the two Negro clubs which appeared at the Stadium. The score would be close, too."[77]

The *Courier's* insults – which smacked in part of racism – notwithstanding, it was apparent that the new Negro Major Baseball League did not offer spectators the same quality baseball as the true Negro major leagues did. By early August, Brown's best players had defected to the New York Lincoln Giants,[78] and the only Gophers that the Minneapolis press was covering were the University of Minnesota Golden Gophers, who were preparing for the coming football season. It is unclear at what point the league folded, but it appears to have been a well-intentioned yet poorly implemented venture that failed to last an entire season.[79]

Brown, in poor health and divorced from his wife, Hattie, returned to Texas after the 1942 season and settled in San Antonio, which is close to his hometown of San Marcos. He was not there long before he died on January 21, 1943. Negro League historian James Riley has provided a wild account of Brown's death that, as of the year 2021, proliferates on the Internet and in print. According to Riley, "Brown enjoyed nightlife and liked to gamble, and it eventually led to his death. In an incident relating to his gambling, he was thrown out of a moving car and died from a broken neck."[80]

It is a peculiar tale of a violent death, but there is no truth to it. The *Defender*, in announcing Brown's death to its readership, noted that Brown "had been seriously ill since the close of the 1942 baseball season."[81] The doctor who filled out Brown's death certificate listed Brown's cause of death as cardiac failure and observed that an enlarged liver and general edema were contributing factors. The secondary causes indicate that Brown likely consumed excessive amounts of alcohol, but he never achieved notoriety in the press for bad behavior that resulted from drunkenness and was not killed after a night of drinking and gambling.

On Sunday, January 24, 1943, Jim Brown was buried in San Marcos-Blanco Cemetery in San Marcos, Texas.[82]

SOURCES

All player statistics and team records were taken from Seamheads.com, except where otherwise indicated.

Ancestry.com was consulted for US Census information; military records; and birth, marriage, and death records.

NOTES

1   "Lyons, Torrienti [*sic*] and Jim Brown Sign with Am. Giants," *Chicago Defender*, January 13, 1923: 10.

2   James A. Riley, *The Biographical Encyclopedia of the Negro Baseball Leagues* (New York: Carroll & Graf Publishers, Inc., 1994), 121.

3   Jim Brown's death certificate lists his mother's maiden name as Emma Giles. However, the 1910 census shows that Emma's widowed mother, Liza Ford, was living with the Brown family at that time and lists Emma Ford as an alternate name for Emma Brown. It is possible that Liza Ford could have been twice widowed, by husbands with the surnames Giles and Ford, or that Jim Brown's death certificate was in error about the name Giles (as it was about his year of birth, listing 1895 rather than the year 1892 that is corroborated by numerous other official documents).

4   "Negro Baseball," *Shreveport Times*, July 6, 1914: 8.

5   "Dallas Black Giants Win," *Dallas Morning News*, July 4, 1915: 6.

6   Multiple sources erroneously list Dave Brown as also having been born in San Marcos, Texas; however, Dave Brown was born in Marquez, Texas. There is no evidence that the two players were related; even if they were kin, they certainly were not members of the same immediate family.

7   "American Giants Open Sunday: 'Rube' Foster Will Present the Greatest Team of His Career," *Chicago Defender*, April 12, 1919: 11.

8   Except for the Jewell's ABCs, all the major Western Independent Clubs from 1919 became members of the NNL in 1920; two additional squads – the Indianapolis ABCs and the Kansas City Monarchs – also were founding members of the circuit.

9   "American Giants Take Kansas City's Measure," *Chicago Defender*, August 28, 1920: 6.

10 "American Giants, 2; Knoxville, 1," *Chicago Defender*, October 9, 1920: 6; James A. Riley, *Of Monarchs and Black Barons: Essays on Baseball's Negro Leagues* (Jefferson, North Carolina: McFarland & Company, Inc., 2012), 74.

11 Paul Debono, *The Chicago American Giants* (Jefferson, North Carolina: McFarland & Company, Inc., 2007), 80.

12 Chicago's 4-3-1 record against the Bacharach Giants was derived from the game accounts found in Bill Nowlin's timeline for the 1920 American Giants in the present volume.

13 "Pitchers Brown and Rile Jump to the Outlaws," *Chicago Defender*, February 17, 1923: 10.

14 "Detroit Americans Face Fosters in 2-Game Fight," *Chicago Defender*, October 20, 1923: 9.

15 "American Giant Nine Plays 5-5 Tie with Tigers," *Chicago Tribune*, October 21, 1923: 2-7.

16 Debono, 96.

17 "American Giants Bow, 7-1, Before Detroit Majors," *Chicago Tribune*, October 22, 1923: 26.

18   "Rube Foster's Giants Beat Detroit Tigers,"
      Chicago Tribune, October 23, 1923: 25.

19   Hattie Mae's surname may have been "Trymise" or
      "Trymire" since both variants appear in legal records.

20   "Foster Releases Several Ball Players: Leroy Grant Among
      Those Unfortunates," *Chicago Defender*, March 7, 1925: 12.

21   "Trio of American Giants," *Pittsburgh Courier*, March 14,
      1925: 7. Since the *Courier* referred to Brown as a left-hand-
      ed batter, it is unknown whether Brown had given up on
      switch-hitting or was simply a better hitter from the left side.

22   Frank A. Young, "American Giants in Tip Top Shape Hand Chicago
      Blues 5 to 3 Trimming," *Chicago Defender*, April 18, 1925: 9.

23   Debono, 105.

24   Debono, 110.

25   "White Teams Fall Before American Giants Attack,"
      Chicago Defender, September 10, 1927: 9.

26   "White Teams Fall Before American Giants Attack."

27   "White Teams Fall Before American Giants Attack."

28   Kyle McNary, *Black Baseball: A History of African-Americans & the
      National Game* (New York: PRC Publishing Ltd., 2003), 112. In 1926
      Atlantic City's Claude "Red" Grier threw a no-hitter against Chicago in
      Game Three of the World Series; it was the high point of Grier's career as
      he won only one game in 1927 before his career ended at the age of 23. In
      the 1927 World Series, Atlantic City's Luther Farrell pitched a seven-inning
      no-hitter in Game Five; although the game was called early due to darkness,
      the victory went in the books. Farrell fared better than Grier after his World
      Series no-no and won a career-high 16 games during the 1928 ECL season.

29   McNary, 112.

30   "Jim Brown Operated on at Douglass Hospital," *Chicago Defender*, July
      7, 1928: 8. No primary or secondary sources list the nature of Brown's
      surgery. However, a July 14 news article mentioned about the American
      Giants that "Russ has been moved to the short field and Davis, the right
      fielder, has been shifted to first since Jim Brown injured his leg." Thus,
      it is entirely possible that Brown had surgery on his injured leg. (See
      "American Giants Play Stars Today," *Detroit Free Press*, July 14, 1928: 15.)

31   "Davis Draws Suspension for Fighting," *Chicago
      Defender*, September 1, 1928: 9.

32   "Davis Draws Suspension for Fighting."

33   Debono, 122.

34   "Shoots First Sacker; Pitcher to Hoosegow," *Lincoln*
      (Nebraska) *Journal Star*, June 1, 1929: 8.

35   "Poindexter Claims Shooting Accidental," *Chicago Defender*, June 15,
      1929: 8. Although Poindexter apparently incurred no legal consequences for
      the shooting, he was banished by the NNL later in the month of June (see
      "Jim Brown, Russ Face Suspension, *Chicago Defender*, June 29, 1929: 8).

36   "Jim Brown, Russ Face Suspension."

37   "Kansas City Wins First Half of National League 1929 Season/
      Kansas City Hands American Giants No-Hit, No-Run Game; Lead
      Series Two Games to One," *Chicago Defender*, July 6, 1929: 8.

38   "Kansas City vs. Am. Giants on June 21st,"
      Chicago Defender, June 21, 1930: 9.

39   "Giants Face Kansas City on July 11th/Willie Foster Succeeds Jim
      Brown as Giant Pilot," *Chicago Defender*, July 12, 1930: 9.

40   "New Faces to Be Seen in American Giants Line-Up as Result of
      Drastic Shake-Up," *Chicago Defender*, August 23, 1930: 8.

41   "New Faces to Be Seen."

42   "New Faces to Be Seen."

43   "Houston Nine in Chicago for 1st Time," *Chicago Defender*, September
      13, 1930: 8. (See also: "Grays Beat Am. Giants; Black Buffs Here/
      Foster Only Giants Pitcher to Stop Homesteads; Jim Brown and C.
      White Sparkle," *Chicago Defender*, September 13, 1930: 8).

44   "New Faces to Be Seen."

45   "Foster Resigns Managership of Am. Giants,"
      Chicago Defender, February 7, 1931: 8.

46   Debono, 129.

47   "Cleveland to Play Team from Chicago," *Chicago Defender*, May 23, 1931: 9.

48   Dan Burley, "Nashville Elite Giants Beaten Twice by Columbia
      Giants at Chicago, 4-1; 5-2," *Chicago Defender*, June 6, 1931: 8.

49   "St. Louis Here for 5-Game Series," *Chicago Defender*, June 6, 1931: 9.

50   Dan Burley, "Columbia Giants Win Series from Cincinnati; Leave for
      St. Louis for 5-Game Stand," *Chicago Defender*, July 4, 1931: 8.

51   "Giants Off for Games in Texas/Former Giant Players on Tour of Southland/
      Leaves to Play Ball in Texas," *Chicago Defender*, August 22, 1931: 8.

52   "Ex-American Giant Players Win Game,"
      Chicago Defender, October 3, 1931: 9.

53   "Elites to Play/Local Negro Ball Club Will Meet Chicago Outfit,"
      Nashville Banner, April 7, 1932: 15. In a distressing display of how
      quickly even a prominent person can fall from the public consciousness,
      the *Banner* printed the following correction in this article: "A story in
      Wednesday's paper stated that Rube Foster was managing the Giants. That
      was incorrect, since Foster is dead. The club is a memorial to Foster."

54   "Jim Brown's Team in League: Franchise of Cleveland to
      Chicagoan's 9," *Chicago Defender*, April 30, 1932: 9.

55   "Cleveland to Welcome Jim Brown's Team,"
      Chicago Defender, May 7, 1932: 8.

56   "Monroe Beats Cleveland in Straight Sets,"
      Chicago Defender, May 14, 1932: 9.

57   "Black Caps Away," *Louisville Courier-Journal*, May 28, 1932: 12.

58   "Louisville Eyes Flag: Jim Brown's Gang Cops 3-Game
      Set," *Chicago Defender*, July 16, 1932: 9.

59   "Louisville Quits Southern League," *Chicago Defender*, July 30, 1932: 9.

60   "Louisville Quits Southern League"; "Jim Brown's Team
      Victor," *Chicago Defender*, August 20, 1932: 8.

61   "Leads Mates into Training," *Chicago Defender*, March 18, 1933: 8.

62   "Nashville to Start Drills," *Chicago Defender*, March 25, 1933: 9.

63   "Elite Giants Train in New Orleans, La.," *Nashville Banner*, April 2, 1933: 11.

64   "Jim Brown's Ball Team Wins a Pair," *Chicago Defender*, May 26, 1934: 16.

65   "Jim Brown's 9 to Tour Coast Starting Soon,"
      Chicago Defender, July 21, 1934: 17.

66   "Jim Brown Quits House of David to Play with
      Cole," *Chicago Defender*, May 18, 1935: 13.

67   "Jim Brown Quits House of David to Play with Cole."

68   "Jim Brown to Manage Palmer House Stars,"
      Chicago Defender, December 2, 1939: 22.

69   "Chicago All-Stars Bring Classy Club Here on Tuesday,"
      Davenport (Iowa) *Daily Times*, July 12, 1940: 16.

70   "Palmer House Boys Feted at Boosters Club,"
      Chicago Defender, December 14, 1940: 20.

71   "Chicago, Detroit, Boston, St. Paul, Baltimore, Minneapolis
      Form Loop," *Atlanta Daily World*, March 25, 1942: 5.

72   "New League Has No Axes to Sharpen," *New York Amsterdam Star-News*, April 4, 1942: 13.

73   "St. Paul Gophers Open Season Sunday June 21," *Chicago Defender*, June 20, 1942: 20.

74   "City Negro Nine Loses League Game," *Minneapolis Star*, June 29, 1942: 19.

75   Charlie Johnson, "Charlie Johnson's Lowdown on Sports: 'Cheating' the Spectators," *Minneapolis Star*, July 1, 1942: 28.

76   Charlie Johnson, "Charlie Johnson's Lowdown on Sports: Saperstein's Explanation," *Minneapolis Star*, July 10, 1942: 20.

77   "Unorthodox and Funny in Spots, Negro Baseball," *Waterloo* (Iowa) *Courier*, July 2, 1942: 9.

78   "Autos Expect Stiff Tussle with Giants," *Saint Joseph* (Michigan) *Herald-Press*, August 18, 1942: 11.

79   "Bury Jim Brown, Famous Am. Giant Catcher, in Texas," *Chicago Defender*, February 13, 1943: 21. In this article, the *Defender* made the claim that Brown ended the 1942 season as the manager of the traveling New York Lincoln Giants team. Although this author was unable to discover any other corroboration for this claim, it is entirely in the realm of possibility and would indicate that the Minneapolis-St. Paul Gophers (and perhaps the entire Negro Major Baseball League) folded in August 1942.

80   Riley, 121.

81   "Bury Jim Brown, Famous Am. Giant Catcher, in Texas."

82   "Bury Jim Brown, Famous Am. Giant Catcher, in Texas."

ELWOOD "BINGO" DEMOSS

BY BILL JOHNSON

He was, by wide acclaim, one of the finest second basemen to play in the segregated era, as well as before the formal creation of a Negro League. Elwood "Bingo" DeMoss played alongside not only John Henry "Pop" Lloyd, but on various teams whose rosters included a figurative "Who's-Who" of Black baseball in the first two decades of the twentieth century.

DeMoss had a career-high .314 batting average and .409 on-base percentage in 67 NNL games for the American Giants in 1920.

(Courtesy Noir-Tech Research, Inc.)

He went on to manage in the cities of Detroit, Akron, Cleveland, and Chicago, and even managed the West All-Stars in the 1936 East-West game. Historian James Riley called DeMoss "…the greatest second baseman in black baseball in the first quarter (of the twentieth) century . . . the consummate ballplayer, excelling at all phases of the game."[1]

There are few known, verifiable details about DeMoss' early life. Based on review of various official United States census documents,[2] along with digitized marriage records[3] and DeMoss' draft registration for World War I, Elwood was born on September 5, 1889, in Topeka, Kansas, as the youngest of five children of Mansfield and Alie (Perkins) DeMoss. Mansfield was born in Tennessee in either 1844 or 1845. It is therefore likely that he was born a slave, and liberated by the end of the United States Civil War. By 1910, Alie (alternatively spelled Eley in some official documents) was a widow, Mansfield having been 15 years her senior.[4] She supported her family by working as a housekeeper in the Topeka area. Of note, that 1910 census lists Alie, 20-year-old Elwood, and the other children as able to read and write. Elwood achieved a seventh-grade education,[5] which was a particularly impressive achievement, given the humble beginnings of the family and the challenges faced by the newly-liberated, non-White families throughout the nation.

Regardless, Elwood DeMoss was also a talented athlete, and while some accounts state that he began his baseball career in 1905 with the Topeka Giants[6], it was more likely 1906.[7] His first documented games as a professional came in 1910, for the Oklahoma Monarchs and the Kansas City Giants. The 20-year-old played second base for those teams that season, and displayed such prowess at bunting and defense that he returned to the Giants for the 1911 season, playing for manager "Topeka" Jack Johnson,[8] who was also at the helm of the 1906 Topeka Giants. Of note, during his brief time with Oklahoma, DeMoss played alongside a young slugger, Louis Santop, the first of many future Hall-of-Famers with whom he would team.

James Riley, in his encyclopedia, summarized DeMoss' skill set as follows: "A scientific clutch hitter with superior bat control and exceptional eye-hand coordination, he was a good contact hitter and could place the ball where he wanted. A natural right-field hitter, he was a skilled hit-and-run artist and a superb bunter . . . Jocko Conlon, who before becoming an umpire played exhibitions against the Chicago American Giants, said that DeMoss could drop a bunt on a dime."[9] While there is no definitive account of how DeMoss was anointed "Bingo," the existing narrative is that it derived from his ability to "place a bunt anywhere he wanted on the field."[10] Kansas City Monarchs catcher Frank Duncan once observed that, "I've never seen a man bunt a ball like DeMoss. Looked like when you play pool and draw a ball back. How he did it, I don't know, but he sure did it."[11]

From Kansas, DeMoss joined the French Lick Plutos and then C.I. Taylor's West Baden Sprudels in 1912. In 1913, 24-year-old DeMoss married Virgil Williams, a woman a year younger than himself. They would have no children, and she passed away in 1935 at the age of 45.

In May of 1915, DeMoss followed manager Taylor to Indianapolis, where he joined C.I.'s brother Ben Taylor, as well as Oscar Charleston and Dizzy Dismukes, in pacing the ABCs to a 37-25 record[12] and a first place finish among the Western Independent Clubs. In two particular games against Rube Foster's Chicago American Giants, on June 21 and July 18, DeMoss scored three runs in eight at-bats, despite producing only one hit.[13] Foster was later quoted as saying "'Bingo' is a ballplayer at all times, and from head to foot. However, his big assets are from the shoulders up."[14]

In Indianapolis, though, DeMoss ran into a bit of trouble. In one now-notorious incident during the fifth inning of a game between a White All-Star team captained by Donie Bush and Foster's ABCs, umpire Jimmy Scanlon made a bang-bang call at second base that favored the White base runner. DeMoss, who had made the tag at second base and knew the runner should have been called out, charged the arbiter and punched him in the face. Before the fight could really get going, right fielder Oscar Charleston raced in and hit Scanlon in the face as well, this time opening a wound and knocking the umpire to the ground. Players from both sides rushed the field, and only immediate police action prevented the potential riot. Charleston and DeMoss were both shuttled off to jail[15] so the game could finish, and the maelstrom dissolved. Both players were later released on bail, and DeMoss was eventually fined five dollars after the case was tried the following December.[16] Manager C.I. Taylor later said, "I am very grieved over the most unfortunate and degrading affair pulled off by DeMoss and Charleston. Umpire Scanlon was wholly blameless. His decision might have been questionable, but there is not one word that can be said justifying the perpetrators of that unfortunate and untimely happening . . . I believe that if DeMoss had any idea that things would have turned out as they did he would not have raised a hand to push the umpire. Remember we are not trying to shadow him for his actions. He needs no defense—he was wrong. But knowing him as I do, I am fully convinced that his conduct was worse than his heart."[17]

Another incident occurred the following spring, in a pool hall owned and operated by DeMoss. In 1916, Judge James Collins, " . . . of the criminal court, ordered Elwood DeMoss, colored, poolroom keeper and ball player, to the county jail because DeMoss had failed to pay a fine of twenty-five dollars and costs imposed by the court April 7 . . . members of the A.B.C baseball team began wondering where they would get a second-baseman to take DeMoss' place . . .". The court refused to release DeMoss early, after his conviction for allowing minors in his establishment, because the player had had the chance to pay his fine but "never set foot in the courtroom."[18]

In 1917, DeMoss found himself playing for Foster's American Giants, the team with which he would serve until 1925. During the offseasons before 1916 and 1917, "Bingo" travelled to Palm Beach, Florida, to play for Foster's other squad, the Royal Poinciana Hotel team, one of the greatest squads ever cobbled together before the 1920 creation of the Negro National League. In addition to DeMoss at second base, the shortstop was John Henry "Pop" Lloyd, a man whom Babe Ruth called the finest player ever.[19] Bruce Petway, possibly a better catcher than even Josh Gibson, was behind the plate, while Oscar Charleston and Pete Hill patrolled the outfield. It was an exhibition team that carried four future Hall of Famers on the roster, and they dominated the rival Breakers Hotel for two seasons. The latter team was no slouch-laden squad, featuring the aforementioned Louis Santop, along with Spottswood Poles, and Cyclone Joe Williams.

DeMoss had registered for the draft, but the Great War (World War I) ended before he was summoned to active duty. He replaced 35-year-old Pete Hill as Chicago's team captain, and then helped guide the American Giants to the first three Negro National League flags (1920-1922).[20]

It was during the 1925 season that DeMoss, in an unusual situation, saved the first Negro National League from an even earlier demise. Paul DeBono summarized:

"On the morning of the last of the three-game series in Indianapolis, when the American Giants awoke at the boarding house of Frieda Eubanks on the near west side of Indianapolis, Rube Foster did not get up with the rest of the team. Normally Rube was one of the first ones to greet the dawn, and as the morning wore on, the players became concerned at the absence of their fearless leader and began to search the house. Finally, Bingo DeMoss, aided by some of the other players, broke down the bathroom door where they found Rube Foster passed out, lying against the gas heater, his arm badly burned, the odor of natural gas heavy in the air. Rube was rushed to the hospital. Bingo DeMoss placed a long distance call to Sarah Foster and urged her to "come at once if you want to see Rube alive."[21]

Foster survived, but would be institutionalized later that year, and died in a sanitarium in 1930.

Following that incident, though, and before leaving the team for medical reasons, Foster engineered DeMoss' transfer back to Indianapolis, along with that of George Dixon, in large part to reinforce an ABC squad whose roster had been raided by an array of eastern and southern teams.[22] DeMoss left Indianapolis after the 1926 season and joined the Detroit Stars. He not only played for the Stars between 1927 and 1930, but managed the team as well. After the 1930 season, Detroit released DeMoss, who hung up his glove and retired as a player.

There remains a debate on whether "Bingo" DeMoss is worthy of enshrinement in the National Baseball Hall of Fame in Cooperstown. He made the preliminary ballot for consideration by the 2006 Special Committee On The Negro Leagues, a committee that selected only 17 players from a group of 55, but his case has not been reviewed since. As statistics from the Negro Leagues are considered somewhat less complete than those kept in "organized" (segregated, non-Black) baseball, it is not necessarily useful to rely only on what has been preserved, as that necessarily omits and ignores all that happened that wasn't recorded. Modern evaluators are left with the observations of those that saw particular players in action. Dave Malarcher, a tremendous player and manager in his own right, noted that DeMoss "had the courage, confidence, and ability written all over his face and posture. He was the smartest, the coolest, the most errorless ball player I've ever seen."[23]

Chicago Defender columnist Russ Cowans had watched baseball, Black and White, since before the 1920 establishment of the first Negro National League, and in a 1957 column wrote:

"I was talking to Halley Harding . . . the talk turned to DeMoss, and these are his words about Bingo: "He was without doubt the greatest ball player I've ever seen. He was playing second base when I joined the Stars, and his keen knowledge of the game made us

Elwood "Bingo" DeMoss spent 21 years manning the keystone sack for 11 different teams, including the American Giants' 1920 championship squad.

(Courtesy Graig Kreindler)

the best double-play combination in the Negro National League. He also made me a better shortstop."[24]

Cowans added, "But best of all, Bingo was always a gentleman."[25]

In short, the consensus has been that "Bingo" DeMoss was fast, a brilliant bunter, and a peerless defender at second base. Eight years earlier, Cowans had asked whether or not Jackie Robinson was "the greatest Negro second sacker of all time?"[26] In querying several long-time baseball observers, DeMoss was instead chosen for that honor. It was no hometown choice, as the selected team included Oscar Charleston, Josh Gibson, Cristobal Torriente, John Henry Lloyd, Bill Francis, Ben Taylor, and Satchel Paige.[27] On that list, only Francis and DeMoss have not yet been elected to the Hall of Fame.

DeMoss took that "keen" knowledge spoken of by Harding and used it in several managing stints. In 1933, the Columbus Blue Birds folded and were replaced in the league by the Cleveland Giants. That club had been put together "with Bingo DeMoss . . . in charge of the team."[28] He worked at various jobs outside baseball for a few years, and in 1935 his wife, Virgil, passed away. In 1936 he accepted the managerial spot on the Chicago American Giants, replacing Dave Malarcher. In 1937, "Candy" Jim Taylor, a younger brother of his early mentor and manager C.I. Taylor, replaced DeMoss at the Chicago helm. That year "Bingo" was accorded the honor of managing the West team, against Oscar Charleston's East squad, in the East-West All Star game. DeMoss' team lost, 10-2, but the reward was in being chosen. It provided a defacto credibility on the old infielder's ability to manage at the highest levels of professional baseball.

There is not much recorded about DeMoss' employment after he was fired, but in the 1940 U.S. Census, he listed his occupation as "Ticket seller for a Baseball park" at an annual salary of $480.00. He was living with his brother Willis and five lodgers in a home valued at $3,500. Although Virgil had died in 1935, Elwood was listed on the census as "married."[29] DeMoss' 1965 obituary observes that he was survived by a wife, Maranda, and two daughters, Bessie Dearborn and Norma Jean Jackson.[30]

In 1942 and 1943, DeMoss returned to the diamond as manager of the semiprofessional Chicago Brown Bombers,[31] and in 1944 was hired by Dr. J. B. Martin to again skipper the American Giants when the former could not reach a contractual agreement with Ted "Double Duty" Radcliffe.[32] This tour of duty lasted a year as well, and DeMoss' final managerial shot came in 1945 with Branch Rickey's United States Baseball League, again managing a team called the Chicago Brown Bombers.[33]

DeMoss walked away from organized baseball in 1946, but stayed in Chicago for the rest of his life. A popular member of the community, he served as treasurer for the "Old Ball Players Club",[34] a group dedicated to helping old, Black ballplayers that had fallen on hard times financially. On Tuesday, January 26, 1965, at the age of 75 and after what was termed a "long illness," Elwood "Bingo" DeMoss died at Cook County Hospital in Chicago.[35] He was interred at Burr Oak Cemetery in Alsip, Illinois, a final resting place for a number of prominent Black Chicago baseball players, including Jimmie Crutchfield, "Candy" Jim Taylor, Ted Trent, and John Donaldson.

NOTES

1   James Riley, *The Biographical Encyclopedia of The Negro Baseball Leagues* (New York: Carroll & Graf Pub; 1st edition, April 1, 1994), 228-229.

2   1910 United States Census. Accessed January 30, 2019.

3   Mansfield and Alie DeMoss certificate of marriage. Accessed January 30, 2019.

4   Ancestry.com digitized records. Accessed January 25, 2019.

5   1940 United States Census at Ancestry.com. Accessed February 1, 2019.

6   Justic B. Hill, "Bingo Was His Name," at *MLB.com*. Accessed January 30, 2019.

7   There is no evidence that the team existed prior to 1906. An article from the *Topeka Daily Capital,* dated September 9, 1906, (page 2) discusses how the team wasn't formed until after 1905.

8   1911 Kansas City Giants team page at Seamheads.com. Accessed January 24, 2019.

9   Riley (1994), 228.

10   2013 Shawnee County Sports Hall of Fame Induction Ceremony -- Elwood 'Bingo' DeMoss; Online. Accessed: January 31, 2019

11   John B. Holway. Unpublished ms, *BINGO*, 3; cited in Leslie Heaphy, ed., *Black Baseball and Chicago* (Jefferson, North Carolina: McFarland 2006), 64-66.

12   1915 Indianapolis ABCs team page at Seamheads.com.

13   The information is culled from data collected by Larry Lester and accessed on December 28, 2018.

14   A. Monroe, "So They Say: DeMoss, Ballplayers 'Best' Choice Dies," *Chicago Defender,* February 1, 1965.

15   *Indianapolis News,* October 25, 1915: 12.

16   "A.B.C. Players Are Fined," *Indianapolis News,* December 9, 1915: 2.

17   "Manager Taylor Regrets A.B.C. Trouble," *Chicago Defender,* November 6, 1915: 7.

18   *Indianapolis News,* October 14, 1916: 28.

19   Riley, 489.

20   Negro League Baseball Museum/Kansas State
      archives, online: Accessed: January 5, 2019.

21   Paul DeBono, *The Chicago American Giants* (Jefferson,
      North Carolina: McFarland and Co., 2006), 54.

22   NLBM/KSU archives, and also corroborated by data gath-
      ered by Larry Lester, accessed December 28, 2019.

23   Larry Lester, S. J. Miller, and D. Clark *Black Baseball in
      Chicago* (Jefferson, North Carolina: McFarland, 2000), 66.

24   Russ Cowans, "Russ' Corner: Old Ball Players To Have
      Their Day," *Chicago Defender*, January 17, 1957: 24.

25   Cowans, "Russ' Corner: Old Ball Players To Have Their Day."

26   Cowans, "Russ' Corner," *Chicago Defender*, July 23, 1949: 15.

27   Cowans, "Russ' Corner," 1949.

28   "Columbus Drops Out of the League and Cleveland Gets
      Its Berth," *Chicago Defender*, August 26, 1933: 8.

29   1940 United States Census. Online at Ancestry.
      com, accessed February 1, 2019.

30   "Old Baseball Great 'Bingo' DeMoss Dies,' *Chicago
      Daily Defender*, January 27, 1965: 25.

31   "Brown Bombers Leave Today For Training Camp," *Chicago
      Tribune*, April 5, 1942: 27, and "Leading Negro Nines Play
      2 Games Today," *Chicago Tribune*, June 20, 1943: 35.

32   DeBono, 165.

33   Lester, Miller, and Clark, *Black Baseball in Chicago*, 66.

34   Cowans. "Old Ball Players To Have Their Day." 24, as well as
      uncredited articles "Old Ball Players Set Date for Installation,"
      Chicago Defender, March 7, 1964: 14; and "Old Ballplayers
      Honor Williams," *Chicago Defender*, January 15, 1966: 17.

35   "Old Baseball Great 'Bingo' DeMoss Dies,"
      Chicago Defender, January 27, 1965.

GEORGE "TUBBY" DIXON

BY BILL JOHNSON

George Dixon, called Tubby most likely due to his stoutness, was a talented catcher who played for 15 years in segregated professional baseball. Most notably, he played with Rube Foster's Chicago American Giants during the 1920 season, the initial foray in organized Negro League baseball. That iteration of the NNL later folded, but after the second Negro National League reemerged in 1933, Dixon again showed up on the Cleveland Giants' roster.

George Dixon was born on January 4, 1896, in Greenwood, South Carolina, to Chester and Carrie Dixon.[1] Chester was a blacksmith by trade, and evidently a successful one as he owned their home. George had a sister, Sarah, two years his senior. Dixon's 1917 military draft registration card notes that he was "short" with a medium build, that he was unmarried, and that his sole dependent at the time was his unnamed mother. Although little is clear about Dixon's early life, the Seamheads. com Negro League database notes that he attended Brewer College in Greenwood.[2] While such a postsecondary institution has never existed, it is likely that Dixon did attend the Brewer Normal School in his hometown. That school was founded by the American Baptist Association in 1872 "as a school for newly emancipated African Americans."[3] At the time, the school had male and female dormitories and was managed by the Board of Missions of the Congregational Church.[4] As the student population was almost exclusively African American, it is reasonable to assume that Dixon was educated there, a Black student in a racially divided community.

Starting with a seven-game stint on the Royal Poinciana Hotel team in Palm Beach, Florida, during the 1916-1917 winter season, Dixon joined the Chicago American Giants on a full-time basis in 1917. A right-handed thrower but left-handed batter with an obvious mind for baseball, he proved to be a natural catcher. In one of his early games in 1917, Dixon caught Dick "Cannonball" Redding's 16-strikeout effort against the Roseland Eclipse.[5] Later, against the rival ABCs, he contributed one of only three American Giants hits off Indianapolis pitcher William "Dizzy" Dismukes in a 3-1 victory. He added the sole Chicago error as well, but he handled pitcher Tom Johnson well enough that the ABCs scratched out only five hits.[6] Sharing starting responsibilities with Bruce Petway, Dixon provided valuable contributions in a series of wins over the New York Cubans.[7] Dixon closed out the 1917 season with two hits in a 9-3 American Giants win over a collection of White major-league players.[8]

Negro League historian James Riley summarized Dixon's introduction to big-time baseball, writing that "Dixon was considered 'a real find' when he arrived with the Chicago American Giants in 1917 along with Rudy Tyree as half of a much-heralded 'Pony battery.' Initially the young left-handed hitting backstop started strong but he leveled-off and finished with a .253 batting average. ..."[9]

Dixon returned to Palm Beach and the Royal Poinciana Hotel for the winter season, and then headed north to Chicago for the 1918 campaign. In a late May game against Jose Junco and the Cuban Stars, he had a team-high three hits and paced Chicago to a 7-6 win at Schorling Park.[10] In July he helped Chicago to another win over Cristobal Torriente and his Cuban squad.[11] Dixon had emerged as a powerful hitter, with a fine throwing arm and innate leadership ability, but whose one notable deficiency was his lack of running speed. He was not among the American Giants called up for military service in World War I, and he continued to play for the American Giants until 1922. His 1920 season, in particular, contributed to Chicago's inaugural championship, and his .324 batting average and .854 OPS were the best in his Negro National League tenure. His 34 runs batted in also proved to be a career high and placed him third on the team behind Torriente and Bingo DeMoss.

Dixon was involved in some memorable games along the way. In June 1921 he and Jim Brown were the catchers for Chicago pitchers Tom Johnson and Tom Williams in a wild game in Indianapolis, one in which Dixon's powerful bat was critical. Trailing the ABCs 10-0 after three innings, the American Giants scored nine runs in the eighth inning to put the game back within reach. Indianapolis followed that up with eight more tallies in the bottom of the inning, making the score 18-9, but Chicago added nine in the top of the ninth to knot the game. "The American Giants staged a sixteen-run rally off eleven bunts, six successive squeeze plays, and Dixon and Tonchetti's (Torriente's) home runs with the bases full, and held the ABCs to an 18 to 18 tie," the *Chicago Tribune* reported.[12] In October the American Giants "won the eastern colored baseball championship" by defeating the Bacharach Giants, 5-4.[13]

In 1922 the 26-year-old appeared in 28 games for the American Giants, batting .250 with two home runs in 28 games. The team used Jim Brown as the primary catcher, and Chicago posted a 37-24-1 record in winning the Negro National League. Overall, the American Giants won 45 games against a slate of opponents that went

beyond league members. Dixon teamed with Oscar Charleston and player-manager Dizzy Dismukes on the 1923 Indianapolis ABCs. He performed well, hitting .281 in 61 league games, but played most of the next year, 1924, for the Birmingham Black Barons.[14] Back with the American Giants for some exhibitions in October, the 28-year-old finished his last genuinely productive season with a .278 batting average in 54 games.

(Courtesy Noir-Tech Research, Inc.)

Backstop George "Tubby" Dixon hit a career-high .324 – 71 points above his career batting average – for the 1920 NNL champions while splitting the starting catching duties with Jim Brown.

Dixon returned to the American Giants for 1925, but as historian James Riley chronicles, "Rube Foster did some housecleaning and unconditionally released many veteran players. Dixon was dispatched to the Indianapolis ABCs along with Bingo DeMoss to balance the league, and hit .258 in 1926, his last in Indianapolis."[15] Dixon spent 1926 playing for the Indianapolis ABCs, but that team folded at the end of the season. Riley, in his biographical magnum opus, states that Dixon also played for the Cleveland Elites in 1926. Authoritative databases at Seamheads. com and Baseball-reference.com show only that Dixon played the entire year in Indiana, but it is possible that Dixon caught on with the Elites late in the season. The Elites were a one-year team, becoming the Hornets for 1927, and may have had roster fluidity that was neither captured nor archived. Regardless, Dixon did spend the next season in Cleveland with the Hornets (1927), and the Tigers (1928). After a break, Dixon returned to the Cleveland Cubs in 1931, and played his final big-league game for the 4-24 Cleveland Red Sox in 1934. He was relegated to backup catching responsibilities for those years, and by age 38 he was out of professional baseball entirely.

In a sad but not uncommon (for the time), item, the *Chicago Defender* on August 17, 1940, reported that "George Dixon, former catcher of the Chicago American Giants … died August 4 in the (Cleveland) city hospital. According to Sport Calhoun who knew Dixon well, the body [was] unclaimed."[16] Per Dixon's death certificate, he had died due to complications from liver cancer.[17]

From his birth in 1896 to his passing at age 44, George Dixon's life was brief and, as of the twenty-first century, relatively anonymous beyond his time in professional baseball. He clearly had a passion for the sport and an uncommon set of skills in most phases of the game, and he played in both versions of the Negro National League alongside and against some of the greatest ever to take the field.

SOURCES

Statistical data is taken from the website www.seamheads.com, unless otherwise noted.

NOTES

1   United States military registration card, dated June 5, 1917, and witnessed by Marcella Reed.

2   George Dixon, George Dixon – Seamheads Negro Leagues Database. Accessed: June 8, 2021.

3   The Brewer School, online: History of our School – Our School – Brewer Middle School (gwd50.org). Accessed June 8, 2021.

4   "Brewer Normal Dormitory Burned on Monday Night," *Greenwood* (South Carolina) *Evening Index,* January 16, 1913: 5.

5   "Army Man Drills Fosters; Blank Roseland, 4 to 0," *Chicago Tribune,* May 7, 1917: 20.

6   "Foster's Men Down Hoosier Team, 3 to 1, and Even Up Series," *Chicago Tribune,* June 12, 1917: 11.

7   "American Giants Trim Cubans by Hard Hitting," *Chicago Tribune,* August 16, 1917: 11; "Giants Beat Cubans Twice," *Chicago Tribune,* August 26, 1917: 16.

8   "Fosters Defeat All Stars, 9 to 3," *Chicago Tribune,* October 22, 1917: 15.

9   James Riley, "George Dixon," in *The Biographical Encyclopedia of the Negro Baseball Leagues* (New York: Carroll & Graf, 2002), 268. www.seamheads.com lists Dixon's batting average for 1917 as .248, not the .253 that Riley cites.

10 "Fosters Divide Holiday Games with Islanders," *Chicago Tribune,* May 31, 1918: 13.

11 "Fosters Beat Cuban Nine, 8-4," *Chicago Tribune,* July 5, 1918: 9.

12 "American Giants in Tie," *Chicago Tribune,* June 29, 1921: 19.

13 "American Giants Win Ball Title," *Chicago Tribune,* October 24, 1921: 18.

14 "Black Barons Drop Opening Battle to Cleveland Outfit," *Birmingham News,* August 17, 1924: 66.

15 Riley, 268.

16 "Catcher Dixon Dies; Body Is Unclaimed," *Chicago Defender,* August 17, 1940: 24.

17 Certificate of Death: George Dixon. State of Ohio, Department of Health, file number 49044, dated August 28, 1940.

WILLIAM "BUCK" EWING

BY THOMAS KERN

Catcher Buck Ewing had a cup of coffee with the 1920 American Giants. He batted .306 for the 1929 Homestead Grays but lost playing time to 18-year-old Josh Gibson the following year.

(Courtesy Noir-Tech Research, Inc.)

George Lippe: *"Buck Ewing was simply terrific."*[1]

William "Buck" Ewing had the good fortune of being in the right place at the right time at least twice during his otherwise itinerant Negro League career. He found himself on the Chicago American Giants in 1920 at the outset of his career as Rube Foster's franchise won the inaugural Negro National League title by an eight-game margin over the Detroit Stars. Later, in 1929 and 1930, Ewing played for the Homestead Grays when it was on the cusp of becoming a heavyweight Negro League franchise. However, the rest of Ewing's career, which involved separate stints in upstate New York – where he married and put down roots – also presents compelling tales. Ewing's career is emblematic of what Black baseball was for most of its players, a peripatetic journey whose stops were often obscure and which entailed little of the limelight of big-time Negro League play.

William Monroe Ewing was born in Massillon, Ohio, on January 31, 1903.[2] Although he never rose to the heights of fellow Ohioans and Negro League Hall of Famers Sol White (from Bellaire) and Ray Brown (from Ashland Grove), he earned his paycheck for over two decades in the game, launched by his start with Rube Foster.

Much of what is known about Ewing's early life exists courtesy of an interview he gave to Allen Long when Ewing was in his 70s. According to

Long, Ewing's father "labored as a coremaker in a [Massillon] foundry. His mother passed away during his infancy. His sister, Mary, went nearly the entire way through the public school system. ... He also had a pair of older brothers. A first cousin, Wade Johnston, wound up as a starting flychaser for the magnificent Kansas City Monarchs."[3] According to the Massillon City Directory, his father, Reuben, worked for Massillon Iron and Steel Company.[4]

Ewing reminisced that he did not start playing baseball until he was 10, but by the age of 15, he thought he was pretty good. When he stopped growing, Ewing topped out at 6-feet-2 and around 200 pounds. He threw right-handed and batted left-handed and found his niche as a more than serviceable catcher.

When Ewing was 16 or so, a local Baptist minister arranged a tryout for him with the Chicago American Giants. Rube Foster liked Ewing well enough to sign him, but the team was already well stocked with veteran catchers Jim Brown and George Dixon. Instead of a roster spot, Foster "instructed Ewing to spend the summer touring with an inter-racial squad from Winnipeg, Manitoba."[5] The Winnipeg squad Long referred to was in fact the Winnipeg Colored Giants, which served as a farm team for all Negro National League teams in 1920. A newspaper in Valley City, North Dakota, described the makeup of the Colored Giants when they came to play the Valley City Squad. "The Colored Giants are made up of young players that are not quite old enough and well-seasoned to make [the Negro National League franchises] so are "farmed out" to this traveling organization where they will finish their baseball education."[6]

Ewing appeared on the American Giants roster in 1920, but records show he played sparingly. Foster was known to favor veteran players. However, Foster was an accumulator of talent and wisely signed and allocated players to feeder teams so he could assess their ability and generate revenue from the exhibition games these teams played. It was while playing for the Winnipeg team that Ewing began developing his catching skills. Allen Long notes that in a game against tiny Valley City, quite possibly the aforementioned game, "Ewing actually picked off an enemy runner off third base while nonchalantly glancing in a different direction."[7] A look at the game summary for that June 1, 1920, contest shows Ewing as catcher retiring a runner on third in the bottom of the ninth for the first out, helping to ensure an eventual 6-5 victory.[8]

It was while playing that year that Ewing gained his nickname from the fans for another Ohio native who made it to the major leagues: William B. "Buck" Ewing, the Hall of Fame catcher-manager who played for and managed the New York Giants and Cincinnati Reds.[9]

Ewing's time on the American Giants gave him exposure in the newly formed Negro National League and although Foster had no room for him (Dixon and Brown remained entrenched behind the plate and were joined by Poindexter Williams in 1921), Ewing was seen as a promising catcher and was signed by the Columbus Buckeyes in 1921. The Dayton Marcos had been sold to Columbus businessmen Harry St. Clair and Dr. Howard Smith who immediately moved the club to Columbus and renamed them the Buckeyes. Future Hall of Fame shortstop John Henry Lloyd was hired as player-manager and Sol White became a coach and adviser. The Buckeyes failed to excel on the field or at the box office and finished sixth out of eight teams with a 25-38 record. At season's end the team was dissolved, and Lloyd moved east to manage the Bacharach Giants.

Ewing backed up Mack Eggleston at catcher while with the Buckeyes and played in 17 games, batting .306. Ewing was part of the headlines in the Buckeyes' league debut against the Chicago Giants on April 30, 1921. He pinch-hit in the top of the ninth with the Buckeyes down 5-1 and two outs:

> "Eggleston [the starting catcher] was due to bat, but Lloyd sent up 18-year-old William Monroe "Buck" Ewing to pinch-hit. Pregame coverage in the *Chicago Whip* highlighted Ewing, predicting that the Massillon, Ohio, native would be "a revelation to the baseball devotees all over the circuit.
>
> On this occasion the hype was justified. Ewing connected for a long opposite-field home run over the right-field wall. The crowd at Neil Park "went dippy for a few minutes," the *Chicago Defender* observed. "Ewing emulated another Ewing," the *Columbus Dispatch* noted, evoking the name of nineteenth-century star – and Ohio native – Buck Ewing. Only two other right-handed hitters had ever homered over Neil Park's right-field wall. Chicago's advantage was down to 5-3."[10]

That was the last of the scoring. Giants starter John Taylor completed the game by striking out Buckeyes right fielder George Brown.

Ewing also played in at least seven games that year for the Cleveland Tate Stars, batting .333. The Tate Stars were an affiliate member of the Negro National League, managed by Candy Jim Taylor and owned by businessman George Tate. Player loans were not uncommon and Ewing's movement to the Tate Stars that year ensured him playing time that he would not have had with the Buckeyes. With the disbanding of the Buckeyes at the end of the 1921 season, the Tate Stars took Columbus's place in the Negro National League in 1922. However, saddled with debt due to poor management, the Tates withdrew from the league and became an independent team in 1923.

By 1922, at the age of 19, Ewing had had a taste of the higher echelons of Negro League ball, playing for Foster and serving under renowned managers Lloyd and Taylor. Long notes that Ewing's next team was the Bacharach Giants and a renewed connection with Lloyd, who moved from Columbus after its demise to manage the Bacharachs, a team he had previously played for. However, Seamheads has no game records with Ewing on the Bacharachs roster. What is known is that Ewing's 1922/1923 offseason was spent in Tonawanda, New York, where he worked at a steel mill. Looking for a team in 1923, he sought advice through the informal player network. Although they did not know each other that well, fellow catcher Louis Santop, Hilldale's star player, facilitated Ewing's next step: a catching gig with Chappie Johnson's Philadelphia Royal All Stars.[11]

George "Chappie" Johnson was born in Bellaire, Ohio, Sol White's hometown, and was one of the early stars of Black baseball. Johnson was a catcher and had played for the Page Fence Giants in the 1890s and then the Chicago Union Giants, Leland Giants, and Philadelphia Giants. He is given credit for being the first catcher – Black or White – to wear shin guards and other protective equipment.[12]

During his playing career, the well-respected Johnson caught Rube Foster, Dizzy Dismukes, and Frank Wickware, among others. Johnson became best known for the semipro teams he later assembled, first out of Philadelphia, and then upstate New York. W. Rollo Wilson captured the nomadic aspect of Black baseball in an August 4, 1923, column in the *Pittsburgh Courier*, noting that "Chappie Johnson's Royal Stars have returned from a successful road trip of several weeks. Out of 92 games played, says Chappie, but 18 were lost."[13] Johnson also fielded teams under the monikers Colored Stars, Wonderers, and Colored Quaker Giants. In 1923 his Philadelphia Royal All Stars applied for membership in the Philadelphia Baseball Association's colored division alongside Hilldale, the Philadelphia Giants, and Philadelphia Stars. They were that good.

Ewing started showing up in the 1923 box scores with Johnson's Philadelphia-based team. Presciently, a game Chappie's team played in Schenectady against the Schenectady Knights of Columbus (the Caseys) became a foreshadowing of sorts for Johnson, who the following year stepped in to fill the void in upstate New York Black baseball. It had been occupied briefly the decade before by the Mohawk Giants, a team for which Johnson himself had played in 1913-1914. However, in mid-1914, the team severed its local connection, as reported by the *Berkshire Eagle*, "claiming they were not receiving their salaries and could not afford to play ball for the sport." The article continued: "Rube Foster, who has been identified with colored ball players for years and has managed the Chicago American Giants for several seasons, advanced the players funds with which to leave for Indianapolis and it is understood the team will hereafter represent Louisville, Ky., and French Lick Springs, Ind."[14] In the years following, several local White athletic clubs filled Schenectady's semipro baseball void created by the Giants' demise. The longest lasting of the teams – the Caseys – survived from 1920 until August 1923, when they disbanded.

Area promoter Hank Bozzi played a strong role in rehabilitating the local game and when the opportunity presented itself to ally with Chappie Johnson and provide a Schenectady home for Johnson's All-Stars in 1924, Bozzi became co-owner with Johnson. Schenectady-based, the All-Stars played most of their games far and wide to take on all comers, often roaming far afield in New York, Massachusetts, and Pennsylvania. That April, the *Glens Falls* (New York) *Post-Star* unveiled Johnson's inaugural team:

> "Among Chappie's stars who have arrived and are ready to start practice session are Bill Ewing, catcher; Babe Hobson, second baseman; Bobby Dean, shortstop; Sam Warmack, left fielder; Lefty Hill, right fielder; Will Raymond, catcher; Don Perry, first baseman; Lewis Mormon, third baseman, and Frank Wickware, Sam Cooper, Nate Pierce, and Ray Haskins, pitchers."[15]

In *The Mohawk Colored Giants of Schenectady*, Frank M. Keetz writes, "[T]he main attraction on the Chappies, other than Chappie himself, was a young catcher from Ohio named William 'Buck' Ewing. … Johnson was known as an astute teacher of white as well as black players and Ewing could not have encountered a better manager. Ewing became a fine defensive catcher and emerged in 1924 as a slugging power hitter."[16]

Over the next three years (1924-1926) during Johnson's time as co-owner, manager, and occasional fill-in player, Ewing anchored the lineup as catcher for Chappie's All Stars. In fact, a successful debut with them in 1924 attracted national attention to Ewing and, as a result, the New York Lincoln Giants ostensibly signed him for the 1925 season. The January 31, 1925, issue of the *New York Age* had Ewing penciled in as manager Judy Gans's catcher.[17] The *Pittsburgh Courier* subsequently wrote, "Buck Ewing, of the Lincolns, is said by observers to be the brightest prospect coming into the Eastern Loop this year."[18]

However, Ewing opted out of a return to a big-time team, having settled in comfortably in upstate New York. The April 11, 1925, edition of the *Pittsburgh Courier* revealed how happy Johnson was with his catcher, likely working his magic to retain Ewing's services, praising him to the hilt, and making him the centerpiece of his All-Stars:

> "Chappie claims that Buck Ewing is the greatest catcher in baseball and that he will be star of the men in the iron masks for the next decade. He says that he is the catcher who can teach young pitchers how to PITCH and how to THINK. He is the biggest gate attraction on his squad."[19]

A year later, *Courier* columnist William G. Nunn added his own insight, writing, "Ewing, the big catcher, with Chappie Johnson, is one of the best in colored baseball, according to reports from the East."[20]

In 1927 Johnson abruptly severed connections with the team, but Ewing remained and was elevated by Bozzi to manager. The team became Ewing's All-Stars for both 1927 and 1928. Ewing had found a home.

In the five-year stretch from 1924 to 1928 when Ewing was ensconced in Schenectady, the team played an endless schedule of games in the tri-state area, against semipro teams – Black and White – and the occasional bigger matchup with Negro League heavyweights. Because the Johnson, and then Ewing, All-Stars lived outside of the official Negro Leagues, their statistical records have not been recorded. Further, the box scores of the All-Stars' games were only intermittently captured in the local papers. Keetz's history of

the Mohawk Colored Giants, assembled from local newspaper stories, offers as good a composite picture as any on Ewing, who was lauded for his power and his presence as a superb catcher.

A typical storyline in Ewing's early years in Schenectady was epitomized by August 8 and August 10, 1924, games between the All-Stars and semipro teams in Kingston and Glen Falls. Keetz writes:

> "Chappie's team downed Kingston 15-5 "before a record crowd" in Amsterdam. … Ewing "hit the longest home run ever seen in Amsterdam." It went "long and far over the centerfield fence in Jollyland Park. … Two days later, Ewing "hit a ball so far in Glen Falls it was "lost" in the high grass."[21]

Ewing's first years in upstate New York established him as a particularly good ballplayer – a big fish in a small pond. Added to his catching and hitting skills, his assuming the mantle as player-manager for the All-Stars in 1927 helped to complete his game. A contest against the Brooklyn Cuban Giants headlined "Brainiest Baseball of the Season" underscored Ewing's emergence as a field tactician who kept his team in the game early despite pitcher Rube Wise's eight walks. Ewing went 2-for-3 with a triple and a stolen base in a 7-3 win. With the game tied at 3-3 in the bottom of the sixth, "Ewing's club strained ahead with a run in the sixth inning and gradually after that the "home club pulled off into a lead that eventually became safe and secure."[22]

In the summer of 1928, Cumberland Posey enticed Ewing to play for his Homestead Grays in several fall exhibitions in what served as an audition for a full-time place with the Grays in 1929. Given the praise lavished on Ewing by Johnson and the African American newspapers, Posey's interest was hardly surprising. Posey's catchers of the mid-1920s were journeymen – George Britt, Charlie Spearman, W.P. Young, and then, in 1928, Benito Calderon and Rags Roberts. Ewing was an upgrade and rather than remain in Schenectady in 1929 for what would have been the third year running of Buck Ewing's All-Stars, Ewing opted for the limelight on an up-and-coming Grays team.

In 1929 Ewing played in 63 games for the Grays, all but two as the starting catcher (he also played first base and right field). Ewing hit .306 with an on-base percentage of .367 and a slugging percentage of .435 and played alongside Vic Harris, Walter Cannady, and John Beckwith. It was not until the following year that the Grays lineup included Oscar Charleston and Judy Johnson; without them in 1929, the Grays lacked a consistent offense and finished fourth in the American Negro League, with a record that was barely over .500. However, Ewing was the catcher for a decent starting rotation – Smokey Joe Williams (at the age of 43), Lefty Williams, Sam Streeter, and the versatile George Britt.

Ewing's size featured in one of his more notorious games in 1929, a May 17 contest between the Grays and Hilldale. Posey, manager of the Grays at the time, was known for his umpire-baiting. According to Posey's biographer James E. Overmyer:

"He began riding the home plate umpire as early as the third inning, refusing to leave the field when the ump tossed him out of the game, and was allowed to stay on the bench. With everyone thus set on edge, more fireworks broke out in the ninth inning. The potential tying run for the Grays was called out on a close play by the same ump. Somebody from the Grays pushed the umpire and Homestead Grays catcher Buck Ewing slugged the arbiter."[23]

Things got more heated, the benches emptied, and Posey and Ewing were suspended by the league for several games. Posey knew he could count on Ewing and his place on the team seemed secure. The icing on the cake for Ewing that year was his only documented trip to the Caribbean for winter league play in Cuba. Ewing played for Santa Clara alongside Frank Warfield, Mule Suttles, and, in his only foray to Cuba, Satchel Paige. Ewing batted .304 on a team that came in second to Cienfuegos.[24]

The American Negro League survived just one year, and in 1930 the Grays played as an independent team. Just as Posey had used the 1928 fall barnstorming swing to audition Ewing, in the autumn of 1929, Posey signed Oscar Charleston, George Scales, Jake Stephens, and Judy Johnson for fall exhibitions and then outspent rival owners to retain them for his 1930 squad.

Ewing began 1930 as Homestead's starting catcher. And then came a July storyline that lives in Negro League lore. Judy Johnson's recollections set the stage for the event. On July 25, the Kansas City Monarchs arrived in Pittsburgh to play the Grays at Forbes Field – a midsummer marquee event for the Black community. The Monarchs came with their own lighting system so that the game could be played at night and

ensure a larger gate after the end of the workday. Johnson recalled:

"We were in the clubhouse trying to discuss signals, because we had never played a night game. Buck Ewing was catching. When Buck got down to give the signal, why [Smokey Joe Williams] couldn't even see his hand. … Williams misunderstood the signal, and Ewing split his hand right down. My sub-catcher was in right field, he wouldn't come in to catch, he was afraid. Here we are, Forbes Field is packed. Josh Gibson was sitting in the stands, him and a bunch of boys who played sandlot baseball. I asked if he would catch. "Yes sir, Mr. Johnson!" I had to hold up the game, let him go in the clubhouse and put on a suit."[25]

The debut of Josh Gibson was a big deal for the Grays and all of Negro League baseball. Ewing was out of the lineup for a while with a broken hand, but he still played in nearly half of the Grays' independent schedule that led to a 45-15-1 record. Once Ewing was able to catch again, Posey inserted Gibson in the outfield to keep his bat in the lineup. Negro League historian Mark Ribowsky wrote, "[W]hile Posey was not ready to yank Ewing, he was gradually making room for Josh around the field and inching him higher in the order."[26]

The handwriting was on the wall for Ewing, and Posey did not offer him a contract for 1931. In Ewing's recollections with Allen Long, the St. Louis Stars "swapped five players, including the fabled Ted "Double Duty" Radcliffe to the Grays for Ewing in the spring of 1931. [Ewing] declined to recognize the transaction."[27] Whether it was the Missouri weather (as noted by Long) or "tough traveling and lower pay during the harsh depression era," according to Keetz, Ewing instead contacted Bozzi about a return to what was now the Mohawk Giants, a name that Bozzi had resuscitated in 1929 after Ewing left Schenectady to join the Grays. In any event, the March 21, 1931, *Pittsburgh Courier* noted that the trade had taken place and hyped the important acquisition by the Grays of Radcliffe in particular. However, rather than report to St. Louis, "[Ewing] chose to return to Schenectady and Bozzi's Mohawk Giants. He never left his adopted town where he eventually died as a respected citizen."[28]

Ewing joined the 1931 Mohawks, managed by Ed Kemp, who had played with Johnson and then Ewing's All Stars in the mid-1920s. Ewing resumed his player-manager role for Bozzi in 1932. Throughout the 1930s, the Giants played in the Schenectady City Twilight League but traveled farther afield as well. (In 1933, the team purportedly had a record of 72-21-11 against all comers.) Ewing was at the center of all things: "Area fans simply said, 'Buck is manager.' Saying the word Ewing was not necessary in Schenectady. It was superfluous. Almost everyone knew who Buck was."[29] Ewing briefly interrupted his time with the Mohawks in 1936 when he went down the road to Albany to manage and play for the Albany Black Sox, ostensibly for the money.

Ewing returned to the Giants during the 1937 season, and then resumed managerial duties in 1938.[30] He remained on the team as a regular and later as a backup catcher through 1941 when, at the age of 38, he stepped away from the game. The Giants were struggling and Bozzi relinquished control of the team in the spring of 1942, unable to assemble a credible squad because of a manpower shortage in World War II. His successor fared no better and the Giants resurfaced for one more year in 1943, with Bozzi back at the helm and Ewing joining his protégé for one more go-round.[31]

The *Bennington* (Vermont) *Evening Banner* captured the now 40-year-old Ewing and his legacy well when it wrote on August 31, 1943, regarding a forthcoming game between Bennington and the Mohawks:

"Old Buck Ewing is still with the Mohawk Giants. ... He and Curley Williams [of Bennington] used to have quite a battle every time they met. ... Sometimes the Bennington fireman [Williams] breezed it by but not often. Those aging legs of Buck, however, no longer bend easily at the knee, so Buck is a first baseman now, rather than a catcher. ... The popular Buck, who is probably better known to baseball fans of New York State and parts of Vermont than many of the minor league stars, must have passed his 40th birthday. ... Buck is the oldest player in point of service with the Giants. He has played with all of Hank Bozzi's great clubs. They still say John McGraw once tried to pass Buck off as a Cuban [in order to circumvent the color barrier and sign him], but this has never been substantiated."[32]

After stepping away from baseball, Ewing took a job with Schenectady-based General Electric for a dozen years, followed by work with Campbell Plastics, another local firm. He also served as a part-time scout for the Cleveland Indians and worked in maintenance jobs until retirement.

Ewing married twice and had a son from his first marriage. He and his second wife were married for more than 30 years. On September 1, 1979, Ewing died at the age of 76. The *Schenectady Gazette* eulogized him, writing:

"Perhaps more important on this sad occasion, however, is that all of us remember Buck Ewing as he had shown himself to be in the half century, he lived in Schenectady ... as fine a man as he was a ball player."[33]

Fittingly, after his many years in Schenectady, the city renamed the main baseball field in the downtown Central Park the William Buck Ewing Memorial Diamond. Ewing had played many a game at Central Park in the 1930s. Keetz writes, "It was the field where thousands sat in the wooden grandstand and "lined the hillsides beyond the outfield and along the baselines during the throes of the Depression Thirties to watch in particular the Mohawk Giants."[34]

The fact that Ewing had not played continually on the top tier of Negro teams probably obscured how good he really was. George Lippe, an adviser to the Chicago White Sox in the 1950s, observed, "Buck Ewing was simply terrific. Too bad baseball didn't lift the color line soon enough for that guy. If he had been given a big-league chance, he would have been every bit as good as Roy Campanella. On that, I'd bet my bottom dollar."[35] More realistically, a Schenectady sportswriter, Hall Buell, opined that Ewing "was a major league talent in a minor league setting."[36]

SOURCES

Unless otherwise noted, all statistical references are from Seamheads.com.

NOTES

1   Quoted in Allen Long, "Historically Speaking: Buck Ewing," *Black Sports*, June 1973: 30.

2   James A. Riley, *The Biographical Encyclopedia of The Negro Baseball Leagues* (New York: Carroll & Graf, 1994), 272.

3   Long: 30.

4   Ancestry.com.

5   Long: 30.

6   "Valley City Fans See Real Baseball," *Valley City* (North Dakota) *Weekly Times Record*, June 3, 1920: 4.

7   Long: 30.

8   "Valley City Fans See Real Baseball."

9   Long: 30.

10 John Fredland, *April 30, 1921: Chicago Giants defeat Columbus Buckeyes in Negro National League debut*, SABR Games Project. https://sabr.org/gamesproj/game/april-30-1921-columbus-buckeyes-defeat-chicago-giants-in-negro-national-league-debut/.

11 Long: 30.

12 Kyle McNary, "Chappie Johnson," *Pitchblack Baseball*, https://www.pitchblackbaseball.com/chappie-johnson.

13 W. Rollo Wilson, "Eastern Snapshots," *Pittsburgh Courier*, August 4, 1923: 6.

14 "Baseball Notes," *Berkshire Record* (Pittsfield, Massachusetts), July 16, 1914: 16.

15 "Chappie Johnson and His Dorpian Team Gets Going," *Glens Falls* (New York) *Post-Star*, April 10, 1924: 6.

16 Frank M. Keetz, *The Mohawk Colored Giants of Schenectady* (Schenectady, New York: Frank M. Keetz, 1999), 32.

17 William E. Clark, "Sports Comment," *New York Age*, January 31, 1925: 6.

18 W. Rollo Wilson, "Eastern Snapshots," *Pittsburgh Courier*, March 14, 1925: 7.

19 W. Rollo Wilson, "Eastern Snapshots," *Pittsburgh Courier*, April 11, 1925: 13.

20 William G. Nunn, "Diamond Dope," *Pittsburgh Courier*, August 28, 1926: 15.

21 Keetz, 33.

22 "Wise Issues Many Passes but Does Well in Trouble," *Glens Falls Post-Star*, June 21, 1927: 8.

23 James E. Overmyer, *Cum Posey of the Homestead Grays* (Jefferson, North Carolina: McFarland & Company, 2020), 102-103.

24 Jorge, S. Figueredo, *Cuban Baseball: A Statistical History, 1878-1961* (Jefferson, North Carolina: McFarland & Company, 2003), 182-184.

25 John B. Holway, *Josh and Satch: The Life and Times of Josh Gibson and Satchel Paige* (New York: Carroll & Graf, 1992), 23.

26 Mark Ribowsky, *The Power and the Darkness: The Life of Josh Gibson in the Shadows of the Game* (New York: Simon & Schuster, 1996), 59.

27 Long: 31.

28 Keetz, 64.

29 Keetz, 77.

30 Keetz, 106, 113.

31 Keetz, 142.

32 "All Set for Gala Game on Labor Day," *Bennington* (Vermont) *Evening Banner*, August 31, 1943: 6.

33 Keetz, 150.

34 Keetz, 150.

35 Long: 30.

36 Keetz, 151.

JUDY GANS

BY DAVE WILKIE

As a ballplayer, Judy Gans is a bit of an enigma. On the one hand, his official statistics paint him as a good, but not great, player. On the other, acknowledgment of his greatness by newspaper writers and his peers can be found scattered throughout the early pantheon of Black baseball history. Hall of Fame manager Wilbert Robinson referred to Gans as "the colored Ty Cobb."[1] Hall of Fame manager Bill McKechnie once claimed that there were at least 25 Black players who could play for any team in the country, and mentioned Gans by name, along with Bullet Rogan, Oscar Charleston, Satchel Paige, and Josh Gibson.[2] While playing for the Paterson Smart Set in 1912, Gans was touted as a rival of Home Run Baker,[3] which was high praise for a player whose name has been all but forgotten when the greats of the game are talked about.

Robert Edward Gans was born on July 16, 1886, most likely in Cleveland, Ohio.[4] His father was Zechariah Gans and his mother was Sarah. Both are listed as being from Pennsylvania in the 1920 census. His 79-year-old mother and his sister, Barbara Newman were living in Cleveland in 1944 when Gans met them for a publicized visit.[5] Zechariah's fate is unknown.

Gans could have just as easily been a football star and his athletic prowess was on display for some of the best professional White teams in Buffalo in 1908, 1909, and 1910. He saw action with the Oakdales and the Black Rock Cycle Club, and played alongside fellow Blackball great Pete Hill on a Pittsburgh-based team, the Fighting Tenth.[6] Between 1905 and 1910

Gans shuttled back and forth between his two loves, football and baseball. While playing in his hometown of Washington, Pennsylvania, he was later compared favorably to local gridiron star Charlie West, who in 1922 was the first African American to play quarterback in a Rose Bowl.[7]

Gans also made a name for himself by training White baseball teams in Ohio and Western Pennsylvania during this time. The left-handed Gans pitched batting practice and hit fungoes and was with a ballclub in Canton, Ohio, when he got his big break. In 1907 Bill McKechnie was playing third base for an Ohio-based team and persuaded manager Ed Murphy to give the young trainer a whirl on the mound during an exhibition game with the Nebraska Indians. The first batter doubled, the next walked, and the third was hit by a pitch. It was not the most auspicious start, but Gans quickly settled down and struck out the next 12 hitters. The barnstorming Nebraska Indians were impressed enough to sign him, thus beginning Gans's long, illustrious baseball career.[8]

Gans next showed up in the press in 1908 as a starting pitcher for the Cuban Giants in the National Association. In a mid-August game, he went the distance in a 5-1 victory over a team from Atlantic City; he also chipped in with two hits.[9] In October, in what must have been a thrill, the 22-year-old Gans signed on with a team calling itself the Brooklyn Royal Giants and steamed to Cuba to play against teams from Habana and Almendares. In 16 games the Giants broke even with an 8-8 record, and Gans fared well on the mound with a 2-2 mark and a 2.73 ERA. One of his victories was a hard-fought 2-1, complete-game masterpiece against the Habana Club. His batting skills had not caught up with his pitching quite yet, and he hit a miserable .095 (2-for-21) on the trip.[10] Gans must have taken to Cuba because he next hooked up with a team from Matanzas, losing two games with a respectable 3.00 ERA for the fourth-place squad.

After a final interlude with football, with the Fighting Tenth, Gans began the 1911 season with the Cuban Giants. Soon afterward he settled in with the team that he spent most of his career with, the Harlem-based New York Lincoln Giants. This was a powerhouse team in its inaugural season of 1911, and featured such superstars as Louis Santop, George Wright, John Henry Lloyd, Spottswood Poles, and Dick "Cannonball" Redding. As the starting center fielder, Gans hit .308 and stole five bases in 10 games.[11]

What was known as the kidnapping of players was a popular pastime for owners of Black ballclubs of the time, and Dick Coogan, White owner of the Paterson

Judy Gans patrolled the outfield for the 1920 American Giants. Although he was unimpressive with the bat, Gans' intangible assets earned him the esteem of his peers as one of the best contemporary outfielders.

(Courtesy Noir-Tech Research, Inc.)

Smart Set of New Jersey, was one of the best. In 1912 he managed to "kidnap" Gans and pitcher Danny McClellan from the Lincoln Giants to stock his already formidable club.[12] The Smart Set team was a short-lived but highly competitive outfit, and this was the team for which Gans took off as a hitter. In 19 games, against all competition, Gans stroked 23 hits for a .351 average, including 6 triples, 4 home runs, and 23 runs scored. He also played stellar defense in left field with 41 errorless putouts and 8 assists.[13]

What should have been a highlight of the 1912 Smart Set season was marred by controversy when the team met the major-league New York Giants in a late May contest at Olympic Park in Paterson, New Jersey. With the hard-fought bout tied 3-3 after nine innings, interim Giants manager Wilbert Robinson argued with the umpire about the introduction of new baseballs for the 10th inning. He pulled his players off the field in protest, causing the game to be forfeited in favor of the home team. Regardless, the Smart Set proved they belonged on the same field as the legendary Giants, and Gans was the star of the show for the Paterson team. He knocked out two hits, including a double, and played outstanding defense in left, as he recorded six putouts, including a running one-handed grab of a blast off the bat of Giants shortstop Art Fletcher.[14]

The Smart Set were a scorching 24-7-2 going into late July when Gans was once again "kidnapped" and returned to the Lincoln Giants.[15] The Smart Set struggled the rest of the way, going 12-7-1 without him.[16] Coogan attempted to "kidnap" Gans again to begin the 1913 season, but Gans was now a fixture with the mighty Lincoln Giants.[17]

The 1912 and 1913 Lincoln Giants had stars at every position on the field. Joining the already-stacked 1912 team were first baseman Bill Pettus and Hall of Fame hurlers Cyclone Joe Williams and Ben Taylor to form what could only be called one of the greatest baseball teams ever assembled.[18] The Giants finished with the best record among all the top Eastern Independent Clubs with Gans acquitting himself nicely by getting on base frequently and showing good speed on the basepaths.

Another trip to Cuba was in the cards for Gans and the Lincoln Giants for the 1912-1913 winter season. Things started off slowly for the team as it played 13 games against Almendares and Habana and struggled to a 5-8 record.[19] According to Pop Lloyd, the departure of many of the Lincoln players and the failure of some to show up caused the five Giants – Lloyd, Spottswood Poles, Dick Redding, Cyclone Joe

Williams, and light-hitting Bill Francis – to jump to the Fe team for the remainder of the season. With the addition of these players, the Fe squad won the Cuban National League championship.[20] Gans was certainly a big reason for its success as he pounded the ball to the tune of a .356 batting average, with 4 three-baggers and 19 stolen bases. The team stole an amazing 136 bases in just 34 games as it drove the opposition batty with its speed.

A curious side note to the 1913 season had Gans, Cyclone Joe Williams, and Grant "Home Run" Johnson all beginning the year with the Schenectady Mohawk Giants, a first-year and ill-fated team that played against Eastern Independent squads such as the Lincoln Giants, Brooklyn Royal Giants, and Paterson Smart Set. All three players were back with the Lincoln Giants just a few weeks after the start of the season.[21]

The Florida Hotel League or Coconut League was a highly competitive rivalry between two hotels in Palm Beach, Florida, that stocked their teams with some of the best players in Black baseball history. Gans's first appearance in the league was in 1912, and by January of 1914 he was a veteran of the circuit.[22] His team, the Breakers Hotel, featured legends Bruce Petway, Pete Hill, John Henry Lloyd, Louis Santop, and Cyclone Joe Williams. Their rivals, the Poinciana Hotel, included Spottswood Poles, Dizzy Dismukes, Bill Pettus, and Frank Wickware.

Gans's defense stood out in one 1914 contest. According to the *Palm Beach Daily News*, "Gans, in the left garden, deserves great credit for the showing he made and the four flies he pulled down. He had to show great speed to get under them in the first place and in all but one instance after he got his hands on the ball he landed in a heap. Twice he stumbled over the mounds near the tall coconut trees and the other time he came in from deep left and gathered in a short fly that many thought he did not catch."[23] The Breakers captured the 1914 title, winning nine games and losing six.[24]

Gans fell in with Rube Foster's Chicago American Giants next, after being invited, along with Cyclone Joe Williams and John Henry Lloyd, to join the team on a trip to the Pacific Northwest. All three players took up Foster's offer and were scheduled to compete against teams in the Pacific Coast League. At the last minute, PCL President Allen Baum objected to Black players playing against PCL teams, which effectively canceled most of their schedule. The Portland Beavers were the only team to go against Baum and play Foster's team.[25]

Gans immediately got into hot water with his new boss. He recounted the story thusly:

> It was a damp day. Petway was on second and two were down and I was at bat. Rube signals for me to lay one down. Higginbottom, a lefthander, was working for Portland and Rube figured that if he tried to field the ball and turn to throw me out at first Petway could score. Well, Petway started up on the pitch, the ball was in the alley, and I knocked it into the bleachers for a home run. As I reached the plate with the winning score, as it later proved to be, George Moore, the fight manager, handed me a fifty-dollar bill and other fans threw money at me amounting to $87.50 all told. I went on to the bench and Rube drawled, "That was a sweet hit, son." "Yes, I sure laid into that one," I said. "Boys told me you could hit," added Rube. "Got yourself some money too, didn't you?" "Yes sir," I answered. "Suppose you wait for me to check up after the game and we'll go back to the hotel together," said the boss. I was getting all puffed up and saw myself getting a feed on Rube as we got in a taxi together. He threw his arm back of me and started to talk. "How did you like working for Sol White down east? Do they have any discipline down there?" "Oh, so so," as I lolled in my seat. "By the way, son, how much money did you collect?" And I told him $87.50. "Well, boy, let papa tell you something. If the Giants had lost that game today, the paper would have been full of what happed to Rube Foster's team. I am the manager of the club. I told you to lay it down and you hit a home run. Son, that home run is gonna cost you that $87.50 and $25 more. Now, the next time you hit a home run when I tell you to bunt, you'll remember that, won't you?"[26]

The 1914 Chicago American Giants were a dominant team with a sparkling 43-14 record, and they easily outpaced the second-place Indianapolis ABCs among the top Western Independent Clubs. Gans uncharacteristically struggled, hitting only .243 with one home run in 169 at-bats.

The following season he was back in familiar territory, but with the Lincoln Stars, an offshoot of the Lincoln Giants, formed when the owners of the Giants lost control of the team.[27] By the end of August, Gans and Lloyd found their way back to the Chicago American Giants to finish out the 1915 season when the owner of the Stars was unable to pay them after drinking away all of his profits.[28] The American Giants also made an appearance in the California Winter League and bested their White competitors, 9 games to 5. It was a historic occasion as it marked the first time an all-Black baseball team had won the California Winter League championship. In spite of his team's success, Gans struggled again, batting only .158 in 13 games.[29]

In February 1916 Gans was back in Cuba with San Francisco Park, a team made up of Chicago American Giants players. Gans hit a solid .300 in 15 games, including four multiple-hit games, but the team had a disappointing 5-9-1 record.[30] Once the team returned home, it fared much better and again finished with a top mark of 40-26-3. Gans continued his regular-season struggles and lost his starting left-field spot to Pete Hill. He managed to rekindle some of his spark on the mound with a complete-game shutout against the ABCs in June and two complete-game victories in August that included another shutout.[31]

In 1917 Gans lived a vagabond lifestyle as he jumped from team to team. The season began with a short stint with the Chicago Giants, followed by another with the Indianapolis-based Jewell's ABCs. In a late July game with the ABCs, Gans was credited with 20 putouts while manning first base.[32] The 1917 season ended with Gans once again suiting up for the Lincoln Giants, this time patrolling center field.

The year 1918 started off well enough for Gans as he began to regain his stroke at the plate, but the clouds of war were about to catch up to him and a number of his teammates. Gans was back with the Chicago American Giants when he, Frank Wickware, and first baseman Leroy Grant were drafted and ordered to report between August 1 and August 5.[33] An article in the *Chicago Defender* mentioned Gans's wife joining him early in the season in anticipation of his enlisting in the US Army.[34] She threw a surprise party for her husband on his birthday, attended by many of his teammates and friends, just days before he left for the service.[35] It is not known how long Gans and his wife, Emma, had been married at this point, but the 1920 census lists them as living in Chicago with eight other roommates, including fellow baseball star Jose Mendez. Emma, who was from Alabama, was 30 years old at the time. Their union dissolved at some point;

the next census indicated that they were divorced and living separately by 1930.

Gans's stint in the Army lasted less than a year, from July 31, 1918, to May 19, 1919.[36] He was a sergeant in the 803rd Pioneer Infantry and received a warm welcome upon his return to the American Giants.[37] Gans spent his time during the war in France and told many tales of his experiences overseas, including how the people there were quite familiar with the exploits of the Chicago American Giants.[38] Gans was well-known for his ability to spin a yarn, but his gift for gab did not help to keep his team from finishing in second place, nor did it prevent his hitting from declining further as he was able to contribute only an underwhelming .200 average.[39] Occasionally he still pitched, and he spun a four-hit shutout against the All Nations Team in late May, shortly after his return from military service.[40]

The 1920 Chicago American Giants won the inaugural Negro National League championship, easily outdistancing the Detroit Stars and Kansas City Monarchs. The newly minted league was the brainchild of American Giants owner and manager Rube Foster. Gans was the starting left fielder for what many consider to be one of the great Negro League teams of all time, but his play on the field was less than stellar as he hit a meager .208 for the champs. However, Gans occasionally chipped in, as he did on June 19, when he swatted a two-run home run and a double in a 10-5 victory over the Oak Parks.[41]

Gans was traded to the Detroit Stars for speedster Jimmie Lyons in December of 1920, but does not appear ever to have played for owner Tenny Blount's team.[42] In an attempt to create equity among the NNL's teams, newspapermen were chosen to select players for the 1921 squads, which took roster-building out of the owners' hands. As a result, Gans remained with the American Giants and Lyons with the Stars for the time being.[43] In a show of how fluid these teams' rosters often were, Lyons ended up as a member the 1921 American Giants anyway and Gans moved back to the Lincoln Giants, where he finished out the remainder of his career.

The 1921 and 1922 seasons were solid ones for Gans, as he batted .267 and a resurgent .333 respectively. But the team struggled to play .500 ball. Gans now spent more time at the right-field position. His entire 1923 season was lost when on April 22 he broke his right leg with a triple compound fracture. He had fractured his left leg in 1921 and these two injuries effectively ended his ability to be a productive player.[44]

Gans accepted a new challenge for the 1924 season when he replaced Cyclone Joe Williams as the manager of the Lincoln Giants. Hopes were high for the season after owner James J. Keenan invested heavily in the team by adding new players and turning Protectory Oval, the team's home ballpark, into a big-league-quality facility.[45] The May 31 edition of the New York Age asserted, "The fans now realize that under Judy Gans the team has improved 100 percent."[46] But the team did not quite live up to expectations and finished in third place. The poorer-than-expected performance was due in part to the numerous injuries to the pitching staff, which led to the 37-year-old Gans taking the mound on more than one occasion.[47]

The Lincoln Giants fell apart in 1925, and Gans lost control of his team. Allegedly, at the start of the season he had advised the owner of the Giants to cut the pay of some players and to release Gerard Williams and Benny Wilson because they wanted more money. This failed to go over well with players in the league and, whether it was true or not, they refused to sign with the Giants.[48] As a result, the team's roster was decimated. Quality pitching was in especially short supply, and the Lincoln Giants' team ERA ballooned to 8.24. It came as no surprise that the team finished in last place in the Eastern Colored League, with a woebegone 7-41-2 record. In mid-August, with the team sitting at 3-31-2, Gans resigned as manager.[49]

Gans was unable to stay away from baseball for long, and he took on a variety of projects. In 1927 he managed the Eastern Colored League All-Stars, a formidable independent team; a newspaper referred to him as crafty and jolly.[50] He also pitched for Chappie Johnson's Stars and in 1928[51] played for Louis Santop's Broncos, for whom he mashed seven hits in two games.[52] It was rumored that Gans would manage the 1928 Cleveland Tigers, but this would never materialize as the Tigers were led by Frank Duncan, Harry Jeffries, and Sam Crawford that season.[53]

Gans was also at the forefront of a movement to secure more Black umpires for Negro League baseball.[54] An editorial in the Philadelphia Tribune in 1927 commented on the problems of White umpires in Black baseball: "Regardless of the reasons for colored ball games having white umpires it is a disgusting and indefensible practice. It will require much thought and perhaps time and money, but the owners of ball clubs owe it to their patrons to discontinue a practice that is a reflection upon themselves, the ballplayers and the Negro race."[55]

Gans himself became a trailblazing Negro League umpire and called his first game in a May 2, 1929, matchup; fittingly, the game involved the Lincoln Giants and the Hilldale Club.[56] The pressure must have been immense, as indicated in the April 20, 1929, edition of the Pittsburgh Courier. W. Rollo Wilson wrote, "The whole movement depends on Judy Gans. If he proves the point, then other veterans will be drafted into service."[57] Gans performed well at his new job and was still umpiring as late as 1938.[58]

Gans was married again in 1937, to Elvera C. Gardiner. The couple remained together until his death in 1949, although very little is known about her.[59]

In 1940 Gans was recognized as a member of the Brotherhood Civic Goodwill Club in Philadelphia, an organization formed in 1884 to spread goodwill and to urge support to Black businesses and labor.[60] In 1944 he was still living in Philadelphia, where he was working as an aerial manager for the US Army Signal Corps.[61]

Judy Gans died on February 13, 1949, at the Naval Hospital in Philadelphia. His death certificate listed his occupation as bartender. He was buried at the National Cemetery in Beverly, New Jersey.[62]

Judy Gans's legacy lived on with Negro League legend and Hall of Famer Judy Johnson who, when elected to the Hall of Fame in 1975, had this to say about his namesake: "One of the old-timers on my first team was named Judy Gans. I resembled him, and my middle name is Julius, so they started calling me Judy too."[63]

Dizzy Dismukes – baseball lifer, crafty pitcher, manager, and longtime personnel director for the Kansas City Monarchs – named Gans the seventh-best outfielder in baseball history, ahead of Rap Dixon and Cool Papa Bell, in a 1930 piece he wrote for the Pittsburgh Courier. He insisted that Gans "must be given credit for being one of the game's greatest fielders."[64] Judy Gans was considered great in his time. He had power, even in the Deadball Era, was known for his speed and exceptional fielding ability, and excelled when called upon to toe the rubber. He played with some of the most iconic teams in Black baseball history, including the 1912 New York Lincoln Giants and the 1920 Chicago American Giants. He was also a pioneering umpire. As with many of the pre-1920 players, his statistics fail to tell the entire story of his career. Judy Gans was a star, and that is how he should be remembered.

SOURCES

All statistics, unless otherwise noted, were taken from the Seamheads Negro Leagues Database at seamheads.com.

NOTES

1 "Manager Shackelton's Club Will Play Famous Colored Nine on Sunday Morning," *Paterson* (New Jersey) *Morning Call*, July 16, 1914: 3.

2 John B. Holway, *The Complete Book of Baseball's Negro Leagues: The Other Half of Baseball History* (Fern Park, Florida: Hastings House Publishers, 2001), 372.

3 *Middletown Orange County Times Press*, June 28, 1912.

4 Most sources, including Seamheads.com, list Washington, Pennsylvania, as Gans's birthplace, but his death certificate and Social Security records list Cleveland as his place of birth. "Ohio" is prominently displayed on his tombstone.

5 "Fined $100 For Making the Home Run That Won the Game," *Cleveland Call and Post*, November 4, 1944: 6B.

6 "Judy Gans to Manage Lincoln Gts. This Year," *Pittsburgh Courier*, March 7, 1925: 6.

7 *Philadelphia Tribune*, September 15, 1927: 10. See also https://www.washjeff.edu/100th-anniversary-of-historic-game-by-dr-charles-f-west-the-first-black-quarterback-to-play-in-rose-bowl-game/. Accessed January 2, 2022.

8 "Judy Gans to Manage Lincoln Gts. This Year," *Pittsburgh Courier*, March 7, 1925: 6.

9 "Cuban Giants Land," *Philadelphia Inquirer*, August 19, 1908: 11.

10 Severo Nieto, *Early U.S. Blackball Teams in Cuba: Box Scores, Rosters and Statistics From the Files of Cuba's Foremost Baseball Researcher* (Jefferson, North Carolina: McFarland & Company Inc., 2008), 78-91.

11 Limited box scores are available from this time period and only games against major-league-caliber teams are included in the Seamheads Negro League database.

12 Lester A. Walton, "In the World of Sport," *New York Age*, August 15, 1912: 6.

13 The author's own research from *Paterson Morning Call* box scores, 1912. This includes games against all competition, not just the major-league-equivalent teams as determined by Seamheads.com.

14 "Smart Set Team Played New York to a Standstill," *Paterson Morning Call*, May 27, 1912: 3, 13.

15 Lester A. Walton, "Kidnapping Players the Latest Game," *New York Age*, August 15, 1912: 6.

16 Author's own research from *Paterson Morning Call* box scores, 1912.

17 "Baseball Game at Olympic Park," *Paterson Morning Call*, April 1, 1913: 3.

18 The 1912 Lincoln Giants featured four Hall of Famers: Louis Santop, John Henry Lloyd, Joe Williams, and Ben Taylor. The team also included likely future Hall of Famers Dick Redding, Spottswood Poles, and Bill Pettus.

19 Severo, *Early U.S. Blackball Teams in Cuba*, 105.

20 Wes Singletary, *The Right Time: John Henry "Pop" Lloyd and Black Baseball* (Jefferson, North Carolina: McFarland & Company Inc., 2011), 52-53.

21 https://agatetype.typepad.com/agate_type/2011/04/schenectady-mohawk-giants-1913.html. See also *Berkshire Eagle* (Pittsfield, Massachusetts), April 22, 1913: 11.

22 William F. McNeil, *Black Baseball Out of Season: Pay for Play Outside of the Negro Leagues* (Jefferson, North Carolina: McFarland & Company Inc., 2007), 16.

23 McNeil, *Black Baseball Out of Season*, 18.

24 "Baseball Season Ends on Florida Fields," *Brooklyn Daily Eagle*, March 18, 1914: 21.

25 Paul Debono, *The Chicago American Giants* (Jefferson, North Carolina: McFarland & Company Inc., 2007), 48.

26 W. Rollo Wilson, "Sport Shots," *Pittsburgh Courier*, February 2, 1929: A6.

27 https://thebrooklyntrolleyblogger.blogspot.com/2020/10/a-team-grows-in-harlem-new-york-lincoln.html.

28 Debono, *The Chicago American Giants*, 57.

29 William F. McNeil, *The California Winter League: America's First Integrated Professional Baseball League* (Jefferson, North Carolina: McFarland & Company Inc., 2002), 54-55.

30 Severo, *Early U.S. Blackball Teams in Cuba*, 206-217.

31 "Gans Scores Shutout," *Chicago Examiner*, June 20, 1916; "Baseball," *Chicago Tribune*, July 9, 1916: B22; "Amer. Giants, 6; St. Louis, 3," *Chicago Tribune*, July 13, 1916: 11.

32 "Hoosier Ball Club Wins Ten Round Go From Fosters, 5 to 4," *Chicago Tribune*, July 24, 1917: 11.

33 "Draft Hits Rube Foster's Club Hard," *Chicago Defender*, July 27, 1918: 9.

34 "Williams Is a Find," *Chicago Defender*, March 2, 1918: 7.

35 "Judy Gans Surprised," *Chicago Defender*, July 27, 1918: 9.

36 Ancestry.com: Military Burial Records.

37 Ancestry.com: Find a Grave.

38 "Giants Recruits Work Hard," *Chicago Defender*, April 5, 1919: 11.

39 "Pow Wow Pickups," *Philadelphia Tribune*, March 10, 1938: 13.

40 "American Giants Blank All Nations," *Chicago Defender*, May 31, 1919: 11.

41 "Oak Parks Lose, 10-3," *Chicago Tribune*, June 20, 1920: A3.

42 "Jimmy Lyons Comes to American Giants," *Chicago Defender*, December 11, 1920: 6.

43 Larry Lester, *Rube Foster in His Time: On the Field and in the Papers with Black Baseball's Greatest Visionary* (Jefferson, North Carolina: McFarland & Company Inc., 2012), 115.

44 "Judy Gans to Manage Lincoln Gts. This Year," *Pittsburgh Courier*, March 7, 1925: 6.

45 "Many New Players in Lincoln Giants Line-Up," *Bridgewater* (New Jersey) *Courier-News*, March 14, 1924: 16.

46 "Lincoln Giants Set Pace for Eastern League Flag Race," *New York Age*, May 31, 1924: 6.

47 "Giants and Hilldale Divide Doubleheader," *Pittsburgh Courier*, August 30, 1924: 13.

48 William E. Clark, "Sport Comment," *New York Age*, July 3, 1925: 6.

49 "Judy Gans Resigns as the Manager of the Lincoln Giants," *New York Age*, August 22, 1925: 6.

50 "Gans' Stars Downs Trenton with Hackett on Mound," *Philadelphia Tribune*, August 25, 1927: 10,

51 "Hilldale Pries Off Lid with Victory," *Wilmington* (Delaware) *Evening Journal*, April 15, 1927: 27.

52 "Lou Santop's Broncos Win from Red Sox," *Philadelphia Tribune*, June 14, 1928: 11.

53 "Bingo DeMoss to Manage Detroit; Gans to Tigers," *Baltimore Afro American*, March 3, 1928: 1.

54 W. Rollo Wilson, "Sport Shots," *Pittsburgh Courier*, April 21, 1928: A4.

55   Neil Lanctot, *Fair Dealing & Clean Playing: The Hilldale Club and the Development of Black Professional Baseball, 1910-1932* (Syracuse, New York: Syracuse University Press, 2007), 200.

56   "Hilldale Loses to Lincolns, 4-3, in Opener," *Pittsburgh Courier,* May 4, 1929: A5.

57   W. Rollo Wilson, "Sport Shots," *Pittsburgh Courier,* April 20, 1929: B5.

58   Chester L. Washington Jr., "'Sez Ches,'" *Pittsburgh Courier,* April 23, 1938: 17.

59   Ancestry.com: US Marriage Index.

60   "Brotherhood Holds Its 56th Anniversary," *Philadelphia Tribune,* October 17, 1940: 3.

61   "Fined $100 For Making the Home Run That Won the Game," *Cleveland Call and Post,* November 4,1944: 6B.

62   Ancestry.com: Certificate of Death.

63   "Johnson Selected to Hall," *Charlotte Observer,* February 11, 1975: 23.

64   "Dismukes Names His 9 Best Outfielders," *Pittsburgh Courier,* March 8, 1930: 14.

JELLY GARDNER

BY JEB STEWART

Floyd "Jelly" Gardner was a prototypical leadoff hitter who played 13 seasons in the Negro Leagues, from 1919 to 1931, most notably for Rube Foster's Chicago American Giants. The speedy Gardner stood just 5-feet-6½ and weighed 160 pounds, and his basestealing prowess created constant pressure on opposing defenses. He was a left-handed hitter, threw right-handed, and played all three outfield positions well.

Gardner was born on September 27, 1895, in tiny Russellville, Arkansas.[1] His parents were Alec Floyd Gardner and Josie (Smith) Gardner, and he had a younger sister named Annie.[2] His father worked as a farm laborer.[3] Although Russellville was a segregated rural community of fewer than 4,000 people, Gardner attended the Russellville Public School for eight years.[4] He enrolled in high school at Arkansas Baptist College in Little Rock,[5] where he later took college courses for two years as well.[6]

At Arkansas Baptist, Gardner tried out for the baseball team and made the squad as an infielder.[7] He initially batted cross-handed until a coach taught him how to properly grip a bat.[8] He may have played professionally as early as 1913 with the Hot Springs Giants or the Missouri Pacifics of Little Rock.[9] By 1916, Gardner had joined the independent Longview Giants in Texas during his school's summer break. He later recalled, "You didn't get much pay down there, you mostly played for your board and rent."[10]

The following year he returned to Texas and played with another club, the Texas All-Stars.[11] Gardner was

After beginning the 1920 season with the NNL's Dayton Marcos, Floyd "Jelly" Gardner joined the American Giants in July and became Chicago's starting right fielder.

listed as one of the best players on the All-Stars, which reportedly had a record of 66-16-3 when they traveled east to play five games against the Indianapolis ABCs.[12] The series did not go well, as the ABCs easily swept the first four games.[13] In the third game, Indianapolis won, 11-1, as Jim Jeffries allowed only two hits, one of them to Gardner.[14] For Gardner, the trip was not a complete disaster. On July 29, the All-Stars faced the Chicago American Giants. Although Texas lost, 7-5, Gardner had three hits and scored a run, which his future manager, Rube Foster, surely noticed.[15]

On June 17, 1917, Gardner registered for military service, listing "ball player" as his usual occupation on his registration card. World War I soon interrupted Gardner's plans to play professional baseball when he was drafted.[16] By May 4, 1918, he enlisted in the US Army; on June 10 he sailed on a transport ship, the *Agamemnon*, from Hoboken, New Jersey, to Brest, France.[17]

Gardner served as a private in Company F in the 365th Infantry, 92nd Division, which was nicknamed the Buffalo Soldier Division and "was one of only two all-black divisions to fight in the United States Army in World War I."[18] Little has been documented regarding Gardner's military service, but his division served on the front lines and "saw action primarily in one of the last Allied operations of the war – the Meuse-Argonne Offensive that began in September and ended with the Armistice on November 11, 1918."[19] Gardner returned to the United States aboard the *Olympic* on February 17, 1919.[20] He was discharged by the Army on March 19, 1919, just in time for baseball season.[21]

Gardner initially lived in Chicago and worked various jobs at restaurants and hotels, but he soon joined the Detroit Stars.[22] The Stars were the top Western independent club in 1919, finishing with a record of 27-14, which was one game better than the Chicago American Giants.[23] In early July, Foster saw his Giants lose three straight to the Stars. Gardner had a hit, scored two runs, and stole a base in the finale, as the Stars won, 11-3.[24] The speed game suited Gardner well, as he recalled to baseball historian John Holway:

"I wasn't a power hitter, I was a punch hitter. Punch it by the first baseman, slow balls to the shortstop, drag it to the second baseman. And I was a fair bunter: If you didn't bunt too hard you were safe – I mean, I was. Or you'd fake like you were going to bunt, the third baseman would come in, you'd push the ball right by him. I got a double on those lots of times."[25]

Despite his success in Detroit, Gardner did not get along with the Stars' owner, Tenny Blount. He bitterly suggested Blount should not even have owned a team because he also "*ran* a gambling house."[26] The following year, he joined the Dayton Marcos in the newly formed Negro National League, although details of his signing are lost to history. For the first few months, he played left field for Dayton. His last reported game with the Marcos was on July 19, 1920, as he contributed a hit in a 3-1 loss to the American Giants.[27]

By the beginning of August, the American Giants had won 15 in a row,[28] and Foster acquired the 24-year-old Gardner to become Chicago's starting right fielder. Foster employed "intimidation, psychology, speed, and the bunt-and-run" as his principal offensive strategies,[29] which made Gardner an ideal fit for Chicago. The American Giants featured Bingo DeMoss, George Dixon, Leroy Grant, and Cristóbal Torriente as the primary run producers in the lineup.

Foster recognized Gardner as one of the fastest players in the game, particularly in running down the line to first base.[30] He immediately made Gardner his leadoff hitter, elevating him from the low place in the batting order he had occupied with Detroit and Dayton.[31] Gardner was so fast that, many years later, when Homestead Grays owner and columnist Cum Posey selected him for his all-time, all-American baseball team, he was effusive in his praise of Gardner's speed, writing:

"I pick Jelly Gardner as the best run-getter and lead-off man I have seen in forty years. No lead-off man in recent years has had the aggressiveness and the ability to reach first base in as many ways as he did. In my opinion he was the only player I ever saw that could steal first base."[32]

For his part, Gardner later expressed pride that he "was always the 'lead-off' (first-place) hitter in the line-up and was never removed for a pinch hitter."[33] With Gardner at the top of the lineup, the American Giants completed the 1920 campaign as champions of the Negro National League with a 43-17-2 record, which was good for a commanding eight-game lead over second-place Detroit. Chicago won NNL pennants again in 1921 and 1922.

On June 13, 1922, Foster moved Gardner out of his usual leadoff spot and batted him seventh. Gardner responded with three hits in four at-bats, a sacrifice, three runs scored, and a stolen base in a wild 19-16 loss to the St. Louis Stars.[34] At season's end, the American Giants won the NNL again in a close race with the Monarchs.

Baseball historian James Riley observed that Gardner's "performance [with Chicago] was inversely related to the team's success. In his first three seasons, he batted only .182, .219, and .236, [but] the American Giants won the Negro National League pennant each year."[35] However, additional box scores from the years 1920-22 have come to light and have helped to determine that his batting average during this time frame was .254 and his on-base percentage was a more respectable .324.[36] He also contributed 60 stolen bases during this period,[37] leading the NNL in 1922 and finishing third the following year. Gardner later remembered Foster would often use smoke from his pipe to convey signs to him on the basepaths.[38]

Gardner was one of the speediest players in the game.[39] Teammate Dave Malarcher called him "a terror" on the basepaths and "a whiz in the outfield," as he described Gardner's aggressive game to John Holway:

"[I]f he's running and you lay the ball down the least bit to the right side of the pitcher if he's a right-hander, the third baseman is going to move off the bag – he's got to move off. I have seen Jelly score from first on balls like that. If the guy makes a not too perfect throw to first base, you just come on home, instead of just going to third. It was really marvelous.

He made one of the two greatest catches I've ever seen. It was down in Baltimore, one of those great big parks. They didn't even have a right field fence, right field was like a pasture. The bases were filled, and Jelly had to run like everything and finally jumped in the air and reached out and caught it with his bare hand. That Gardner was a great little outfielder."[40]

By 1923, newspapers began referring to Gardner as "Jelly."[41] According to baseball historian Jim Yeager, because he was "[s]hort, round, and jovial, Gardner was tagged with the nickname 'Jelly Roll' by his teammates. Nicknames had a way of catching on in the early days of baseball in America, and Floyd 'Jelly Roll' Gardner was never Floyd. He was simply called 'Jelly.'"[42]

Despite his affable nickname, Gardner had a reputation for hard-nosed play on the field. He was always willing to argue with umpires and to fight opposing players.[43] Off the field, he was known for late nights in speakeasies and shot houses during Prohibition.[44] Gardner later recalled that Foster did not care what he did outside the ballpark.[45] While his manager overlooked Gardner's after-hours shenanigans, he expected him to take his job seriously, and he had no tolerance when Gardner failed to follow his orders in a game. As Foster's son Earl told baseball historian Robert Peterson:

"One time Jelly Gardner was sent up to bunt and he tripled. He came back and sat down on the bench. The old man took that pipe he smoked – he always had it – and he popped him right across the head. And he fined him and told him, 'As long as I'm paying you, you'll do as I tell you to do.'"[46]

Gardner played well in 1923, batting .280 with a .377 on-base percentage, as he led the American Giants in steals (21) and runs (70). However, Chicago had an off-year and finished 3½ games behind the Kansas City Monarchs. It was the first of four straight NNL pennants for the Monarchs from 1923 to 1926, while Chicago slipped to second place three times. For his part, Gardner performed well for the American Giants during this time-frame as he batted .301 and averaged 64 runs scored and 14 stolen bases. He also posted a career-high batting average (.325) and on-base percentage (.432) in 1924, as he paced Chicago in plate appearances, at-bats, hits, and walks. He then spent the winter in Cuba playing for Santa Clara and Matanzas, where he batted .288.[47]

Before starting the 1925 campaign, the American Giants played an exhibition against the Chicago Blues, regarded as "the strongest white club in the city."[48] Gardner collected three hits including two doubles in the 5-3 win, which left newspapers predicting a pennant for Foster.[49]

On April 27 the American Giants opened the NNL schedule on the road at Rickwood Field with a four-game series against the Birmingham Black Barons. In front of 10,000 fans, one of the largest crowds ever to see a Negro League game in Birmingham, the American Giants crushed the Black Barons, 15-6. Gardner's home run keyed a six-run outburst by Chicago in the fifth inning.[50] He also made "several spectacular catches" in the outfield.[51] The *Pittsburgh Courier* – perhaps reporting on Gardner's performance for the *entire* series – noted that he collected four hits, including a home run and two doubles in the game.[52] Chicago then swept the remaining three games from Birmingham.[53]

Despite the early success, the American Giants soon cooled off and the Monarchs moved into first place by late spring.[54] Kansas City won the NNL by 3½ games over the second-place St. Louis Stars.[55] Although Chicago finished 57-41-2, it fell to third place, a disappointing 10 games behind the Monarchs.

The 1926 season proved to be transitional for both the American Giants and Gardner, who was now 30. Chicago traded its best player, Cristóbal Torriente, to the rival Monarchs before the season.[56] Rube Foster managed the first half for Chicago, but the American Giants sank to fourth in the standings.[57] Foster was suffering from a mental illness and took a leave of absence during the second half; he was replaced as manager by third basemen Dave Malarcher.[58] The American Giants bounced back to finish 57-24-3. Gardner had an excellent year at the plate, leading the team with a .315 batting average, a .424 on-base percentage, and 57 runs scored.

With Torriente, Kansas City had the best overall record in the NNL once again. However, Chicago managed to win the second-half title and faced the Monarchs in a best-of-nine NNL Championship Series for the right to meet the champion of the Eastern Colored League in the Negro League World Series.[59]

Unfortunately for the American Giants, the first four games of the series were in Kansas City and the Monarchs won each of the first three games.[60] The next day, Chicago managed to eke out a 4-3 win behind the strong pitching of Rube Currie.[61] After the series shifted to Chicago, the Monarchs won Game Five, 11-5, to take a commanding four-games-to-one lead, but "[i]n one of the most dramatic comebacks in the history of post season play, the Chicago American Giants won the final four games of the series."[62] For the NNL championship series, Gardner posted a .472 on-base percentage, which was the highest for either club, along with a .752 OPS, which was only second to Torriente's .783.

After defeating the Monarchs, the American Giants faced the Atlantic City Bacharach Giants in the Negro League World Series. Through six games, Chicago repeated its poor start from the NNL series and trailed Atlantic City three games to one (with two games ending in a tie). Even so, Gardner made two key defensive plays, which may have prevented the Bacharach Giants from sweeping the series.

In the sixth inning of Game Two, with the American Giants leading 7-5 and the bases loaded, Ambrose Reid of the Bacharach Giants singled to right, scoring Willie Jones. However, Gardner prevented a run by throwing home to catcher John Hines, which made Chano Garcia scurry back to third. Hines then picked off Hubert Lockhart at second, and shortstop Sanford Jackson threw the ball back to Hines, who tagged Garcia out at the plate to complete the improbable 9-2-6-2 double play, which ended the threat in Chicago's 7-6 win.

Next, in the sixth inning of Game Four, and with the Bacharach Giants leading 4-3, Garcia hit a triple to start the bottom of the inning.[63] Rats Henderson then hit a fly ball to right. This time Garcia did not retreat, but Gardner fired home to Hines to nail him.[64] Although the game ended in a 4-4 tie, without Gardner's throw Chicago would have lost the game and probably the series.

After eight games, the Bacharach Giants led the series four games to two and needed just one more win to become Negro League champion for 1926. Facing elimination in each contest, the American Giants won the last three games of the Series. The final contest was scoreless until the bottom of the ninth as Lockhart battled Chicago's Willie Foster. Lockhart was nearly untouchable through eight innings, allowing only two hits and one walk, while Foster struggled, as he surrendered 10 hits and three walks after nine frames. Gardner opened the bottom of the inning with a base hit to left field; he moved to second on Malarcher's sacrifice bunt. Left fielder Sandy Thompson then singled to center to drive Gardner home for the winning run in the 1-0 victory.

Although Gardner batted only .222 in the World Series, he led both teams with 12 walks, scored 8 runs, stole 3 bases, and had an on-base percentage of .417.

By 1927, John Henry "Pop" Lloyd told sportswriter Rollo Wilson that Gardner was already worthy of being considered an all-time great.[65] He was one of the heroes of the American Giants' championship squad but soon got into a contract dispute with owner John Schorling, who was now running the team due to Foster's mental illness.[66] He held out for the spring and into the summer before becoming a free agent and joining Pop Lloyd's Lincoln Giants of the Eastern Colored League in July.[67]

Lloyd was delighted with the signing, which he believed gave him the strongest outfield in baseball, and Gardner's fleet feet and strong throwing arm made an immediate impact. The *Pittsburgh Courier* reported that "playing against the Camden team here Sunday, July 17, Gardner saved the game for the home team by an accurate throw from centerfield to home plate and also prevented the score from being tied up in the ninth inning by a star one hand catch off the centerfield fence."[68] Sportswriter William G. Nunn gushed over his speed, observing that "Gardner has absorbed the Rube Foster style of play, and he has the speed of a greyhound, both afield and on the bases."[69]

Gardner batted .286 for the Lincoln Giants based on limited box scores, which are available for only five of his games in 1927.[70] Even with Gardner at the top of the lineup, Lincoln could not catch Atlantic City, which won both halves of the ECL. Lincoln finished with a disappointing 10-15 record and mired in sixth place 12½ games behind the Bacharach Giants. Back in Chicago, Malarcher and his American Giants surely missed Gardner at the top of the order. Despite his absence, they won the NNL pennant and again defeated the Atlantic City in the Negro League World Series, which was the last one played until 1942.

That winter, Chicago and Detroit competed to sign Gardner for the 1928 campaign.[71] Although Bingo DeMoss of the Stars insisted he had already inked Gardner to a deal, by the beginning of the season Gardner had returned to the American Giants, albeit only briefly.[72] Later that summer, the independent Homestead Grays announced Gardner's signing. The *Pittsburgh Courier* vaguely reported that his acquisition came as a surprise because "no advance notice was given of Gardner's intention of joining the Grays."[73] Baseball historian Paul Debono concluded that Gardner had jumped his contract with Chicago.[74] He played well for the Grays, batting .292.

That offseason, Homestead played an eight-game series against a collection of barnstorming players from the American League who included Jimmie Foxx.[75] In the first game, Gardner batted leadoff. He went 2-for-4 with a double, stole two bases, and scored three runs as the Grays beat the All-Stars, 8-4.[76] He batted a respectable .280 for the series, which the two teams split.

For Gardner, 1929 was nearly a mirror image to the previous year. This time, he was expected to open the season with Homestead.[77] However, by Opening Day, sportswriter Rollo Wilson reported that "Jelly Gardner has taken French leave from the Grays and that Cum Posey is searching for another fly-chaser."[78] In fact, he had already returned to Chicago.[79] Even with Gardner's return, the American Giants limped to a 19-24 record and fifth place in the NNL standings in

the first half.[80] Although they bounced back to finish 51-40, this was only good for third place, a distant 17½ games behind the Monarchs.

Gardner batted .315 with an impressive .419 on-base percentage and was the American Giants' second-best offensive player behind Pythias Russ.[81] He nearly won the league's stolen-base title as well.[82] However, his skills soon began to decline as the new decade got underway.

By 1930, Gardner was 34 years old and was no longer an everyday player in Chicago's outfield. According to the available statistics, he batted only .232 and stole just a single base in 34 games for the fourth-place American Giants. Late that fall, Rube Foster, the man who had originally signed him for Chicago in 1920, died after a long illness.[83]

The following year, Gardner signed with the Detroit Stars, the team for which he had plied his trade in 1919 as a young prospect. His offensive abilities continued to decline; he batted only .215. On July 9 he had one final flash of glory as he homered in Detroit's 10-7 win over the Cleveland Cubs.[84] Despite his heroics, Gardner could not help the Stars escape fourth place as they finished with a 25-33 record. After the season the Rube Foster-founded NNL collapsed.

Years after he retired, Gardner told John Holway that he returned to play for the American Giants in 1933, although no contemporaneous news reports confirm this.[85] Both his Hall of Fame questionnaire, which he completed in 1972, and his player clip file report he played for Homestead in 1932 and 1933.[86] Once again, no newspaper sources confirm this.

After retiring from baseball, Gardner briefly worked for the US Post Office.[87] He then worked for many years for the Gulf, Mobile and Ohio Railroad as a waiter and Pullman porter.[88] He married Dorothy Haynes on November 29, 1950, and the couple had two children, Floyd Alec Gardner, and Judie Marie Gardner.[89] On July 29, 1951, he played in his last reported game – a two-inning old-timer's exhibition contest – to honor Rube Foster at Comiskey Park.[90]

Gardner died in Chicago on March 28, 1977, at the age of 81.[91] He is buried in Saint Mary Catholic Cemetery and Mausoleum in Evergreen Park in Cook County, Illinois.[92]

Based on the currently available statistics for league games, Gardner batted .280 during his career with a solid on-base percentage of .373, an OPS+ of 102, and 146 stolen bases. In 1952 the *Pittsburgh Courier* selected him as an immortal of the game.[93] Throughout his career, he was frequently cited in newspaper accounts as being not only one of the fastest players in the game but also as possessing one of the deadliest arms.[94] Rollo Wilson argued that Gardner was good enough to play in the major leagues.[95] In his 13 games against big-league clubs, he batted .292 with 5 stolen bases and 10 runs scored.[96]

Gardner appeared on the preliminary ballot of the 2006 Special Committee on the Negro Leagues Election to the Baseball Hall of Fame but failed to garner enough votes to make the final ballot.[97] However, it remains an open question as to whether he is deserving of induction.

For his part, Gardner believed he was a better hitter than Ty Cobb,[98] although this claim was certainly an exaggeration, which stands in marked contrast to the available evidence. In 1974 sportswriter Doc Young of the *Chicago Defender* interviewed an anonymous old-time Negro League player who declared that "Jelly Gardner was a better player than Cool Papa Bell," adding, "I played against Cool Papa Bell and I know he wasn't an all-around star. He could run fast but he couldn't throw and he couldn't hit with power."[99] The player cited an East Coast bias as the reason voters overlooked Gardner and others.[100]

Dave Malarcher assessed Gardner as "one of the greatest Negro ballplayers we had. ... He should be in there in the Hall of Fame, and I happen to know that better than anybody. He wasn't a great slugging hitter, but he knew how to go everything at bat to get on base. He was fast, he could bunt, he could run, he was daring. And he was a run-maker, because anything you did behind him, he'd score."[101]

On December 16, 2020, Major League Baseball announced that seven professional Negro Leagues that operated from 1920 to 1948 had been designated as having "Major League status."[102] Consequently, Gardner has finally been recognized as a major-league player for 12 of his 13 seasons in professional baseball. With his rating as a big leaguer now established, it may be time to reevaluate his Hall of Fame candidacy.

SOURCES AND ACKNOWLEDGMENTS

All player statistics and team records were taken from Seamheads.com, except where otherwise indicated.

The author wishes to thank fellow SABR member Joe DeLeonard for reviewing this article and offering helpful suggestions. Cassidy Lent, a reference librarian at the National Baseball Hall of Fame and Museum, generously provided Jelly Gardner's Hall of Fame player clip file and questionnaire, along with John Holway's excellent article on him.

NOTES

1   Jelly Gardner's National Baseball Hall of Fame questionnaire.

2   Gardner questionnaire; Arkansas. Pope County. 1900 US Census.

3   Arkansas. Pope County. 1900 US Census; Arkansas. Pope County. 1910 US Census; Arkansas. Pope County. 1920 US Census.

4   Jelly Gardner questionnaire.

5   The school provided courses for students in grammar school, high school, and college. "Arkansas Baptist College," *Arkansas Democrat*, August 31, 1919: 67.

6   Jelly Gardner questionnaire.

7   John Holway, "Historically Speaking: Jelly Gardner," *Black Sports*, September 1974: 60.

8   Holway: 60.

9   Jim Yeager, "Floyd Gardner: They Called Him 'Jelly,'" January 20, 2020: accessed at https://onlyinark.com/sports/floyd-gardner-they-called-him-jelly/; "'Jelly' Gardner and George Johnson Both from 'Lone Star State' Scale Heights," *Pittsburgh Courier*, February 21, 1925: 6.

10   Holway: 60.

11   https://www.seamheads.com/NegroLgs/player.php?playerID=gardn01jel.

12   "Jeffrey and Johnson Will Do Pitching for Taylor's A.B.C.s," *Indianapolis Star*, July 22, 1917: 45.

13   "Taylor's Team Twice Trims Texas Team," *Indianapolis News*, July 23, 1917: 11; "Jeffries Allows Team Only Two Hits and Taylor A.B.C.s Win," *Indianapolis Star*, July 24, 1917: 11; "Taylor's Squad Wins Again from the Texas All-Stars," *Indianapolis Star*, July 25, 1917: 10. According to baseball historian Paul Debono, the game between the All-Stars and the American Giants was played on "Texas Day ... in which his home state was honored." Paul Debono, *The Chicago American Giants* (Jefferson, North Carolina: McFarland & Company, Inc., 2007), 65.

14   "Jeffries Allows Team Only Two Hits and Taylor A.B.C.s Win," *Indianapolis Star*, July 24, 1917: 11.

15   "Fosters Score Five in One Round and Beat Leaguers, 7-5," *Chicago Tribune*, July 30, 1917: 11.

16   "'Jelly' Gardner and George Johnson Both from 'Lone Star State' Scale Heights," *Pittsburgh Courier*, February 21, 1925: 6.

17   US Army Transport Service Arriving and Departing Passenger Lists, 1910-1939.

18   Ephrem Yared, 92ND INFANTRY DIVISION (1917–1919, 1942–1945), March 9, 2016: accessed at https://www.blackpast.org/african-american-history/92nd-infantry-division-1917-1919-1942-1945-0/.

19   Yared. According to baseball historian Jim Yeager, Gardner was briefly listed as missing in action in a local newspaper. Jim Yeager, "Floyd Gardner: They Called Him 'Jelly,'" January 20, 2020: accessed at https://onlyinark.com/sports/floyd-gardner-they-called-him-jelly/

20   US Army Transport Service Arriving and Departing Passenger Lists, 1910-1939.

21   US Department of Veterans Affairs BIRLS Death File, 1850-2010; Gardner questionnaire.

22   Holway: 60; James A. Riley, *The Biographical Encyclopedia of the Negro Baseball Leagues* (New York: Carroll & Graf Publishers, 1994), 306.

23   https://www.seamheads.com/NegroLgs/year.php?yearID=1919. All statistics in this biography are from Seamheads or Retrosheet.org.

24   "Detroit Stars Make It Sweep with Chicago," *Detroit Free Press*, July 8, 1919: 16.

25   Holway: 60.

26   Holway: 60.

27   "American Giants Trim Dayton Nine Again, 3-1,"
     Chicago Tribune, July 20, 1920: 14.

28   "Chicago Club Here Tomorrow," *Kansas City Times*, July 30, 1920: 12.

29   Tim Odzer, "Rube Foster," accessed at https://sabr.org/
     bioproj/person/andrew-rube-foster/#_ednref10.

30   William G. Nunn, "Diamond Dope," *Pittsburgh Courier*, April 10, 1926: 14.

31   Debono, 77. With the Stars and Marcos, Gardner usually batted at the
     bottom of the lineup. "Stars Work Hard Scoring Odd Run on Doyle's Boys,"
     Detroit Free Press, April 28, 1919: 12 (batted sixth); "Corrigan Field Is
     Opened with Stars' Victory," *Detroit Free Press*, May 31, 1919: 16 (batted
     seventh); "Second Contest Is Annexed by Detroit Stars," *Detroit Free Press*,
     June 1, 1919: 26 (batted seventh); "Detroit Stars Again Wallop Pittsburghers,"
     Detroit Free Press, June 24, 1919: 21 (batted seventh); "Detroit Stars
     Make It Sweep with Chicago," *Detroit Free Press*, July 8, 1919: 16 (batted
     eighth); "Whitworth Is Master Over Blount's Cast," *Detroit Free Press*,
     July 28, 1919: 11 (batted seventh); "Stars Pummel Foster's Club in Third
     Game," *Detroit Free Press*, July 29, 1919: 16 (batted seventh); "Marcos
     6; Am. Giants 5," *Chicago Tribune*, June 20, 1920: 14 (batted second).

32   Chester Washington, "Sez Ches," *Pittsburgh Courier*, March 6, 1943: 18.
     Posey also selected Buck Leonard (1B), George Scales (2b), George Monroe
     (3b), Willie Wells (ss), Pete Hill (lf), Oscar Charleston (cf), and Josh Gibson
     (c) as position players for this team along with pitchers Satchel Paige, Bullet
     Joe Rogan, Slim Jones, Joe Williams, Rats Henderson, and Willie Foster.

33   Gardner questionnaire.

34   "Battling Bee Won by St. Louis Stars Over Chicago Giants,"
     St. Louis Globe-Democrat, June 14, 1992: 16.

35   Riley, 305.

36   This includes Gardner's performance with Dayton in
     1920 as those numbers are not separated.

37   This includes Gardner's performance with Dayton in
     1920 as those numbers are not separated.

38   Robert Peterson, *Only The Ball Was White* (New
     York: Oxford University Press, 1970), 109.

39   "Both Clubs Traveling Fast," *Kansas City Times*, July 2, 1924: 14.

40   Holway: 58.

41   "Orange Opens Season Sunday," *Bridgewater* (New Jersey)
     Courier-News, April 12, 1923: 12; "Am. Giants, 5; Kansas
     City, 1," *Chicago Tribune*, August 26, 1923: 23.

42   Jim Yeager, "Floyd Gardner: They Called Him 'Jelly,'" January 20, 2020;
     accessed at https://onlyinark.com/sports/floyd-gardner-they-called-him-jelly/.

43   Yeager; Riley, 305-06; Posey's Points, *Pittsburgh Courier*, April 12, 1941: 16.

44   Riley, 306; Holway: 60.

45   Holway: 60.

46   Peterson, 111.

47   Gardner player file at the National Baseball Hall of Fame.

48   "Am. Giants Play Like Champions and Win 5-3,"
     Pittsburgh Courier, April 18, 1925: 12.

49   "Am. Giants Play Like Champions and Win 5-3."

50   "Chicago Takes Opener from Black Barons,"
     Birmingham News, April 28, 1925: 16.

51   "Am. Giants Take Opener from Barons,"
     Pittsburgh Courier, May 2, 1925: 13.

52   "Am. Giants Take Opener from Barons." This is at odds with the box
     score published in the *Birmingham News*, which showed that Gardner

went 1-for-6 in the first game. "Chicago Takes Opener from Black
Barons," *Birmingham News*, April 28, 1925: 16. In the second game of
the series, Gardner went 2-for-5 with a double and a run scored in the
12-2 win. "Chicago Wins Second Clash from Rushmen," *Birmingham
News*, April 29, 1925: 16. Only a line score has been located for the
third game of the series, which the American Giants won, 12-10.
"American Giants Rally to Defeat Birmingham," *Chicago Tribune*,
April 30, 1925: 15. In the fourth game of the series, Gardner went
2-for-4 with a double and a run scored in the 9-8 win. "Black Barons
Lose Four in Row to Giants," *Birmingham News*, May 1, 1925: 23.

53   "Black Barons Lose Four in Row to Giants,"
     Birmingham News, May 1, 1925: 23.

54   "Chicago Giants Here Tomorrow," *Kansas City Star*, May 27, 1925: 14.

55   https://www.seamheads.com/NegroLgs/year.php?yearID=1925&lgID=NNL.

56   Peter C. Bjarkman, "Cristóbal Torriente," accessed at
     https://sabr.org/bioproj/person/cristobal-torriente/.

57   Debono, 110.

58   Debono, 110.

59   "The Pennant to Chicago," *Kansas City Times*, September 13, 1926: 10;
     "Sports Notes," *Parsons* (Kansas) *Daily Sun*, September 14, 1926: 2.

60   "Kay See Wins Three," *Pittsburgh Courier*, September 25, 1926: 14.
     The first two games were hotly contested with Kansas City claiming
     one-run wins, 4-3 and 6-5. "Kansas City, 4; Giants, 3," *Chicago Tribune*,
     September 19, 1926: 32; "Monarchs Trim Fosters in Negro Title Game,
     6-5," *Madison* (Wisconsin) *Capital Times*, September 20, 1926: 10. In
     Game Three, the Monarchs won easily, 5-0. "Kay See Wins Three."

61   "Play-Off Championship" Series, Center for Negro League Baseball
     Research, 3, accessed at http://www.cnlbr.org/Portals/0/RL/
     Negro%20League%20Play-Off%20Series%20(1925-1929).pdf.

62   "Play-Off Championship" Series.

63   Frank A. Young, "Atlantic City Invades West, Leading Chicago 2
     to 1 In World's Series," *Chicago Defender*, October 9, 1926: 11.

64   Young: 11.

65   Rollo Wilson, "Sports Hots: Press Box & Ringside,"
     Pittsburgh Courier, April 2, 1927: 18.

66   "World Champs Open Season Next Sunday,"
     Pittsburgh Courier, April 16, 1927: 17.

67   Rollo Wilson, "Sports Hots: Press Box & Ringside," *Pittsburgh Courier*,
     July 23, 1927: 16. "'Jelly' Gardner Now on Roster of Lincoln Giants,"
     Pittsburgh Courier, July 23, 1927: 16. Paul Debono noted that Gardner
     signed with the Homestead Grays. Debono, 116. However, it was
     pitcher Ping Gardner who joined Homestead, not Jelly Gardner. "'Ping
     Gardner to Twirl for Grays," *Pittsburgh Courier*, July 9, 1927: 17.

68   "'Jelly' Gardner Now on Roster of Lincoln Giants."

69   William G. Nunn, "Sport Broadcast Talks,"
     Pittsburgh Courier, August 6, 1927: 16.

70   https://www.seamheads.com/NegroLgs/team.php?-
     yearID=1927&teamID=NLG&LGOrd=3.

71   "Baseball Gossip of the National League,"
     Pittsburgh Courier, March 17, 1928: 16.

72   "Baseball Gossip of the National League"; Q.J. Gilmore, "Doings of the
     National League," *California Eagle* (Los Angeles), May 25, 1928: 9.

73   "Grays Win Both Games Saturday," *Pittsburgh Courier*, August 4, 1928:
     16; "Homestead Grays Have Real Collection of Ball Players; Lineup of
     Team Is Announced," *Warren* (Pennsylvania) *Tribune*, August 22, 1928: 6.

74   Debono, 120.

75 "Grays Set for Big Leaguers," *Pittsburgh Courier*, October 6, 1928: 17.

76 "Grays Beat Big Leaguers in First 2 Tilts," *Pittsburgh Courier*, October 13, 1928: 16.

77 C.L. Washington, "'Ches' Says," *Pittsburgh Courier*, March 29, 1929: 17.

78 Rollo Wilson, "Sports Hots: Press Box & Ringside," *Pittsburgh Courier*, April 27, 1929: 17.

79 "M'Donald Holds Akron Scoreless; Grays Win Sparkling Opener, 4-0," *Pittsburgh Courier*, April 27, 1929: 16; "Can't Stop the Monarchs," *Kansas City* (Missouri) *Times,* April 30, 1929: 13; Debono, 123.

80 "National League Standings," *Birmingham Reporter*, June 29, 1929: 7.

81 https://www.seamheads.com/NegroLgs/team.php?-yearID=1929&teamID=CAG&LGOrd=1&tab=bat&sort=R_a.

82 "American Giants Open Series Here," *Detroit Free Press*, May 17, 1930: 17.

83 "'Rube' Foster, Negro Baseball Pitcher, Dies," *St. Louis Post-Dispatch*, December 10, 1930: 26.

84 "Homers by Gardner, Dean Give Stars Win," *Pittsburgh Courier*, July 11, 1931: 14.

85 Holway: 60.

86 Gardner questionnaire; Hall of Fame player file.

87 Holway: 60.

88 Holway: 60.

89 Gardner questionnaire.

90 Russ J. Cowans, "Rube Foster Honored at Chisox Park," *The Sporting News*, August 8, 1951: 34.

91 https://www.findagrave.com/memorial/224134327/floyd-gardner.

92 https://www.findagrave.com/memorial/224134327/floyd-gardner.

93 "Courier Experts' 'Roll of Honor,'" *Pittsburgh Courier*, April 19, 1952: 16.

94 "Both Clubs Traveling Fast," *Kansas City Times*, July 2, 1924: 14; "Dismukes' Diamond Dope," *Pittsburgh Courier*, November 15, 1924: 7; "'Jelly' Gardner and George Johnson Both from 'Lone Star State' Scale Heights," *Pittsburgh Courier*, February 21, 1925: 6; William G. Nunn, "Diamond Dope," *Pittsburgh Courier*, April 10, 1926: 14; Rollo Wilson, "Sports Hots: Press Box & Ringside," *Pittsburgh Courier*, November 18, 1928: 18; Chester Washington, "Sez Ches," *Pittsburgh Courier*, March 6, 1943: 18.

95 Rollo Wilson, "Sports Hots: Press Box & Ringside," *Pittsburgh Courier*, September 3, 1927: 18.

96 Todd Peterson, ed., *The Negro Leagues Were Major Leagues: Historians Reappraise Black Baseball* (Jefferson, North Carolina: McFarland & Company, Inc., 2020), 233.

97 https://www.baseballreference.com/bullpen/2006_Special_Committee_on_the_Negro_Leagues_Election.

98 "The World Series That Never Was Played," *Chicago Tribune*, October 18, 1970: 30.

99 A.S. "Doc" Young, "Good Morning Sports!" *Chicago Defender*, May 14, 1974: 21.

100 A.S. Young.

101 Holway: 58.

102 https://www.mlb.com/news/negro-leagues-given-major-league-status-for-baseball-records-stats.

LEROY GRANT

BY FREDERICK C. BUSH

Negro League historian James A. Riley portrays Leroy Grant as a "hulking first sacker [who] was susceptible to bonehead plays in the field and on the bases, and evidently made some critical errors during the 1917 season."[1] In truth, although Grant did have some rough times in 1917, he was considered by many of his peers and contemporary observers to be one of the premier first baseman in all of baseball. Grant was most often compared to Hal Chase, his White counterpart, and both men plied their trade in New York City in 1912-13, Chase for the Yankees and Grant for the Lincoln Giants. Sports columnist Alvin Moses wrote of Grant, "He could bat, field, and run the bases like a frightened gazelle – in fact some of the stops and plays he executed around the initial bag appeared incredible. If he possessed any diamond weaknesses, we were never able to discern them."[2]

Riley also describes Grant as "evidently temperamental and moody," which is an apt depiction of Grant's demeanor.[3] Moses, in his post-career retrospective on Grant, likened him to another White contemporary, declaring, "His was a flaming, fiery spirit, not unlike that of the one and only Tyrus Cobb. ... Grant was always willing to fight, but not in the manner that ... true fighting men were wont to. Leroy thought it the most ethical thing in the world to assault a fellow player with a bat or anything at hand in lieu of such an implement of warfare."[4] Grant's often dour mien might be a reason why, despite "all of his color and dash, he lacked the adulation of the fans."[5] His

quick and violent temper certainly impacted the event that dominated his life after professional baseball and contributed to tragic circumstances until his death at the age of 62.

(Courtesy Noir-Tech Research, Inc.)

First baseman Leroy Grant provided an intimidating presence on and off the field for the American Giants. An excellent glove man, he was compared to such White major-league contemporaries as Hal Chase and Jake Daubert.

Leroy Grant was born on April 15, 1889, in Houston, Texas, to Ned and Mary (Thomas) Grant. Ned was a laborer who worked such odd jobs as he could find, while Mary kept house and raised the children. Leroy had at least four older brothers – Edward, William, John, and Abernethy – who ranged from 18 down to 10 years his elder; public records about the family are spotty, and Leroy appears to have had additional siblings (including at least one sister). His mother's fate is also unknown as, at the time of the 1910 US Census, 22-year-old Leroy was living with only his 65-year-old father and two young nephews, Ellsworth, 5, and Frank Clark, 3. Ned Grant's marital status was still listed as "married," but no further record of Mary is to be found.[6]

At the time of the 1910 Census, Leroy's occupation was listed as "Professional Bead [sic] Player." The Texas Colored Baseball League was formed in May 1910 but did not last long, breaking up in July of the same year.[7] The Houston Black Buffaloes were one of the franchises in that short-lived circuit; the team had been around prior to the TCBL's formation and continued to play after the league folded. Although not certain, it is quite likely that Grant played for the Black Buffs or one of the other TCBL squads. Rube Foster, a fellow Texan, who owned, managed, and pitched for the Chicago American Giants, was always on the lookout for new talent. At some point that year, he discovered Grant and signed him to a contract for the 1911 season.

Grant was still a diamond in the rough during his first season with Foster's independent ballclub, and he batted .248 in 34 games while putting up a .974 fielding percentage that was right in line with the .973 cumulative average for first basemen on the Western Independent teams. Grant did not receive much mention in the press other than appearing in box scores. However, in July, the *Chicago Defender* noted, "Grant, the star first sacker of the American Giants, is improving every day."[8]

In January 1912 Grant traveled with Foster and pitcher Frank Wickware, another American Giants player, to Cuba, where all three played for the Fe team during the winter season. Fe finished in last place, but Wickware posted a stellar 10-3 record. Foster pitched in only two games (with no decisions), while Grant found his way into only three contests and was a meager 1-for-10 at the plate.[9]

Two additional members of the Fe team were pitcher Dick "Cannonball" Redding and catcher Louis Santop, who both played for the New York Lincoln Giants. Grant moved east and joined the Lincoln Giants for the 1912 season. Foster often became angry and indignant when players he discovered defected to other squads, but he may not have viewed Grant's loss as a major blow to his team. The fact was that Grant's play still needed improvement, although he was doing his utmost to better his game.

Grant's new squad, the Lincoln Giants, was the dominant independent team in the East in 1912, and he played alongside four future Hall of Famers. Included among that distinguished crew were shortstop-manager John Henry "Pop" Lloyd, catcher Santop, pitcher-first baseman Ben Taylor, and fastball ace Cyclone Joe Williams.[10] Unlike his teammates, Grant was overmatched: He played in 16 games and batted a paltry .196.

In December the Lincoln Giants traveled to Cuba to play a series of games against the Almendares and Habana teams. The winter visitors did not fare particularly well, posting a 5-8 record against the two Cuban squads. Redding was the only pitcher to post a winning record (2-1); Wickware, who had been so dominant the previous year, went 2-2 while Williams bottomed out at 1-5. Grant played in all 13 games and performed no better with the bat than he had back home, going 8-for-39 (.205).[11]

Grant persevered, however, and the 1913 campaign marked his breakout season. He raised all of his offensive numbers, in particular his batting average, which saw an almost 70-point increase to .262 in 17 games against the East's top teams. The press took notice of the resemblances to counterparts in the White major leagues. In July the *Buffalo Commercial* raved that the Lincoln Giants team "has today a dark fellow who, with the exception of Chase and [Jake] Daubert, is the best first baseman playing ball today."[12] The reporter extended the comparison, stating, "Grant exhibits footwork around the initial bag much the same as Chase does. He picks up the worst kind of throws out of the hard gravel and reaches for wild ones and gets them with the same grace that marked Chase when he was trying."[13]

Grant's progress as a player was even more amazing considering his weak performance in 1912. The *Commercial's* reporter reminded readers that Grant "joined the Lincoln Giants last summer and was so poor as a player that Manager [sic] Rod McMahon tried to wish him on any colored team that would have him. He had a contract, and McMahon had to hold on to him."[14] Now, Grant was playing so well that he no longer needed to worry about job security.

In July and August 1913, the Lincoln Giants played a home-and-away "championship" series against the Chicago American Giants for supremacy in Black baseball. When the series moved from New York to Chicago, it was reported that "[b]etween 7,000 and 10,000 fans were present at Schorling's park" [*sic*] on July 27 for the first game in the West.[15] Although neither team belonged to a league and the championship was an unofficial one, the game had a World Series atmosphere:

"Every automobile and taxicab available on the South Side was engaged for the day. Street cars were packed and jammed and thousands walked. The Eighth Regiment band of the K. of P.'s furnished music for the waiting throng. Extra chairs were used for the occasion, benches were made especially to accommodate the massive crowd. It was a beautiful sight."[16]

Cyclone Williams, who dominated much of the series, held Foster's squad in check this day, pitching an 8-0 shutout and adding a three-run homer in the sixth inning to support his own cause. Williams's home run "was knocked so high over the fence that it looked as though it would drop in the lake," and the ball landed "just a few feet from the Bull Durham [so that it was] thought that the tobacco people will award him $25.00."[17]

Although Grant did not distinguish himself in the series, he did his part as the Lincoln Giants claimed the championship over his former team. Foster tipped his cap to the New Yorkers, saying, "I am one who takes his hat off to the victorious Lincoln Giants. Their great playing and wonderful defense was never surpassed, if equaled, on any diamond."[18]

Grant returned to New York for the 1914 and 1915 seasons. The Lincoln Giants continued to be a powerhouse squad in the East, and Grant, now a wizard with the glove, kept improving with the stick. In 1914 Grant batted exactly .300 and had a .347 on-base percentage, and in 1915 he raised those figures to .309 and .371, respectively. In both seasons, the Lincoln Giants played exhibition games against two White major-league teams, the New York Giants and Philadelphia Phillies, posting 1-1-1 and 1-3 records. Grant struggled in 1914, batting .182, but in 1915 he led all Lincoln Giants with a .385 batting average in the four games.

Grant had come such a long way from his first season with the Lincoln Giants that Cyclone Williams took him to Florida in the winter as a member of his Breakers Hotel team in the Florida Hotel League. The Breakers won the title over the Poinciana Hotel, nine games to six, but Grant struggled to an .083 batting average in the six games he played. Nonetheless, he had proven his mettle, and Foster was willing and able to lure him back to the Chicago American Giants for the 1916 season.

Grant's homecoming to Chicago was a rousing success in 1916. Although his batting average fell, it was still a solid .278, and it was obvious how much he had improved since his first stint in the Windy City. The accolades started coming early in the season as the *Chicago Defender* dubbed him "Home-run" Grant after he hit a long ball in an 11-0 whitewashing of the University of Oregon on April 14 in Eugene, Oregon.[19] In regard to Grant's fielding, the *Defender* reported on a May 7 game against the West End team at Schorling Park, "When the infield work of the Giants started, Grant immediately caused much concern [to the West Enders] by his all-round work around the first sack and it was a revelation to the fans who applauded every play."[20]

The most notable aspect of the 1916 season was the intense rivalry between the American Giants and the Indianapolis ABCs, who engaged in a bitter dispute over which squad was champion of the West that year. In October, the ABCs won four of five games in a "postseason" series between the two teams and declared themselves champions. Foster, much embarrassed by his team's performance, pointed out that the American Giants had won three of four games (with a fifth ending in a tie) in August; thus, Foster argued, nothing had been settled between the two teams. The dispute made obvious the fact that "it remained impossible to decide which team was the best without the benefit of an organized league."[21]

In the winter Grant again participated in the Florida Hotel League, though he switched over to the Poinciana Hotel team, managed by Foster, and played against his old teammate, Cyclone Williams, who still managed the Breakers Hotel squad. Grant batted .220 in 14 games as the Poinciana team captured the title with 7-6-2 record, holding Williams winless (0-4) in the process.

Grant had found the sweet spot in his baseball career as he had become a solid all-around performer and competed for championships wherever he played. In 1917 all of that came crashing down. Grant's batting average and fielding percentage were almost identical to those of the previous season (.271 and .975 in 1917 compared to .278 and .974 in 1916) and he cut his errors from 17 to 15, but there was no forgiveness for his miscues.

The *Defender*, which had hailed the hero Grant in 1916, turned on him after a fielding error coupled with a baserunning blunder resulted in a tough 12-inning loss to the Kansas City All-Nations team in the first game of a doubleheader at Schorling Park on September 9, 1917. Cannonball Redding had joined the American Giants in 1917 and "up till the ninth frame [he] had held the boys from Kansas City hitless" as he engaged in a pitching duel with K.C.'s John Donaldson.[22]

In the fateful – or as the *Defender* termed it, "fatal" – 12th inning, Grant's drop of shortstop Pop Lloyd's throw on Cristobal Torriente's two-out grounder gave the All-Nations team a reprieve. After catcher Clarence Coleman drew a walk, Donaldson doubled to drive in Torriente with what turned out to be the winning run. As if the situation were not awful enough for Grant, he had the chance to score the tying run in the bottom of the inning but erred again.

Grant led off the Giants' half of the inning with a double and advanced to third on George Dixon's sacrifice. Redding hit a long fly ball to center field, and the *Defender* described what happened next:

"Instead of Grant holding the bag until he saw whether the outfielder was going to catch the ball or not, knowing if he didn't he had plenty of time to score from third with the tying run, he started for home, getting about one-fourth of the way there, seeing the ball caught, he had to return, touch the bag and then try to beat the throw. Torrenntti [*sic*] then had plenty of time to set himself and throw, which he did as true as an arrow and bone-headed Grant was caught five feet off the bag."[23]

It was a tough way to lose the game but was not representative of Grant's play throughout the season. Nevertheless, the *Defender's* reporter excoriated the American Giants' first baseman, writing, "Both teams had good support till the twelfth, when Grant saw visions of some fried chicken and hot biscuits and he dreamed a long dream, only to awaken and find out he was the cause of defeat."[24]

Despite the *Defender* columnist's mean-spiritedness toward Grant on this occasion, he was a key performer on an American Giants squad that dominated the West in 1917. Chicago finished the season with a 49-14-2 record against other top Black teams while no competitor finished with a record over .500. At least Grant was able to vacation in Florida as part of the

Foster-led Poinciana Hotel team in the winter. This time Grant batted .214 in 13 games as Poinciana again won the title with a 9-5 record against the Breakers Hotel.

As if to stem the tide of criticism, Grant played like a man possessed in 1918. He was in the middle of the best season of his career – .348 batting average, .411 on-base percentage, and .981 fielding percentage – when Uncle Sam came calling in July as the United States had entered the World War in the previous year. Grant had been on such a tear that the *Defender* now deemed him "the greatest first baseman that ever wore the American Giants uniform" when it reported that he and teammates Judy Gans, Frank Wickware, and Bobby Williams had all been ordered to report for Army service between August 1 and 5.[25] In spite of the loss of key personnel, Chicago still had the best record among the Western teams, finishing 20-8-2 in a season abbreviated by various wartime restrictions.

In 1919, Grant returned from the war – along with Gans, Williams, and pitcher Tom Johnson – and Foster added Oscar Charleston and Cristobal Torriente to his strong squad. In another abbreviated season, Chicago finished 27-16 but had stiff competition from the Detroit Stars club that finished with a barely better 27-14 mark.

The most striking event that took place in 1919 was a late-July/early-August riot that caused the team's home field, Schorling Park, to be temporarily occupied by National Guard troops. The events began on July 27:

"Eugene Williams, a black youth, was swimming near a 'white beach' and was attacked by a stone-throwing white male. The youth drowned, and when the police arrived, they did not take action against the perpetrator. A riot broke out that would last five days and claim the lives of 23 blacks and 15 whites. The South Side of Chicago became a war zone; children were among the dead, homes were burned, shops looted, there were volleys of gunfire and territorial wars fought over certain neighborhoods."[26]

Although the city of Chicago was scarred by the events, "[t]he riot hardly fazed Rube [Foster], who in the days immediately following remained busy laying the groundwork for an organized league."[27]

On February 13, 1920, Foster and his fellow owners in the West met at the Paseo branch of the YMCA in Kansas City, Missouri, and formed the Negro National

League. Chicago dominated the early years of the NNL, claiming the first three league championships (1920 through 1922). In the NNL's inaugural season, the American Giants rolled to a 43-17-2 league record (a .717 winning percentage) to claim the pennant by eight games over the Detroit Stars. At the conclusion of the season, Foster took his team on a swing through the South, where it won 14 consecutive games and defeated the Negro Southern League's champion, the Knoxville Giants, five times. Next, the team traveled northeast to take on the Atlantic City Bacharach Giants in a series of games played at Philadelphia's Shibe Park and Brooklyn's Ebbets Field. This series was to serve as "a dress rehearsal for what Rube envisioned as the black World Series."[28] Chicago emerged with a 4-3-1 record in the series against the East's top independent club of 1920, and the American Giants reigned supreme in 1920.[29]

Grant, who was living as a roomer in his employer Foster's home in 1920, remained the team's starting first baseman throughout the season, even though he slumped to a .213 batting average. His temper came to the fore in a July 31 game against the Kansas City Monarchs, the team that eventually supplanted the American Giants for NNL dominance, at K.C.'s Association Park. In the bottom of the first inning, John Donaldson – playing center field on this occasion – slid hard into Grant at first base. A fistfight between the two players ensued, and "[a] special detachment of officers rushed on the field and quelled the disturbance."[30] In the end, "[t]he affair amounted to Grant putting the big southpaw [Donaldson] to the ground and then both were banished from the game."[31] The American Giants, minus Grant, prevailed by a 9-7 score.

In 1921 the American Giants picked up where they had left off the previous season. Foster's team claimed its second straight NNL pennant as their 44-22-2 record resulted in the league's best winning percentage (.667); the Kansas City Monarchs won more games, posting a 54-41 (.568) league ledger, but finished 4½ games behind Chicago. In 1922 Chicago won the pennant by virtue of having an almost infinitesimally greater winning percentage than Kansas City: the American Giants' 37-24-1 record gave them a .607 winning percentage compared with the Monarchs' 47-31-2, .603 mark. It was the end of the American Giants' dominance of the NNL and also heralded the decline of Grant's career, although he still managed batting averages of .251 and .267 as the team's regular first baseman in those two seasons.

In 1923, as the American Giants finished in second place behind the Monarchs, the *Defender* noted that Grant "was seldom seen in the lineup"; it reported that he had been transferred to the Indianapolis ABCs in August.[32] The primary reason for Grant's lack of playing time was no doubt the dismal .194 batting average he posted in 30 games for Chicago. The move to Indianapolis, where he batted .238 in seven games, was temporary; it turned out that Foster had sent Grant to help Indianapolis because they "were short of a first sacker."[33] Although the ABCs were an NNL rival, Foster had been looking out for the good of the league as well as that of his own team.

Grant managed to hang on with Chicago for one last season in 1924 – and played in three games for the NNL's Cleveland Browns – but his batting average with Chicago plummeted to .180 in 29 games. The American Giants again placed second behind the Monarchs, and Foster began to make wholesale changes prior to the 1925 season. On March 7 the *Defender* reported, "The axe fell and fell heavy upon the heads of several players of the American Giants this week," and noted that Grant was one of a number of "heroes of many a battle" who had been unconditionally released while other teammates had been assigned to rival NNL squads.[34]

Grant returned to Schorling Park on September 8, 1928, along with former American Giants left fielder Jimmie Lyons, as a member of the semipro Michigan City (Indiana) Wonders. The Wonders lost a 5-3 game to the Evanston (Illinois) Giants that day, but Grant and Lyons "were well received by the crowd: Many still believe Grant, with his coaching off first would still be an asset to the Giants."[35] Grant did have a brief future in coaching – or rather, managing – but with the Michigan City club rather than the American Giants. However, before that job opportunity presented itself, Grant's hot temper caused his life to take a wrong turn in 1929.

Early in the year, Grant was fined $35 and sentenced to 90 days in jail for assault and battery. He was released on July 13, 1929, after serving his time, but events took a turn for the worse just a few months later. In the early morning hours of November 26, Grant stabbed a man named C.D. Frieson to death in front of a cabaret in Michigan City. According to the news account of the incident, "The stabbing occurred after a brawl. The men had been fighting over a mutual sweetheart, Miss Rosalie Jackson. Grant escaped and police said the girl refused to talk."[36] Grant was on the lam, and "[a] dragnet was set by Gary [Indiana] police" to capture him; the police believed that Grant "would try to escape to Gary and go into hiding. ... He was suffering from a crippled foot and wore a slipper on the member when last seen."[37]

On January 3, 1930, it was reported that an indictment for murder had been returned against Grant, though at that time he was still being sought.[38] Grant was eventually captured by the authorities in Grand Rapids, Michigan, on June 18 and was returned to Michigan City to stand trial on the murder charge.[39] There is considerable irony in the fact that, while Grant was set to go on trial for murder, his former American Giants teammate, pitcher Dave Brown, was playing for semipro teams in the Midwest under the alias Lefty Wilson while evading a murder charge of his own stemming from an April 28, 1925, incident in New York City.

A few months later, on November 13, it was reported that "Michigan City's prison baseball nine had a new first base recruit today with admission of Leroy Grant, colored giant, to serve a two to twenty-one years sentence for manslaughter. Grant ... was known as one of the best first basemen of his race. While in jail here [La Porte] ... Grant has been keeping in training throwing a baseball at the jail wall." [40]

The very next day, Grant threw himself upon the mercy of the court as he requested a new trial. Whether he had been the recipient of poor legal advice or just had not understood his plight, "Grant said he pleaded guilty to the manslaughter charge because he thought the penalty was a one-to-10-year sentence. Grant said he was willing to stand trial on a charge of first-degree murder. The judge granted a new trial, and the state approved."[41]

Grant's trial never took place, perhaps because he could not afford legal representation, so his sentence for manslaughter stood. He was paroled on February 1, 1934, and found immediate employment in baseball. A brief paragraph in the *Defender*'s February 17, 1934, edition stated, "Leroy Grant, great first baseman with Rube Foster, is now manager of the Michigan City Giants at Michigan City, Ind. Grant and club owner, Kemp, visited the offices of The Chicago Defender last week and both looked fine."[42] Grant had kept baseball at the forefront of his activities by playing for the prison team throughout his incarceration, and a brief article in early April reported, "Spring training of the Indiana state prison baseball squad has begun. ... Prospects for another good team [are] bright. ... Only one man, Leroy Grant, colored Michigan City star, has been lost by 'graduation.'"[43]

Grant completed the terms of his parole and was discharged from his sentence completely on January 31, 1935. It should have been the beginning of a new lease on life, but he was unable to stay out of legal trouble. In 1936 Grant was fined $110 and sentenced to 180 days in jail for public intoxication (and presumably creating a disturbance). Then, for a time, he managed to walk the straight and narrow. However, in 1941, he was fined $213.50 and again served a 180-day jail sentence for assault and battery.

Grant was still out of prison in April 1942, when he filled out a World War II draft registration card. He was residing in Michigan City and listed as his contact person Clarence Kemp, owner of the city's semipro baseball team with whom he had visited the *Defender's* offices in 1934. Within less than a year from this time, new circumstances resulted in Grant losing his freedom for the remainder of his life. Official records do not indicate the manner in which Grant again ran afoul of the law, but he was admitted to Logansport State Hospital, a psychiatric facility, on January 13, 1943, and was declared by the State of Indiana to be legally insane. He was diagnosed with paranoid schizophrenia and was transferred from Logansport to the Indiana Hospital for Insane Criminals (IHIC) in Michigan City on March 30, 1943.[44]

Grant's health continued to decline during what was to be his permanent incarceration at the IHIC, and, on May 2, 1949, he was transferred back to Logansport State Hospital, where he could receive better treatment for the physical ailments that now plagued him as well. Grant remained institutionalized at Logansport until his death on May 7, 1951. His death certificate listed the following conditions as contributory causes of death: pulmonary tyberculosis [*sic*], generalized arteriosclerosis, and schizophrenic psychosis. His body was donated for scientific study to the Anatomical Board of Indiana University.

Grant's prison records and death certificate both listed him as a widower, but no record of his marriage has been uncovered. Thus, the identity of his wife remains a mystery, though Grant's prison records indicate that the couple did not have any children.

Grant's crimes cannot be excused or dismissed, but his isolation in his final years and the fact that he suffered from physical and mental illnesses were tragic. It was an unfortunate end to the life of a player about whom Alvin Moses had written in 1927 in the *Pittsburgh Courier*, "When one attempts to assemble great first basemen, just remember that LEROY GRANT belongs – and that's that."[45]

ACKNOWLEDGMENT

Thanks to Michael Vetman, archivist for the Indiana Archives and Records Administration, for providing official documents about Leroy Grant's prison terms and transfers to hospital facilities.

SOURCES

Except where otherwise indicate, all player statistics and team records were taken from Seamheads.com.

Ancestry.com was consulted for US Census information, military records, and birth and death records.

NOTES

1   James A. Riley, *The Biographical Encyclopedia of the Negro Baseball Leagues* (New York: Carroll & Graf Publishers, Inc., 1994), 331. Grant was not as "hulking" as Riley thought him to be. Riley lists Grant as standing 6-feet-4 and weighing 215 pounds; however, on Grant's World War II draft registration card, he is listed as 5-feet-11 and 174 pounds.

2   Alvin J. Moses, "In Baseball's 'Hall of Fame' – Leroy Grant – The Wizard – First Baseman," *Pittsburgh Courier*, June 4, 1927: 16.

3   Riley, 331.

4   Moses.

5   Moses.

6   Leroy's brother, William, died in Houston on June 23, 1938. His death certificate indicates that both Mary Grant's maiden name and exact place of birth in the state of Louisiana were unknown to Texas officials at that time; also unknown is whether she and Ned Grant split or she predeceased her husband.

7   Mike Vance, ed., *Houston Baseball: The Early Years, 1861-1961* (Houston: Bright Sky Press, 2014), 259.

8   "American or Chicago Giants Which?" *Chicago Defender*, July 8, 1911: 1.

9   Jorge Figueredo, *Cuban Baseball: A Statistical History, 1878-1961* (Jefferson, North Carolina: McFarland & Company, Inc., 2003), 97-100.

10   Williams may be better known today by the nickname Smokey Joe; however, at this point in his career, most news accounts referred to him as Cyclone Joe.

11   Severo Nieto, *Early U.S. Blackball Teams in Cuba: Box Scores, Rosters and Statistics from the Files of Cuba's Foremost Baseball Researcher* (Jefferson, North Carolina: McFarland & Company, Inc., 2008), 105, 113.

12   "Most Ball Players Develop Themselves," *Buffalo Commercial*, July 10, 1913: 4.

13   "Most Ball Players Develop Themselves."

14   "Most Ball Players Develop Themselves." Rod "Jess" McMahon and Ed McMahon were co-owners of the team; Pop Lloyd was the manager in 1912.

15   Cary B. Lewis, "Lincoln Giants Win First Two Games in Championship Series – American Giants Win Third Game – Great Games on Saturday and Sunday," *Indianapolis Freeman*, August 2, 1913: 4.

16   Lewis.

17   Lewis.

18   Paul Debono, *The Chicago American Giants* (Jefferson, North Carolina: McFarland & Company, Inc., 2007), 47.

19   "Giants Drub U. of O.," *Chicago Defender*, April 15, 1916: 7.

20   Mr. Fan, "American Giants Win," *Chicago Defender*, May 13, 1916: 7.

21   Debono, 62.

22   Mister Fan, "Grant Dreams; Redding Loses Hard Game: Bonehead Play Gives All Nations 12-Inning Win," *Chicago Defender*, September 15, 1917: 10.

23   "Grant Dreams; Redding Loses Hard Game."

24   "Grant Dreams; Redding Loses Hard Game."

25   "Draft Hits Rube Foster's Club Hard," *Chicago Defender*, July 27, 1918: 9.

26   Debono, 71-72. See also: Gary Ashwill, "White Racial Violence & the Negro Leagues: The Chicago Riot of 1919," June 14, 2020, https://agatetype.typepad.com/agate_type/2020/06/white-racial-violence-the-negro-leagues-the-chicago-riot-of-1919.html.

27   Debono, 73.

28   Debono, 80.

29   Chicago's 4-3-1 record against the Bacharach Giants was derived from the game accounts found in Bill Nowlin's time-line for the 1920 American Giants in the present volume.

30   "A Late Rally Beats Monarchs," *Kansas City Star*, August 1, 1920: 14.

31   "Rube's Crew Flays Monarchs," *Chicago Whip*, August 7, 1920: 6.

32   "Foster Begins to Wreck Once Great Machine," *Chicago Defender*, August 11, 1923: 9.

33   "Leroy Grant Back in City: Had Been with Indianapolis," *Chicago Defender*, September 1, 1923: 9.

34   "Foster Releases Several Ballplayers: Leroy Grant Among Those Unfortunates," *Chicago Defender*, March 7, 1925: 12.

35   "Evanston Is Winner over Michigan City," *Chicago Defender*, September 15, 1928: 8.

36   "Negro Fatally Stabbed," *Seymour* (Indiana) *Tribune*, November 26, 1929: 1.

37   "Search for Michigan City Killer," *Munster* (Indiana) *Times*, November 26, 1929: 17.

38   "Maloney Is Sentenced," *Munster Times*, January 3, 1930: 25.

39   "News Briefs," *Bedford* (Indiana) *Daily Times*, June 18, 1930: 3.

40   "Prison Nine Recruit," *Indianapolis News*, November 13, 1930: 26.

41   "Objects to Sentence; Now to Stand Trial," *Muncie* (Indiana) *Evening Press*, November 14, 1930: 10.

42   "Leroy Grant Is Manager of Nine," *Chicago Defender*, February 17, 1934: 8.

43   "Prison to Have a Good Team," *Valparaiso* (Indiana) *Vidette-Messenger*, April 10, 1934: 6.

44   The Indiana Hospital for Insane Criminals (IHIC) was built by prison labor in 1910 and admitted its first inmates in 1912. The IHIC facility was demolished in 1954, but Logansport State Hospital was still open as of 2021.

45   Moses.

TOM JOHNSON

BY FREDERICK C. BUSH

The early life of pitcher Tom Johnson, one of the star hurlers for the 1920 Chicago American Giants team that won the inaugural Negro National League pennant, is largely shrouded in mystery. What is known is that he had two outstanding seasons for Rube Foster's squad, including the 1920 campaign, in which he pitched to a perfect 11-0 record for Chicago. In total, he carved out a nine-year career in the Negro Leagues that concluded with a 62-40 record (.608) against Negro major-league-caliber competition. After his playing days ended, Johnson moved from the mound to behind the plate and worked games as an umpire. His life was tragically cut short, however, when he died at the age of 37 from an illness first contracted during his military service in World War I.

Thomas Jefferson Johnson gave his date of birth as April 22, 1889, on his World War I draft registration card. He also listed his place of birth as Bryan (Brazos County), Texas; however, no other information about his birth family or background is available on this document. The 1900 US Census lists only one Black family with a son named Tom Johnson living in Brazos County. The date of birth given for Tom in the census does not match the date he gave on his draft card – this was not an unusual circumstance as misinformation about dates and the spellings of names abounds in census records – but his mother's background hints that this Tom may indeed have been the American Giants' pitcher. According to the census, Tom Johnson was the stepson of Jon Hays, a farmer,

and the biological son of Sallie Hays; also living in the house were two additional stepchildren, Dora and Elizah Johnson, as well as the couple's children, Charley and Viola Hays.[1]

(Courtesy Noir-Tech Research, Inc.)

Righthander Tom Johnson was a perfect 11-0 for the American Giants in NNL play. Amazingly, his 1.84 ERA placed him only third among the team's starters behind Dave Brown's 1.82 and Tom Williams' 1.83 marks.

The one clue that this was Tom Johnson the pitcher lies in the fact that his mother's birth state was listed as Georgia. Tom Johnson was given the nickname College Boy because he attended Morris Brown College in Atlanta, Georgia, prior to becoming a professional ballplayer. If Johnson finished his secondary school education in Texas – which is not a certainty – then there were already numerous Black colleges for him to choose from in his native state, including nearby Prairie View Normal and Industrial College (now Prairie View A&M University), which is 55 miles from Bryan; Tillotson College and Normal Institute and Samuel Huston College, both located in Austin (and now joined as Huston-Tillotson University); and Wiley College in the East Texas city of Marshall. Since Tom's mother was from Georgia, she probably still had family in that state, and it is conceivable that the extended family connection – perhaps not only to his mother but also to his biological father – prompted Tom to go to Georgia to continue his education.

Johnson's first season as a professional ballplayer was spent with the New York Lincoln Giants in 1911. As professional Black teams barnstormed through Atlanta, they no doubt saw Johnson pitch for the Morris Brown team while he attended college.[2] The Lincoln Giants sent out the siren call of a baseball career that Johnson followed, first to the Northeast and later to the Midwest. Louis Santop, a fellow 22-year-old from Tyler, Texas, was the starting catcher for the Lincoln Giants, so it is possible that he convinced his fellow Texan that New York City was a good place to play baseball.

Whether or not Santop held any such sway over Johnson, the two formed the battery for the Lincoln Giants in what likely was the first professional shutout, and perhaps even the first professional victory, that Johnson pitched, on July 16, 1911, at Olympic Field in New York City. In a three-team doubleheader, Dick "Cannonball" Redding took the mound for the Lincoln Giants and hurled a 3-0 victory over New London in the first game. Johnson went to the hill in the nightcap against Central Islip and matched Redding by throwing a five-hit, 1-0 shutout.[3] The 1911 season was a learning experience for Johnson, who finished 1-2 and had a sparkling 1.52 ERA against the East's other top independent Negro League clubs.[4] Although there was no league at that time, the Lincoln Giants finished with the second-best record among the Eastern squads with their 9-6-1 ledger putting them behind only the Cuban Stars' 18-11-1 record.

Toward the end of the season, there was an early push by the *New York Age* for White baseball to integrate. The newspaper pointed out that the Detroit Tigers had played (and lost) a series in Cuba against a team composed of Cubans and four Negro League players the previous winter. It posited that a progression from light-skinned Cubans to dark-skinned Cubans to dark-skinned African American players would be a logical advancement toward full integration. Columnist Lester A. Walton wrote:

> "It is strange that the big league managers are opposed to colored men of this country playing in the National and American Leagues. In all other form of sport the Negro is not barred from competing, except, of course, in the South. White and colored runners take part in the same events, the Caucasian and Negro meet in the fistic arena, and white and colored jockeys ride rival horses on the different race courses. Then, if there is no race prejudice on the race track, in the prize ring and on the cinder path, why should there be on the baseball field?"[5]

It took another 35 years for the integration of White baseball to begin, and Johnson did not live long enough to see that day. However, he became a successful pitcher in the Black major leagues and, as his first professional season came to an end, he tossed a three-hit, 7-0 shutout against the semipro Brightons in early October.[6] At midmonth, the players departed Olympic Field, their home ballpark, to pursue winter ball or to rest. According to the press, "The Lincoln Giants made a great record this season. They participated in 105 games and lost 17."[7]

Considering the stellar ERA that Johnson posted in 1911, which showed that he had true potential, it is odd that he appears not to have played baseball in 1912. Not only does he not appear on any team's roster or in any box or line scores, his whereabouts for the year are unknown. John Henry "Pop" Lloyd, a future Hall of Famer who managed the Lincoln Giants in 1911, resigned as both manager and captain of the team after the season ended. In a letter to team owner Rod McMahon, Lloyd wrote that he was resigning because "the players have not shown the right spirit toward me since I was appointed manager, and rather than force a fellow player to do his best I have decided to give up my positions."[8] Johnson never had the reputation of being difficult or a hothead, so it is unlikely that he did not return to the Lincoln Giants because of any difficulties getting along with or playing for Lloyd in 1911.

Whatever pursuits Johnson engaged in during the 1912 season, he reappeared in the East as a member of the Cuban Giants in 1913. As had been the case during his rookie season, Johnson pitched mostly in games against semipro squads rather than against the other Black titans of the East. He was 0-2 in two games against top squads, although his 0.56 ERA shows that he either lacked run support or had numerous errors made behind him.

The fact that runs came at a premium for the Cuban Giants was also in evidence in many of the games that Johnson pitched against semipro teams. On June 22 Johnson went only four innings of a 14-inning victory over the Pullmans in Buffalo, New York. Gunboat Thompson finished the game and earned the victory, but the press noted that the Cuban Giants "showed great improvement yesterday, the addition of Gordon, Williams and Johnson strengthening the team 50 per cent."[9]

As the June 22 game apparently was Johnson's first appearance in 1913, he had to rebuild some stamina. That effort did not take long, as was evidenced by his pitching all 19 innings in a July 18 game against the semipro Spirellas in Meadville, Pennsylvania. According to the news account of the game, "It was getting too dark to play any longer and the game would be called when the 19th inning was ended," but Meadville's starting pitcher, who also went the distance and whose name was given only as Connell, banged out the winning hit with two outs in the bottom of the frame.[10] Johnson struck out 16 batters while allowing only nine hits and two walks but still suffered a 3-2 setback in what the local newspaper raved was "four hours and 16 minutes of the greatest exhibition of baseball ever seen in Meadville."[11]

Johnson fared better on August 3, when he faced the Pullmans again in Buffalo. He made certain that he could not lose by throwing a two-hit shutout as his "breaks were too fast and clever for [the Pullmans'] bats."[12] This time, his teammates also supported him with their own lumber – something they had failed to do during Johnson's herculean effort against Meadville – and scored nine runs in the victory. The Cuban Giants and their frequently quiet bats did not compete with the East's top teams often, posting a 2-3 record in such games; in comparison, Johnson's former team, the Lincoln Giants, posted the top record of 16-6-1.

In 1914 Johnson led a nomadic baseball existence, starting the year in eastern New York, moving south to Kentucky, and finally traveling west to Chicago to join Foster's American Giants. Johnson began the season in Schenectady, New York, with the independent Mohawk Giants, who were named after the river on which their home city was founded. He lost a tight 4-3 decision to the Pittsfield, Massachusetts, club at that squad's Wahconah Park on April 25. Conditions were less than ideal and, "[b]ecause of the wintry weather, only 400 of the most faithful fans turned out to witness the contest."[13] On May 2 the tables were turned again – as had happened with the Cuban Giants the previous year – and Johnson received overwhelming run support in a 17-0 trouncing of the New York Colored Giants at Schenectady's Mohawk Park.[14]

The weather continued to get warmer, but the same could not be said for the Schenectady club. In mid-July, Johnson lost two hard-fought games to the Indianapolis ABCs at Indy's Northwestern Park. On July 12 his opponent, "[Dicta] 'Spit Ball' Johnson's pitching was too much for the Mohawk Giants" as the ABCs won 4-0, and two days later he took another loss when he went the distance in a 10-inning, 10-9 slugfest at the same venue.[15]

Another two days passed before it was announced that Tom Johnson and the entire Mohawk Giants team would not be returning to Schenectady in 1914. The players claimed that "they were not receiving their salaries and could not afford to play ball for the sport."[16] It was also reported that "Rube Foster, who has been identified with colored ball players for years and has managed the Chicago American Giants for several seasons[,] advanced the players funds with which to leave for Indianapolis and it is understood the team will hereafter represent Louisville, Ky., and French Lick Springs, Ind."[17] The Mohawk Giants finished their abbreviated 1914 campaign with a 3-13 record against the East's other independent Black ballclubs.

Johnson pitched to a 2-0 record in his two appearances for the Louisville White Sox, finishing with a 0.00 ERA in 12 innings. Thereafter, he joined Foster's Chicago-based squad for the first time and posted a 2-0 record with a 1.00 ERA in 18 innings. Thus, after going 1-5 with Schenectady, Johnson was able to even his season ledger at 5-5 and finished the season with a composite 3.03 ERA.

Just as the *New York Age* had encouraged the integration of White baseball at the end of the 1911 season, there were now rumblings in the Chicago press about White teams' refusal to compete against Black squads. Foster's American Giants had challenged the Federal

League's Chicago Whales and had been rebuffed. In turn, a news article goaded:

"A challenge of the American Giants to meet the 'Feds' has been turned down by the 'Feds,' drawing the color line, but strange to say the 'Cubs,' the New York Giants, Detroit and both the American and National teams of Philadelphia have played the colored teams. What is the difference whether they play the black boys in Cuba or at home? Come, be honest, now; ain't you afraid of the black men?"[18]

The taunting did not work – the color line remained drawn in the United States.

While the ChiFeds may have been afraid to play against Black teams, Johnson's fear might have been that he would have to move from team to team again in 1915. Sure enough, the new year ended up being a tale of two seasons as Johnson pitched for both the Indianapolis ABCs and the Chicago American Giants. How Johnson came to pitch for Indianapolis is uncertain, but the two teams were fierce rivals that often tried to lure away each other's star players. Foster, who was now 35 years old and had enough to do as owner and manager of the Chicago team, rarely took the mound anymore. However, on June 23 in Indianapolis, he took his former young pitcher to school as the American Giants delivered an 8-1 whipping to the ABCs. The *Chicago Defender* observed, "It looked as though it might be a real ball game, but, oh, my! in that [eighth] inning Thomas Johnson took the aeroplane, and when he finally got down the Giants had five runs added to their already total of three. They slammed him all over the lot and made him force in two runs by issuing passes with the bases loaded."[19]

In eight appearances (all starts), Johnson pitched to a 3-5 record with a higher-than-usual 4.41 ERA in 63⅓ innings for an ABCs team that finished with the best record in the West at 37-25-1. By late July, he was back with the American Giants in Chicago for a series against the powerful New York Lincoln Stars. The first game, on July 31, was a disaster as he surrendered five runs in the first inning of an eventual 11-3 loss in which he was pulled from the game early; however, he rebounded with a tough-as-nails complete-game 2-1 victory just two days later that marked his best performance that year.[20] Johnson finished the season for Chicago with a 4-4 record with a 2.60 ERA in 62⅓ innings as the American Giants put up a 29-25-3 record against the West's top clubs.

At the conclusion of the 1915 regular season, Johnson took a working vacation in Palm Beach, Florida, where he pitched for the Royal Poinciana Hotel team in its annual winter series against the Breakers Hotel. Johnson's manager there was C.I. Taylor, co-owner and manager of the ABCs, for whom he had toiled in the first half of the year. Although Johnson was 1-0 with a 0.73 ERA in his two appearances (one start), the Breakers Hotel won the series by a count of nine games to six.

In 1916 Johnson notched an early-season victory against the Pacific Coast League's Portland Beavers, a Triple-A-caliber team, in Sacramento, California. The four-game series marked the fourth consecutive year that the two squads had faced one another during Portland's spring training. On April 6, in the first game of the series, Johnson went the distance in an 11-6 victory with only three of the runs he surrendered being earned. The game was not as close an affair as the final score seemed to indicate. Portland scored three runs in the eighth and added another tally in the ninth, and those late "runs that cantered across the plate gave the Beavers a more graceful exit from the awful carnage" that the Chicago squad had inflicted upon them for most of the afternoon.[21] The American Giants also won the second game, but Portland then salvaged a split of the series.

Once the regular season began, the American Giants ruled over their fellow independent squads in the West with a 40-26-3 record, while Johnson put up a 14-4 record of his own. Although the 14 wins marked Johnson's top single-season total against major-league-caliber competition, his 3.40 ERA was a bit higher than usual, and he sometimes had difficulty finishing games. On July 10, in a game against the St. Louis Giants at Chicago's Schorling Park, "Johnson was not only wild in his shots to the plate but made a wide heave to first that earned his retirement with five runs charge to his discredit" in a 6-2 loss.[22]

But as Johnson's record indicates, his mound appearances resulted in far more wins than losses, and on September 2 he made history of a positive kind. Johnson and Dick Whitworth hurled a combined no-hitter – albeit in a shortened game – as Chicago defeated the Cuban Stars West team, 6-0. Johnson exited the game in the fifth and Whitworth finished the next two frames before the game had to be "called in the seventh on account of darkness."[23] Stellar defense helped to keep the Cubans out of the hit column; the *Chicago Defender* noted, "All the credit of the victory doesn't belong to Tom nor to Whitworth. Much credit belongs to [the outfield of] Duncan, Hill, and Gans. Duncan pulled down a drive just it was about to hit the fence."[24]

Little more than a week later, on September 10, Johnson capped off the season by leading the American Giants to Chicago's city championship in a 6-2 triumph over the Gunthers at Schorling Park. In addition to pitching a complete game in which he struck out six batters, he had three hits of his own and scored one run in his dazzling performance.[25]

During the winter of 1916-17, Johnson again pitched for the Royal Poinciana Hotel team in the Palm Beach Championship Series. Poinciana's roster was composed of the Chicago American Giants and was managed by Rube Foster while the Breakers Hotel squad was filled with members of the New York Lincoln Giants and was managed by Cyclone Joe Williams (who later became better-known by the nickname Smokey Joe). The press raved that "[t]he series was the best ever played here and both teams seemed to be pretty evenly matched, with the American Giants a little on the long end with baseball knowledge under the hat."[26] Juan Padron hurled a 2-0 shutout in the final game to give the Poinciana/American Giants team a 7-6-2 edge and the championship. Johnson contributed a 1-1 record and a 3.20 ERA in 19⅔ innings over five appearances (three starts).

By 1917 Johnson was firmly ensconced as a member of Chicago's pitching staff. Foster's aggregation barnstormed through Johnson's old college stamping grounds in March as they prepared for the coming season. Johnson did not get to pitch against his alma mater – Dick Redding defeated Morris Brown College by an 11-2 score – instead spinning a nifty 12-1 victory over Atlanta University on March 20 in which he "held the rah-rah boys to seven scattered hits."[27]

The American Giants were so powerful in 1917, finishing with a 49-14-2 record, that no other Black independent team in the West managed better than a .500 mark. Johnson was 7-3 and had a sparkling 2.57 ERA against the top teams that year. He pitched one of his finest games on June 30 as the American Giants took on the Cuban Stars West in Hammond, Indiana, and Johnson dueled against Eustaquio Pedroso in a tight 1-0 triumph. Chicago first baseman Leroy Grant galloped home to score the game's only run in the bottom of the eighth inning, after which Johnson finished a four-hit shutout by pitching a scoreless ninth.[28] Johnson remained as hot as the weather throughout the summer and pitched another superlative shutout – this time a 2-0 two-hitter – against the Jewell's ABCs on July 22 in Chicago.[29]

One week later, the American Giants and their Texas-born owner, Rube Foster, hosted Texas Day at Schorling Park. According to the *Defender*, "Not only will everyone here from the Lone Star state turn out but many of their friends who hail from the sunny southland. The Texas All Stars will be the attraction. With them are some of the fastest and best ball players of the country."[30] The American Giants celebrated the day with a 7-5 victory, and fellow Texan Tom Johnson got the start in Monday's 7-6 triumph over the All Stars, although Tom Williams earned the win in relief.[31]

After the 1917 season, Johnson did not head back to Florida. Instead, he married Marie Button on Christmas Day in Chicago. The couple's marriage reveals once more the glaring gaps in information about Johnson's early life. On the World War I draft registration card he filled out on June 15, 1917, Johnson had stated that he already had a wife and child. Indeed, the 1930 Census indicates that Marie was 15 years old at the time of her first marriage. That marriage must have been to Tom Johnson, though no record of it has turned up, as the 1920 Census listed both Tom and Marie at 30 years of age and recorded the names and ages of their three children – Malcolm (14), Edward (12), and Mildred (9) – indicating that they had started a family at a young age as well. It was also noted that all three children had been born in Illinois, which brings into question exactly when Johnson had left his birth state of Texas and moved to Illinois, as well as again raising the query as to why he chose to go to college in Georgia. In any case, whether the Johnsons' first marriage was considered invalid because they had both been 15 years old at the time or there was another reason, Cook County (Illinois) marriage records show that they officially tied the knot on December 25, 1917.

Not long after celebrating his nuptials, Johnson was drafted into the US Army. Because he was college-educated, he was commissioned a lieutenant in the 183rd Infantry Brigade at Camp Grant in Rockford, Illinois. Early in the year, Johnson played for the camp's baseball team. In fact, on May 12, 1918, the Camp Grant team arrived at Schorling Park for a game against the American Giants that, thanks to Foster's generosity, was to benefit the Army Eighth Regiment's depleted athletic fund. Baseball was a morale-booster for the troops, but, as the *Defender* reported, "The Clark Griffith bat and ball fund does not reach our boys. Blame this on the kaiser [*sic*]. Two hundred and fifty thousand dollars' worth of these goods are now at the bottom of the Atlantic. This was on its way over there for the boys in the trenches and others doing their bit. It must be made up."[32]

Almost immediately thereafter, Johnson became one of "the boys in the trenches"; he was sent to France, where he served in the 365th Infantry.[33] Although the US military was still segregated at the time, Black units fought alongside White units in numerous battles during World War I. In two separate actions from October 8-November 8 and November 9-11, the 365th had 30 men killed in action, 13 mortally wounded, and another 583 wounded in battle.[34] Johnson survived the horrors of combat and was honorably discharged from the Army on March 29, 1919, at Camp Dix, New Jersey. Although he had not been wounded and had managed to avoid the lethal influenza outbreak that was raging worldwide in 1918-19, he contracted pulmonary tuberculosis, which became a chronic condition that led to his early death.

The 1919 season saw the American Giants and their rivals play fewer games than usual as certain wartime restrictions were still in place and soldiers, like Johnson, were still returning to their teams and civilian life. In Chicago's final season as an independent team, Foster, who had long intended to establish an organized league, "decided to back a new team to be located in Detroit. Wartime labor brought thousands of blacks to Detroit, and Rube figured it was fertile ground to plant another team."[35] The American Giants and Detroit Stars became instant rivals and finished with nearly identical records: Detroit at 27-14 and Chicago at 27-16.

Although Foster did not like it when players jumped from his American Giants to another team, he still took care to support the competition in the hope of maintaining a sufficient number of teams to form a league and, later, to sustain it. Thus, he was not averse to lending a player (or players) to other teams from time to time so that they could continue to compete. In 1919 Johnson returned to the American Giants, for whom he was 4-4 with a 3.74 ERA, but he also was loaned to Detroit for one game in which he pitched seven innings, allowed three unearned runs, and was the winning pitcher of record.

The highlight of Johnson's 1919 campaign came against Detroit on June 17 at Schorling Park. On this date, Johnson was involved in his second no-hitter, and this time he finished the game himself. It was far from a perfect game as six walks and an error by shortstop Bobby Williams combined to give Detroit three

runs in the game, two of which were scored in the first inning. Had it not been for a seven-run outburst by Chicago in the seventh inning, Johnson might actually have lost his no-hitter, but he emerged with a 7-3 victory.[36] The game served as notice that Johnson was picking up where he had left off prior to being drafted into the Army.

The most stunning event that took place in 1919 was a late-July/early-August riot that caused the team's home field, Schorling Park, to be temporarily occupied by National Guard troops. The events began on July 27:

"Eugene Williams, a black youth, was swimming near a 'white beach' and was attacked by a stone-throwing white male. The youth drowned, and when the police arrived, they did not take action against the perpetrator. A riot broke out that would last five days and claim the lives of 23 blacks and 15 whites. The South Side of Chicago became a war zone; children were among the dead, homes were burned, shops looted, there were volleys of gunfire and territorial wars fought over certain neighborhoods."[37]

Although the city of Chicago was scarred by the events, "[t]he riot hardly fazed Rube [Foster], who in the days immediately following remained busy laying the groundwork for an organized league."[38]

On February 13, 1920, Foster and the owners of the other major Western clubs formed the first Negro National League at the Paseo branch of the YMCA in Kansas City, Missouri. The American Giants went on to claim the first three NNL pennants, and Johnson was a major factor in the team's success in the league's inaugural season. The American Giants finished the season with a 43-17-2 record and Johnson was a perfect 11-0 with a 1.84 ERA for Chicago in NNL games. Amazingly, Johnson was only third in ERA on Chicago's pitching staff, finishing just behind Dave Brown's 1.82 and Tom Williams's 1.83. Johnson again was loaned to Detroit at times and pitched to a 2-2 record in four games (all starts) – with a much higher 4.21 ERA – for the Stars that kept him from being undefeated in league play.

Although he suffered two losses with Detroit, Johnson could do no wrong for most of the season. He won shutouts such as the 5-0 whitewashing he gave the Kansas City Monarchs on May 24.[39] He triumphed in low-scoring games like the pitchers' duels against Jose Leblanc and the Cuban Stars West on May 31 and the

10-inning complete game versus the Bacharach Giants on August 9 that ended with identical 3-2 scores.[40] And he was victorious in several routs, including Detroit's 11-3 victory over the St. Louis Giants on September 18 and Chicago's 13-1 thrashing of the Bacharachs on October 7, the latter being a game in which he allowed only one hit.[41] The 1920 season was a triumphal march through the NNL for Lieutenant Tom Johnson and the Chicago American Giants.

As the 1921 season began, Johnson had no idea that it would be his last in a baseball uniform. He was now 32 years old, but that hardly marked him as over the hill, and he was coming off a phenomenally successful 1920 campaign. The American Giants picked up where they had left off and captured their second consecutive NNL pennant with a 44-22-2 record, but Johnson was inconsistent and pitched to only a 7-8 ledger with an inflated 5.10 ERA in 121⅔ innings.

Although he was inconsistent that year, one highlight transpired on May 30 – Memorial Day – when "Lieut. Tom Johnson, overseas veteran, missed the chance to parade with his old outfit, the remnants of the 365th Infantry, 92d Division, and twirled for Foster."[42] Johnson no doubt made his fellow veterans proud as he hurled the American Giants to a 10-4 victory over the Cuban Stars at Schorling Park.

One month later, on June 28, Johnson was the starter in a most unusual game against the Indianapolis ABCs at Indy's Washington Park. Although Johnson was no longer on the mound in the latter stages of the game, over the course of the eighth and ninth innings, "[t]he American Giants staged a sixteen run rally off eleven bunts, six successive squeeze plays, and Dixon and Tonchetti's [sic] home runs with [the] bases full, and held A.B.C. to an 18 to 18 tie."[43]

Johnson's finest moment in the 1921 season took place on July 6, when he threw the final shutout of his career, a four-hit, 1-0 victory over the NNL rival Kansas City Monarchs in Chicago.[44] His pitching went steadily downhill from that point forward. In his last mound appearance, on October 15 against the Hilldale Club in Darby, Pennsylvania, Johnson and Tom Williams had their offerings knocked "all over the lot" in a 15-5 loss.[45]

Johnson departed for spring training with the American Giants in March 1922.[46] However, before the start of the regular season, the *Defender* reported on April 15 that "Jack Marshall, Tom Williams, and Tom Johnson are not with the club. The absence of these seasoned veterans of the mound has weakened the Giants to some extent."[47] Marshall and Williams had

moved to other teams, but Johnson spent the majority of the 1922 season in the hospital as his pulmonary tuberculosis had become an active ailment again.[48] Although he recovered from this bout with the illness, he lacked the stamina needed to continue pitching. Since Johnson wanted to stay around the game he loved, he became an umpire for NNL games.[49]

However, Johnson was unable to conquer his illness permanently. On September 2, 1925, he was admitted to a home for disabled veterans in Milwaukee, but he was discharged again on October 15. Johnson lingered for another year as a homebound convalescent until he died on September 22, 1926, leaving behind his wife and three children. He was buried in Lincoln Cemetery in Blue Island, Illinois, on September 25. Foster and his American Giants baseball team sent a "floral piece in the shape of a baseball diamond" to honor their deceased teammate.[50]

SOURCES

All player statistics and team records were taken from Seamheads.com, except where otherwise indicated.

Ancestry.com was consulted for US Census information; military records; and birth, marriage, and death records.

NOTES

1   The Census indicated that Sallie Hays had given birth to nine children, eight of whom were still living in 1900. Since there were only two Hays children at that time (and three Johnson children living with their mother and stepfather), it is quite likely that the other three siblings were also Johnson children who were either already adults or were being raised by relatives.

2   A 1916 article in the *Chicago Defender* referred to Johnson as "the ex-college star," confirming that he had been discovered while pitching at Morris Brown College; see Mister Fan, "American Giants Beat City Champions," *Chicago Defender*, September 16, 1916: 7.

3   "Lincoln Giants Score Two Shut-outs," *New York Age*, July 20, 1911: 6.

4   Johnson participated in additional games, such as the victory over Central Islip, but records for games against semipro and college squads are not counted as part of official Negro League statistics at the present time (2021).

5   Lester A. Walton, "In the World of Sport," *New York Age*, September 28, 1911: 6.

6   "Minor Baseball," *Brooklyn Times Union*, October 2, 1911: 4.

7   Lester A. Walton, "In the World of Sport," *New York Age*, October 19, 1911: 6.

8   Lester A. Walton, "In the World of Sport," *New York Age*, November 9, 1911: 6.

9   "Cuban Giants Win Out in Fourteenth," *Buffalo Times*, June 23, 1913: 12.

10 "Meadville's Base Ball History Knows Only One Game Like That Great Nineteen-Inning Victory," *Meadville (Pennsylvania) Evening Republican*, July 19, 1913: 5.

11 "Meadville's Base Ball History."

12 "Pullmans Cleaned to Queen's Taste," *Meadville Evening Republican*, August 4, 1913: 5.

13   "Pittsfield Club Again Trims Mohawk Giants," *North Adams* (Massachusetts) *Transcript*, April 27, 1914: 8.

14   "Mohawk Giants Win at Schenectady," *New York Age*, May 7, 1914: 6.

15   "A.B.C.'s in Victory," *Indianapolis Star*, July 13, 1914: 8; "Another for A.B.C.'s," *Indianapolis Star*, July 15, 1914: 4.

16   "Baseball Notes," *Berkshire Evening Eagle* (Pittsfield, Massachusetts), July 16, 1914: 16.

17   "Baseball Notes."

18   "Englewood Happenings," *Suburbanite Economist* (Chicago), September 25, 1914: 1.

19   "Circus Game to Giants 8 to 1," *Chicago Defender*, June 26, 1915: 7.

20   "American Giants Leading in Lincoln American Series," *Chicago Defender*, August 7, 1915: 7.

21   "Giants Beat Portland," *Chicago Defender*, April 8, 1916: 7.

22   "Johnson's Miscues Cost Foster Game," *Chicago Defender*, July 15, 1916: 5.

23   "No-Hit, No-Run Game to American Giants," *Chicago Defender*, September 9, 1916: 7.

24   "No-Hit, No-Run Game to American Giants."

25   Mister Fan, "American Giants Beat City Champions," *Chicago Defender*, September 16, 1916: 7.

26   "American Giants Win Palm Beach Championship," *Chicago Defender*, March 31, 1917: 7.

27   "American Giants, 11; Morris Brown, 2," *Chicago Defender*, March 31, 1917: 7; "American Giants, 12; Atlanta U., 1," *Chicago Defender*, March 31, 1917: 7.

28   "American Giants Beat Cubans in 1-0 Battle," *Chicago Defender*, July 7, 1917: 9.

29   "American Giants Still on Rampage/Jewel's A.B.C.'s Fall before Onslaught," *Chicago Defender*, July 28, 1917: 10.

30   "Texas Day Will Be Observed at the American Giants Park Sunday," *Chicago Defender*, July 28, 1917: 10.

31   "Texas Stars Lose Two Close Games," *Chicago Defender*, August 4, 1917: 10.

32   "183d Brigade, Led by Lieut. Tom Johnson, Invades Chicago Sunday, *Chicago Defender*, May 11, 1918: 9.

33   Brett Kiser, *Baseball's War Roster: A Biographical Dictionary of Major and Negro League Players Who Served, 1861 to the Present* (Jefferson, North Carolina: McFarland & Company, Inc., 2012), 31-32.

34   "92D Division: Summary of Operations in the World War," https://history.army.mil/topics/afam/92div.htm, accessed March 16, 2021.

35   Paul Debono, *The Chicago American Giants* (Jefferson, North Carolina: McFarland & Company, Inc., 2007), 69.

36   "Foster's Giants Cop Again, 7 to 3," *Chicago Tribune*, June 18, 1919: 18.

37   Debono, 71-72. See also: Gary Ashwill, "White Racial Violence & the Negro Leagues: The Chicago Riot of 1919," June 14, 2020, https://agatetype.typepad.com/agate_type/2020/06/white-racial-violence-the-negro-leagues-the-chicago-riot-of-1919.html.

38   Debono, 73.

39   "Monarchs Lose Second," *Chicago Defender*, May 29, 1920: 9.

40   "Amer. Giants, 3; Cubans, 2," *Chicago Tribune*, June 1, 1920: 24; "Bacharachs Lose in Tenth," *Chicago Defender*, August 14, 1920: 6.

41   "Detroit Stars Defeat St. Louis Giants, 11-3," *St. Louis Post-Dispatch*, September 19, 1920: 60; "American Giants Cop, 13-1," *Chicago Tribune*, October 8, 1920: 21.

42   "American Giants Beat Cuban Stars in Holiday Fray/ Tom Johnson, Overseas Veteran, Celebrates Memorial Day Beating Islanders," *Chicago Defender*, June 4, 1921: 10.

43   "American Giants in Tie," *Chicago Tribune*, June 29, 1921: 19. The *Tribune* butchered the spelling of Cristobal Torriente's last name as "Tonchetti."

44   "American Giants Take 1-0 Battle," *Chicago Tribune*, July 7, 1921: 12.

45   "Hilldale, 15; Am. Giants, 5," *Chicago Defender*, October 22, 1921: 10.

46   "National League News: American Giants Leave for South Monday," *Chicago Defender*, March 11, 1922: 10; "Foster's Crew Are on Their Training Trip," *Chicago Defender*, March 18, 1922: 10.

47   Mister Fan, "Rogers Park Opens Season Against Rube," *Chicago Defender*, April 15, 1922: 10.

48   James A. Riley, *The Biographical Encyclopedia of the Negro Baseball Leagues* (New York: Carroll & Graf Publishers, Inc., 1994), 443.

49   Riley, 443; "Tom Johnson, Vet Pitcher, Passes Away," *Chicago Defender*, October 2, 1926: 10.

50   "Tom Johnson, Vet Pitcher, Passes Away."

DAVE MALARCHER

BY RICHARD J. PUERZER

Dave Malarcher was an erudite, disciplined, and reverent man known appropriately as Gentleman Dave. As a player, he was a small (5-feet-7 and 150 pounds during his playing days), speedy, and smart third baseman, whose play embodied the methodology of one of his mentors, Rube Foster. Malarcher later became a manager, utilizing what he learned from Foster and his other great mentor, C.I. Taylor, to great success. Malarcher led his teams to multiple championships and always had the respect of his players. As was written in an article when he left baseball, "he was a perfect model for young ballplayers – he was a credit to baseball in Chicago and the nation over."[1]

David Julius Malarcher was born on October 18, 1894, in Whitehall, Louisiana. He was the youngest of 11 children, with seven sisters and three brothers. His mother, Martha (Campbell) Malarcher, had been born into slavery and later worked as a midwife and caretaker for the children in the homes of plantation owners. His father, Henry Louis Malarcher, was a field laborer on the local sugarcane plantations. Martha Malarcher valued education and made sure that all her children received some teaching. One of Dave's older sisters ran the first school that he attended. Malarcher reported having a pleasant childhood that included swimming in the Mississippi River and playing baseball.[2]

In 1907 Malarcher moved to New Orleans, where he worked as a laborer for a wealthy family. While there he attended New Orleans University, which offered African American children opportunities that

"Gentleman Dave" Malarcher was the starting third baseman for the 1920 Chicago American Giants.

ranged from elementary education to college-level studies. Malarcher continued to attend New Orleans University through his college years and played for the school's baseball team, serving as team captain.[3] From 1913 to 1916, Malarcher also played for the New Orleans Black Eagles, a strong semipro team that played throughout Louisiana and East Texas. It was at this time that Malarcher developed his ability to switch-hit. While playing in a game for the Black Eagles against the Indianapolis ABCs, who were barnstorming their way north from a trip to Cuba in the winter of 1915-1916, Malarcher caught the attention of C.I. Taylor, the ABCs' owner and manager.[4] Taylor offered Malarcher $50 a month to play for the ABCs, and he jumped at the chance, although he joined the ABCs to play in the summer and continued to attend college in the winter.[5]

Malarcher joined a strong Indianapolis team. The 1916 ABCs featured such great players as Bingo DeMoss, Dizzy Dismukes, 19-year old Oscar Charleston, and three of C.I. Taylor's siblings: Ben Taylor, Candy Jim Taylor, and Steel Arm Johnny Taylor. In addition to learning from his fellow players, Malarcher was under the tutelage of one of the greatest baseball mangers of his or any time, C.I. (for Charles Isham) Taylor. Taylor had an enormous impact on Malarcher, teaching him a great deal, especially about how to run a baseball team. Taylor stressed physical conditioning, nurturing his players as they developed, and he concerned himself with what his players did off the field, including strongly discouraging them from drinking both in and out of baseball season.[6] As a 21-year-old rookie, Malarcher played 16 games at second base and two games at shortstop and compiled a slash line of .275/.339/.373. After the season, Malarcher returned to college in New Orleans. In 1917 he rejoined the ABCs as the starting right fielder. In addition to the 39 games he played in right field, Malarcher also played 13 games at third base, three games at second, one at shortstop, one as a pitcher, and three games as a catcher when both catchers on the team were out with injuries. For the season, Malarcher posted a slash line of .233/.308/.285. He began to show what would become his trademark patience at the plate and he led the team in sacrifice hits.

The 1918 season started with the threat that the United States' entry into the Great War would impact professional baseball and its players. Malarcher and several of his teammates had registered for the draft and were notified that they could be conscripted at any time. Malarcher returned to the ABCs and assumed a new starting position, third base, which became his primary position for the remainder of his playing career. He had a strong arm and gained renown as one of the best defensive third baseman in Negro League history.[7] Batting second in the order, Malarcher played in 39 games before he was drafted in late July. He compiled a slash line of .250/.364/.297 and, despite leaving in midseason, led the team in walks and sacrifice hits. Malarcher's approach at the plate embraced the small-ball strategies employed by C.I. Taylor.

After being drafted, Malarcher reported to Camp Dodge in Johnston, Iowa, on August 22, where he was assigned to the 809th Pioneer Infantry Regiment, an African American unit. A number of his ABCs teammates and other Negro League players also served in the 809th. Malarcher shipped out to France, arriving in September, but never saw action as the war ended soon after he arrived (on Armistice Day, November 11, 1918). While in France, Malarcher played baseball for his unit's baseball team in the American Expeditionary Force League. His baseball prowess was also on the mind of a stateside rival baseball manager. While stationed in St. Luce, France, Malarcher received a letter from Rube Foster, the Chicago American Giants' owner and manager, inviting him to play for the American Giants after his military service.[8]

Malarcher was discharged from the Army on August 2, 1919.[9] Upon his return to the United States, he was given $60 by the Army and returned to Indianapolis. He wanted to go to Louisiana to see his mother and girlfriend but did not have enough money to make the trip. Malarcher requested a $75 loan from C.I. Taylor, who declined to lend the money right away; thus, Malarcher decided to head to Chicago to see Rube Foster. Foster lent him the money without hesitation, establishing a business and personal relationship between the men for years to come.[10] In addition, Foster facilitated the signing of Malarcher to play the remainder of the 1919 season with the Detroit Stars.[11] Foster had backed the Stars' ownership; therefore, he had in interest in the team's success. Oscar Charleston joined Malarcher in playing out the season with the Stars. Malarcher played only eight games for Detroit, all at third base, but showed little rust from his time away, collecting 11 hits and scoring eight runs in the limited action.

In 1920 Malarcher played for Foster's Chicago American Giants in the newly formed Negro National League. Then 25 years old, Malarcher was the best third baseman in the Negro Leagues. The 1920 Chicago American Giants were a great team, led on offense by Cristobal Torriente, who posted a league-leading 1.085 OPS, and Bingo DeMoss, who had a .799 OPS. Malarcher had a .669 OPS for the season. The team's pitching staff, which featured Dave Brown, Tom Williams, and Tom Johnson, was the strength of the team. For the season, the American Giants' team ERA was 2.32, which was 1.20 runs per game better than the league average. The team finished with a record of 43-17-2 in the Negro National League, far and away the best record in the league. In addition to having on-field success, Malarcher also experienced joy away from the baseball diamond when he married Mabel Sylvester on June 16, 1920.[12]

Malarcher quickly became a disciple of Foster's brand of scientific baseball, and his skill set matched up well with Foster's approach to manufacturing runs. Malarcher was a patient hitter and a fast and smart baserunner, and was proficient at advancing runners – an ideal Deadball Era player. Additionally, Malarcher was eager to learn from Foster, both in terms of baseball strategy and in terms of leadership and business management. These skills benefited Malarcher later in life both as a manager and in his post-playing career.[13]

The 1921 Chicago American Giants relied on pitching, defense, and manufacturing runs to finish atop the Negro National League standings once again with a record of 44-22-2 in league play. Malarcher batted only .209 for the season, but he continued to draw walks and steal bases, and he also contributed solid defense at third base.

In 1922 the American Giants captured the Negro National League pennant for the third consecutive season. Malarcher, however, had a tough season, suffering multiple injuries that sidelined him for the majority of the campaign. In May he tore ligaments in his chest, reportedly near his heart, which kept him on the bench.[14] When he came back, he was spiked while attempting to steal second and had to be carried off the field. Power-hitting John Beckwith, one of the most feared hitters in the game, took Malarcher's place in the lineup while he was out. Malarcher eventually returned and had a dramatic hit in one of the most intense games of the 1922 season. On August 16, the American Giants faced off against the Bacharach Giants at Schorling Park in Chicago. Beckwith started the game at third base but was replaced by Malarcher when the scoreless game went into the ninth inning. The game continued to be a scoreless affair until the bottom of the 20th inning, when Cristobal Torriente drew a leadoff walk, advanced to second on a sacrifice

bunt, and scored on Malarcher's base hit to give the American Giants a 1-0 win.[15]

Malarcher was healthy again for the 1923 season and, at age 28, was entering the prime of his career. He manned the hot corner once again, with John Beckwith moving over to first. For the season, Malarcher hit .304/.386/.411, batting over .300 and slugging over .400 for the first time in his career. Despite Malarcher's strong season and stellar performances from teammates Beckwith and Torriente, the American Giants regressed as a team and did not finish in first place for the first time since the inception of the Negro National League.

After the season, the American Giants faced the American League's Detroit Tigers in a three-game set. Although Ty Cobb did not play in the series, the Tigers still featured Harry Heilmann, Heinie Manush, and Bobby Veach in their lineup. The American Giants fortified their lineup by adding Oscar Charleston. The teams played to a 5-5 tie in the first game, the Tigers prevailed by a score of 7-1 in game two, and the American Giants won game three, 8-6.[16] Malarcher had an excellent series, batting .364 and playing flawlessly at third base. After the 1923 season Commissioner Kenesaw M. Landis decreed that only all-star White teams could play Negro League teams in the future as Negro League teams were regularly defeating White major-league teams.

Malarcher again manned third base for Chicago in 1924 and had another solid season, batting .280 and leading the team in runs scored with 69 (over 77 games) while also stealing 22 bases. Nevertheless, the American Giants finished a distant second to the Kansas City Monarchs, who defeated the Eastern Colored League's Hilldale Club in the first Negro League World Series.

In 1925 Malarcher was paid $225 a month, with a $500 bonus at the end of the season.[17] He split his time between third base and second base, covering the keystone sack while regular second baseman Bingo DeMoss left the team for a time in midseason. On offense, Malarcher had perhaps his best season and was arguably the best hitter in the American Giants lineup, sporting a slash line of .324/.410/.381 and again leading the team in runs scored and stolen bases. The American Giants, however, did not have great season, finishing in third place behind the Monarchs and St. Louis Stars.

The 1926 season proved to be a monumental one in the life of Dave Malarcher as well as in the history of the Negro Leagues. After their third-place finish in 1925, Rube Foster chose to dismantle much of the American Giants roster. He traded Cristobal Torriente, the team's best player over the previous six seasons, to the Kansas City Monarchs, and dealt Bingo DeMoss and two other players to the Indianapolis ABCs. The trades made for a younger roster for the American Giants, and perhaps also brought about greater parity in the league. Malarcher took over as Chicago's team captain, a role that had previously belonged to the departed DeMoss.[18] His pay was increased to $250 a month, reflecting his increased responsibility and importance to Foster's squad.[19] The team played well over the first half of the season; however, during that period, Rube Foster occasionally displayed erratic and unstable behavior. At the halfway mark in the season, Foster agreed to a vacation, and Malarcher took over as manager. Later that summer, Foster was arrested after several violent incidents. He was eventually deemed mentally irresponsible and was committed to an asylum in Kankakee, Illinois, where he remained until his death on December 9, 1930. Rube Foster, the most important figure in the history of the Negro Leagues to that point, never returned to baseball.[20]

Despite the turmoil of the first half of the season, the American Giants had played well. In the second half of the season, under Malarcher, they excelled. Pitcher Willie Foster, Rube's half-brother, blossomed and became the rotation's ace. The American Giants won the second half of the Negro National League season with a record of 30-7-2 and earned the right to face the Monarchs in a best-of nine championship series. Although the American Giants lost the first three games, they came back to win three of the next four. The teams agreed that if two more games were required, they would play a doubleheader. Willie Foster matched up against Kansas City's ace pitcher and manager, Bullet Rogan, in game eight of the series, and the American Giants prevailed, 1-0, on a ninth-inning run. Incredibly, with the series on the line, Foster and Rogan both pitched the second game of the doubleheader as well. With darkness coming on, the teams agreed to limit the game to five innings. Foster again was dominant, and the American Giants won, 5-0, which propelled the team to the Negro League World series, in which they faced the Atlantic City Bacharach Giants.

The nine-game World Series was scheduled to be played in Atlantic City, Baltimore, Philadelphia, and Chicago. After the first game ended in a tie, Atlantic City won four of the next seven games (with another tie game in the mix), including a no-hitter thrown by

Red Grier. The Bacharachs stood one victory away from winning the series, but the American Giants again staged a comeback and won the final three games of the series, with Willie Foster pitching a 1-0 shutout in the clinching game. Malarcher had led the team through the challenges of the season, and through two tough series comebacks, to a championship.[21]

The 1927 season marked a time of continued change for the American Giants. It was clear that Rube Foster would not return to the team, so Malarcher was named as the permanent manager. The team got out of the gate fast and won the first half of the season. Malarcher held down third base and provided a steady managerial hand. The Birmingham Black Barons won the second-half title to set up a championship series against the American Giants. Included on the Black Barons' pitching staff was 20-year-old Satchel Paige, who started one game in the series but did not factor in

(Courtesy National Baseball Hall of Fame)

Malarcher became manager of the American Giants in 1926, leading the franchise to Negro League World Series championships in 1926 and 1927 and to the Negro Southern League title in 1932.

the decision. The American Giants toppled the Black Barons four games to one to advance to the Negro League World Series, a best-of-nine set against the Atlantic City Bacharach Giants. Chicago took the first four games in the series but then lost three in a row to Atlantic City. However, the American Giants were able to clinch a second straight World Series title, with Willie Foster again winning the final game.[22]

The 1928 campaign was a tumultuous one for Malarcher and the American Giants and began with a dispute over the ownership of the team. After Rube Foster had been institutionalized, his wife, Sarah Foster, had tried to assert her rights to the ownership of the team. Foster's White business partner, John Schorling, rebuffed Sarah Foster and took full control of the team for himself. Then, halfway through the 1927 season, Schorling sold the team to William Trimble, a White racetrack owner. As time passed, it became clear that Trimble was not a fully committed owner: He paid low salaries and devoted little attention to the team. As if these challenges were not enough for Malarcher, in mid-May he broke a bone in his shoulder, leaving him unable to play or to manage the team. He missed more than half the season and, in his absence, veteran pitcher George Harney took over the managerial duties. Several other players suffered injuries during the season, forcing the team to sign other players and use a multitude of lineups during the season. Despite all of this, the American Giants were able to win the second-half league title. This time around, Chicago faced the St. Louis Stars, who featured a lineup that included Cool Papa Bell, Mule Suttles, and Willie Wells, in a nine-game championship series. (There would be no World Series, because the Eastern Colored League had disbanded earlier in the season.) The Stars prevailed in the series, five games to four.[23] After the season, Malarcher threatened to leave the Giants, asserting that he had not been compensated as manager of the team since Trimble assumed ownership.[24] After a meeting with Trimble did not resolve the matter, Malarcher made good on his threat and left the team. He said he preferred to devote his time to his insurance and real estate businesses, which he had previously pursued only in the offseason.

Malarcher was out of the Black major leagues in 1929 and 1930. Although he did work full-time in insurance and real estate, he also led semipro teams – the American Eagles in 1929 and the All-Stars in 1930 – that featured some former players from the American Giants. The teams played locally in Chicago.[25] The end of 1930 brought about another event of huge impact,

the death of Rube Foster on December 9. At his funeral, Malarcher's wife, Mabel, sang a solo as a part of the service.[26]

In 1930 William Trimble, recognizing the challenges of owning a team during the Depression, sold the team to Charles Bidwill.[27] However, the remaining American Giants players jumped to other teams, and Bidwill was unable to field a team in 1931. Meanwhile, Malarcher took a leadership role in a newly formed team that became known as the Columbia American Giants, a squad that essentially took the place of the Chicago American Giants in the still-extant Negro National League. The league was a shadow of its former self, however, without a formal schedule or any plans for playoffs.[28] After playing into early July and posting a record of 6-17-1, Malarcher decided to drop out of the NNL and turned the team into a semi-pro squad.

In 1932 the American Giants team was revived under the ownership of Robert Cole, a Black Chicago-based undertaker who had acquired the franchise. One of the first things Cole did was to hire Malarcher as manager. The team, now referred to as either Cole's American Giants or the Chicago American Giants, played in the newly formed Negro Southern League. All indications were that the team would have a good season after it signed Willie Foster to anchor the pitching staff and Turkey Stearnes to lead the offense. Malarcher, 37 years old and having not played since 1928, was now a full-time manager, although he made appearances in two games during the season. The American Giants won the first half of the season and finished the season with a 34-12 record in NSL games. They faced the Nashville Elite Giants, the league's second-half champions, in a best-of-seven championship series and won the pennant in seven games.[29]

In 1933 the second incarnation of the Negro National League, led by Pittsburgh Crawfords owner Gus Greenlee, began play, and Cole's American Giants returned to the NNL fold. The American Giants ended up playing most of their home games at Perry Stadium in Indianapolis after they were no longer able to play in Chicago because Schorling Park, their home ballpark since 1910, was being converted to a dog-racing track.[30] Willie Foster and Turkey Stearnes returned to the team, and Cole and Malarcher were also able to sign Mule Suttles and Willie Wells to give the team a potent offense. The American Giants averaged 7 runs per game for the season and finished with a 41-22-1 record. The American Giants believed that they had the best record in the first half of the season, and were entitled to a playoff. However, the Pittsburgh Crawfords were named the league champions by their owner and the league commissioner, Gus Greenlee.[31]

In 1934 the core of the American Giants – Stearnes, Wells, Suttles, Willie Foster, and manager Malarcher – all returned to the team, and the team itself returned to Chicago for its home games after the dog-racing track failed. Over the course of the season, Malarcher experienced the best and worst of Black major-league baseball.

A personal high point took place when Malarcher managed the West team in the second annual East-West All-Star Game, the biggest event in the Negro League season. The game was played on August 26 at Comiskey Park and drew a crowd of 30,000. The game was a pitching duel, with Willie Foster pitching the final three innings for the West and Satchel Paige pitching the final four innings for the East, and the East winning, 1-0.[32]

The American Giants finished with a 28-20-3 record and won the league's second-half title. The Philadelphia Stars, winners of the first half, took on the American Giants in a wild best-of-seven championship series. However, the culmination of the series eventually drove Malarcher out of baseball. The American Giants won the first two games in the series, but the Stars came back until the series was tied at three games apiece. The seventh game in the series ended in a tie, thus extending the series by another game. In the eighth game, the Stars won, 2-0, to capture the pennant.[33] However, Malarcher was upset about the events that unfolded during the final game and filed multiple protests. His primary complaint concerned the fact that Stars slugger Jud Wilson had punched umpire Bert Gholston during the game but had not been ejected. League Commissioner Rollo Wilson agreed that Jud Wilson should have been removed from the game, but he did not allow Malarcher's protests to stand.

Malarcher was bothered by what he saw as a growing lack of sportsmanship in the game as well as what he saw as mismanagement of the league. The events in the final game of the series against the Stars were the breaking point for him. He wrote a letter to the sports editor of the *Chicago Defender* (which published it on January 19, 1935), in which he criticized the commissioner for his lack of action regarding the incidents in the final game of the 1934 championship series.[34] Malarcher decided it was time to leave professional baseball and tendered his resignation with a 12-page letter to Robert Cole in mid-February of 1935. Asked why he was resigning, Malarcher simply responded,

"I like baseball and I always will, but I think the time is here for me to step out."[35] He was only 39 years old when he walked away from a successful managerial career.

After leaving baseball, Malarcher worked as a real estate broker for several decades. He briefly returned to the American Giants as their business manager in 1940 but stayed in the position for only one year.[36] Malarcher's wife, Mabel, died in 1946; the couple did not have any children. The death of his wife inspired Malarcher to begin to write poetry, an avocation he continued to practice for the remainder of his life. In 1948 Malarcher wrote a poem, "Sunset Before Dawn," after he had attended a game and watched former Negro League players who were now playing in the White major leagues. Malarcher described the poem as concerning "the host of Negro players, now deceased – the great ones whom the great majority of America's fans did not see."[37]

Sunset Before Dawn

By David Malarcher

Thou wert among the best

Who wrought upon this earth,

O dead! Thine *endless* rest

Is merit of thy worth …

O, minds of fleetful thought!

O dead who lived too soon!

What pity thou wert brought

To twilight ere the noon!

But sleep thou on in peace,

As orchids which did bloom,

Like pure unspotted fleece

Within the forest's gloom.

In 1978, when Malarcher was a member of the Society for American Baseball Research, he published a paean to Oscar Charleston in SABR's *Baseball Research Journal*.[38]

For the remainder of his life, Malarcher lived in the same home he had built in 1927 at 6441 Vernon Avenue and attended Woodlawn A.M.E. Church in Chicago. "Gentleman Dave" Malarcher died at the age of 87 on May 11, 1982, in Chicago.[39] He was buried in Saint James Methodist Cemetery in Convent, St. James Parish, Louisiana.

SOURCES

Unless otherwise noted, Seamheads.com was used for all Negro League player statistics and team records.

Thanks are extended to Cassidy Lent, manager of reference services at the National Baseball Hall of Fame and Library, for providing a copy of David Malarcher's Hall of Fame player file.

NOTES

1   "Malarcher, Ideal Leader, Quits Baseball For Good," *Chicago Defender*, February 16, 1935: 17.

2   John Holway, *Voices From the Great Black Baseball Leagues, Revised Edition* (New York: Da Capo Press, 1992), 41-42.

3   Holway, 44.

4   Paul Debono, *The Indianapolis ABCs* (Jefferson, North Carolina: McFarland, 1997), 66.

5   Holway, 44-45.

6   Debono, *Indianapolis ABCs*, 74.

7   Steven R. Greenes, *Negro Leaguers and the Hall of Fame* (Jefferson, North Carolina: McFarland, 2020), 188.

8   Debono, *Indianapolis ABCs*, 80-82.

9   From survey found in Malarcher's Hall of Fame player file.

10   Debono, *Indianapolis ABCs*, 82.

11   Paul Debono, *The Chicago American Giants* (Jefferson, North Carolina: McFarland, 2007), 71.

12   From survey found in Malarcher's Hall of Fame file.

13   Debono, *Chicago American Giants*, 77.

14   Debono, *Chicago American Giants*, 87.

15   "The Game Play by Play," *Chicago Defender*, August 26, 1922, 10.

16   Debono, *Chicago American Giants*, 96.

17   From contract found in Malarcher's Hall of Fame file.

18   Debono, *Chicago American Giants*, 108.

19   From contract found in Malarcher's Hall of Fame file.

20   Debono, *Chicago American Giants*, 110.

21   Debono, *Chicago American Giants*, 111-114.

22   Debono, *Chicago American Giants*, 118-119.

23   Debono, *Chicago American Giants*, 120-121.

24   "D. Malarcher Threatens to Quit Giants," *Chicago Defender*, April 13, 1929: 8.

25   Debono, *Chicago American Giants*, 126.

26   Debono, *Chicago American Giants*, 128.

27   Bidwill later owned the Chicago Cardinals of the NFL.

28   Debono, *Chicago American Giants*, 130.

29   Debono, *Chicago American Giants*, 132.

30   Debono, *Chicago American Giants*, 133.

31   Debono, *Chicago American Giants*, 135.

32   Larry Lester, *Black Baseball's National Showcase* (Lincoln: University of Nebraska Press, 2001), 61.

33   Debono, *Chicago American Giants*, 137.

34   Dave Malarcher, "Chicago Hits Ruling by Baseball Head on Protest," *Chicago Defender*, January 19, 1935: 17.

35   "Malarcher, Ideal Leader, Quits Baseball for Good," *Chicago Defender*, February 16, 1935: 17.

36   "Malarcher Becomes Business Manager of American Giants," *Chicago Defender*, May 18, 1940: 24.

37   Holway, 57.

38   David J. Malarcher, "Oscar Charleston," *Baseball Research Journal* (Cooperstown, New York: SABR, 1978), 68.

39   David Malarcher obituary, *Chicago Tribune*, May 14, 1982: C27.

JACK MARSHALL

BY CHRIS HICKS

Jack "Boss" Marshall stood 5-feet-9 and weighed 167 pounds. He was a right-handed pitcher, both a starter and a reliever. Most of his seven seasons in the Negro National League were with the Chicago American Giants; he appeared on the rosters of the first two teams to win Negro National League pennants. He also played in the NNL for the Detroit Stars and the Kansas City Monarchs.

Marshall was born on May 11, 1895, in Carrollton, Missouri, to Sam and Lenora Marshall.[1] Sam and Lenora both grew up in the area. According to the 1880 census, Lenora lived with her mother, Rachel, and a sister named Pearlie. Sam lived with his mother, Sarah, and his grandfather, Reuben, who was well-known in the White and Black communities. The local newspaper ran an obituary, rarely seen for Black community members at the time, noting that he had been enslaved by Killus Callaway in Howard County, Missouri.[2] Sam and Lenora married on August 7, 1890, when Sam was 27 and Lenora was 22. Their first child, Leota, came in 1891, followed by Jack in 1895. About a week after Jack was born, Sam was working off a $2 fine in nearby Keytesville, Missouri, for drunkenness. In 1900 Sam and Lenora lived with her family with their two children. He worked as a day laborer, and she stayed at home. Sometime after that, Sam left the family, and no further conclusive records could be found about his life. By 1910, the household had moved to Kansas City, Missouri, and everyone lived in Kansas City for the rest of their lives. Marshall's aunt Pearl was the breadwinner of the family, working as a masseuse throughout her life. His mother Lenora never remarried and occasionally worked as a laundress, maid, or cook to provide supplementary income for the household.

It is unclear exactly when Jack started playing baseball. By 1917, at age 22, he was pitching for Brown's Tennessee Rats. When he registered for the World War I draft that June, he listed his trade as "minstrel troupe," working for W.A. Brown in Holden, Missouri, where the Tennessee Rats were based. The group was a combination minstrel show and barnstorming team that toured the Midwest. The players put on comedic-style baseball games during the day, and then they performed shows with singers, musicians, and skits at night.[3] One such example of the Rats' itinerary involved a two-game weekend series against the Brandeis Department Store team. Their appearance on Sunday, July 29, was part of an "athletic carnival" that featured such things as "wrestling, base ball, tug of war, shadow wrestling, and other classy events."[4] Not everyone appreciated such antics, including a South Dakota newspaperman who called a portion of a 1916 game "a vaudeville performance by the visiting negro team that exasperated the Minnesotans, amused the crowds, but included little baseball."[5]

On June 11, 1918, Marshall was drafted into the US Army in Kansas City, Missouri. He never left Fort Leavenworth, Kansas, where he worked in the Army Service School there. He was honorably discharged on December 18, 1918, making him available to play the next baseball season.

In 1919 Marshall joined the Chicago Union Giants for the season. That summer came to be called the Red Summer because of the many eruptions of racial violence throughout the United States. These race riots often occurred in industrial cities that had seen a large influx of Black migrants, who had trekked north looking for better work and social conditions than they found in the rural South. Much tension centered on employment and union membership, and strikes across the country contributed to this racial tension.

Like many other cities, Omaha, Nebraska, experienced labor unrest related to a national Teamsters' Union strike. By the beginning of the summer, "local boilermakers, bricklayers, tailors, telegraphers, teamsters, and truck drivers had already walked off their jobs."[6] On June 21 the Central Labor Union in Omaha threatened to add an additional 30,000 striking workers to the already numerous crowds. In response, the police outlawed public gatherings. Strikebreakers, including "eight Negros from Kansas City," required the protection of a hastily gathered 150 new police deputies.[7] On June 25 the mayor called on the American Legion to do the jobs of the strikers, and they responded by promising that "anything savoring of anarchy in Douglas County shall be put down by the Legion."[8] Many concessions were made to mollify the strikers, and many had returned to work by June 27.[9]

On June 30, 1919, the Union Giants arrived in Omaha to play the Armours. a company team of White players from the Armour packing plant. During the first game of the doubleheader, a "45-minute riot" broke out. It started originally as a fight between Jimmy Collins and Turner, a first baseman for the Union Giants. When Collins slid into first base, Turner accused Collins of spiking him. Marshall then came in from right field to get involved in the dust-up. He punched Collins above his left eye, causing a wound that needed two stitches. This punch incited the fans, both Black and White, to join the fight, clearing the benches and the stands. Some gathered baseball bats and other impromptu weapons, adding tension to the situation. The police chief, named Eberstein, happened to be at the ball game with his son Russell. He pushed back the gathering mob, waving his gun at the crowd. He arrested Marshall. The fans continued to hurl venom, but the police chief's action defused further threat of physical violence. More law officers arrived, taking Marshall to jail in handcuffs. The game then continued, and the second game was also played without incident. The Armours swept the doubleheader.[10]

The next day, Marshall was fined $25 for disturbing the peace and was released from custody.[11]

On August 3, 1919, the Chicago Union Giants were to play the White Eagles of Gary, Indiana.[12] The week before, on July 27, a Black boy floated across an invisible line in the water that separated segregated

(Courtesy Noir-Tech Research, Inc.)

Although Jack Marshall was third in innings pitched on the 1920 American Giants' pitching staff with 113 1/3, he was saddled with a hard-luck 6-7 record in NNL play.

beaches in Chicago. This began riots marked by murder, arson, and other acts of violence. Chicago Mayor William Hale Thompson requested that the state militia and National Guard be activated, resulting in nearly 10,000 troops pouring into the city; these troops did not leave until August 8.[13] The Gary team canceled the game, citing a "considerable sentiment" against the White Eagles playing a Black team given the "seriousness of the Chicago race riot situation."[14] It is unclear whether the players for the Union Giants would have been in Chicago at the time of the riot, but it is unlikely. They played in Omaha on July 27, beating the Armours while Chicago exploded. Omaha had a race riot at the end of September, resulting in the attempted lynching of the mayor and the lynching of Will Brown, a 41-year-old Black packinghouse worker.[15]

In 1920 the Negro National League was formed by Rube Foster and other Midwestern team owners in Kansas City, Missouri. The league consisted of eight teams and played a 60-game schedule. Foster decided to distribute the star players to different teams. Then there would be some parity among the teams, and each club would have a "draw" so fans would flock to the gates and watch the game. Fans were not thrilled with their favorite players being assigned to other teams but learned to accept it. When it was time for spring training, Foster had several players, including Marshall, show up for tryouts in case the players he had told to report did not arrive at Schorling Park.[16]

Marshall impressed Foster. He was one of the new players added to the Chicago American Giants roster, joining the club as a pitcher. The team was considered the favorite to win the championship. Foster himself was sure his team would come out on top, stating that there was "no fear of the future of the Giants" and that "ultimate success is sure."[17] The team finished the season in first place with a 43-17-2 record in league play. In 17 games (13 starts), Jack Marshall amassed a 6-7 record in league games with nine complete games and a 3.41 ERA. One of his more impressive wins was a 13-inning, 1-0 shutout on June 3 against the visiting Cuban Stars West. Six days later, he shut out the St. Louis Stars, 6-0, on a three-hitter.

Foster saw enough from Marshall to bring him back for the 1921 season. Star players Bingo DeMoss, Dave Malarcher, and Cristóbal Torriente also returned. In January, Foster took his team to Palm Beach, Florida, where the players worked for the Royal Poinciana Hotel as porters, bellhops, and in other service jobs while playing as a company team for the resort.[18] Other Negro League teams also brought players to resorts in the area. Hilldale made up the team for the Breakers Resort. These teams formed the Florida Hotel League, which played from January to early March, allowing the players to earn money while also providing preparation for the Negro National League season.[19] After the last game in Florida, the American Giants barnstormed their way to Chicago for the start of the regular season.

The *Chicago Defender* thought Marshall was a likely candidate to pitch for the American Giants' on Opening Day, May 7, but the nod went instead to teammate Dave Brown.[20] For the 1921 NNL season, Marshall had a 6-4 won-lost record in 14 games (11 starts) with 9 complete games and a little over 91 innings pitched. On June 4 he shut out the Columbus Buckeyes in the first game of a doubleheader on three hits. Malarcher and Torriente scored the only runs for the American Giants in the pitchers' duel.[21] Rube Foster's trust in his team was well-founded, and the American Giants repeated as Negro National League champions.

The 1922 season brought a change of scenery for Marshall, who was sent to the Detroit Stars. Foster overhauled his pitching staff, acquiring all new pitchers, save for Dave Brown.[22] Marshall made his Stars debut on April 16, pitching in relief in a combined five-hit shutout of the Cowpers, a local White amateur team. The *Detroit Free Press* said that the addition of Marshall and other players had "greatly strengthened the Stars."[23] Marshall pitched respectably for the Stars, ending 1922 with a 6-5 record over 19 games (12 starts), 7 complete games and 112⅔ innings. He also made three appearances for the New York Lincoln Giants after the NNL season and pitched to an 0-1 record.

In 1923 Marshall returned to the Chicago American Giants. The pitching staff was considered "weak," and it was said that Foster was using "a patchwork of journeymen (some of whom struggled with drinking problems) and 'flash in the pan' throwers."[24] Despite winning championships with these types of pitchers, the pitching staff in 1923 found it difficult to achieve success as none of them had the ability to overpower hitters.[25] Marshall struggled mightily, appearing in 17 games and posting a 2-6 record.

Marshall looked to rebound in 1924. He went to spring training in Texas with the team, but ended up being left along with fellow pitchers Dicta Johnson, Harry Kenyon, and Fulton Strong.[26] He then reported for training with his hometown Kansas City

Monarchs.[27] However, he pitched in only three games and had an 0-1 record despite posting a 3.45 ERA that was better than the league average (112 ERA+). His last appearance for the team came in a late-May doubleheader against the Indianapolis A.B.C.'s.[28]

At the beginning of 1925, Marshall was back with the Chicago American Giants, but his second stint with the team was short-lived. Once again, Rube Foster unconditionally released multiple players at the beginning of the season. Marshall was among the group, who also included veterans George "Tubby" Dixon, Tom Williams, and Dick Whitworth. The move was made in accordance with a new rule that "all players held in reserve or upon whose services options are held, must be placed on salaries by clubs holding them on May 1."[29] Marshall did not appear again in any box scores until 1928.

Jack Marshall was living in Kansas City, Missouri, according to a 1924 city directory. On November 15, 1927, he married Helen Hayes Gibbs in Jackson County, Missouri.

In 1928 Marshall returned to the Negro National League for a second stint with the Detroit Stars. Several other former Monarchs were members of the team. Marshall and Rube Currie, George Mitchell, and Grady Orange were said to be responsible for most of the Stars wins through mid-May.[30] The recurring message of newspaper accounts of Marshall's outings was that he was giving up a low number of hits in his outings. He had a career-best 10-5 record 142⅓ innings pitched. On July 28 Marshall gave up five hits and three runs in a 9-3 complete-game win against the St. Louis Stars, the team that went on to win the league championship.[31]

During Marshall's second term with the Stars, the city's underworld was dominated by the Purple Gang, otherwise known as the Sugar House Gang. The gangsters, primarily Jewish, were a known group of bootleggers who "supplied Al Capone with Old Log Cabin, his favorite whiskey."[32] The Purples were also involved in many other "sin industries," including prostitution, which was rampant in Detroit in the late 1920s because there were so many more men than women living in the city. In 1926 there were 711 brothels operating in the open "within a one-mile radius of City Hall."[33] According to Ted "Double Duty" Radcliffe, Jack Marshall had a brothel in the late 1920s, likely in 1928, the year he played for the Stars. These dealings meant that he would likely have had to have some "understanding" with the Purples. Even so, Radcliffe spoke of run-ins with the police:

"[Jack] had a couple of good girls. He was what we called a 'player.' It was raided two or three times. I was in it one time, but the policeman recognized me and let me go."[34]

Marshall returned once more to the Chicago American Giants in 1929. Showing he still had something left in the tank at age 34, he turned in a solid performance against the St. Louis Stars, one of the best teams in the league after winning the championship the previous year. In the third game of a five-game series, on September 14, he gave up 10 hits and four runs and helped himself at the plate with an RBI base hit in two at-bats. The American Giants won the game, 9-4, taking three of five games in the series.[35] After a 4-6 season in 1929, Marshall finished his pitching career with a 34-36 record with 42 complete games and a 4.26 ERA in 108 appearances (77 starts).

In 1930 Marshall reported on the US Census that his occupation was "baseball club." However, no records were found to show what team he may have played for. Even though he and Helen Gibbs had married in 1927, the couple seems to have parted ways. He was living with his mother, Lenora, Aunt Pearl, and a cousin named James Walker. Meanwhile, Helen was living with her family and working as a maid for a private family. Marshall listed himself as single while Gibbs indicated that she was divorced.

By 1934 Marshall and Helen Gibbs had reconciled and were living with his family at 2726 Woodland Ave. On May 5, 1936, Helen gave birth to daughter Mary Alice in Kansas City; she was the couple's only child. By 1939, the Marshalls had bought a home at 1914 Montgall Avenue in Kansas City. According to the 1940 census, Marshall worked as a laborer on a sewer project. His World War II draft card from 1942 indicates that the couple may have had another falling-out, since his address is listed on it as 2012 Askew. His mother and aunt still lived on Woodland, so he had not returned to their residence. This new address may also have been related to his work for the WPA, the New Deal employment program.

Marshall eventually settled into a post-baseball career with the Kansas City Department of Public Works. By 1955 he had once more reconciled with Gibbs, and they moved their family into another house they purchased at 2534 Garfield Avenue in Kansas City. However, they later returned to the old neighborhood; at the time of their deaths they were living at 3310 Montgall, about two miles north of their first home. Jack died on his 66th birthday, May 11, 1961, in Wadsworth, Kansas, which is present day

Leavenworth. He is buried in the Fort Leavenworth National Cemetery.

ACKNOWLEDGMENTS

The author thanks Bill Nowlin and Frederick C. Bush for research assistance.

SOURCES

Unless noted, all statistics come from Seamheads.com, all genealogy information comes from Ancestry.com, and all directory information comes from the Heritage Quest database.

NOTES

1   This seems to be the accurate birthdate based on the majority of records, including his military records. The exception that gets cited in other places is from his World War I draft registration card, which lists 1893.

2   *Chariton Courier* (Keytesville, Missouri), November 23, 1900: 3.

3   Donn Rogosin, *Invisible Men: Life in Baseball's Negro Leagues* (Lincoln: University of Nebraska Press, 2020), 55.

4   "Athletic Carnival When Tennessee Rats Come," *Omaha Daily Bee*, July 27, 1917: 7.

5   "Tennessee Rats Win Game 6 to 3 Against Jasper, Minn., Here," *Sioux Falls* (South Dakota) *Argus-Leader*, July 28, 1916: 3.

6   Michael L. Lawson, "Omaha, a City in Ferment: Summer of 1919," *Nebraska History* 58 (1977), 395.

7   Lawson, 396.

8   Lawson, 396.

9   Lawson, 397.

10 "Free-for-All Riot Marks Armour Game," *Omaha World Herald*, June 30, 1919.

11 "Jack Marshall," *Omaha World Herald*, July 1, 1919.

12 "May Call Off Union Giant Game," *Munster* (Indiana) *Times*, July 31, 1919: 5.

13 Karen Christianson, project director, "Mayor Requests State Militia, *Chicago 1919: Confronting the Race Riots*, https://exhibits.chicagocollections.org/1919/militia.

14 "May Call off Union Giant Game'" "Gary Cancels Game with Union Giants," *Munster Times*, August 2, 1919: 5.

15 Lawson, 415.

16 "'Rube' Assigns Players to Giants," *Chicago Defender*, March 20, 1920: 9.

17 "Giants Mobilizing," *Chicago Defender*, April 3, 1920: 9.

18 Layton Revel and Luis Munoz, "Forgotten Heroes: David 'Gentleman Dave' Malarcher," Center for Negro League Baseball Research, 2014.

19 Paul Debono, *The Chicago American Giants* (Jefferson, North Carolina: McFarland & Company, Inc., 2007), 82-83.

20 "League Season Opens Saturday at Giants Park," *Chicago Defender*, May 7, 1921: 11.

21 "American Giants Win," *Chicago Tribune*, June 5, 1921: 18.

22 Debono, 88.

23 *Detroit Free Press*, April 17, 1922: 12. Information about the Cowpers is from Chris Rainey, "Fred Schemanske," SABR BioProject.

24 Debono, 93-94.

25 Debono, 93-94.

26 Debono, 98.

27 "Monarchs to Start Training," *Kansas City* (Missouri) *Times*, April 2, 1924: 14.

28 "Play Two Games Today: Rain Postponed Yesterday's Monarch-Indianapolis Contest," *Kansas City Times*, May 20, 1924: 14.

29 Debono, 103.

30 "Former Mates to Battle," *Kansas City Times*, May 18, 1928: 17.

31 "Detroit Stars Win over St. Louis Nine," *Detroit Free Press*, July 29, 1928: 27.

32 Richard Bak, *Turkey Stearnes and the Detroit Stars* (Detroit: Great Lakes Books, 1994), 130.

33 Bak, 131.

34 Bak, 131.

35 "St. Louis Stars Drop Three Games to American Giants; to Play Baltimore Black Sox," *Chicago Defender*, September 14, 1929: 9.

CARROLL RAY "DINK" MOTHELL

BY BILL NOWLIN

"Mothell was the greatest utility man in the game of baseball. He could step in at any position, except pitcher, and you'd never notice that the regular player was missing."

– Cool Papa Bell[1]

Playing a variety of positions over the years, the versatile Dink Mothell was a member of three Kansas City Monarchs teams that finished as league champions – the 1924, 1925, and 1929 Monarchs. In 1924 he most often played center field; in 1925 it was left field; and in 1929 he usually manned first base. In 1926, with Mothell as second baseman, the Monarchs finished with the best overall record in the league and were the first-half champions, but the second-half champion Chicago American Giants prevailed five games to four over the Monarchs in a Negro National League championship series.[2]

Mothell did pitch, too, at one point, and acquitted himself well, thus having played at all nine positions.

As Phil Dixon has perceptively pointed out, because Negro League rosters were often limited to between 14 and 17 players, having someone with the versatility to fill in at a number of positions meant that "utility men like Wade Johnston, Hurley McNair, Sam Bankhead, Carroll (Dink) Mothell, and others weren't viewed as second-stringers, but, rather, as highly valued contributors."[3]

Mothell's career in the Negro National League began in 1920 with the Chicago American Giants. He played briefly with them – as a catcher – before joining the Monarchs. The 1920 Chicago American Giants were the league champions, making him a member of yet another championship team.

Carroll Ray Mothell was the middle of three sons born to Samuel "Sandy" Mothell and Scottie Lee (Pillow) Mothell. He was born on August 13, 1897, in Topeka, Kansas. His brothers were Claude C. Mothell (1895-1965) and Ernest D. Mothell (1900-1973).

Sandy Mothell (born in 1874) never got to see his son Ernest; Sandy died of consumption at his home on May 15, 1900.[4] Ernest was born in August.[5]

Sandy Mothell was a military veteran, who had served in the Spanish-American War as a volunteer with the 23rd Kansas Infantry. His parents, Ben and Eliza Mothell, had come to Topeka from Tennessee. Ben Mothell worked as a railroad laborer. Samuel (Sandy) had been born in Tennessee.[6]

Sandy Mothell had served as a private in Company A of the 23rd Kansas Voluntary Infantry regiment, alongside a couple of his brothers-in-law, Edward Pillow and Charles Pillow.[7] The whole unit was from Topeka, an African American regiment that served in Cuba from August 1898 to March 1899. Fourteen of the unit's members died in the service, 12 of them due to disease and 10 of those in Cuba. Pvt. Mothell was discharged from the service at Fort Leavenworth, Kansas, on January 21, 1900, and returned home to Topeka.

The Pillow family also came to Topeka from Tennessee. Charles and Celia Pillow were Scottie's parents and thus Dink Mothell's maternal grandparents. Charles was a Civil War veteran, and at the time of the 1885 census was listed as a laborer. SABR member Jan Johnson reports that he was a charter member of the Fort Pillow GAR Post in Topeka and one of the founding members of the Lane Chapel C.M.E. Church. After her husband's death, Scottie Mothell moved into the Pillow household with her three sons. She did not marry again.[8]

The Mothells worked at a number of jobs. Charles Pillow was a school janitor at the time of the 1900 census. His sons, Charles and Edward, were, respectively, a day laborer and a railroad section man. Scottie had no employment status indicated. In 1910 she was listed as a housekeeper for a private family; the younger Charles was a driver for a paint store and Edward was listed as a brick mason.

In 1920 Charles still worked as a teamster for the paint company. Ernest's occupation was grocery delivery. Carroll's first occupation listed was in 1920 as a "laborer, not employed."[9]

Carroll Ray Mothell was known by at least two nicknames – Deke, and, most commonly, Dink. Carroll's schooling saw him through eighth grade.[10] He grew to stand 6-feet tall, with a listed weight of 175 pounds.

As early as age 17, Dink had played some in and around Topeka with a team called the Topeka Giants.[11] He recalled, "We had a fellow around here by the name of Jack Johnson – a prizefighter – 'Topeka Jack,' we called him. He had a little team around here called the Topeka Giants, and I played with him on occasion. That would be around 1914."[12] He threw right-handed but, as he told John Holway, "I was a switch-hitter. When I first started playing, they fed me so many curve balls from the right side that I knew I had to do something to stay in the league, so I switched over. As a kid I was a cross-handed [switch] hitter. I had more power from the right side but I struck out a lot less from the left side; it looked like I could see the ball better."[13] In at least one clipping from 1917, "D. Mothel" was listed as a pitcher on the team.[14] One interesting pregame advertisement from the June 14 *Mayetta* (Kansas) *Herald* promoted a game three

days later between Johnson's Giants and the Mayetta Indians. It declared, "This is Topeka's crack team of colored boys. Jack Johnson is the greatest short-stop and Dick Mothell the greatest catcher in the country."[15]

Mothell first showed up in professional baseball with the 1920 Kansas City Monarchs for manager Jose Mendez, listed as a catcher on the team.[16] He had been doing construction work around Topeka and making, he said, about $130 a month. "In March 1920 I wrote to team owner J. L. Wilkinson of the Monarchs and told him about myself. A couple of weeks later I got a contract. ... I'm supposed to get 120 down in Kansas City."[17] He added, "I didn't like catching, but they only had one catcher, a Cuban named [Vicente] Rodriguez."

His departure from Topeka was noted in the *Topeka Plaindealer*, a brief note saying, "He is a star catcher."[18]

Mothell told Holway more about his brief time with the team: "We went barnstorming around Oklahoma, Missouri, Nebraska. We traveled in automobiles, and we slept in different places; in a small town you'd have maybe two or three players in this residence, two or three in another residence, like that. It was hard to find rooms; sometimes we'd just sleep in the automobiles."[19]

Researcher Jan Johnson believes that Mothell may have caught the first road game ever played by the Monarchs – albeit a nonleague game – in Beloit, Wisconsin, on April 22, 1920.[20]

In a road game on May 9, Mothell played second base against the St. Louis Giants, batting seventh in the order and without a base hit. He batted in the eighth spot, catching Rube Currie, against the Chicago American Giants on May 23 in Chicago. He is listed with one base hit and committing one error. Dave Wyatt of the *Chicago Defender* wrote, "The K.C. catchers put the visitors in an awful hole, especially Rodriguez, while Mathol [*sic*] was flashy in spots, but wobbled in the pinches."[21] The hit may have been his first as a pro. On May 29 and 30, he played third base against Indianapolis. In the 14-inning game on the 29th, he was again hitless (0-for-5) but did get credit for a sacrifice.[22] He was 1-for-4 on May 30.[23] A note in the *Defender* said, "The Monarchs are expecting a fellow soon, Rogan by name, and big leaguers who have seen him work pronounce him the best ever. He is with the 24th regiment and will report the middle of June. Mathol, the Kansas City catcher, is playing the ball of his life at third base, but the team is sadly in need of a second baseman."[24] On June 5 Mothell played third in a 7-3 home win against the visiting

Cuban Stars. He was hitless but scored one of the runs.[25] In an article datelined June 11, he is shown at third base again, with two base hits – one a double – in an 8-7 come-from-behind win against Indianapolis.[26]

It was tough to travel the way teams did. Even though Mothell wasn't playing much, a couple of the older players said he should ask for more money. He did, but Wilkinson declined, so Mothell quit the Monarchs.

Rube Foster of the Chicago American Giants had seen him play well in a game – perhaps the May 23 game in Chicago – and when he heard that Mothell and the Monarchs had parted ways, Foster sent a sportswriter to talk with him. Mothell was disinclined to get back in baseball, but he said his mother told him, "This is your second chance."[27] He got a raise from Foster, all of $5 more per month.

Mothell wasn't used much, saying, "I'd sit on the bench, pinch-hit every now and then." Where he had liked Jose Mendez, the Monarchs' manager, he said he really didn't like Foster, allowing that he was a good organizer but too "tough on his ball players, a lot tougher than he should have been."[28] Mothell is shown as appearing in four games for the 1920 Chicago American Giants. One of his teammates in Chicago was Bingo DeMoss, another Topekan. Mothell said he caught in only two games; one was on September 4, when he went 1-for-4 against the Detroit Stars. He was listed as "Matholl" in the *Chicago Whip* box score.[29] Seamheads shows his stats for the year as appearing in 21 games for the season, with 84 plate appearances and a .169 batting average. He had two extra-base hits, both doubles, and eight runs batted in.

What Mothell did for the next three years is difficult to pin down. He next turns up in the Seamheads database in 1924. Mothell told Holway that he quit Foster's team in 1922, which suggests that he had played for them, at least to some extent, in 1921. He said he worked for the Santa Fe railroad but would also "play with little teams around here [Topeka], catching."[30] Carroll Mothell may have been the Mothel who pitched a five-hit shutout for the Topeka Cubs on April 30.[31]

Dink's younger brother Ernest played baseball, too, a pitcher, reports Jan Johnson: "Along with Dink, I'm showing him in roster lists of the 1917 Topeka Giants, the 1921 Topeka Cubs, and I think the 1921 Topeka Giants. Both brothers also played for the Chanute Black Diamonds at least once in 1921."[32]

In 1923 Dink wrote to Wilkinson again and was brought to spring training with the Monarchs in Dallas. Mothell said, "I thought I had made the club. But Wilkie had another team, his farm club, called the All Nations and he sent me out with the All Nations in 1923. We played Nebraska, Iowa, South Dakota, Minnesota, Canada. I played first base, second base, outfield. I came back to Kansas City in 1924, and played a utility role, going in when somebody got hurt."[33]

The All Nations team was quite a team, winning over 120 games in a very busy year and at one point reportedly winning 44 consecutive games. Players whom Wilkinson had put on the team also included Newt Allen, Ted Alexander, John Donaldson, and Jose Mendez.[34]

"Dink" Mothell played only a brief role for the 1920 American Giants, but he was a member of three Kansas City Monarchs championship squads in the mid- to late-1920s.

Wilkinson shut down the All Nations club after the 1923 season.[35] Mothell was on the reserve list for the Monarchs at year's end.[36]

Mothell joined the team for spring training. One interesting game was a preseason game behind prison walls at the United States Penitentiary at Fort Leavenworth. More than 3,000 prisoners watched the April 19 game, an 11-1 win for the Monarchs. Mothell and Frank Duncan shared catching duties.[37]

In 1924 Mothell got a good deal of work, appearing in 70 known regular-season games (the Monarchs team showed a record of 57-22) and hitting for a .276 batting average and an on-base percentage of .376. He drove in 46 runs and scored 53. He had 11 doubles and five triples and stole six bases. He was already proving his versatility. Existing statistics show him catching in 12 games and playing first base in 14, second base in 2, third base in 5, left field in 3, center field in 34, and right field in 9. The trade that wasn't – Phil Dixon writes, "In 1924, Kansas City offered seven players in a trade for Cool Papa Bell of the St. Louis Stars. When St. Louis demanded that Mothell be one of the seven men included in the deal, Kansas City was forced to refuse the trade."[38]

Mendez and the Monarchs finished first in the Negro National League, five games ahead of the second-place Chicago American Giants. The Monarchs played the Eastern Colored League champions, Frank Warfield's Hilldale Club of Darby, Pennsylvania, in the "World's Colored Championship," winning five games to four, with one tie game. Mothell played in the Series but was injured badly in Game Three – hit by a pitch badly enough that he "had to be carried off the field."[39]

The two teams took the Series to its final game, in Chicago, on October 20. Mendez held Hilldale to three hits and the Monarchs won, 5-0. Mothell played first base. Kansas City scored all five runs in the bottom of the eighth. Three runs were in when Mothell came to bat with one out, Mendez on third, and Allen on second. He singled to center field, driving in the fourth and fifth runs.[40]

Many years later, when Mothell was asked what he considered to be his outstanding achievement in baseball, he replied, "There were a few, but I consider being one of few players to play in the first Negro World Series. Oct. 3-24."[41]

His last game of 1924 may have been an exhibition game in Topeka, when the Monarchs played the White Eagles, a local semipro team named after an area petroleum company. Pitching for the White Eagles was right-hander Jesse Barnes, who had pitched for the Boston Braves that year. Mothell homered over the right-field fence, part of a 16-1 shellacking that was not all Barnes's fault (his team committed eight errors).[42]

In 1925 the Monarchs were the first-half champions and also the ultimate NNL champions after defeating the St. Louis Stars in the NNL Championship Series.[43] One standout day for Mothell was the June 21 doubleheader sweep of Birmingham (6-5 and 4-3), when he was 4-for-6 with a stolen base in each game. On September 14, also against the Barons, he doubled and tripled in a game and – perhaps not surprisingly – was also hit by a pitch.[44]

Mothell played a lot of left field, but his versatility was perhaps well exemplified by four games against the Chicago American Giants at the end of August and into the beginning of September. Mothell played right field, first base, right field, center field, center field, and second base.[45]

At the beginning of September, the Monarchs had been trailing the St. Louis Stars, but then reeled off four straight wins, leaving them just five games behind in the standings.

During the NNL championship series against the Stars, the Monarchs lost the services of both Mothell and Bullet Rogan, Mothell suffering his injury in the last playoff game against St. Louis in Chicago.[46] He was "confined to bed."[47] With both men out, the Monarchs lost that final game and, in October, the World Series to the Hilldale club.[48]

In 1926 the Monarchs finished with the best record in the NNL, 60-22.

Mothell began the season playing left field and leading off. By June he was more frequently handling second base and batting further down in the lineup.[49] When the team clinched the first-half pennant with a July 5 doubleheader sweep of the Cubans, Mothell played third base in both games. Seamheads shows him with a .290 batting average for the year, his best year to date.

The Monarchs were the first-half champions in the NNL. In late August, writer (and Negro League umpire) Bert Gholston selected Mothell as the utility player for his all-star team.[50]

The second-half champion Chicago American Giants matched up against the Bullet Rogan-managed Monarchs in a playoff series. The first game of the series was at Kansas City's Muehlebach Field. Chicago was down 3-0, then scored three runs in the top of the sixth. In the bottom of the sixth, with two outs and Cristóbal Torriente on third, Mothell singled over second base with the go-ahead and ultimately winning run.[51] The series ran nine games, and Mothell appeared in eight of the nine games playing second base, batting .233, and driving in five runs. Chicago came out on top.

After the season was over, Mothell kept playing ball all winter long. Rogan recruited Mothell and a number of others to play California winter baseball for the Los Angeles Royal Giants.

The Pacific Coast News Bureau noted one game early in December when Mothell moved from first base to right field, and said he "saved the Giants several times with brilliant throws to the bases or plate. Mothell showed the greatest arm ever seen at the Sox Park."[52]

The Giants played well into March 1927, giving Mothell year-round employment as a ballplayer.[53]

The 1927 Monarchs dipped in the standings. Mothell kicked off Opening Day in Memphis with a single and triple in a 6-0 win. He had the winning hit – a bases-loaded single – in the bottom of the 10th inning of the August 7 game against Memphis.[54]

The American Giants won the first-half championship over the Monarchs and Kansas City ended the season in third place, percentage points behind St. Louis.

Mothell never hit a lot of home runs. Seamheads shows 18 homers over the course of his 12 years and 612 games. One came on June 25, 1927, against visiting Cleveland – his home run and an RBI single helping produce a 6-5 win.[55] He no doubt enjoyed a real spurt during some nonleague games in September. Against the Wichita All-Pros, he was 3-for-6 with a triple and a homer on September 17, 3-for-5 with another homer on the first game on the 18th, and 2-for-4 with a double in the second game.[56] On July 21 he won a game against Emporia that was tied, 3-3, going into the ninth. There was one out and a man on base. Mothell hit a "single down the foul line into right field. It was lost in the weeds" and went for a home run.[57]

Throughout the season, there were always a large number of games played against various semipro and other teams. Against the Concordia Travelers, Mothell had a three-home-run game on July 27 in Salina.[58] Playing Arkansas City on September 21, 1927, he hit two home runs in a 16-0 win.[59]

One remarkable game, while barnstorming during the season, saw Mothell steal four bases against Emporia on September 14.[60]

Bert Gholston again selected Mothell for his all-star team.[61] He wrote of Mothell, "He is one of the best second basemen in the circuit. His fielding is the talk of the day throughout the league. He is an ideal running mate for any good shortstop. He can range far to the left or right with perfect ease and he is deadly on slow hit balls that require accurate fielding and a quick throw."[62]

After the season, it was winter ball again, this time playing for a team billed as the Cleveland Colored Stars.

Mothell mostly played second base for the Monarchs in 1928. The team again contended but wound up in second place. For three years in a row, Mothell's stats show four home runs each year. One came in Chicago on June 29 as the Monarchs no-hit the American Giants, 4-0, behind the pitching of Alfred "Army" Cooper (7⅓ innings) and Chet Brewer.[63]

His batting average shows as .298, the highest of his career for a full league season.

After the season, the Monarchs played against a number of teams in Kansas, Nebraska, and Colorado. Mothell continued on westward after that, and in the winter of 1928-29 he played with the Cleveland Giants. (The team name seemed to change from year to year but many of the players remained the same, from the 1926 Royal Giants to this year's edition.) They won the California Winter League title.[64]

In 1929 the Monarchs ended up on top once again, finishing first. Mothell played first base in almost every game. One standout game early on was the May 25 season opener, against visiting Memphis, an 8-3 win in which he hit two doubles.[65] A 4-for-5 game against the Cuban Stars on August 19 was another memorable one, three singles and a double helping the team win its 14th game in a row.[66]

Mothell was part of a triple play in a touring game in June against the Okmulgee Merchants, a close game the Merchants won in 11 innings. In the bottom the eighth, with two on base, a Merchant lined the ball to Newt Allen at second base. He threw to shortstop Halley Harding who then threw to Mothell at first base.[67]

In an August 6 game against Detroit, the team batted around and Mothell was one of four Kansas City batters who had two base hits in one inning.

The Monarchs won the first-half flag, beating the St. Louis Stars, 18-6, on September 2, to clinch the league championship. Mothell got in a fist fight with John Henry Russell of the Stars, who claimed Mothell had spiked him.[68] The 16 stolen bases Mothell is credited with in 1929 represented his personal best in league play, one more than the 15 he had stolen in 1928.

In an October 5 postseason game in San Antonio against the Cuban All-Stars of San Luis Potosi, a Cuban/Mexican team said to be Mexico champions, Mothell was key in a four-run third inning. He singled in two runs, advanced to third base, and then stole home.[69]

The Monarchs were both first-half and second-half champions of the NNL.

Once again, Mothell joined Rogan, Newt Allen, Biz Mackey, and Newt Joseph in California Winter League ball. This year the team was dubbed the Philadelphia Royal Giants. Mothell primarily played first base. One notable win was on October 19 against a White team stacked with players including Bob Meusel, Irish Meusel, Fred Haney, and Tony Lazzeri. Mothell was one of five Royal Giants to homer in the 12-9 win.[70] Ten days later, Jimmie Foxx and Al Simmons joined the opposition, but still went down to defeat, 10-3.

In 1930 the St. Louis Stars reigned supreme while the Monarchs placed second. It's perhaps surprising that Kansas City did as well as it did.

The season started normally. In fact, playing a pre-season game at night in Waco on May 5, 1930, the Monarchs prevailed 8-0. Honors went to Mothell, with two bases-loaded triples – one in the first inning and one in the ninth. Both would almost certainly have gone for grand slams except for ground rules due to canvas stretched around the outfield, but the star of the game was Johnny Markham, who pitched a no-hitter, said at the time to be the first night-game no-hitter.[71]

Rogan suffered medical misfortune about halfway through the season. Mothell took over as manager in midseason. The team had been 26-10 in league games under Rogan, but then was 16-28 under Mothell. The entire team suffered a combination of injuries and illness that resulted in half the team being unable to fully contribute. Rogan had to be hospitalized and was in "very serious condition in a Kansas City hospital"; a July 28 report predicted that he would be out for the remainder of the season.[72] Army Cooper and L.D. Livingston were in an automobile accident. Newt Allen was injured during a game. LeRoy Taylor and Halley Harding both had to stop playing due to illness. It's not surprising that the team's performance swiftly went downhill.

At least one report, in the *Chicago Defender*, referred to Mothell as "Captain Mothel," saying in a story datelined Pittsburgh that he "has played bang-up ball in the three games here."[73] He hit a three-run homer in the June 19 game.

Mothell's defense was appreciated, too. A note in the *Kansas City Times* read, "The playing of Mothell this season at first base has been one of the features."[74] Monarchs owner J.L. Wilkinson had permanent lights installed at Muehlebach Field and more than 50 night games were played there in 1930.[75]

In the winter of 1930-31, Mothell played some baseball in Cuba. He is shown with six at-bats for Santa Clara and 41 for Cienfuegos, with a combined record of .195, including two triples and one stolen base.[76]

The Monarchs were an independent ballclub in 1931, no longer a part of the Negro National League. Rogan is listed as manager. Mothell is shown as batting .320 in 19 games, playing both second base and first base.

The comings and goings are a little unclear. In mid-July, Mothell ("late of the Kansas City Monarchs") played first base for Gilkerson's Union Giants ("one of the fastest semi-pro outfits on the road") which had traveled to Ogden, Utah, to play a local team there.[77] Just a few days earlier, he was with the Monarchs playing a game in Manhattan, Kansas, and losing to Elden Auker.[78]

By mid-August, J.L. Wilkinson had re-signed Mothell and he was back with the Monarchs. On August 13 the Monarchs beat the Omaha Packers, 4-3.[79] Three days later, the Cuban House of David team drew a Depression-era crowd of 8,500 to Muehlebach Field. The Monarchs took both games, 5-4 (in 13 innings) and 4-3. Facing Luis Tiant the elder in the first game, Mothell was 2-for-5 with a base on balls.[80] Next, the team headed to Chicago to play the Chicago Mills team.

One of the last games of the season was in Kansas City against a visiting team of major leaguers who included Lloyd and Paul Waner. The Monarchs won, 4-3, with Mothell hitting an eighth-inning double to deep center and scoring the tying run on a ball hit by Newt Allen, who moments later scored on a hit by Tom Young.[81]

After the season, writing in the *Pittsburgh Courier*, Cum Posey named Mothell as the right fielder on his "All-America Ball Club."[82] *Kansas City Call* sportswriter A.D. Williams wrote: "When Mothell first entered the big show some eleven years ago we found him to be a player of remarkable ability. Through all these years we have watched his work, checked him at every turn and find him to have a record hard to beat. His career in the NNL is one that any player should feel proud to claim. Men like Dink are not found every day."[83]

The 1932 season again saw the Monarchs as an independent club, managed by Mothell. The team's record was 13-5, first among the independent clubs. Mothell played third base in almost all the games. In April, he served as "captain" and played for the Cleveland-based Wakeman Red Caps.[84]

It was in 1932 that Mothell got his first known work pitching during a game. He was with the East-West League's Cleveland Stars at the time and played second base in both games of the June 18 doubleheader in Pittsburgh. The Crawfords won the first game, 10-2. In the second game, Cleveland had a 3-1 lead after seven innings, but starter Nelson Dean appears to have run into trouble in the bottom of the eighth and been charged with four runs. At some point during the difficulty, Dean was replaced. Mothell moved from second base to the pitcher's mound, Joe Ware moved in from left field to take Mothell's place at second, and Orville Singer entered the game in left field, batting in Dean's spot in the lineup. When the inning was over, the Crawfords had taken the lead, 4-3, but the Stars scored four runs in the top of the ninth and won the game. Mothell had one base hit in the game; whether his hit came in the ninth and may have contributed on offense, we do not know. Seamheads shows him pitching in just one game – this one – and working to six batters, allowing one hit, and retiring the other five without a walk or a strikeout. It would appear that he was the winning pitcher in the game.

Mothell appeared in 15 games and hit for a .214 batting average. He is credited with four sacrifices and four stolen bases, driving in five runs and scoring 10. There was another spiking incident, noted in the *Defender*: "Mothel showed poor sportsmanship while going into second."[85]

Riley writes, "When the East-West League folded during the season, the ultimate utility man returned to Kansas City, where he added another starting position to his list, as the regular third baseman."[86] It was a short season, the start uncertain and delayed until the beginning of July due to the Depression. As he had done with Cleveland, Mothell appeared in 15 games for the Monarchs; he had nine base hits in 55 plate appearances (.196), with five RBIs and eight runs scored. He stole five bases. Six walks and one hit-by-pitch gave him a .302 on-base percentage. Seamheads lists the team in first place among independent clubs. One newspaper article from August had Frank Duncan as the team's manager, and one in September had Mothell as "manager and third baseman of the club."[87] Needless to say, there were many more than 18 games

played during the season, but the majority of these contests were barnstorming games against non-major-league caliber opponents.[88] The *Kansas City Times* declared that the team's August 14 sweep of a double-header over the Cuban Stars gave them 32 consecutive victories.[89] The October 3 paper said the Monarchs had won 73 of 76 games.[90]

After the season, the Monarchs planned to take the train to Mexico and play a slate of games there, from October 22 to November 8, against the Mexico City Aztecs.[91] Prohibition was in force in the United States, so readers of the *Baltimore Afro-American* may have been titillated by a photograph in the December 24 issue showing Mothell with Frank Duncan, Turkey Stearnes, Newt Allen, and others posing holding bottles of gin, whiskey, and champagne before their return to the States.[92]

One newspaper later characterized Mothell as "quiet but efficient"[93] – but at the same time he clearly had at least on occasional playful side. A 1930 photograph shows him jokingly holding a shotgun pointed at teammate Halley Harding, while the Monarchs bus driver watches with a smile.[94]

The 1933 Monarchs are shown on Seamheads as playing only six games, as an independent club, with a record of 4-2. Bullet Rogan was back as manager, after his year and a half apparently dealing with medical issues.[95] He had returned in October 1932. Mothell is shown as playing second base in the six games, going 5-for-23 at the plate. Clearly, they played many more, but newspaper coverage seems sparse – perhaps because the Depression had taken even deeper hold. The team largely played on the road. In his biography of Rogan, Phil Dixon says the Monarchs traveled in "three Ford touring cars for the southern states, up to the Dakotas, across to the Pacific Northwest and into Canada."[96] He says the Monarchs played more games in Winnipeg – eight – than the four they played in Kansas City itself.

There was a game against the House of Davids, who beat the Monarchs, 7-5, in Emporia, Kansas. Mothell played second base and was 2-for-3 with a double and a stolen base.[97] The two teams sometimes barnstormed together.

After the 1933 season, Mothell became a baseball ambassador, traveling as one of 12 all-stars who played baseball "for two days in Japan and for a short time in China; then they remained in The Philippines until early February."[98] The team had departed San Francisco on the *SS President Lincoln* in November and returned to Los Angeles from Honolulu on April

6, on the *SS President Cleveland*. Among the participants were Monarchs Newt Allen, Chet Brewer, Andy Cooper, Mothell, and Bullet Joe Rogan. The team played an eight-game series in Hawaii on their way back. Mothell hit .323 during those games, including "a triple off of former Royal Giants pitcher Ted Shaw secured an 8-5 victory over the Hawaiian Mutual Telephone ball club on March 21."[99]

An article in the *Courier* said the Monarchs "are not part of any league" and that after the 1934 season "they will go to South America for a series of games with teams in Brazil, Argentina, and the Canal Zone."[100]

In 1934 the Monarchs again played most of their games on the road. Their stats on Seamheads show them with a 3-6 record and no home ballpark. Mothell is shown in seven games at second base, going 7-for-28 (.250).

The June 30, 1934, *Baltimore Afro-American* presented all-star choices by Dan Burley, and Mothell was one of three second basemen chosen for his team, not for 1934 but for all time. The other two were George Scales of New York and Dick Lundy of Newark.[101]

In August the Monarchs became the first African American team to play in the venerable but previously segregated *Denver Post* tournament. Drawing sizable crowds, they prevailed in five games and progressed all the way to the championship game before losing, 2-0, to Grover Cleveland Alexander's House of David team.

There was one oddity that happened during the fifth inning of the August 5 game against the Denver Athletic Club. The game had been scoreless. Nate Joseph reached second base on an infield hit and an errant throw by the Denver shortstop. Manager Sam Crawford had John Donaldson pinch-run for Joseph, and he advanced to third base on pitcher Cooper's sacrifice. Crawford then had Mothell pinch-run for the pinch-runner Donaldson. Turkey Stearnes singled and Mothell scored the first run of what became a 4-3 Monarchs win. The *Denver Post* tried to explain it: "It seems Donaldson was substituted because he was a faster runner; Mothell because he was smarter. At least that's the story!"[102]

The Monarchs then traveled, playing Alexander's team in Colorado Springs, Wichita, La Crosse, and Tulsa. They also took on a number of other teams, such as Dizzy Dean's All-Stars, at games in Oklahoma City, North Dakota, Wichita, Kansas City, Des Moines, Chicago, and Milwaukee. It was, wrote Dixon, "one of the most profitable campaigns in their history," and

he quoted the *Kansas City Times* as saying they had "played 143 games winning 127."[103]

The team played its final game on October 15.

In the year he turned 38, Dink Mothell retired from baseball in 1935 "because of problems in his right shoulder."[104] That said, he did show up from time to time, playing a bit that summer with the McNair Paseo Taverns of Kansas City, a semipro team with several members drawn from the ranks of former Monarchs and Chicago American Giants players. The McNair team lost an August 18 game in Emporia but Mothell provided a thrill by stealing home.[105]

He is said also to have worked some games as an umpire.[106]

Mothell returned to Topeka and lived out his life with most of his acquaintances unaware of his years with the Monarchs. He never married and had no children. After his passing, family friend Wilber Douglas Jr. – whose father had played with Mothell on the Topeka Giants – said he worked numerous odd jobs, mostly doing custodial work. "That's about all he could get in those days. I really don't think many people he worked for knew anything about his baseball career." He added, "Dink was a very likeable fellow. But when he talked with us kids about ball, he was very stern about how he did it. He made us listen, that's for sure."[107] Douglas donated Mothell's uniform to the Negro Leagues Baseball Museum.

Mothell died in a Topeka hospital on April 24, 1980, survived by his aunt, Mrs. Janie Hollis. He was 82, retired, and a member of the Lane Chapel CME Church.

He was not forgotten, but fuller recognition came just over 30 years later.

The Society for American Baseball Research Negro Leagues Committee raised funds to place a tombstone on his previously unmarked grave. The tombstone dedication occurred in June 2011 and was featured on *NBC Nightly News*. The inscription reads:

Topeka's "Super Substitute" Legendary second baseman in Negro Leagues Baseball as a member of the Kansas City Monarchs. Mothell played at least one game at each position during his 15 seasons in the Negro Leagues.

"Mothell was a soft-spoken man," SABR's Larry Lester said at the dedication. "Not everyone is a self-promoter." Family friend Jocelyn Lyons learned much about his baseball history during the ceremonies. "I didn't know all this as a kid," He said, "I just knew him as Uncle Dink. I knew him as grandpa's best friend."[108]

A couple of months later, on August 6, 2011, the *Topeka Capital-Journal* named Dink Mothell as number 50 on its list of Top 100 Athletes in Shawnee County, Kansas, history.[109] Carroll Ray "Dink" Mothell was inducted into the Kansas Baseball Hall of Fame on February 4, 2012.

ACKNOWLEDGMENTS

Many people helped in developing this biography. Special thanks to Jan Johnson, who provided considerable assistance. Thanks as well to Gary Ashwill, Phil Dixon, Kevin Johnson, Mike Lynch, and Mark Schremmer.

NOTES

1 Phil Dixon with Patrick J. Hannigan, *The Negro Baseball Leagues* (Mattituck, New York: Amereon House, 1992), 100.

2 https://www.seamheads.com/NegroLgs/year.php?yearID=1926&lgID=NNC.

3 Dixon with Hannigan, 24.

4 *Topeka Plaindealer*, May 18, 1900.

5 The date of his birth is uncertain. When he registered for the draft in World War I, he reported it as December 16, but when he reregistered for the draft in World War II, he gave his birthdate as August 13.

6 State of Kansas census, 1885.

7 Charles was listed with the surname Pillows. Mothell was listed as Sandy Mathell.

8 Email to author from Jan Johnson on January 7, 2021.

9 Carroll Mothell does not turn up in the 1930 census, though we do see his brothers Claude (a janitor at the State House in 1930 and janitor at a commercial bank in 1940) and Ernest (laborer in a mattress factory in 1930 and machinist in a mattress factory in 1940). Carroll Mothell was living in Kansas City in 1940 and is listed as a janitor in a public office building.

10 Carroll Ray Mothell player questionnaire from the National Baseball Hall of Fame.

11 A photograph of him with the 1918 Topeka Giants appears in Dixon with Hannigan on page 88.

12 Dink Mothell interview with John Holway, presented in John Holway, *Black Ball Tales* (Springfield, Virginia: Scorpio Books, 2008), 58. Gary Ashwill has written a two-part biographical portrait of Topeka Jack Johnson. See "Topeka Jack Johnson, Parts 1 and 2," AgareType. com, February 21, 2016 and April 6, 2016 at: https://agatetype.typepad. com/agate_type/2016/02/index.html and https://agatetype.typepad.com/ agate_type/2016/04/topeka-jack-johnson-part-ii.html. Accessed March 3, 2021. In 2016, Jan Johnson was the local Topeka coordinator for a grave marker installation for Johnson and prepared biographical remarks.

13 Holway, 58.

14 "Drill Before Game," *Topeka State Journal*, June 2, 1917: 7. This was likely a mistake. In the actual game, he was the catcher. See "Giants Defeat Battery 'A,'" *Topeka State Journal*, June 4, 1917: 3. A clipping from September shows Dick as catcher and "E. Mothel," quite likely Ernest, as pitcher. "Knights vs. Giants," *Topeka State Journal*, September 22, 1917: 7. Both Mothells were mentioned as competitive tennis players, with "Carol Mothel" playing in the boys' semifinals at Ripley Park. He was a few days shy of 21 years old at the time. See "Tennis Finals Tonight," *Topeka Daily Capital*, August 8, 1918: 2.

15 Advertisement from page 4 of the *Mayetta* (Kansas) *Herald*. Amusingly, the next line of the ad proclaimed "Funny Jokes a Specialty."

16 "Here Are the Fans; Take Your Choice," *Chicago Defender*, May 1, 1920: 9. He was listed as Mathell.

17 John Holway, *Black Ball Tales*, 58.

18 "Seen and Heard During the Week," *Topeka Plaindealer*, April 9, 1920: 3.

19 Holway, *Black Ball Tales*, 58, 59.

20 "Leaguers Lose First," *Beloit* (Wisconsin) *Daily Call*, April 23, 1920: 4. The battery was presented as "Correy" and "Mathell."

21 Dave Wyatt, "American Giants Win in 11th," *Chicago Defender*, May 29, 1920: 9. In newspaper accounts, throughout this career, his name was most often rendered as "Mothel." It was a rare article that spelled it correctly.

22 "Monarchs Lost Long Game," *Kansas City Times*, May 30, 1920: 12.

23 "Monarchs Won in Big Rally," *Kansas City Times*, May 31, 1920: 6.

24 "Kansas City Notes," *Chicago Defender*, June 5, 1920: 9.

25 "Cuban Stars in a Defeat," *Kansas City Star*, June 6, 1920: 14A.

26 "Monarchs Win Final from Indianapolis," *Chicago Defender*, June 11, 1920: 9.

27 Holway, 59.

28 Holway, 59-60.

29 "Star Lose First to Giants," *Chicago Whip*, September 11, 1920: 5.

30 Holway, 60.

31 "Cubs Shut Out Oskaloosa," *Topeka Daily Capital*, May 1, 1922: 7.

32 Jan Johnson email to author, March 1, 2021. Some clippings the *Chanute* (Kansas) *Daily Tribune* in both August and September 1920 show a Mothel catching. In a few 1921 clippings, there is a D. Mothel catching and an E. Mothel playing shortstop for Chanute. And there is one that shows E. Mothell at shortstop with D. Mothell, playing left field and then pitching the final 7⅓ innings of a game against the Humboldt Grays. "Humboldt 6, Diamonds 3," *Chanute Daily Tribune*, June 6, 1921: 4. The July 24 game against Overbook featured the Topeka Giants battery of "D. Mother" and "E. Mother." See Topeka Giants 12; Overbrook 3," *Topeka State Journal*, July 25,1921: 3. Johnson adds, "There was an older Mothel(l) player, James. He was on Topeka Jack's 1906 and 1907 Topeka Giants teams, and again in 1917." How James might have been related is unknown. He is likely the James Mothel born in Topeka in 1879.

33 Holway, 60.

34 Phil S. Dixon, *Wilber "Bullet" Rogan and the Kansas City Monarchs* (Jefferson, North Carolina: McFarland, 2010), 86.

35 Phil Dixon with Patrick J. Hannigan, 100.

36 "National League's Player Reserve List," *Chicago Defender*, December 15, 1923: 8.

37 "K.C. Monarchs Down U.S. Prisoners, 11-1," *Chicago Defender*, April 26, 1924: 9.

38 Phil S. Dixon, 71.

39 "Negro Clubs in the Game," *Kansas City Times*, October 6, 1924: 9. The game ended as a 6-6 tie game after 13 innings. See also Frank A. Young, "Hilldale Leads in World Series," *Chicago Defender*, October 11, 1924: 1.

40 "The Title to Monarchs," *Kansas City Times*, October 21, 1924: 12.

41 Carroll Ray Mothell player questionnaire from the National Baseball Hall of Fame.

42 "Monarchs Trim Eagles," *Topeka Daily Capital*, October 27, 1924: 2. Barnes won 15 games for the Braves in 1924 but lost 20. In 13 years in the majors, he won 152 games. The article used the name "Claude Mothell" but it was brother Carroll (Dink) who was on the Monarchs.

43 https://www.seamheads.com/NegroLgs/year.php?-yearID=1925&lgID=NNC&tab=standings.

44 The Monarchs won in 13 innings, 2-1. The one run was said to be the first run the Barons had scored against Monarchs pitching in three consecutive games. Mothell scored one of the two runs. For reasons unknown, Rogan started in right field and Mothell in center, but at some point they switched positions. "A Long Game to the Monarchs," *Kansas City Times*, September 15, 1925: 10.

45 "Kansas City and American Giants Split Two-All in Four-Game Series at Chicago," *Chicago Defender*, September 5, 1925: 8. Mothell switched positions during two of the games.

46 On page 59 of his book on Bullet Rogan, Dixon quotes the *Kansas City Call*'s *Baseball Extra* of October 1925 saying that both were out due to injuries. And "it is absolutely certain that neither of them will get in the post-season classic this year."

47 Frank Young, "Hilldale Now Leads Kansas City in Championship Series," *Chicago Defender*, October 10, 1925: 8.

48 Dixon, 60, 61.

49 James Riley says that Mothell "[a]ssumed the duties at second base, enabling Newt Allen to fill the void left when Dobie Moore's career was ended in a shooting incident early in the spring." James A. Riley, *The Biographical Encyclopedia of the Negro Baseball Leagues* (New York: Carroll & Graf, 1994), 572.

50 "Bert Gholston's All-Star team," *Kansas City Call*, August 27, 1926: 7.

51 "Monarchs Off in Lead," *Kansas City Star*, September 19, 1926: 24. Mothell singled in the sixth the next day and scored the tying run. Moments later, the Monarchs made it 6-5 for another win.

52 "Giants Lose First Doubleheader Game," *Pittsburgh Courier*, December 11, 1926: 14. The ballpark was White Sox Park.

53 See, for instance, "Colored Giants Will Send Strong Team Against Suds," *Bakersfield* (California) *Morning Echo*, March 6, 1928: 6. Likewise, in 1928, the *Pittsburgh Courier* noted that Frank Duncan, Newt Allen, and Mothell had all returned from California and would spend "a few days with local fans" before joining Bullet Rogan to head to Hot Springs to prepare for the 1928 season. "Baseball Gossip in the National League," *Pittsburgh Courier*, March 17, 1928: 16.

54 "Monarchs Win, Then Lose," *Kansas City Times*, August 8, 1927: 9.

55 "Kansas City Keeps Up a Dizzy Pace," *Chicago Defender*, July 2, 1927: 9.

56 "Kansas City Stops Wichita League Club," *Chicago Defender*, September 24, 1927: 9.

57 "Lose Game in Ninth," *Emporia Gazette*, July 22, 1927: 10.

58 "Monarchs Lift Eight Balls from Park in Turning Back Travelers," *Salina Journal*, July 28, 1927: 18. See also "Sports Far and Near," *Birmingham Reporter*, August 13, 1927: 7.

59 "Monarchs Humble Arkansas City," *Kansas City Times*, September 22, 1927: 11.

60 "Lose to the Monarchs," *Emporia Daily Gazette*, September 1, 1927: 5.

61 Bert Gholston, *Kansas City Call*, September 23, 1927: 6.

62 Quoted in Dixon with Hannigan, 119.

63 "American Giants Held Hitless," *Chicago Tribune*, June 30, 1929: A7.

64 Dixon, 132.

65 "Monarchs, Win, 8 to 3," *Kansas City Star*, May 26, 1929: 87.

66 "No. 14 to Monarch String," *Kansas City Times*, August 20, 1927: 12.

67 "Merchants Defeat Monarchs 3 to 2 in 11-Inning Game," *Okmulgee* (Oklahoma) *Sunday Times Democrat*, June 9, 1929: 7.

68 "Pennant to Monarchs," *Kansas City Times*, September 3, 1927: 19.

69 "K.C. Monarchs Downs Cuban-Mexican Team," *Chicago Defender*, October 12, 1929: 8.

70 James Newton, "Watching the Scoreboard," *Chicago Defender*, November 2, 1929: 8.

71 "A No-Hit Game at Night," *Kansas City Star*, May 6, 1930: 10.

72 "Rogan Out for Rest of Season," *Chicago Defender*, August 2, 1930: 8. Phil Dixon wrote of speculation mentioning lockjaw, a virus, and an eye operation among explanations at the time, but historians still don't know the actual ailment(s) that kept him out of baseball for more than a season. Dixon, 100.

73 "Monarchs Split 2 Night Games With Homestead Grays But Are beaten in Daytime," *Chicago Defender*, July 26, 1930: 8.

74 "The Cubans Here Today," *Kansas City Times*, June 7, 1930: 19.

75 "A Game on Here Tonight," *Kansas City Times*, August 1, 1930: 14.

76 Jorge S. Figueredo, *Cuban Baseball: A Statistical History, 1878-1961* (Jefferson, North Carolina: McFarland, 2003), 192, 195.

77 "Union Giants to Oppose All-Stars in Ogden Matinee," *Ogden* (Utah) *Standard-Examiner*, July 24, 1931: 8.

78 "Auker Holds Monarchs to Seven Hits; Travelers Win, 5-2," *Manhattan* (Kansas) *Mercury*, July 28,1931: 3. Two years later, Auker was pitching for the Detroit Tigers.

79 "Monarchs Nip Western 9 in Tough Battle," *Chicago Defender*, August 22, 1931: 8.

80 "Monarchs Top Cubans Twice Before 8,000," *Chicago Defender*, August 22, 1931: 8.

81 "K.C.'s Win Before 8,000," *Chicago Defender*, October 10, 1931: 9.

82 "Posey's All-America Ball Club," *Pittsburgh Courier*, October 10, 1931: A5.

83 Williams was quoted in Dixon with Hannigan, 136.

84 "Red Caps Have Good Squad to Oppose Bakers," *Sandusky* (Ohio) *Register*, April 28, 1932: 8.

85 "Notes of the Game," *Chicago Defender*, September 4, 1932: 9.

86 Riley, 572.

87 The August 8 *Kansas City Times* referred to "Manager Duncan." See "Monarchs Win, 8-1, 4-2," *Kansas City Times*, August 8, 1932: 10. A September 9 column contained the phrase characterizing Mothell as manager; Duncan was on the team. "Three Pitchers Give Up 22 Hits," *Battle Creek Enquirer*, September 9, 1932: 19.

88 Statistics against nonleague opponents are naturally not included in official Negro League statistics.

89 "Monarchs' String Grows," *Kansas City Times*, August 15, 1932: 10. They won number 33 the following day. It's not clear when the streak ended.

90 "Monarchs Make it 73," *Kansas City Times*, October 3, 1932: 12. Earlier, see "Only 2 Losses in 65 Games," *Kansas City Star*, September 22, 1932: 12. The October 9 *Star* said they were 75-3; see page 56.

91 "Monarchs Prepare to Invade Mexico," *Baltimore Afro-American*, September 24, 1932: 17.

92 "Train Now Leaving for Ol' Mexico," *Baltimore Afro-American*, December 24, 1932: 18.

93 "Kansas City Monarchs to Show Wares with Sealeys in Night Game," *Hutchinson* (Kansas) *News*, September 25, 1930: 10.

94 Dixon with Hannigan, 160.

95 Rogan had spent 1932 playing for a nonleague team in Jamestown, North Dakota. See Dixon, 107-111.

96 Dixon, 139.

97 "Davids Defeat Monarchs, 7-5," *Emporia Gazette*, August 22, 1933: 6.

98 Janet Bruce, *The Kansas City Monarchs: Champions of Black Baseball* (Lawrence: University of Kansas Press, 1985), 86, 87.

99 Kazuo Sayama and Bill Staples Jr., *Gentle Black Giants: A History of Negro Leaguers in Japan* (NBRP Press, 2019), 358.

100 "Monarchs Facing Heavy Schedule," *Pittsburgh Courier*, April 28, 1934: A4.

101 Dan Burley, "All-Time Team of Athletic Stars," *Baltimore Afro-American*, June 30, 1934: 19.

102 Walter Judge, "Kansas City Colored Stars Defeat Denver A.C., 4 to3," *Denver Post*, August 6, 1934: 17.

103 Dixon, 150.

104 Dixon, 151.

105 "Emporia Wins by Late Rally, 5-4," *Emporia Daily Gazette*, August 19, 1935: 3.

106 Dixon, 183.

107 Mark Schremmer, *Topeka Capital Journal*, August 7, 2010.

108 Mark Schremmer, "Negro Leagues Star to Receive Grave Marker," *Topeka Capital Journal*, June 4, 2011.

109 Jan Johnson notes that the *Capital-Journal* updated its rankings in 2020. Mothell is now number 59 in the Top 125. Rick Peterson, "Charting Shawnee County's Top 125," *Topeka Capital Journal*, August 23, 2020: B2, and August 30, 2020: B2.

JOHN REESE

BY ROBERT NASH

As his nicknames, Speed Boy and Sparkplug,[1] suggest, John Edward Reese was a fleet-footed outfielder who put together a 12-year career at the highest levels of professional baseball in the Negro Leagues. Although he spent most of his career as a reserve outfielder, he was talented enough to play in the outfield alongside some of the greatest players in history. When his playing days were largely over, he had a brief, but highly successful run as a manager, steering the St. Louis Stars to the last two pennants of the Negro National League in 1930 and 1931.

Reese was born on April 19, 1895,[2] in Pensacola, Florida. Little is known of his early life, but the 1910 US Census shows him still living in Pensacola with his mother, Carrie Reece, and stepfather, James Reece.[3] James Reece was listed as a bay man in the ship-loading field. Although he adopted his stepfather's surname, Reese himself spelled it "Reese." On occasion, however, various sources, including box scores, continued to render his last name as "Reece."

By 1915 Reese was a student at Morris Brown College in Atlanta. One of Georgia's Historically Black Colleges and Universities (HBCU), Morris Brown was founded in 1881 under the auspices of the African Methodist Episcopal Church. In the 1917-1918 Morris Brown catalog, a John E. Reese is listed as a junior in the Commercial Department.[4] The aim of the department was "to give a theoretical and practical education to young men and women who are looking forward to business careers."[5] While at Morris Brown, Reese was a member of the school's baseball team.

A rare box score from 1915 shows "Reese" playing center field and scoring two runs in a 9-5 victory over crosstown rival Morehouse College.[6] In the following year, Reese and two teammates were touted for fielding which "created a sensation," in a losing effort to visiting Howard University.[7]

In early April 1917 the United States declared war on Germany. Reese was one of the millions of young American men who were required to register for the military draft in June 1917 as the nation prepared to enter the First World War. At that time, he put down Morris Brown as his residence. He gave his occupation as janitor, with B.J. Davis at the Odd Fellows Building in Atlanta as his employer. Benjamin J. Davis Sr., a prominent African American of Atlanta, was the founder and editor of the *Atlanta Independent*, a weekly newspaper that began publication in 1903. Reese also listed a mother and 3-year-old child as dependents. Since he indicated his marital status as single, it is unclear if the mother listed was his own mother, or the mother of his child (if he had fathered one).[8]

Reese was not called into military service, and in 1918 he made his way north to begin his career as a professional baseball player with the Hilldale Club of Darby, Pennsylvania. Located on the outskirts of Philadelphia, Darby had been home to a Black amateur team since 1910. Under the leadership of its primary owner and team president, Ed Bolden, Hilldale became a fully professional team in 1917.[9] Reese joined four other recent Morris Brown College alumni on the team's roster: Elias "Country" Brown, McKinley "Bunny" Downs, Daniel "Shang" Johnson, and Tom Williams. The 1918 team also included future Hall of Fame catcher Louis Santop; and a young Judy Johnson made a very brief appearance with the team that year before beginning his own Hall of Fame career in earnest several years later.

As an independent Black team with no league in which to compete, Hilldale scheduled games against other professional Black ballclubs, as well as White semipro, industrial, and military teams. A local newspaper declared that Hilldale "played the strongest teams obtainable."[10] Sunday games in Philadelphia were prohibited by the blue laws in force at the time, so many Hilldale players, including Reese, made the short trip to Atlantic City, New Jersey, where there were no restrictions on Sunday games, to play for the Bacharach Giants. Although Reese struggled at the plate during his first season as a professional, he regularly started in the outfield, primarily as the center fielder for both Hilldale and the Bacharach Giants.

At the end of Reese's first season with Hilldale, a September game was scheduled against a barnstorming team advertised as the World Champion Boston Red Sox. The Red Sox had just defeated the Chicago Cubs in the 1918 World Series. While the "Red Sox" team that Hilldale faced did in fact have four members of the 1918 Red Sox, the rest of the team was composed of current or former players from other teams. Reese led off for the home team in the bottom of the first inning with a single off Bullet Joe Bush of the Red Sox and scored Hilldale's first run. Hilldale was behind 4-3 going into the bottom of the ninth inning, but when Bush refused to accept a new ball in place of one that had been removed from play, the game was awarded to Hilldale by forfeit.[11]

Reese was one of seven players from the 1918 Hilldale squad who returned for the 1919 season. Taking over the starting spot in left field, he had a strong season at the plate. At the end of the season, Hilldale faced off against the Bacharach Giants in what the local press in a bit of hyperbole proclaimed was "for the colored baseball championship of America."[12] The game was played at Shibe Park, the first time Black baseball teams were permitted to play on the home field of the American League's Philadelphia Athletics. Hilldale did not fare well against the Giants and Cannonball Dick Redding. Redding gave up only three singles in the game, one of them to Reese, on the way to a 10-0 shutout.[13]

Reese apparently made his offseason home in Pennsylvania: The 1920 Federal Census shows a John Reese living as a boarder in Philadelphia in early January of that year. The census taker recorded the respondent's occupation as "Ball Player," and his industry as "Team," leaving little doubt that he was John Reese of the Hilldale Club.[14] In any case, Reese would not be living in Philadelphia for much longer.

(Courtesy Noir-Tech Research, Inc.)

John Reese played an important role as a reserve outfielder, appearing in 41 league games for the 1920 American Giants. As manager, he piloted the St. Louis Stars to NNL championships in 1930 and 1931.

In February 1920 Black team owners at the behest of Rube Foster met in Kansas City, Missouri. The meeting resulted in the creation of the first organized league for Black teams. The new league was called the Negro National League. Many years later, in December 2020, the league was officially recognized by Major League Baseball as a major league.[15] As the primary mover for the new league, Foster became its first president. A former outstanding pitcher himself, Foster owned and managed the Chicago American Giants, one of the most successful teams in Black baseball. Foster's Giants had competed against Hilldale in previous seasons and, as he was always on the lookout to improve his team, Foster recruited Reese and pitcher Tom Williams away from Hilldale to join the Giants for the 1920 season in the new league.

In a preseason review, a reporter for the *Chicago Defender* wrote that "Reese, the new outfielder, comes here from the Hilldales of Philly. He has been facing all the high class twirling of the eastern hurlers, and if there are any thing to the signs, then he supplies that punch the fans so feared might be missing."[16] Reese was projected to be in the starting outfield alongside veterans Judy Gans and future Hall of Famer Cristóbal Torriente.[17] Reese did indeed win a starting position in Chicago's outfield, but partway through the season he was replaced in the starting lineup when the Giants acquired Floyd "Jelly" Gardner from the Dayton Marcos. Reese, however, remained a regular contributor down the stretch as the Giants won the pennant in the Negro National League's inaugural season.

Reese began the 1921 season with Tenny Blount's Detroit Stars. His new teammates included two future Hall of Famers, player-manager Pete Hill and pitcher Andy Cooper. Reese played left field and batted second for his new team as it got off to an excellent start. By the end of June, Detroit had raced to a league-leading record of 17-3.[18] Reese was in the lineup for an early-season highlight when his teammate, veteran right-hander Big Bill Gatewood, tossed the Negro National League's first no-hitter en route to his career-best season at age 39.[19]

By early July, however, Reese was back with the American Giants. He got some extra playing time at the end of that month when he replaced left fielder Jimmie Lyons in the starting lineup. Lyons had fallen 25 feet down a hotel elevator shaft when the Giants were on the road for a series against the Cincinnati Cuban Stars.[20] Although Lyons quickly recovered from the fall to reclaim the starting job, Reese still ended up logging the fourth most games in Chicago's

outfield as the Giants won their second consecutive league title. He remained with the Giants throughout the 1922 season in his familiar reserve outfielder role behind the well-established starters Torriente, Lyons, and Gardner as Chicago captured its third straight league pennant.

After three championship years with the Giants, Reese opened the 1923 season with the Toledo Tigers. Toledo was one of the Negro National League's two new teams, along with the Milwaukee Bears. The pair replaced the Cleveland Tate Stars and Pittsburgh Keystones, who had left the league after only one season. Reese started in the outfield for the Tigers, playing all three positions and leading the team in stolen bases and runs scored. Toledo was unable to finish out the league season, ending its only year of play in July. Reese and six of his Tigers teammates were quickly picked up by the St. Louis Stars. One of the former Tigers, veteran third baseman Candy Jim Taylor, took over as player-manager. Although the Stars finished the season with one of the worst records in the league, Reese again played all three outfield positions and batted .316 down the stretch for his new team. His combined statistics for the 1923 season with Toledo and St. Louis represented career highs for him in almost all offensive categories.

Reese's first few seasons with St. Louis were among the best of his career. The Stars began to build a strong team that in a short time challenged the Chicago American Giants and the Kansas City Monarchs for league supremacy. When Reese arrived on the team in 1923, it already had a young pitcher who was soon converted into one of the greatest center fielders in Negro Leagues history, Cool Papa Bell. Nineteen-year-old shortstop Willie Wells joined the team in 1924 to embark upon his Hall of Fame career as St. Louis improved its record and returned to the top half of the league standings.

In 1925 the Negro National League instituted a split season with the league champion to be determined by a postseason playoff between the first- and second-half winners. By then, Reese had again become a reserve outfielder, although still a useful one. His performance in an early-season doubleheader led the *St. Louis Argus* to report that Reese "proved that he can still hit, and his throwing arm has returned to form. He played a great game getting two hits in the first game and connecting once in the second contest. So, this gives the Stars much needed reserve strength."[21] The Stars finished second in the first half of the season, then took first-place honors in the second half to set up the league's first postseason playoff against the Kansas City Monarchs. Reese was used as a pinch-runner and defensive replacement in four games as the Stars lost a tightly contested series to the Monarchs, 4 games to 3.

For the 1926 season, the St. Louis lineup was bolstered by the addition of the third future Hall of Famer to its lineup, slugging first baseman Mule Suttles. Reese played only sparingly in 1926, but he took over as the team's manager partway through the season.[22] He then led the Stars to an impressive 40-17-2 record to end the season, but it was only good enough to finish behind the second-half winners, the Kansas City Monarchs.

Despite his successful stint as manager, Reese was not brought back to lead the team in 1927. The 1926 season also effectively marked the end of Reese's career as a player. He apparently appeared in no games in 1927 or 1929, and in only one game in 1928. As a result, he was not a part of the Stars' first league championship in 1928. They easily won the first half of the season before facing the second-half winners, the Chicago American Giants. In a hard-fought nine-game series, the Stars dethroned the two-time defending champions, in the process becoming the only team other than the Giants or the Kansas City Monarchs to win a Negro National League title.[23]

It later turned out that Reese's career with St. Louis was not yet finished after all. Subsequent to a three-year absence, he returned as the team's manager in 1930. Under Reese's leadership the Stars won the season's first half. Reese occasionally inserted himself into the lineup, mostly as a pinch-runner, but in a mid-July contest he played in right field and led off for St. Louis. He went 2-for-4, including a triple, and scored two runs in a win over the Louisville Black Caps.[24] Ahead of an August series with the Nashville Elite Giants, Reese demonstrated his competitive leadership by commenting, "If we can 'take' the champions [i.e. the Monarchs] three straight … why can't we sop up the tailenders."[25] The Detroit Stars, managed by Reese's old Chicago American Giants teammate Bingo DeMoss, won the second half of the season. They faced off in another tight series, which St. Louis won 4 games to 3 by taking the final two games. Reese even got himself back on the playing field as a pinch-runner in the fourth game of the series.[26] The Stars were honored with a parade in St. Louis followed by a banquet at a local YMCA, where Reese was presented with a "St. Louis Stars, World's Champions, 1930" banner.[27]

Reese returned to manage the Stars for the 1931 season. In an early season matchup, the Stars faced the Indianapolis ABCs, a team managed by Reese's former St. Louis teammate and manager, Candy Jim Taylor. In a lead-up to the contest, the *Chicago Defender* recognized Reese as "one of the most astute bosses in the game today," adding, "It is a deep problem to determine what will be the outcome when he matches his wits with those of Jim Taylor, called the second Rube Foster by close followers of the game."[28] In August the *St. Louis Globe-Democrat Sunday Magazine* ran a feature profiling the Stars' success. John "Sparkplug" Reese was described as a "baseball graduate from that most renowned of all Negro baseball clubs – Rube Foster's American Giants of Chicago." The story went on to say that Reese was "a wily field general whose rule of strategy may be confined to a single sentence … 'Sock 'em and keep 'em socked.'"[29]

For the 1931 season, the depleted Negro National League was down to only six teams. Under Reese, the Stars easily won both halves of a shortened season and were declared the league's uncontested champions. But the economic difficulties of the Great Depression brought the 12-year run of the league to a sad end after the 1931 season.[30] The Stars did have a chance to cap off their final season at the beginning of October by winning both games they played against the Max Carey All-Stars, a barnstorming team of current and former major leaguers. Although the All-Stars included future Hall of Famers Bill Terry, Paul Waner, and Lloyd Waner, they did not have much luck against one of the Negro Leagues' best teams. In the first game, the Stars' Ted Trent struck out Paul Waner and Babe Herman twice, and Bill Terry four times.[31] The All-Stars fared even worse in the second game, getting overwhelmed, 18-1.

Although Reese had demonstrated his leadership capabilities in two-plus seasons as the St. Louis manager, it appears that his career in baseball came to an end in 1931, along with the demise of the Negro National League. His post-baseball life is largely a mystery. He gave an Atlantic City address in 1937 when he applied for a Social Security account number.[32] In 1944 he and Freddie Inez Thomas were married in West Palm Beach, Florida.[33] The 1945 Florida State census shows he and his wife living in West Palm Beach,[34] and West Palm Beach was apparently his home for the remainder of his life. He died on October 5, 1966, of undisclosed causes at the Freedman's Hospital in Washington, D.C., and his remains were to be returned to West Palm Beach for burial. In addition to his wife, he was survived by two daughters, Hortense Reese Green and Catherine Reese; a son, John Edward Reese Jr.; six grandchildren; and 12 great-grandchildren.[35]

SOURCES

Unless otherwise indicated, statistics and team records were obtained from the Seamheads Negro Leagues Database (seamheads.com), baseball-reference.com, and retrosheet.org.

NOTES

1   James A. Riley, *The Biographical Encyclopedia of the Negro Baseball Leagues* (New York: Carroll and Graf, 1994), 657.

2   Reese's World War I draft registration card, dated June 5, 1917, lists his birthdate as April 19, 1895, but his Social Security application dated September 1, 1937, lists a birthdate of April 15, 1897.

3   1910 United States Federal Census, accessed from Ancestry.com.

4   *Morris Brown College Catalog, 1917-1918*, 61, Atlanta University Center-Robert W. Woodruff Library, https://radar.auctr.edu/islandora/object/auc.007.catalog%3A1917.01.

5   *Morris Brown College Catalog, 1917-1918*, 50.

6   "Morris Brown Defeats Morehouse," *Savannah Tribune*, April 3, 1915: 1, accessed from the America's Historical Newspapers database.

7   "At Morris Brown," *New York Age*, April 20, 1916: 2, accessed from the America's Historical Newspapers database.

8   World War I draft registration card for John Edward Reese, Precinct 4C, Atlanta, Georgia, June 5, 1917, accessed from Ancestry.com.

9   For more information on the Hilldale Club see Neil Lanctot, *Fair Dealing and Clean Playing: The Hilldale Club and the Development of Black Professional Baseball, 1910-1932* (Jefferson, North Carolina: McFarland, 1994), and Courtney Michelle Smith, *Ed Bolden and Black Baseball in Philadelphia* (Jefferson, North Carolina: McFarland, 2017).

10   "Hilldale Building Strong Team," *Philadelphia Inquirer*, February 20, 1919: 14, accessed from Newspapers.com.

11   For a detailed account of the game, see Bill Nowlin, "The One Time the 'Boston Red Sox' Played a Black Team," *Baseball Research Journal* 50: 1 (Spring 2021): 80-84.

12   "Hilldale and Giants Battle for Title Today," *Philadelphia Inquirer*, September 8, 1919: 13, accessed from Newspapers.com.

13   "Bacharach Giants Crush Hilldale," *Philadelphia Inquirer*, September 9, 1919: 14, accessed from Newspapers.com.

14   1920 United States Federal Census, accessed from Ancestry.com.

15   In addition to the Negro National League (1920-1931), the other six leagues recognized as major leagues were the Eastern Colored League (1923-1928), American Negro League (1929), East-West League (1932), Negro Southern League (1932), Negro National League (1933-1948), and Negro American League (1937-1948).

16   David Wyatt, "Nothing Lacking to Make Giants Great, 'Rube' Has Fine Team by All the Dope," *Chicago Defender*, April 10, 1920: 11.

17   Wyatt.

18   *Chicago Defender*, July 2, 1921: 10.

19   See Donna L. Halper, "June 6, 1921: Bill Gatewood of Detroit Stars throws Negro National League's first no-hitter," SABR Games Project, https://sabr.org/gamesproj/game/june-6-1921-bill-gatewood-of-detroit-stars-throws-negro-national-leagues-first-no-hitter/, accessed December 22, 2021.

20   "Jimmy Lyons Falls Down Elevator Shaft," *Chicago Defender*, July 30, 1921: 11.

21   "St. Louis Stars Win Series from the Memphis Red Sox," *St. Louis Argus*, May 15, 1925: 6, accessed from the Internet Archive (archive.org).

22   Branch Russell started the season as the team's manager and was replaced by Dizzy Dismukes before Reese took over managing duties.

23   See Kevin Johnson, "St. Louis's Forgotten Champions of 1928," Bob Tiemann, ed., *Mound City Memories –Baseball in St. Louis* (Cleveland: SABR, 2007), 41-44.

24   "St. Louis Stars Beat Louisville Black Caps to Sweep Series, 6-0," *St. Louis Globe-Democrat*, July 16, 1930: 18, accessed from Newspapers.com.

25   "Nashville in St. Louis for 5 games," *Chicago Defender*, August 23, 1930: 9.

26   For a detailed account of the 1930 NNL Championship Series, see "St. Louis Wins 1930 Series in Seven Games," in Robert L. Tiemann, ed., *St. Louis's Favorite Sport* (St. Louis: SABR, 1992), 48-51.

27   "St. Louis Ball Fans Fete Flag Winning Stars," *Chicago Defender*, October 11, 1930: 9

28   "A.B.C.'s Return Home for Opening Game with St. Louis Stars Friday Night, June 26," *Chicago Defender*, June 27, 1931: 8.

29   "The St. Louis Stars Are the World's Champion Negro Baseball Team," *St. Louis Globe-Democrat Sunday Magazine*, July 26, 1931: 8, accessed from Newspapers.com.

30   After a one-year absence, a second Negro National League was organized in 1933, mostly with teams that were not part of the first Negro National League.

31   "Trent Fans Bill Terry Four Times," *Chicago Defender*, October 10, 1931: 8.

32   US Social Security Act Account Number Application for John Edward Reese, September 1, 1937.

33   State of Florida Bureau of Vital Statistics Marriage License for John Edward Reese and Freddie Inez Thomas, West Palm Beach Florida, February 16, 1944.

34   Florida State Population Census, 1945, West Palm Beach, accessed from MyHeritage. Library Edition.

35   John E. Reese obituary, *Washington Evening Star*, October 6, 1966: 31: B-7, accessed from Genealogybank.com.

ARVELL "BILL" RIGGINS

BY KEVIN LARKIN AND FREDERICK C. BUSH

Arvell "Bill" Riggins, a shortstop-third baseman who played from 1920 to 1935, was an under-appreciated player whose professional career began at the same time as the first Negro National League.[1] Riggins hit for a solid .292 average over the course of his career in Black baseball's major leagues but has remained less well known than some of his peers because he toiled primarily for squads that were not of championship caliber. Despite his teams' lack of success at reaching the playoffs, the infielder made a name for himself in the Midwest, where he played seven years with the Detroit Stars, before moving East and splitting the latter part of his career between three New York-area teams.

Arvell Riggins was born in the area around the future town of Colp, Illinois, on February 7, 1900, to Daniel and Ida (Miller) Riggins. Colp, founded in 1901, was named after farmer-turned-mine-owner John Colp and is in the formerly coal-rich area of Williamson County in Southern Illinois. Colp sold his mine to the Madison Coal Corporation in 1906 and the new owners named the area around the mine No. 9.[2] Although Colp and No. 9 existed side by side, distinct boundaries were drawn. According to Ron Kirby, a former Colp resident who worked to preserve the area's history, "In defining areas, we spoke of the village of Colp, as the 'white camp,' which were streets outside of the incorporated town where whites only lived; the 'black camp,' signifying No. 9; and the 'yellow camp,' which was geographically on the

highway to Herrin and identified by the yellow company houses."[3]

Riggins may have lived in nearby Dewmaine, a village several miles to the south that had been founded in 1899 and is now a ghost town, as there is some question regarding which settlement was his true birthplace.[4] The name Dewmaine was inspired by two names from the Spanish-American War in 1898: the *USS Maine*, the ship that exploded and accelerated the onset of the conflict, and Commodore George Dewey, the American hero of the Battle of Manila Bay.

In addition to its colorful name, Dewmaine had an equally interesting origin. Samuel T. Brush, general manager of the St. Louis and Big Muddy Coal Company in nearby Carterville, brought the first Black miners to the area to break a strike by White union miners in May 1898, just three weeks after the Battle of Manila Bay. The union laborers returned to work in July but went on strike again in May 1899. Brush brought additional Black workers to Dewmaine, which resulted in violence. One woman died when the new workers' train was fired upon, and another five Black men were killed at the Carterville train station.[5] Brush, like John Colp, sold out to the Madison Coal Company in 1906, and his mine in Dewmaine became known as the No. 8.[6]

It is possible that Arvell's father, Daniel Riggins, had been among the first group of Black miners to arrive in the area in 1898. Daniel and Ida Miller were wed in Williamson County on May 4, 1899, and the couple embarked upon married life and started a family amid the violent events precipitated by the early union unrest among the area's coal mines.[7]

When Arvell Riggins registered for the World War I draft in September 1918, he listed the Madison Coal Company as his employer. In 1920, baseball became his escape route from a life in the mines, an unhealthy occupation that would not have been available to him much longer in any case, as the No. 8 mine ceased operation in 1923 and the No. 9 closed in 1930.[8]

At the time of the 1920 census, Riggins was already married to Jeanette "Jennie" Jefferson, and the couple was living with Jennie's family in Colp. The exact date of their marriage is unknown, though the year 1919 is most likely. Their first child – Arvell Jr. – was born on July 21, 1920, in Colp.[9] Young "Baby" Riggins's photograph was featured in the *Chicago Defender's* June 18, 1921, edition to accompany an article about the Detroit Stars' June 12 doubleheader sweep of the Columbus Buckeyes. Jennie and Arvell Jr. had

Arvell Riggins at the outset of a 14-year career in the Negro Leagues during which he played on seven different teams and finished with a lifetime .292 batting average in league play.

(Courtesy of the Ronald W. Kirby Special Collection in the Morris Library, Southern Illinois University, Carbondale, Illinois)

attended the games at Detroit's Mack Park that day and the *Defender* claimed that "[t]he youngster took good pains to applaud his daddy when he singled" in the first game.[10] The couple eventually welcomed two more sons into the family, William (b. 1922) and Lonnie (1924).

Riggins had embarked upon his professional baseball career in March 1920, just four months before his first son's birth. It is unknown whether Riggins honed his skills on a school team, company team, or simply on the sandlots, but Rube Foster discovered him and assigned him to his Chicago American Giants squad of the new Negro National League to start the 1920 season.[11] The 5-foot-8, 160-pound Riggins, a switch-hitter who threw right-handed, played in only three league games for Chicago before being reassigned to the Detroit Stars. He became Detroit's starting shortstop and batted .275 in 59 games for owner Tenny Blount's team, which finished in second place, eight games behind Chicago. Riggins's performance during the regular season earned him the honor of joining the St. Louis Giants in a postseason series against teams of White major-league all-stars. He went 1-for-8 at the plate in two games played.

In December 1920 Riggins and outfielder Judy Gans were officially traded to the Detroit Stars in exchange for outfielder Jimmie Lyons.[12] Thus, Riggins returned as Detroit's shortstop in 1921 and appeared in 80 of the Stars' 85 games against fellow Negro major-league teams. His hitting improved significantly as he raised his batting average 30 points to .305 and posted a .351 on-base percentage. Detroit finished the season with a 38-46-1 record that included a 30-33-1 ledger in NNL play, which put them in fifth place, 12½ games behind the champion Chicago American Giants.

If there was a knock against Riggins at this point in his career, it involved his fielding. He committed a whopping 48 errors in 75 games at shortstop, and his .883 fielding percentage was below the league average of .907. Events in a 3-2 loss to Hilldale at Razzberry Park in Camden, New Jersey, on September 7 were typical of Riggins's misadventures in the field. Detroit led, 2-1, entering the ninth inning, but Riggins "paved the way for the Hilldale triumph by permitting [Connie] Rector's weak grounder to go through his legs after [Otto] Briggs and [Phil] Cockrell had been retired."[13] Although Stars reliever Bill Holland issued two bases-loaded walks that resulted in Hilldale's game-tying and winning tallies, Riggins's error had made the tough loss possible.

Nonetheless, Riggins was one of the NNL's noteworthy performers as was evidenced by the fact that he again appeared in the postseason, albeit in only a single game. This time, he played for the New York Lincoln Giants against the Bears, a team of White semipros led by former New York Giants pitcher Jeff Tesreau, who stymied Riggins into a 0-for-4 appearance with the bat. In the field, Riggins registered three putouts and three assists, but as was often the case, he also made an error.

In 1922 Riggins appeared in 81 games at shortstop for Detroit. His defense improved dramatically as he cut down his number of errors to 33, and his .922 fielding percentage was above the league average of .915. As fate would have it, however, his offense declined accordingly. Riggins hit only .247 for the season, 58 points less than in the previous season. In Detroit's first season under new manager Bruce Petway (Pete Hill had skippered the team from 1919 to 1921) the Stars improved to a 50-34-1 record. The team was 42-31-1 in NNL play, which was still only good enough for fourth place, but it had closed the gap considerably; the Stars finished only 2½ games behind first-place Chicago.

Riggins once again played in the postseason as he joined the St. Louis Stars for a three-game series against the American League's Detroit Tigers, managed by Bobby Veach. St. Louis won two games against the Tigers, who were without the services of Ty Cobb and Harry Heilmann. Riggins started all three contests at shortstop but had just one hit in nine at-bats and made two errors.

In 1923 Riggins put his offense and defense together and had his all-around breakout season for Detroit. He appeared in 71 games at shortstop during the NNL season and fielded his position at a .923 clip. (The league average was .918.) Although he made 36 errors, his fielding percentage now showed that number to be an indicator of his great range – rather than a shaky glove – as increased chances meant the increased possibility of errors. At the plate, Riggins batted .302 (80-for-265) and had a .379 on-base percentage; he scored 59 runs and drove in 43. The Stars finished the NNL season with a 39-27 record (41-30 overall) but were relegated to a third-place finish behind the league's two powerhouses, the first-place Kansas City Monarchs and the Chicago American Giants.

Riggins remained a member of the Stars as Detroit played a three-game series against the American League's St. Louis Browns in October. The Stars once again captured two of three games against a team of White major-leaguers, taking the first two games by identical 7-6 scores before losing the third game, 11-8. Riggins' postseason struggles continued as he managed only a 1-for-12 batting line (.083) in the three games.[14]

Riggins, who had blossomed into a star, continued to ply his trade at shortstop for Detroit for three more years, from 1924 through 1926. He posted batting averages of .305, .267, and .300 during those seasons, and his fielding remained steady. Although Riggins's batting average was subpar by his standards in 1925, he was still an offensive force and stole 26 bases, which placed him second in the league behind Cool Papa Bell, who stole 30 bags for St. Louis.

In both 1925 and 1926, the Stars played a 100-game NNL schedule, an unusually high number of league games for a Negro League squad, and Riggins played 94 and 91 games respectively. Although Detroit continued to be an above-average team, the Stars finished in third place in the NNL in 1924 with a 35-28-1 mark and then placed fourth in each of the next two seasons with records of 56-44 (1925) and 52-47-1 (1926).

Besides appearing in 91 games as shortstop of the Detroit Stars in 1926, Riggins also assumed the managerial reins from Petway and guided the team to a 44-34-1 record before being replaced by Candy Jim Taylor, who had skippered the Cleveland Elites for most of the season. The Stars had fared better under Riggins: Taylor led the team to an 8-13 ledger. Detroit finished a distant fourth, 16½ games behind the Kansas City Monarchs.

On March 8, 1927, in a surprising move, Detroit traded the veteran Riggins to the NNL's newest team, the Cleveland Hornets, for first baseman Stack Martin and 22-year-old shortstop Halley Harding.[15] Prior to a game against the Black Barons in early May, the *Birmingham News* raved that Riggins was "rated as one of the greatest negro shortstops in the country. He is a great fielder, bats in clean-up position and is fast on the bases."[16]

The Cleveland team did not lack for hitting, with Riggins batting a career-high .341, left fielder Tack Summers hitting .355, right fielder Ernest Duff coming in at .318, and first baseman Edgar Wesley knocking the cover off the ball at a .424 clip. The pitching staff, however, was another story. The leading winners on the staff, Square Moore and Slim Branham, had a mere two victories apiece. Moore, Branham, and Howard Ross all had ERAs north of 6.00, while Frank Stephens barely missed joining the three with his 5.93 mark. However, Percy Miller outdid them all with a 9.33

ERA over 45⅓ innings pitched, though he somehow managed to escape with a 1-2 record. Oddly, Nelson Dean, who led the staff with 65⅓ innings pitched and had a 3.44 ERA (119 ERA+) was saddled with the worst record at 1-9. In the end, the Hornets fared as well as most expansion franchises do, especially with such wretched pitching, and finished the season with a 13-36 record (14-38 overall) that placed them seventh in the NNL, ahead of only the Memphis Red Sox, who finished at 25-69-3.

By August, Riggins had escaped the purgatory called Cleveland and was playing for owner Cumberland Posey's independent Homestead Grays in Pittsburgh. He manned third base for a mere six games but continued to swing a hot bat as he hit .318 (7-for-22) in his limited appearances. Riggins moved back to his familiar position of shortstop for a series against a team of White major leaguers that was managed by Earle Mack and featured Heilmann and fellow future Hall of Famer Heinie Manush. The Grays won two

Arvell (Orville) Riggins Jr. was ready to follow in his father's footsteps until Riggins Sr. chose not only a new team but also a new family in New York City in 1928.

(Courtesy of the Ronald W. Kirby Special Collection in the Morris Library, Southern Illinois University, Carbondale, Illinois)

of six games from the major leaguers while Riggins played in only two of the contests and went 2-for-7.

The 1928 season found Riggins with the New York Lincoln Giants – the team for which he had played a single game against a White semipro aggregation seven years earlier – as the team's starting third baseman. In announcing Riggins's acquisition, the *Chicago Defender* extolled him as "one of the best hot corner guardians in the business."[17] The New York Lincoln Giants were members of the Eastern Colored League in 1928 and were managed by future Hall of Fame shortstop John Henry "Pop" Lloyd. Riggins appeared in 33 games, batted .270, and fielded his position at a .949 clip (the league average was .907), making only five errors. Although the Lincoln Giants' overall .533 winning percentage (21-17-2) was the best of the ECL's five teams, the team's 9-7-1 record and .563 winning percentage in league games put them in third place behind the first-place Atlantic City Bacharach Giants and second-place Baltimore Black Sox.

Lloyd was still in the manager's seat in 1929 although, after the demise of the ECL, the Lincoln Giants were now a member team of the American Negro League. Riggins again manned the hot corner, though he occasionally played second base, and posted a career-high .344 batting average with a .444 on-base percentage in 66 games played. The Lincoln Giants had a fine season, posting a 40-26-2 league record (45-28-2 overall), but finished in second place, eight games behind the Baltimore Black Sox.

In 1930 Riggins returned for one final season with the Lincoln Giants squad that was now an independent club. He continued to flourish under Lloyd's tutelage and batted .343 for the season, only one point lower than the previous year, as the team's starting third baseman. The powerful Lincoln Giants finished with a 41-14-1 record. Although there was no league in the East that year, only the Homestead Grays finished with a better mark of 45-15-1 among the top independent clubs.

Although Riggins found steady employment with the Lincoln Giants from 1928 to 1930, his personal affairs were on shaky ground. Jennie and Arvell Jr. continued to live in the Detroit area while young William and Lonnie resided with their maternal grandparents, William and Lizzie Jefferson, back in Colp. In the meantime, Riggins abandoned the family that he had started with Jennie and apparently married a woman named Marion Carter in New York in 1929.[18]

According to the 1930 US Census, Riggins (whose first name was misspelled as "Arnell") and Marion were residing at the family home of his new brother-in-law, John L. Carter, in Manhattan. Riggins listed his occupation as manager of a baseball club, even though Lloyd was the skipper of the Lincoln Giants at that time. He also gave his age at the time of his first marriage as 29, which indicates that he claimed his betrothal to Carter was his first marriage, and he claimed that he had been born in Missouri, not Illinois. The misinformation Riggins provided for the census was due to the fact that he was guilty of bigamy when he married Marion Carter and clearly was trying to conceal his first marriage from either his new in-laws, the authorities, or both.

The fate of Riggins's second marriage is unknown, since no record has been found to indicate whether the couple divorced or that Marion died at a young age. The only certainty is that Marion was gone from Riggins's life by the time he registered for the World War II draft in 1942, and he was living in Manhattan with another woman who may or may not have been his third wife.

Amid Riggins's personal intrigue, the Lincoln Giants folded and were replaced in New York City by the Harlem Stars. Riggins was a member of the team but, for the most part, the Stars were such in name only. In mid-July, the *New York Age* reported:

> "The experiment of having Negro teams play at the big-league baseball parks (the Yankee Stadium and the Polo Grounds) when the home team is away, has not met with the success its promoters had hoped for and will be abandoned before the present season is out. ...

> "Bill Robinson's Harlem Stars was the team used in this experiment, and it is problematic whether they will complete the season. At any rate, the owner of the Lincoln Giants, James J. Keenan, plans to return to the semi-pro baseball field with another colored team for the Catholic Protectory Oval next season, and hopes to reclaim many of his old players, now with the Harlem Stars."[19]

The *Age* identified three problems that had contributed to low attendance, and which presaged the demise of the club: Manager Pop Lloyd "was only able to get together [a] mediocre team on so short notice," the price of admission was too high, and the publicity that past Black teams, like the Lincoln Giants, had "received in former years in the daily press [had] not been given."[20]

(Courtesy Noir-Tech Research, Inc.)

Arvell "Bill" Riggins, pictured here in a Detroit Stars uniform, started his professional career with the American Giants in 1920 but was soon reassigned to Detroit, where he spent seven years as the starting shortstop.

As the Stars attempted to complete the 1931 season, the squad became financially strapped even more by events surrounding an August 16 doubleheader against Hilldale that was held at Yankee Stadium to benefit the Brotherhood of Sleeping Car Porters. According to the *Age*, both the *New York Amsterdam News*, whose "Sports Dean" Romeo L. Dougherty promoted the event, and the Brotherhood failed to pay the Stars or the umpires, although the Hilldale team was paid its share of money from the gate receipts and the Brotherhood was alleged to have received over $400 as well. The *Age* asserted that "benefit performances are becoming a racket in Harlem."[21] Dougherty had already addressed the fiasco three days earlier in his weekly column. Although he claimed, "I make no charge in the matter against anyone," he then assigned blame to the co-promoters of the event when he asserted, "I have carefully studied the situation and found that too many cooks usually spoil the soup and that is what happened on [this] occasion."[22] In the end, while the *Age's* accusations may have been extreme, they were not entirely unwarranted, and the double-header fiasco contributed to the financial instability of the Harlem Stars franchise.

The Stars managed to play a mere 18 games against other prominent Black teams in the East, and had a 6-12 record. Riggins started all 18 games, including 14 at second base and four at shortstop. His batting average dropped precipitously from the .344 and .343 marks of the previous two seasons to .239 as he managed only 16 hits and drew seven walks in the 18 games. Riggins's days as a major contributor to top-caliber Black ballclubs were at an end, though he continued to play occasionally for the New York Black Yankees, the team that rose out of the ashes of the Harlem Stars in 1932.

In 1932 Riggins appeared in only seven games against major-league-caliber competition – six at third base and one as a pinch-hitter – for the independent Black Yankees. One of the games was a highlight of the Black Yankees' season, on August 29 at Pittsburgh's Greenlee Field. It was rare for a Negro League team to have its own ballpark, and Gus Greenlee and his Crawfords team had just held a grand dedication and played an exhibition game on their new grounds. The New Yorkers were the first Black major-league team to face the Crawfords, and the two teams dueled in splendid style as Satchel Paige and the Black Yankees' Jesse Hubbard kept zeroes on the scoreboard until the top of the ninth inning. Riggins

Marker on Dewmaine School Road commemorating native son Arvell "Bill" Riggins, who began 1920 with the American Giants but spent the best years of his career with the NNL's Detroit Stars.

hit a one-out single in the final frame but was not to be the hero on this day as he was forced at second on Ted Page's fielder's choice. Page stole second, advanced to third on catcher Bill Perkins's wild throw, and then scored the game's only run when Clint Thomas singled.[23] For the season, Riggins batted .278 (5-for-18) but drew more walks (6) than he had hits (5) in his limited time with the squad, which finished with a 17-14-1 record against its fellow independent Black teams.

After a two-year hiatus, Riggins returned to the Black Yankees for five games during the 1935 season. His name still carried enough clout that he was named as one of "the well-known colored stars that [would] appear" in a June 23 game against the semipro Bay Parkways at Erasmus Field.[24] In five games against fellow Black professional teams, Riggins batted .231 before calling an end to his career as a ballplayer.

Over the course of his 14 years in the Negro Leagues, Riggins had a .292 career batting average and a .359 on-base percentage. His career 96 OPS+ denotes him as a slightly below-average batter, although in some of his better seasons he certainly had been among the top hitters in his league. In his *Historical Baseball Abstract*, Bill James summed up Riggins as a "good switch hitter and a good shortstop, but a heavy drinker."[25] Although James used the designation "good" rather than "great," Riggins was nonetheless a player of note in the early days of the Negro major leagues and, as such, his services were in demand elsewhere as well.

Riggins, like many ballplayers of his era, also played several seasons of winter-league ball. Early in his career he ventured west to participate in the California Winter League, which was the only integrated baseball league at that time. The 1922-23 season marked Riggins's first stint in the Golden State, during which he played for the St. Louis All-Stars. He returned for the next two seasons and continued to play for the St. Louis teams (Stars in 1923-24 and Giants in 1924-25). After playing elsewhere for a few winters, Riggins joined the Nashville Elite Giants for one final winter in California, in 1930-31. In four seasons out West, Riggins batted .321 (87-for-271) in 72 games.[26] It is likely that Riggins played in far more than those 72 games, however, as the California Winter League did not receive widespread press coverage during the early 1920s.

Riggins spent additional winters plying his trade in the Cuban Winter League, which was renowned for its ardent fans and stiff competition. In three seasons on the island, he played for Habana (1924-25),

Almendares (1928-29), and Santa Clara (1929-30). Riggins batted .301 (80-for-266) and led the league with nine triples in the 1928-29 season.[27] As was the case with the Negro League squads on which he played, Riggins never won a championship; each of his Cuban teams finished in second place.[28]

Riggins remained in New York after his playing days ended, but little is known about his post-baseball years. He registered for the World War II draft in February 1942, at which time he was employed as a longshoreman and listed Iver Mae Moore (the 48-year-old widow of a man named John Moore) as his contact person.

Riggins died on March 8, 1943, in the home he shared with Moore at 53 West 135th Street in Manhattan. He was 43 years old and died of multiple heart-related ailments, including hypertension, coronary thrombosis, and chronic myocarditis. His death certificate listed Moore, who provided all personal information for the document, as his wife. A close inspection of her signature on the document, however, shows that she began to sign her last name with the letter "M" but then wrote "Riggins" over it, casting doubt on whether the couple was married. Moore had Riggins buried in Beverly Hills Cemetery in Putnam Valley, New York, northeast of New York City. In addition to Moore, Riggins was survived by his mother, Ida; his first wife, Jennie; and at least two of their sons, Arvell (Orville) Jr. and William.

Ida Reed, his mother, had remarried after her divorce from Arvell's father, Dan, and died in Chicago in 1947. (Dan had also remarried and had died on March 31, 1942, just one year earlier than his only son.) Jennie Riggins, on the other hand, never remarried and died in Detroit in 1981. Arvell Jr. served in the US Army during World War II and lived to the age of 90; he died in Detroit on November 30, 2010. William Riggins inherited his father's athleticism, and he and his cousin, James Miller (from Ida's side of the family), helped to lead Colp's Herrin Township High School basketball team to the 1941 championship of the Southern Illinois Conference of Colored High Schools.[29] William married a woman named Dorothy Mitchell in 1947 and settled in the Detroit area as well. No information about the life of Arvell and Jennie's third son, Lonnie, is currently known. Also unknown is the fate of Riggins's second wife, Marion Carter, and there is no record that she and Arvell ever had any children.

Although Riggins had a checkered personal life, he had gained a degree of fame as a baseball player in the early years of the first Negro National League. In July 2013 a committee from Colp announced plans to erect a plaque in Riggins's honor on Dewmaine School Road.[30] The idea came to fruition, and Riggins shares the "Hometown Heroes" plaque with fellow Colp native Jimmy Springs, who was inducted into the Vocal Groups Hall of Fame in 2007.

ACKNOWLEDGMENTS

Gratitude is extended to SABR member Dr. Frank Houdek, Emeritus Professor of Law at Southern Illinois University in Carbondale, for the research material he obtained from the Ronald W. Kirby Special Collection at SIU's Morris Library and for traveling to the Colp-No. 9-Dewmaine area to take photos of the plaque that is dedicated, in part, to Arvell Riggins.

Negro League researcher Gary Ashwill has two posts about Riggins on his Agate Type website – "Who was Orville Riggins (May 23, 2007) and "'Baby' Riggins and his dad" (February 8, 2011) – that provided the foundation and direction for further research into events in Riggins's life.

SOURCES

Ancestry.com was consulted for US Census information and military draft registration records, as well as birth, marriage, and death records.

Except where otherwise indicated, all player statistics and team records were taken from Seamheads.com.

NOTES

1   Riggins usually signed his name as Arvell, but several sources spell it Orville. Additionally, Riggins sometimes used the name William or the shortened version, Bill. Riggins' first father-in-law (Jennie's father) was named William and Riggins gave his second-born son that name, but no evidence has come to light to explain why he also used the name for himself at times: However, in the latter part of his career, he became well-known in newspaper articles as Bill Riggins.

2   Mary Beth Roderick, "Colp & No. 9: A Few Miles and a Different Future," *Carbondale* (Illinois) *Southern Illinoisan*, November 20, 2011: 9A-10A.

3   Roderick, "Colp & No. 9."

4   Arvell Riggins listed Colp as his birthplace on his World War I draft registration card in 1918 but gave Dewmaine as his birthplace on his World War II draft card in 1942.

5   "Dewmaine History," Williamson County Illinois Historical Society, https://www.wcihs.org/history/dewmaine-history/, accessed September 25, 2021.

6   Mary Beth Roderick, "Ghost Town: The Rise and Fall of Dewmaine," *Southern Illinoisan*, November 20, 2011: 4A (article begins on 1A).

7   Daniel Riggins was born in Atlanta, Georgia, in 1870. Most of the Black miners brought to Williamson County were from Tennessee, but Riggins obviously could have made his way from Georgia to Illinois via Tennessee. Ida Miller was born in Kentucky, but her family moved to Tennessee and later settled in Colp. It is unknown whether Riggins and Miller knew each other in Tennessee already or met for the first time in Williamson County.

8   Roderick, "Colp & No. 9"; Roderick, "Ghost Town."

9   As was the case with his father, Arvell Jr.'s name had variant spellings. He often signed his name as Arvill (with an "i" rather than an "e") and later used Orville. His official World War II Army enlistment records have the name Orvill (without the "e").

10   "Baby Riggins Sees Detroit Cop 2 Games/Watches Father Perform as Shortstop and Applauds When 'Dad' Singles," *Chicago Defender*, June 18, 1921: 11.

11   "'Rube' Assigns Players to Giants," *Chicago Defender*, March 20, 1920: 9. This article gives Riggins's first name as Orville.

12   "Jimmy [*sic*] Lyons Comes to American Giants," *Chicago Defender*, December 11, 1920: 6.

13   Frank H. Ryan, "Hilldale Wins in Ninth: Pinch Pitcher Forces Home Tying and Winning Runs," *Camden* (New Jersey) *Courier Post*, September 8, 1921: 19.

14   "Browns Lose Again in Ninth," *Detroit Free Press*, October 9, 1923: 24; "Browns Again Fall to Stars," *Detroit Free Press*, October 10, 1923: 15; "Browns Check Stars in Final," *Detroit Free Press*, October 11, 1923: 19.

15   "Cleveland Gets Riggins; Detroit Martin, Harding," *Chicago Defender*, March 12, 1927: 8.

16   "Cleveland to Battle Black Barons Monday," *Birmingham News*, May 1, 1927: 20.

17   "Riggins Now with Lincoln Giants Club," *Chicago Defender*, March 31, 1928: 9.

18   Gwendolyn Young, Arvell (Orville) Riggins Jr.'s daughter, wrote two letters to Ronald W. Kirby (who was researching the history of his native town of Colp) that bear out the fact that Arvell Riggins Sr. abandoned his family. In a letter dated November 18, 2015, Young wrote, "[…] apparently Orville (Arvell) Sr. deserted the family by 1930 once he started playing ball in New York." In a second, undated letter, she wrote, "My dad loved baseball, but he didn't have much respect for Orville Sr. because he deserted the family and was a 'dead beat' [*sic*] dad." (Both letters are contained in the Ronald W. Kirby Special Collection at Southern Illinois University's Morris Library).

19   William E. Clark, "Playing of Negro Baseball Teams in Big League Parks Has Not Met with Success and Will Be Ended," *New York Age*, July 18, 1931: 6.

20   Clark.

21   "Benefit Rackets," *New York Age*, August 22, 1931: 6. See also, "But 3,000 Attend Benefit Games at Yankee Stadium," *New York Age*, August 22, 1931: 6.

22   Romeo L. Dougherty, "In the Sports Whirl: When Is a Benefit Not a Benefit?" *New York Amsterdam News*, August 19, 1931: 12.

23   "Hubbard Pitches Three Hit Game to Beat Paige, 1-0," *Pittsburgh Courier*, May 7, 1932: 15.

24   "Black Yanks Meet 'Parks': Stage Set for Great Clash Between Rival Nines on Sunday," *New York Amsterdam News*, June 22, 1935: 16.

25   Bill James, *The New Bill James Historical Baseball Abstract: The Classic – Completely Revised* (New York: Free Press, 2001), 187.

26   William F. McNeil, *The California Winter League: America's First Integrated Professional Baseball League* (Jefferson, North Carolina: McFarland & Company Inc, 2002), 260.

27   Jorge S. Figueredo, *Who's Who in Cuban Baseball, 1878-1961* (Jefferson, North Carolina: McFarland & Company, Inc., 2003), 358. This book erroneously lists Riggins as playing with Almendares during the 1924-25 season; Figueredo's second volume about Cuban baseball (see Note 28) gives the correct team as Habana.

28   Jorge S. Figueredo, *Cuban Baseball: A Statistical History, 1878-1961* (Jefferson, North Carolina: McFarland & Company, Inc., 2003), 158, 178, 182.

29   "Herrin Township at Colp 'Tigers,'" http://www.illinoishs-glorydays.com/id567.html, accessed October 17, 2021.

30   Bucky Dent, "Colp Negro League Star to Get Honor," *Southern Illinoisan*, July 8, 2013: 1.

CRISTOBAL TORRIENTE

BY PETER C. BJARKMAN

"I think I was playing third base at the time, and he hit a ground ball by me.... It dug a hole about a foot deep on its way to left field. ... In those days Torriente was a hell of a ballplayer. Christ, I'd like to whitewash him and bring him up."

Frankie Frisch (quoted by John B. Holway, *Blackball Stars*)

The legends and hyperbole – like Frankie Frisch's report of a batted ball excavating the infield turf – repeatedly trump the solid factual evidence emerging from much of Cuba's prehistoric era during the final two nineteenth-century decades and initial two twentieth-century decades. We possess the all-too-alluring images provided by fading sepia photographic portraits and dog-eared collectible tobacco cards. There are indeed substantial collections of sketchy box scores and skeletal line scores provided by chroniclers like Severo Nieto and Raúl Diez Muro – as notable for their inconsistencies and glaring inaccuracies as for any substantial record of dimly remembered turn-of-the-century winter-season pennant races. Holes are sometimes only partially filled by enthusiastic contemporary journalistic reports that are (as was the tenor of the times) far more celebratory than anything else. In the end the frustration is always that – in the words of American songstress Kate Wolf – "the picture on the cover doesn't match the one inside."

Modern-era researchers haven't provided all that much to improve the picture. Tampa-based Jorge Figueredo (a sports journalist in Cuba before the 1959 revolution) has done the most to fill in gaps in our knowledge with his detailed statistical summaries and efforts at narrative chronicles for the turbulent decades that comprised Cuba's professional-winter-league saga.[1] But when it comes to resurrecting individual ballplayers, the best of our chroniclers have too often settled for sometimes outlandish fables gleaned from octogenarian stars of the past invested in turning their own careers and those of rivals into the heady stuff of pure folklore. John B. Holway (*Blackball Stars*) repeats legends of Torriente line drives digging two-foot holes in infield turf, or of Martin Dihigo outdoing a *cesto*-using jai alai player with his throws from home caroming off the center-field wall, and of Mule Suttles smashing a 600-plus-foot homer into the wind in Havana's La Tropical ballpark. James Riley (*The Biographical Encyclopedia of the Negro Baseball Leagues*) cannot resist echoing reports that José Méndez once killed a teammate in practice with an errant fastball to the chest, or repeating the oft-quoted lines of Indianapolis manager C.I. Taylor that "If I should see Torriente walking up the other side of the street, I would say, 'There walks a ball club.'" Enticing testimonials, but in the end a bit too reminiscent of tales of Josh Gibson home runs struck in Pittsburgh and landing in New York, or of Cool Papa

Center fielder Cristóbal Torriente, a career .343 hitter, and a star pitcher in the Negro Leagues, is a member of both the Cuban Baseball Hall of Fame and National Baseball Hall of Fame.

(Courtesy Noir-Tech Research, Inc.)

Bell snapping a light switch and landing in bed before the electricity dimmed.

Of the three greatest Blackball-era Cuban icons, Martin Dihigo owns the most substantial legacy, due in part to his well-documented performances both in Mexico and in the United States with the Alex Pompez Cuban Stars. But mostly Dihigo benefited from the fact that the bulk of his long career fell in the better-documented winter and summer Cuban, Mexican League, and Negro League seasons of the 1930s and 1940s. José Méndez stands on the thinnest ground, suffering from an injury-shortened career that restricted his greatest achievements as a pitcher to little more than a single decade in which the bulk of his heroics came in an "American Season" limited to exhibition barnstorming games. Slugger Cristóbal Torriente boasts a greater North American Negro League legacy than Méndez as far as we can tell, but little of the Torriente story can today be documented with much certainty. The highlight North American years for Torriente came at outset of Rube Foster's Negro National League when the Cuban slugger paced the Chicago American Giants to three initial league pennants while reportedly batting .411, .338, and .342.[2] But much of his career was a vagabond journey with a dozen different clubs that was plagued by a penchant for nightlife and excessive drinking and was marked by several personal disputes with club managements that cut short a stopover with the Western Cuban Stars in 1916 and also saw him abandoning the Kansas City Monarchs a decade later after a dispute over some stolen jewelry.[3]

THE BURIED LEGACY OF CUBA'S GREATEST SLUGGER

If there are troubling inconsistencies attached to Torriente's North American Negro League statistics or occasional conflicting reports in slim existing narratives covering his on-field prowess, worse still is the fact that next to nothing is known about Torriente away from the baseball diamond – a gapping void that clouds his legacy still further. Biographical data boils down to a mere handful of consistently reported facts. He was born on November 16, 1893, in the seaport city of Cienfuegos. (One undocumented source suggests the location was a rundown house at 17 Hernan Cortés Street.) He died 44 years later in a pauper hospital in New York, only a half-dozen years after his playing career dissipated with the Atlanta Black Crackers and Cleveland Cubs in the summer of 1932. There are also suggestions that before fading into total obscurity in

New York the hard-luck athlete had resided at least briefly in Ybor City, Florida (a Tampa district), and also that (as reported by Holway among others) fellow Cuban stars Rodolfo Fernández and Martin Dihigo had found him in "poor circumstances" in Chicago sometime in the mid-'30s. Holway reports that it was in fact Dihigo who relocated Torriente to New York for his final years of poverty and illness. We have no information regarding parents or siblings, and no clues about childhood years in Cienfuegos – except for a single undocumented report by Holway that the future ballplayer had joined the army at age 17 and "was assigned to the artillery because he was husky enough to hoist the heavy artillery pieces onto the mules."[4]

About the origins of baseball activities we know only slightly more, although the record is hardly complete. His career was launched as a 17-year-old southpaw pitcher and part-time outfielder with the local Yara Club that claimed a juvenile district amateur championship in 1910. He moved on two years later to a semipro Cienfuegos team for which– like the North American Bambino to whom he would so often be compared in the future – his heavy hitting caused abandonment of pitching assignments and solidified his role as a cleanup slugger and outfielder. At age 20 he entered the island's top professional circuit, debuting on January 5, 1930, with the Habana Reds and hitting .265 in 28 rookie-season games. A year later he moved over to the Almendares Blues, for whom he would perform for five seasons (excluding two winters when he apparently remained in the States throughout the winter months and skipped games in his homeland). After Almendares he returned to the Havana Reds for the bulk of an extended Cuban League career stretching through 1927. His two full decades with stateside Negro League clubs opened with Tinti Molina's Western Cuban Stars (1913-1916), peaked with seven seasons (1919-1925) starring on Rube Foster's Chicago American Giants, and included stopovers with nearly a dozen other clubs, although none of those additional sojourns lasted more than a year or two.

The key source for much of the Torriente legend – or at least the mainstream popularity of that legend – can be traced directly to the writings of John Holway. Holway focuses his laudatory account on a single game at the heart of a much celebrated 1920 "American Season" Havana tour by John McGraw's National League New York Giants, a barnstorming event most famed for the single appearance on the island of the legendary Babe Ruth. Ruth – perhaps intent more on the attractions of Havana night life than any serious offseason slugging – had a rough time against Cuban competition right from the start. He smacked both a single and triple in the opening game with the Havana Reds, yet was struck out three consecutive times by cup-of-coffee Cuban big leaguer José Acosta in the second contest of the series.

But it was the third memorable outing, against Almendares on November 5, 1920, that would find a permanent spot in winter-baseball lore. That was the game in which the muscular local favorite Torriente would smack three towering homers and thus provide heroics seemingly more Ruthian than anything offered by the original Babe himself. Holway is elaborate in his descriptions, stressing the trench-digging groundball that almost cost Frankie Frisch a leg at third base, describing how "the Bambino frowned incredulously" when the Cuban slid into second after his soil-excavating hot liner, and then describing the three Torriente round-trippers as prodigious smashes clearing the left-center-field fence. Ignored or at least discounted was the fact that the Giants "batting practice" hurler that day was not a regular big-league twirler but instead first baseman George "High Pockets" Kelly. Also missing in Holway's narrative are the contemporary press accounts that tell a very different story about that afternoon's ballpark histrionics.

Both a substantial North American Negro Leagues career mostly with the Chicago American Giants, and a respectable tenure in the Cuban League have too long been altogether overshadowed (as underscored by Torriente's bronze Cooperstown plaque) by the amplified accounts of that single afternoon in spacious Almendares Park. Three homers were struck by the Cuban, to be sure. But Roberto González Echevarría– relying on the Havana press accounts of the day – has effectively put the lie to the mythic status of Torriente's lionized one-day slugging feat.[5] The three long blasts off the unpolished pitching of Kelly were all of the inside-the-park variety (the fences were largely unreachable in Almendares Park, where the center-field barrier stood almost 600 feet from home plate) and were likely unenthusiastically pursued by hung-over Giants outfielders. Kelly had apparently volunteered for mound duty on a lark and while Ruth in relief did give up the infamous groundball double, he did not allow one of the homers often reported by enhancers of the legend. A local press account cited by González Echevarría suggests that Giants pitchers were not taking most of the games on the tour very seriously, were in truth lobbing "batting practice tosses" at the Almendares hitters, and were at any rate probably on the day of Torriente's heroics still feeling the effects of excessive partying the previous night.

If mythical trappings infused into more mundane ballpark events have done almost as much to deflate as to elevate Torriente, we also perhaps need to raise an accompanying and equally pesky historical distortion. This is the legend touting the early twentieth-century Cuban winter circuit as somehow representing a legitimate Golden Age of domestic island baseball. This unfortunate reigning portrait of pre-revolution Cuban baseball is nowhere more celebrated than in Roberto González Echevarría's widely circulated 1999 volume *The Pride of Havana*. And here is perhaps the biggest skeleton in the closet. The Cuban league of the first half of the twentieth century – so often romanticized as Cuba's baseball epicenter – was in truth largely a ramshackle affair. Often it wasn't a league at all but merely a short-season tournament, often featuring as few as three teams and perhaps fewer than two dozen games. Seasons were rarely long enough even in the most extended campaigns to provide reliable individual statistics; sometimes the winter seasons were even canceled or curtailed due to economic stress or political unrest. The playing fields were of low quality by modern standards and the competition always uneven. There were indeed a handful of top Blackball stars (mostly American) and later a sprinkling of big leaguers seeking wintertime work. But the significant big-league presence came long after Torriente and Méndez were gone from the scene, only after the end of mid-1940s hostilities with Jorge Pasquel's player-raiding Mexican League, and after inclusion of the Havana circuit under the umbrella of Organized Baseball. In brief, the pre-World War II Cuban winter circuit was hardly a league on which to base much in the way of big-league quality credentials.[6]

It is now almost a platitude that early twentieth-century Negro ballplayers suffered numerous injustices. Their past glories inarguably need to be resurrected and they deserve their long-overdue recognition in the game's annals. We are indebted as fans of the sport and consumers of its history to those who have labored to set the record straight by arduously searching archives of the nation's once prolific African-American press. But at the same time we must here keep the historian's eye sharply focused. The game's past must be recorded with rigor and not turned over to enthusiasts with a "reconstructionist" agenda of their own making. Resurrecting Blackball history should not hinge on the kind of sloppy "scholarship" churned out by writers

like William McNeil who through easy "hocus pocus" methods develop shoddy mechanisms for measuring and enshrining midcentury Cuban leaguers.[7] To be rejected out of hand are lame efforts like McNeil's to elevate Torriente and others by merely transforming their batting and pitching numbers (registered in shorter island seasons) into the precise length of standard big-league seasons, without ever so much as considering relative evidence about the playing conditions or quality of opposition such batsmen and hurlers were actually facing.

In a rather remarkable sleight of hand, McNeil informs us that according to his ingenious "conversion factor," Cristóbal Torriente would have been reasonably expected to smack 17 homers and hit .329 annually in the big leagues (presumably the 1920s and 1930s big leagues of his own era, but that is not specified). Delightful magic if you can stomach it. According to this same unscientific method we might have projected that 2014 American League Rookie of the Year José Abreu (based on his best seasons in a contemporary Cuban League likely far stronger than the four-team circuits Torriente performed in) should have smacked 63 round-trippers in his debut campaign with the Chicago White Sox. Not a very insightful metric but all too characteristic of the less than rigorous enthusiasm of many of today's most ardent Blackball boosters.[8]

Was Torriente, alongside Méndez and preceding Dihigo, part of the greatest group of Cuban players ever produced? He may well have been, through the argument now becomes especially difficult in the light of the achievements on big-league diamonds of a handful of modern-era stars stretching from Liván and El Duque Hernandez to Abreu, Puig, Chapman, and Céspedes. If Méndez mesmerized vacationing big leaguers for a handful of celebrated exhibition outings at most limited to three winters, Chapman has proven unhittable over a half-dozen big-league seasons in one of the sport's greatest offensive eras. If Torriente batted well over .300 and slugged a few seemingly impressive homers in several dozen poorly reported short-season barnstorming circuits, Abreu and Céspedes have slugged away against the best of big-league hurlers in the heat of arduous 162-game pennant races.

Torriente's Cuban League legacy is certainly impressive, even if sometimes distressingly thin. He boasts a legacy certainly the equal of the one attached to Méndez, even if he didn't enjoy quite the same hometown icon status earned by the "Black Diamond" with those politically charged early-century triumphs over big leaguers representing occupying American forces. His record as a hitter is largely unparalleled in his own era. He owned the third highest overall batting mark in league history (.352 in a dozen campaigns), trailing only Americans Jud Wilson (.372 but only six seasons) and Oscar Charleston (.360 across a full decade). Other records include an unsurpassed five times as leader in triples, four times as the home-run leader (although his high was four in 1923 due to the immense league parks), and twice as batting champion. And there were accounts of Torriente's remarkable defense as a rocket-armed center fielder that supplement holes left by missing or spotty statistical records. One can question (and perhaps should question) the level of competition in an era that witnessed no major leaguers on Cuban soil for regular league games outside the exhibitions of the staged early-winter American Season.[9] But that argument can be raised whenever one compares different leagues or eras. Any player must be judged by where he stood against the competition at hand, and Torriente seemed to rank well ahead of most of the field he faced.[10]

Why in the end, then, does a biographical sketch of Torriente, reputedly one of the greatest of all Cuban sluggers and now a certified Cooperstown inductee, divert into a debate about the valuation of resurrected and reconstructed Negro statistics, the scant availability Negro League records and reliable firsthand game accounts, or the likelihood of overestimations of a pre-World War II Cuban winter league? In large part, of course, simply because there is so little else to pursue and so little else to add to the discussions of the void that is in large measure the sum total of the mysterious ballplayer's underreported and under-documented career. But more importantly, such debates become centerpieces of the Torriente story precisely because they seem in the end to constitute his greatest legacy. Even more than his almost equally shadowy Cuban contemporary José de la Caridad Méndez, Torriente is remembered far more for what we don't know, for what has consequently been invented or elaborated, than for what is found in verifiable records or documented events.

Torriente in the end suffered multiple blows from the unfortunate timing of his birth and from the segregated baseball universe into which he was accidentally born. He was denied by his skin color the chance to perform on the main stage of North America's prestigious professional leagues. He thus achieved his greatness not only in the shadows of stateside outlaw

Negro leagues ignored by a mainstream White press, but also in a Cuban winter circuit that was largely off the radar for the game's North American center of gravity during the era in which he played. And when he did finally reach Cooperstown in a belated single-year effort (2006) to enshrine an entire bucket load of long-overlooked Blackball legends, his bronze plaque would trumpet a single renowned moment of his career (outslugging Babe Ruth during the Bambino's 1920 barnstorming tour of Havana) that was little more than an unfortunate distortion of actual events. Unfair as it may be, Torriente's bronze plaque on the walls of Cooperstown would seem to cast him into the all-too-large collection of the game's shakiest fabrications, a cherished myth meriting a place alongside Doubleday's 1839 miraculous-conception invention of American ballplaying, the Babe's 1934 World Series "called shot" in Wrigley Field, Bonehead Fred Merkle's single-handed loss of the 1908 pennant, or Jackie Robinson's sanctioned solo role in the sport's hard-won racial integration.

THE MYSTERIOUS BURIAL OF A LEGENDARY BALLPLAYER

If Fate's existing blows to a legitimate or lasting reputation were not sufficient, an even more painful irony has now arisen to besmirch the sketchy Torriente legacy. The largest amount of ink recently devoted to this lost Blackball legend is now being expended not in any strenuous efforts at uncovering actual on-the-field accomplishments, but rather to ongoing internet debates about the circumstances surrounding his final unfortunate days in a New York paupers' hospital, the ambiguous circumstances surrounding the disposition of his human remains, and the equally mysterious location of his long-ignored bones. If the ballplayer remained lost to mainstream White baseball fandom while he lived, his final resting place today appears to be equally lost to those wishing to celebrate his murky legend.

The small phalanx of Negro baseball enthusiasts might well be excused for their somewhat odd focus given the scarcity of any other leads to pursue about who the living Torriente actually was. But it seems nonetheless a final unwarranted blow to Torriente's legacy that the major efforts are not now being directed toward peeling away overblown legends and replacing them with more substantial documentation, but are instead being focused on resurrecting

Torriente as a cause célèbre because he might be the only Cooperstown Hall of Famer without a properly marked gravesite.[11]

It was long common knowledge (or so we assumed) that within months of his lonely passing in New York the destitute former ballplayer's remains were spirited away to his homeland for proper ceremonious interment by the pre-revolution Fulgencio Batista government. But that charming piece of folklore now appears to be only the final piece of distracting mythology attached to Torriente's star-crossed legacy.

Dedicated Negro Leagues researcher Ryan Whirty wrote on his popular blog site in January 2016 about the revealing discoveries of fellow sleuths Ralph Carhart and Gary Ashwill (including the newly discovered official Torriente death certificate tracked down by Carhart in New York City archives) that combine to suggest the Cuban's remains have in truth never been removed from their mass grave location in New York City. That location appears to be Calvary Cemetery in Queens, where the body may well have originally been dumped along with those of perhaps16 other nameless paupers when the penniless Torriente succumbed to the ravages of alcoholism and TB on April 11, 1938 (at age 44). Torriente is now known to have spent his final several painful years at the Riverside Hospital on the city's North Border Island in the East River. The existing death certificate (which this author has seen)[12] verifies a primary cause of death as pulmonary tuberculosis and the burial place as the Calvary Cemetery, a truly massive facility owned by the New York Catholic Archdiocese and reported to contain more than three million remains (the largest number of any cemetery in the United States).

Confusion over the true location of the ballplayer's body only arose when stories circulated in Cuba (but were never well documented) that within two years (supposedly in 1940) the body was exhumed and removed to the homeland at the joint request of future President Fulgencio Batista and Cuban Sports Ministry director Jaime Mariné. What followed was supposedly an official enshrinement in the Colon Cemetery on the heels of Torriente's election to the 1939 inaugural class of a new Cuban Baseball Hall of Fame. Yet there is no concrete evidence of the reinterment and much speculation exists that the report may have been circulated on the island merely to prop up the popularity of the powerful army colonel who had effectively been controlling the government for much of the previous decade (after the overthrow of dictator Gerardo Machado in 1933) but was now officially

running for the presidency (which he indeed won) in 1940.

Whirty's central aim was to discount the long-standing and seemingly apocryphal story that the newly empowered Batista government actually returned the bones to Havana for relocation in the Colon Cemetery, supposedly as centerpiece for a newly erected monument devoted to multiple legendary Cuban ballplayers.[13] But Whirty further attempts to link the events surrounding the ballplayer's fate to a 1938 assassination attempt aimed at strongman Batista (himself a mulatto) and involving a similarly named white-skinned Havana politician (Cosme de la Torriente). His efforts – in this final case perhaps more valuable in the long run – also extend to uncovering Torriente's lost family connections at the end of the nineteenth century in the southern port city of Cienfuegos.

One line of inquiry pursued by Whirty – largely in an effort to locate a living relative who might perhaps aid in efforts to open the reported New York grave for possible revealing DNA testing – involves a wealthy nineteenth-century Cienfuegos family involved in the sugar-processing trade, a family with the reported surname Torriente. Whirty links this family through marriage to a *de la Torriente* clan that just might be connected with the assassination plotter in Havana, drawing a potential link to Batista and the glimmer of a theory about why the Cuban government might have initially "turned its back on one of its great ball-playing heroes at the time of his death." (Of course the idea that the Batista regime abandoned Torriente to the fate of an unmarked pauper's grave in New York directly contradicts the unproven reports that the Cuban government did in fact have the ballplayer exhumed and returned to the Cuban capital.) Whirty speculates that the Black ballplayer just might have been directly related to an unknown slave on the Cienfuegos sugar plantation owned by wealthy Spaniard Esteban Cacicedo Torriente – a slave who might (as often happens) have formally adopted the sugar baron's hereditary family surname.

But there are flaws in the theory from the start. Foremost is the fact that the surname of the sugar mill owners was not the final name of *Torriente* but the middle name of *Cacicedo*. Spanish double last names feature the surname (patriarchal name) and then the mother's name. It thus seems that even if the slave theory were plausible the ballplayer's adopted family surname would have been quite different. Furthermore, the whole thesis about Batista plotting to have the dead ballplayer interred in a monument at the Colon Cemetery is itself just as seriously flawed, at least as reported, since the ballplayer monument that does indeed feature a relief bust of Torriente (alongside those of Méndez and Antonio García) was not yet there at the time. The pair of tombs erected by the Association of Christian Ballplayers were built in 1942 and 1951, well after Torriente's death and original New York interment.

The real mystery begging resolution for the legions of fans interested in recapturing the sport's pioneering years and its lost Blackball history is in the end, of course, not at all where the bones of the long-dead Torriente may actually reside. A more pressing issue seems to be recovery of details surrounding the substantial lost (and thus also buried) career behind the embellished legends that prop up Torriente the onetime ballplayer. It is not so much where the man is buried that so puzzles, but instead where the true outlines of the living ballplayer have somehow been buried by excessive myth-making and the voids and vagaries of our lost Blackball history.

Faced with a sparsity of reliable records and compelling firsthand accounts that reach behind the hagiography, it today seems that well-meaning amateur historians and later-day Negro Leagues enthusiasts have – with all their perhaps well-meaning efforts – repeatedly clouded the actual (and admittedly substantial) achievements of one of Cuba's earliest homegrown stars under a haze of Bunyanesque myth and less than substantial epic legend. In the end they seemingly have buried rather than resurrected any true semblance of the doubly if not triply ill-fated Cristóbal Torriente.

SOURCES

In addition to the sources cited in the Notes, the author consulted:

Bjarkman, Peter C. *A History of Cuban Baseball, 1864-2006* (Jefferson, North Carolina, and London: McFarland & Company Publishers, 2007).

Rucker, Mark, and Peter C. Bjarkman. *Smoke: The Romance and Lore of Cuban Baseball* (New York: Total Sports Illustrated, 1999).

ONLINE SOURCES

Martínez de Osaba y Goenaga, Juan A. "Cristóbal Torriente: El Bambino … de Cienfuegos," online in *Cubadebate* (March 27, 2014).

Whirty, Ryan. "Who Holds Cristóbal's Fate," online in: *The Negro Leagues Close Up: A Blog About a Century of African American Baseball History* (January 27, 2016).

_____. "Torriente: Slavery, Politics, the Sugar Trade and the Search for Answers," online in: *The Negro Leagues Close Up: A Blog about a Century of African American Baseball History* (January 21, 2016).

_____. "A Mass Grave for a Baseball Legend?" online in: *The Negro Leagues Close Up: A Blog About a Century of African American Baseball History* (January 7, 2016).

NOTES

1   Jorge S. Figueredo, *Who's Who in Cuban Baseball, 1878-1961* (Jefferson, North Carolina, and London: McFarland & Company Publishers, 2003), and *Cuban Baseball: A Statistical History, 1878-1961* (Jefferson, North Carolina, and London: McFarland & Company Publishers, 2003).

2   These are the batting-average numbers provided by James A. Riley (*The Biographical Encyclopedia of The Negro Baseball Leagues*) for those three seasons. (New York: Carroll & Graf, 1994). But such are the vagaries and inconsistencies of Negro League statistics that these numbers do not at all match those provided by John Holway *The Complete Book of Baseball's Negro Leagues: The Other Half of Baseball History* (Fern Park, Florida: Hasting House Publishers, 2001). Riley has Torriente claiming the 1923 Negro National League batting title with a .412 mark, but Holway has him finishing third the same year at .395. Holway's numbers for Torriente are .361 (1920), .346 (1921), and .393 (1922). No matter which source for Negro League numbers one looks at, it is evident that Torriente was a consistent slugger and posted impressively high numbers. But the lack of any consistent reporting or calculations is enough to cloud any specifics when it comes to measuring the Cuban's greatness in terms of baseball's highly cherished yardstick numbers.

3   Riley reports that it was the Cuban's love of nightlife that caused the American Giants to trade him off to Kansas City before the 1926 Negro National League campaign. Since debauchery rarely affected on-field performance, Torriente stroked the ball at a reported .381 clip and led the new club to a first-half league title. But he then apparently quit the squad in mid-August when the team owner refused to compensate him for a lost or stolen diamond ring. His absence was blamed for a second-half dip in the standings, but after returning, he hit .407 in a losing playoff effort against his former teammates, the Chicago American Giants. At least that is Riley's version. Again Holway differs (*The Complete Book of Baseball's Negro Leagues*), crediting Torriente with only a .371 season's average (it is not clear if Holway's numbers reflect only the first half-season or the full year) and a lesser .355 playoff hitting mark.

4   John B. Holway, *Blackball Stars* (Westport, Connecticut: Meckler Books, 1988), 126.

5   Roberto González Echevarría, *The Pride of Havana – A History of Cuban Baseball* (New York: Oxford University Press, 1999), 158-161.

6   One of pre-Castro Cuban baseball's strongest champions, César Brioso, concedes in the epilogue to his recent celebration of a historic 1947 season (*Havana Hardball: Spring Training, Jackie Robinson, and the Cuban League*, University Press of Florida, 2015) that "whatever the Cuban League may have lost in autonomy [by merging with Organized Baseball] it more than gained in stability." Brioso admits that in the first half of the century numerous teams (like Santa Clara, Fé, Matanzas and others) rose to brief prominence only to "fade, withdraw, and disappear forever."

7   William F. McNeil, *Baseball's Other All-Stars (The Greatest Players From the Negro Leagues, the Japanese Leagues, the Mexican League, and the Pre-1960 Winter Leagues in Cuba, Puerto Rico and the Dominican Republic)* (Jefferson, North Carolina: McFarland, 2000).

8   Holway (*Blackball Stars*) offers an only slightly less meaningful metric when he poses as evidence of Torriente's slugging skills a table of performance against White big leaguers in 28 barnstorming exhibitions between 1918 and 1919 against White big-league clubs. The reported .311 batting average and three homers in 90 at-bats certainly suggest a skillful batsman. But what more do we make of exhibitions that were a close equivalent to today's spring-training games. Would any modern-era hitter's spring-training stats be posited as evidence for stature among the game's true greats?

9   Again there is a good deal of distortion here in some of the ordained volumes of Blackball history. And there are again all the false assessments of the Cuban winter league of the first half of the century. Donn Rogosin (*Invisible Men*, 1983; new edition, University of Nebraska Press, 2020) mentions stars like Ruth and Cobb playing in the Cuban circuit, which never happened since their only appearances came in brief preseason exhibition tours. Few White big leaguers of star status played in Cuba. Even in the '50s the dominating Americans were big-league role players like Spook Jacobs, Rocky Nelson, and Dick Sisler.

10   When it comes to statistics alone, perhaps the biggest downside of the case for Torriente as a Hall of Famer of true Cooperstown stature comes from Holway's own compilations in the tables found at the end of his own laudatory chapter (*Blackball Stars*, 133). Compiling known numbers from a two-decade career in North American Negro circuits (excluding all the undocumented barnstorming matches), Holway can report only 57 homers (plus a .338 BA) over 731 documented games and 3,233 plate appearances. Huge parks in Cuba itself explain few long balls on home turf, but the stateside numbers seem less impressive than might be expected. Again the "picture on the cover doesn't match the one inside."

11   Whirty writes (in his January 7, 2016, blog entry) that one of his missions is "to direct attention to the possibility that the Cuban Babe Ruth is now the only Hall of Famer buried in an unmarked grave." The claim itself is not quite correct, of course, because the actual resting place of fellow Cuban Hall of Famer José Méndez is actually also in equal dispute. It is likely that Méndez (or at least the bulk of his bones) rest in a group crypt that houses early-century Cuban ballplayers at the Havana Colon Cemetery. But a marked and undisputed individual gravesite certainly does not exist.

12   A copy was supplied to the author by Ralph Carhart in the fall of 2015, weeks after we had jointly visited the presumed Colon Cemetery resting spot in Havana.

13   The now rather dilapidated ballplayer tombs have been a regular stop of the annual Cubaball tour organized by Canadian SABR member Kit Krieger. Krieger has been personally involved in several efforts to have them restored. It is apparent that some players are interred there but likely in a mass crypt and not individual graves. Méndez and Torriente are two players (along with Antonio García) whose busts appear on one of the tombs. Ralph Carhart (plus this author) revisited this site in 2015 with one of the recent Cubaball tours.

FRANK WARFIELD

BY MARGARET M. GRIPSHOVER

Frank Warfield may be one of the least understood and appreciated stars of the Negro Leagues, and possibly one of the most unjustly maligned. He stood just 5-feet-7-inches tall and was slight in stature, but he was feisty, fast, and, some would say, furious. Yet few player-managers in the Negro Leagues achieved as much as did Frank Warfield.

Frank Warfield was born on April 28, 1899, in the small farming community of Pembroke, in Christian County, Kentucky. He was the only child born to Richard and Lela Rollins Warfield. His mother died when Frank was less than 3 years old. The year of Warfield's birth is up for debate. Kentucky did not routinely issue birth certificates until 1911, but the 1900 Census indicates that Frank Warfield was born in April 1899. In subsequent years, however, documents, including his World War I draft card, incorrectly state that he was born in 1898. His father, Richard Warfield, was born in Christian County in 1876. He was the son of Walter Warfield, who earned his freedom from enslavement by serving in the US Colored Troops Heavy Artillery during the Civil War. Richard Warfield, who worked as a farm laborer in Christian County, married Lela Rollins on September 30, 1899, approximately five months after Frank's birth. When Warfield was born, Pembroke was home to fewer than 700 people.[1] The town was a stop on the Louisville & Nashville Railroad and was known for growing two things — strawberries and tobacco, both labor-intensive crops.

Frank Warfield's journey northward to Indiana followed a path taken by many African American Kentuckians during the first wave of the "Great Migration." From the 1910s to 1940, the majority of African Americans who relocated from the South to cities in Indiana were from Kentucky.[2] Warfield's

(Courtesy Center for Negro League Baseball Research)

Frank Warfield, pictured here in a Santa Clara (Cuba) uniform, had only a brief stint with the 1920 American Giants, but he had a 19-year career in the Negro Leagues, primarily as a second baseman.

father was likely aware of the opportunities in cities like Indianapolis from others who already relocated there and from other sources of information such as newspapers. As early as 1889, Christian County residents were subscribing to the *Freeman*, an African American newspaper published in Indianapolis since 1884.[3] For Richard Warfield, the decision to leave Pembroke followed shortly after the death of his wife, Lela, around 1901. Another motivation to leave Pembroke was to escape the racial injustice and violence that was prevalent in Christian County and western Kentucky.[4] In the early 1900s, lynchings of African Americans in Christian County and neighboring Todd County were not uncommon.[5] Richard Warfield, with his young son in tow, headed first to Louisville, where he worked cleaning railroad cars. After a brief stay in Evansville, Indiana, they moved northward to Indianapolis where they lived off and on for nearly two decades. The Warfields' move to Indianapolis did not, however, insulate them from racism. By the 1920s, the Ku Klux Klan was deeply imbedded in Indiana and counted among its allies the mayor of Indianapolis and other influential politicians, including Governor Edward L. Jackson.[6]

When Richard and Frank Warfield arrived in Indianapolis in 1910, the city of over 233,000 had a large, thriving African American community with many successful Black-owned businesses, including two newspapers with national circulation. Richard Warfield found work as a general laborer. He and his son moved several times within the west side of Indianapolis between 1910 and 1920, with their longest tenure at 408 Smith Street, which was also Frank's last known address in Indianapolis. None of the houses in which Warfield and his father lived are still standing. All were demolished, along with at least 8,000 other structures, to make way for urban-renewal projects and the development of the "Inner Loop" of Interstates 65 and 70.[7]

Frank Warfield's name first appeared in an Indianapolis newspaper not for playing baseball, but rather for gunplay. When he was 11 years old, Warfield was shot in the shoulder by a friend while the boys were playing with a pistol.[8] It was reported that the bullet either grazed Warfield's shoulder or passed through it, and that the 17-year-old boy who pulled the trigger was so mortified by the experience that "his friends believe he may be dead of heart disease due to the fright over the accident."[9] The description of the superficial gunshot wound was likely correct given that Warfield's World War I draft card listed no

visible physical disqualifications, nor did it impact his ability to play baseball.

Nearly three years to the day after the shooting, Warfield's name made the newspaper again, but this time it was for his debut as a baseball player. On June 21, 1913, Warfield appeared in the lineup as the right fielder for the Denison Cubs, a peripatetic team composed mainly of amateur players, many of whom were employees of the Denison Hotel of downtown Indianapolis.[10] Warfield and his team acquitted themselves admirably and were described as doing "as good work as members of the A. B. C.'s. [*sic*]"[11] Warfield spent the summer of 1913 with the Denison Cubs, earning valuable experience against local nines – both White and Black teams. At the age of 14, he was already demonstrating his gifts for stealthy and savvy baserunning."[12] Later in his career, these talents earned him the nickname Weasel Warfield.

Two major events marked Frank Warfield's life in 1914. In March his father, Richard Warfield, widowed for more than a decade, married Lizzie Littlejohn in Indianapolis. It was likely the first time in Frank Warfield's memory that a woman lived in his household. Sharing a home with newlyweds may have been an incentive for Warfield to get out of the house and play baseball, which precipitated his second watershed moment in 1914: playing in his first true semipro and professional baseball games. At the beginning of the 1914 season, Warfield joined the Eastern Black Sox, a semipro traveling team composed largely of former and future players for the Indianapolis ABCs. The Eastern Black Sox fielded teams in 1913 and 1914, before folding in the summer of 1915. The addition of Warfield contributed to the team's prospects, and they had nowhere to go but up; in 1913, they had lost a game to the ABCs by the score of 38-9.[13]

When Warfield hit the road with the Eastern Black Sox during the summer of 1914, they were promoted as "baseball vaudeville" and "baseball jugglers," but also as the "fastest colored baseball team in three states."[14] Warfield spent most of his time tending to the gardens in left field. Soon, at age 15, Warfield experienced his first taste of organized baseball when he suited up as the starting shortstop for the Indianapolis ABCs for a June 28 game against the Louisville White Sox at Spring Bank Park in Louisville.[15] The ABCs defeated Louisville, 11-10, and, despite committing two errors, Warfield copped a walk, swatted a double, and scored on a fly ball.[16] And, even though the ABCs' manager, C.I. Taylor, sent "some subs" to Louisville and saved most of his "regulars" for a home tilt against the Cuban Stars, Warfield's brilliance outshone his bungles, and he caught the attention of one reporter who noted that "Young Warfield is a very fast man on bases and very promising."[17]

Warfield started 1915 where he had left off the year before – playing left field for the Eastern Black Sox and making brief appearances with the Indianapolis ABCs. The 1915 Black Sox lineup was bolstered by former ABCs players George Beard, Bernie Lyons, Otis "Cat" Francis, and Jack "The Poor Fighting Boy" Hannibal. Despite the infusion of veteran talent and a new team manager, the Eastern Black Sox folded in midseason.[18] Less than two weeks after the demise of the Sox, Warfield was picked up by the Indianapolis ABCs to patrol left field for a doubleheader against the Louisville White Sox, but this time it was a homestand and Warfield was on the varsity squad. He was enlisted to fill in a vacancy in the outfield created when Oscar Charleston was "out of the line-up, owing to a bit of misunderstanding with the management."[19] Warfield was planted in left field, while George Shively migrated to center to cover Charleston's usual domain. Indianapolis split the twin bill with Louisville, winning the first game, 5-0, but losing the nightcap, 8-4.[20] Warfield went hitless in four plate appearances in the opener, but showed some promise in the second with two singles and a stolen base, although he also committed an error.[21] The next day, the ABCs downed the Louisville White Sox, 9-0, with Warfield once again blanked at the plate.[22] Warfield's duties with the ABCs in 1915 were short-lived and unremarkable, lasting just three games, and ending with Charleston's return to good graces. Afterward, Warfield found a new baseball home with the French Lick Plutos, a traveling semipro team based in French Lick, Indiana, with a lineup that was nearly identical to that of the defunct Eastern Black Sox.

In 1916, Warfield started out with the newly formed Bowser's Indianapolis ABCs, and finished the season with the St. Louis Giants. In early 1916 Tom Bowser and C.I. Taylor dissolved their partnership in the Indianapolis ABCs, and each formed new teams using their names and the ABC moniker.[23] Warfield, along with former ABC players Oscar Charleston and Bingo DeMoss, chose Bowser's aggregation over Taylor's squad.[24] With DeMoss presiding over second base, Warfield was relegated to patrolling right field. By mid-June, however, Warfield jumped to greener pastures by signing with the St. Louis Giants of the Western Independent Clubs, of which Taylor's ABCs were members. He was just 17 years old and the only

teenager on the Giants' roster. He played in 27 games for St. Louis and posted some flashy numbers for such a young player. Warfield batted .343 and was tied with Jimmie Lyons for the most stolen bases on the team with 17. The St. Louis Giants, however, underperformed in 1916, finishing the season as an also-ran in the Western Independent Clubs standings, winning less than half as many games as the top club, the Chicago American Giants.

During the 1917 and 1918 seasons, Warfield remained with one team – C.I. Taylor's Indianapolis ABCs. In the spring of 1917, he "excited the hometown fans" with his defensive flair as an infielder.[25] But for the bulk of the year, Warfield was relegated to residing in right field, where he made some dazzling catches.[26] As the season wore on, he saw more frequent infield assignments, mainly at second base. Toward the end of 1917, Warfield saw more action at short, especially when the ABCs' regular shortstop, Morten "Specs" Clark, was no longer effective because, according to one sportswriter, Clark's "eyes have gone."[27] Warfield's gifts with the glove offset his mediocre output at the plate as he finished the year with an anemic .214 batting average. The ABCs capped off the regular season by proclaiming themselves as "world's series" champions over the Chicago American Giants, an opinion not shared by Rube Foster, who vehemently disputed the outcome of the series.[28]

Warfield's 1918 season with the ABCs saw him emerge as a full-time infielder. He started the season at shortstop but was also platooned at second with C.I. Taylor's younger brother James "Candy Jim" Taylor. The season was a challenging one for Warfield and the ABCs. As they battled to retain their disputed championship title, they also faced two more formidable foes; human and material resources lost to World War I and the influenza pandemic of 1918. All the clubs in the league played fewer than 50 games, and as the draft took more players to Europe, the number of available opponents dwindled.[29] That summer, the ABCs often found themselves playing mostly local nines and squads composed of military personnel. In one such game, played on the Fourth of July, the ABCs downed the "Aviation" nine, who were in training at the Indianapolis Motor Speedway, with Warfield providing some fireworks of his own by rocketing a home run over the left-field fence.[30]

Despite the ABCs' lineup that included two future Hall of Famers, C.I. Taylor's other brother, Ben Taylor, and Oscar Charleston, they finished the abbreviated season in second place in the Western

Independent Clubs race, losing the title to their nemesis, the Chicago American Giants. Warfield's batting average improved dramatically to .330 in 1918, although he appeared in 28 fewer games than in the previous year. The 1918 season sputtered to an end by early October when the influenza pandemic resulted in the prohibition of public gatherings, including baseball games. What likely would have been the final game of the season, a tilt against the Muncie Greys, the "white champions of Indiana," was nixed by order of the Muncie health board.[31] There was speculation in the press that Warfield would be drafted into the military, but that was not the case.[32] Frank and his father, Richard Warfield, both registered for the draft on September 12, 1918, but neither was inducted into the military. Frank Warfield did his patriotic duties at the close of World War I as a shipping clerk for the Indianapolis Red Cross, boxing up relief supplies and some of the 20,000 Christmas packages sent to doughboys serving in France.[33]

Frank Warfield's 1919 season could be best described as "the same but different." It was the same in that he began the year working as a clerk in C.I. Taylor's billiard parlor and cigar store in Indianapolis, a job he had held in previous years. It was different because he did not play baseball for Taylor's ABCs. In fact, 1918 was the last year that Warfield wore the ABCs' uniform. The reason for this was that Taylor did not field an ABC team in 1919, citing postwar difficulties in securing a worthy roster and shifting his focus toward his other business enterprises.[34]

When Warfield left the employment of C.I. Taylor, he also lost a connection to his mentor and tough taskmaster, and, in a sense, his baseball father figure. Unemployed and undeterred, Warfield packed his bags and baseball acumen, and signed as the starting second baseman with Tenny Blount's newly minted Detroit Stars. Another difference for Warfield in 1919 was that for the first time in his career as a full-time professional baseball player, he did not start the season as a teenager. On April 28, 1919, Warfield turned 20 years old. He played in all but two of Detroit's 41 games. Although his batting average was a meager .215, he made the most of his plate appearances by garnering 22 walks, led the team in triples, and then used his aggressive and savvy baserunning to cross the plate 35 times. Another dissimilarity between 1918 and 1919 for Warfield was that he played for two teams, the Detroit Stars and the Dayton Marcos. In the postseason, Warfield had one start for the Marcos at short, in a losing effort against the Chicago American Giants.[35]

And in an odd twist of coincidence, the "same but different" situation occurred in 1920 – Warfield played 99 percent of the regular season with one team and was added to another team's roster in the postseason. The difference was that in 1919, Warfield had played for the lowly Marcos who never had a winning season as members of the Western Independent Clubs or the Negro National League, whereas in 1920 he joined the Chicago American Giants just in time for their championship run.

Warfield donned his Stars uniform once more in 1920 and took up residence at second base. He resumed his slot as the leadoff man for Detroit and drew the attention of the baseball press and public for his offensive and defensive talents. Warfield started the season off on the right foot in April with "an exhibition of base running never witnessed in Mack Park," and by midsummer was described as "among the best keystone sackers in colored circles."[36]

By the end of the regular season, Warfield had compiled a respectable .281 batting average for the Stars and was second only to former St. Louis Giants teammate Jimmy Lyons in hits and runs scored. The Stars finished the season in second place the National Negro League standings, bested by the Chicago American Giants for the honor of hoisting the pennant.

For Warfield, though, his season was extended after he was picked up by Rube Foster to play in a Negro League "world series" against the Atlantic City Bacharach Giants of the Eastern Independent Clubs. Foster needed an able infielder to step in and fill the vacancy created at shortstop when Chicago's Bobby Williams jumped to the Dayton Macros in mid-September.[37] Warfield appeared in four games for Chicago. He had just two hits during the series, but his fly ball in the second game of a doubleheader on October 17, 1920, resulted in the only run scored and a victory for the Chicago American Giants.[38]

Warfield remained with Rube Foster's American Giants when they took up winter residence in Palm Beach, Florida, as the Royal Poinciana Hotel nine, and played against John Henry "Pop" Lloyd's team that represented the Breakers resort hotel.[39] Warfield was demoted to outfield duties when Bobby Williams returned to the American Giants' lineup in the postseason and reclaimed his residence at second base.[40] On their postseason swing through Southern states, Warfield and the Chicago American Giants crossed bats with local teams in Atlanta and Memphis.[41] Warfield's "spirited winter's play" for Foster's American Giants was duly noted and he was "universally regarded as being without a peer as a second sacker."[42]

Between 1919 and 1922, Warfield made a habit of playing for the Detroit Stars during the regular season and picking up a postseason gig with a different team. This appeared to be a good strategy. He was credited in 1920 for having "aided materially in the big things that the Foster club put over in the East," and, in the 1921 postseason was "holding down the hot corner in the K.C. Monarchs' line up in the post-season scrap." In 1921, the Detroit Stars finished another also-ran season while Warfield continued to hone his skills. The *Chicago Whip* was particularly enamored with Warfield as he "led the attack for the Detroiters this season," adding that as "one of the leading second-sackers in the game, the midget Star has played all positions this season."[43] As the leadoff man for Detroit, he ended the season as the team's top run producer and maintained a .264 batting average. In the 1921 postseason, Warfield was picked up by the Kansas City Monarchs.[44]

In the spring of 1922, Warfield returned for his final season with the Detroit Stars, and he made the most of it. His batting average soared to .318 and led his team in runs scored with 70 trips across the platter. Warfield was described as a "Keystone artist" and on par with the league's other outstanding second baseman, Bingo DeMoss of the Chicago American Giants.[45] But the Stars' new player-manager, Bruce Petway, could not lift the men out of the doldrums and once again Detroit was an also-ran in the Negro National League. As he had done in the three previous years, Warfield picked up a postseason gig, this time as a second baseman with the St. Louis Stars. Warfield was in the lineup for St. Louis when the Stars bested the barnstorming Detroit Tigers in two out of three exhibition games in the Gateway City.[46] Warfield's brilliant baserunning provided the winning run in one of the games when he stole home during a daring double steal.[47] The outcome of the contests between the Stars and the Tigers was highlighted more than a decade later as the first in a series of articles that appeared in the *Chicago Defender* to "show that owners and not the players are the ones keeping the color bar in baseball."[48] After Warfield's season ended in the States, he was enlisted by Tinti Molina's Santa Clara Club to Cuba for winter league play in early 1922. One of his teammates was third baseman Oliver Marcell, with whom five years later he had a notorious and violent altercation that resulted in damaging consequences to the legacies of both players.

The 1923 season signaled major shifts in Warfield's baseball life. His early mentor, C.I. Taylor, had died the previous year, and for the first time in his career, Warfield played for a team that was based neither in Indiana nor in a state that bordered it. It was also the first time that he assumed the role of player-manager, a duty that brought him both accolades and derision. From 1923 to 1928, Warfield was a member of Ed Bolden's Hilldale Club of Darby, Pennsylvania, a suburb of Philadelphia. Joining him in Darby was former Detroit Stars teammate Clint Thomas. Detroit Stars owner Blount lamented the loss of Warfield, and later blamed him for the "Detroit wreckage" of a season.[49] Blount said, "I made every effort to have him remain with us," but he "packed up suddenly and left us."[50] Another addition to Bolden's team was shortstop Pop Lloyd, who assumed the role of player-manager for Hilldale in 1923.[51] Bolden's calculations paid off in the end with Hilldale winning the Eastern Colored League championship. But there was dissension in the ranks. In late September, Lloyd was suspended as manager by Bolden and Warfield was named Hilldale's new captain.[52]

Warfield's new role as player-manager did not sit well with influential sportswriter (later league secretary) W. Rollo Wilson, whose unabashed adoration for Lloyd shaped his reporting on Warfield. Wilson did not hold back in his criticisms of the Hilldale club's management over Lloyd's dismissal and insinuated that Warfield was the instigator of Lloyd's exit. Wilson ranted that "one of the new stars on the team has managerial designs and that he became a little messenger, sub rosa, from the club house to the office."[53] He further alleged that since Lloyd's departure, "morale of the team has suffered," and that Hilldale lost most of its most recent games with Warfield at the helm.[54] He also questioned how the "older and more experienced men would react to such a change" given Lloyd's successes and that he "kept the temperamental stars in line."[55] Wilson demanded to know how there could be so much "ill-feeling on a team which won over seven-tenths of the games played" and claimed that the public was similarly outraged.[56]

In the end, Hilldale did not, as Wilson predicted, fall apart when Lloyd was removed as manager. The reality of the situation was that Lloyd was not as popular in the clubhouse as Wilson believed and was not missed by his players. According to historian Neil Lanctot, Lloyd "seldom endeared himself to the management," and his "handling of the team quickly alienated several players."[57] Wilson's dire predictions that Hilldale would collapse under Warfield's leadership did not come to fruition.[58] In fact, Warfield led Hilldale to pennants in the ECL again in 1924, 1925, and 1926. Meanwhile, Lloyd, who, after being fired by Hilldale was named manager of the Atlantic City Bacharachs, failed to win another pennant. It was not until 1930 that Lloyd bested one of Warfield's teams, when Lloyd's New York Lincoln Giants finished second and Warfield's Baltimore Black Sox were third, to the 1930 champion Homestead Grays.

After Lloyd's ignoble exit from Darby, Wilson continued to use his newspaper column to flog Warfield. He went so far as to try to gin up some discord of his own during the winter season with a column in the *Courier* about how Lloyd and his teammates were being paid more money than Warfield and his Santa Clara mates."[59] Wilson failed to acknowledge that Warfield had a much more successful season that winter in Cuba than did Lloyd. Warfield bested Lloyd in nearly every category, including stolen bases, and Warfield's Santa Clara Club was the 1923-24 league champion. Wilson eventually gave Warfield his due as one of the best second basemen and managers of his era. Nevertheless, in 1958, when Wilson named 11 players that he believed should be in the Hall of Fame, he included John Henry Lloyd and Oliver Marcell, but not Frank Warfield.[60]

In the spring of 1924, and for the first time in his career, Warfield began the season as a player-manager. But before he took the reins as the captain of the Hilldale Club, Warfield's .301 batting average helped the Santa Clara club, considered to be the one of the best teams in Cuban League history, win the winter season championship with a 36-11-1 record.[61] Warfield's first full season as the player-manager of Hilldale was a spectacular success. Hilldale was the champion of the ECL. Lloyd, whose leadership skills were hailed as nonpareil by W. Rollo Wilson in 1923, finished three places behind Warfield in the league standings. Despite losing the "East-West world series" to the Kansas City Monarchs in "ten of the most hotly contested games in diamond history, the 1924 season was a notable one for Warfield."[62] He posted a .309 batting average during the regular season, the best of his career as a player-manager, stole 22 bases, and banged out 14 doubles, another career high.

Warfield headed to Cuba for the winter of 1924-1925, just as he had done in the previous few years. But one statistic attributed to Warfield's postseason engagements that was overlooked was his acquisition of a spouse. Although a marriage license has yet to surface, immigration documents from the winters of 1924 and 1925, indicate that a "Mrs. Frank Warfield" was born in Springfield, Ohio, in May 1898. In both years, the ships' manifests identified Frank Warfield as "married." On March 17, 1924, Frank Warfield of Philadelphia and "Mrs. Frank Warfield" of Detroit arrived in Key West, Florida, from Havana, along with several other ballplayers. On February 20, 1925, when Warfield sailed from Havana to Key West, he was accompanied by "Eva Warfield," of Philadelphia. Eva Warfield's identity is as mysterious as her entrance and exit from Frank Warfield's life. Prior to 1924, and after 1925, she disappears from the public record, and there is no evidence to suggest that the couple had any children. Warfield's marital status on his death certificate states that he was "single" rather than married, widowed, or divorced.

Thanks to W. Rollo Wilson, another puzzling aspect of Warfield's identity surfaced in early 1925. In his column for the *Courier*, Wilson wrote about "Francis Xavier Warfield" and the demise of the Santa Clara club.[63] Wilson continued to use this nomenclature for Warfield into 1926.[64] It is unclear why Wilson baptized Warfield with such a Catholic-sounding name. Warfield never signed a document with a middle name, let alone with "Xavier." No evidence has surfaced to indicate that Warfield was Roman Catholic. No known parish records mention Warfield's name and he was not buried in a consecrated Catholic cemetery. In all likelihood, Wilson was influenced by the name of a popular contemporaneous White baseball player, Francis Joseph "Lefty" O'Doul, who was renamed "Francis Xavier O'Doul" by at least one sportswriter.[65] O'Doul's contributions to the development of baseball in Japan earned him a spot on the 2021 Hall of Fame's Early Baseball Era Committee's ballot, though he fell short of enshrinement.

In 1925, at the age of 26, Frank Warfield became the youngest player-manager to win a World Series when Hilldale avenged its 1924 loss to Kansas City by dethroning the Monarchs in five of six games. No other Negro League player-manager ever accomplished this feat. The youngest White player-manager to win a World Series was Hall of Famer Bucky Harris, who at age 27, led his Washington Senators to victory over the New York Giants in 1924. Young Warfield's success as a manager was noteworthy, especially since the 1925 Hilldale squad was devoid of "squabbling" and "petty grievances," and was adjudged to be the best in the team's history.[66] It is noteworthy that such harmony existed in the Hilldale clubhouse during such a turbulent season. This is especially true for a year overshadowed by poor umpiring and precarious finances.[67] Even the World Series victory was bittersweet given that fewer than 1,500 fans witnessed the final tilt and the payout was meager. As John Holway noted, "Many players felt that they could have made more barnstorming against whites."[68]

The 1926 season was Warfield's last full season as Hilldale's player-manager. Although he scored the most runs on the team that season, his offensive output began a steady decline. It is ironic that after Warfield's career peaked in 1925, W. Rollo Wilson reversed course and began to heap praise on Warfield. Wilson's retort to fans' cries of "wahassamatter [sic] with Warfield?" was, "The Clan Darbie [sic] captain and field manager is perhaps the best second baseman in Negro baseball these days," and, in a complete about-face, asserted that since he replaced John Henry Lloyd in 1923, Warfield "has proved his worth ever since."[69] Despite Wilson's boosterism, Warfield's 1926 season ended with a thud. Hilldale lost the 1926 ECL title to the Atlantic City Bacharachs, and his team and league faced financial and franchise failures.[70] Warfield's gloom deepened in November when his stepmother, Lizzie Littlejohn Warfield, died in Indianapolis from tuberculosis at age 43.

Warfield's final season with Hilldale, 1927, coincided with the team's slide into irrelevance in the ECL. By midsummer, he was demoted from player-manager to just player, and he was replaced as the Hilldale leader by Otto Briggs. One pundit remarked that "it was thought wise to have [Warfield] relinquish the responsibility … as it seems to have affected his playing since Hilldale began going bad this season."[71] Warfield muddled through the remainder of 1927, playing 55 games at second for Hilldale and batting just .219. His defensive skills, however, remained strong. Even longtime critic W. Rollo Wilson acknowledged this when he named Warfield to his "all-Eastern League club."[72] Warfield jumped to the Baltimore Black Sox at the close of the season, playing a handful of games for a familiar face – Black Sox manager Ben Taylor.

The Charm City worked its magic on Warfield in 1929 when he was named player-manager of the Baltimore Black Sox. It was his best team since the 1925 Hilldale club. Warfield led the Black Sox to the championship of the American Negro League, which had been formed from the ashes of the ECL. Sportswriter Wilson initially questioned the wisdom of Black Sox team owner George Rossiter's decision to hire Warfield as manager and believed that Baltimore's

Achilles' heels would be aching at right field and first base, but those predictions proved to be unfounded.[73] Jesse James "Mountain" Hubbard flourished in right field. First base was ceded to Hall of Famer Jud Wilson. Warfield had a "million-dollar infield" with Wilson, Dick Lundy, and the mercurial Oliver Marcell, who was acquired from the Bacharachs.[74] After the regular season ended, Wilson conceded that the "Black Sox deserved to win the pennant" and that Baltimore "had the best club in the league and a highly efficient leader in Frank Warfield."[75] Wilson also acknowledged Warfield's ability to maintain clubhouse cohesion and to control "a half dozen temperamental stars, described as "so many barrels of gunpowder," and thought that "Warfield trod lightly and blithely over them with never an explosion or consequence."[76] Wilson's description of Warfield's ability to keep the peace is important to note since some authors who have written about Warfield decades after his death often have described him as having a reputation for being divisive, hot-tempered, and combative.

During the 1929 season, Warfield faced one of his biggest challenges – managing the talented but temperamental third baseman Oliver "Ghost" Marcell, who was among the players that W. Rollo Wilson described as "barrels of gunpowder."[77] Warfield spent the winter of 1929-1930 in Cuba, as did Marcell. Unfortunately for both men, just before leaving Cuba to return to the United States, long-simmering tensions between player and manager exploded in a dispute over an alleged debt. The exact events that transpired in early February in Santa Clara are clouded by a lack of reliable published accounts and distortions that foster greater sympathy toward Marcell while placing more of the blame on Warfield. The brawl, which erupted during a card game in a Santa Clara hotel, resulted from Marcell's lingering anger from the 1929 season when Warfield took Marcell out of the Black Sox lineup due to Marcell being "not in condition or up to form."[78] Marcell alleged that Warfield owed him money, and demanded that Warfield make good on the debt so Marcell could cover his heavy losses at the poker table.[79] The story goes that "Marcell is said to have made a lunge at Warfield, and in the ensuing scuffle, Marcelle's nose was badly bitten."[80] As a result of the melee, Warfield spent the night in jail and Marcell spent the night in the hospital.[81] Warfield was soon released from custody with no consequences and returned to the United States via Key West on February 3, 1930. Marcell left Cuba four days later.

The outcomes of these unfortunate events had both short and long-lasting impacts on the legacies of both men. The most immediate effect of the fight was that Marcell was traded from Baltimore to the bumbling Brooklyn Royal Giants for what was to become his final season in the Negro Leagues. Despite reports that Marcell had a hair-trigger temper and that he threw the first punch, and that Warfield – the smaller of the two – was only defending himself, Warfield is often portrayed as the bad guy in the fight. In fairness, it is easy to paint Marcell as the more sympathetic character. After all, he lost the end of his nose and resorted to wearing a patch over the nose to hide the disfigurement.[82] In subsequent years, the blame for Marcell's departure from the Negro Leagues in 1930 is often laid squarely on Warfield and the nose-biting incident.[83] In truth, Marcell was already at the end of his career. As Bill Gibson of the *Baltimore Afro-American* put it less than three months after the incident in Cuba, "Since the number of fans are wondering why Ollie Marcelle is not at the hot corner for the Black Sox this season, and probably blaming it upon a little altercation between Marcelle and Warfield in Cuba, last winter, it might be in order to say that had the matter never occurred, Marcelle would have been given the air just the same. … Marcelle's legs have gone back considerably in the past two seasons."[84]

In the end, the Black Sox finished 1930 in third place behind the Eastern Independent Clubs champion Homestead Grays. Warfield continued his downhill slide in 1930, batting a meek .218, and, for the first time since 1914, stealing no bases. One bright note for Warfield's squad that year was the addition of a new pitching phenom named "Kid Satchells" [*sic*] – Satchel Paige, who debuted with the Black Sox in May 1930, but drifted in and out of the lineup for much of the season.[85]

Warfield's final full season with the Baltimore Black Sox in 1931 had some similarities to the previous one – except that everyone kept their noses. The Black Sox finished sixth in the nine-team Independent League that saw Warfield's former team, the Hilldale club, managed in 1931 by Hall of Famer Judy Johnson, win the pennant. For the first time in years, Warfield was not in command of second base, played in only 43 of Baltimore's 60 games, and barely had a pulse at the plate, posting the lowest batting average of his career (.149). And, for the first time since 1915, he produced no extra-base hits. His precipitous decline could be attributed to the stress of managing his players and some of the Black Sox' business dealings. It is more likely,

however, that the 32-year-old Warfield was already suffering from the effects of tuberculosis, the disease that took his life the following year.

In March 1932, it was announced that Warfield would take the helm as player-manager of the newly formed Washington Pilots of the East-West League.[86] The Pilots were a far cry from the Hilldale and Black Sox teams that took Warfield to the top of the game. The team lost a string of games in the spring thanks to an error-prone infield and wildly inconsistent pitching. In their opening home game, at Griffith Stadium, the Pilots committed a half-dozen errors, two by Warfield, in an 8-2 loss to Hilldale.[87] The East-West League was in no better shape than the errant Pilots, and by the end of June, questions arose as to whether or not the entire operation would fall apart before the close of the season.[88] It was reported that teams were struggling to make payrolls and at least one league official "had ceased sending in box scores … because he found it a waste of time and effort."[89]

Undeterred, Warfield shored up the Pilots' infield with the additions of Hall of Fame first baseman George "Mule" Suttles, third baseman Dewey Creacy, and shortstop Jake Dunn.[90] Warfield himself was appearing less frequently in the lineup and ceded dibs on second base to Sammy Hughes. In July Warfield made plans for a series of road games with the Homestead Grays and the Pittsburgh Crawfords.[91] On July 4, 1932, Warfield made what was probably his last plate appearance when he pinch-hit for pitcher Ted Trent in the first game of a doubleheader against the Grays. Warfield went out with a bang. When he came to the plate in the bottom of the ninth, he hit a grounder that was bungled by Grays third baseman Walter Cannady, allowing two runs to score and seal the 4-2 walk-off victory for the Pilots.[92]

On Friday, July 22, 1932, the Pilots opened a weekend series against the Pittsburgh Crawfords at Greenlee Field, but Warfield did not put himself in the lineup. The Pilots were sunk by the Crawfords, 4-3.[93] On Sunday, July 24, in the last game of Warfield's career and the last day of his life, the Crawfords destroyed the Pilots, 14-5.[94] After the game, Warfield and Pilots business manager Douglas Smith were headed back to the Bailey Hotel, located in the Hill District, Pittsburgh's historic African American neighborhood, about a block from Gus Greenlee's Crawford Grill. Along the way, Warfield was suddenly stricken and by the time they arrived at the hotel, he was dead.[95] The time of death was estimated at 6:55 P.M., not long after the end of the Pilots game. Smith signed the death certificate as the "informant." Smith identified himself as Warfield's "friend," but was not so close a friend to know Warfield's correct birth and family information.

There has been much speculation about the circumstances of Warfield's death, likely fueled by rumors among the press and disgruntled players. In one imagined scenario, Warfield's demise was the result of an encounter with a woman in the Bailey Hotel, a conclusion likely drawn from those who adjudged him as a "ladies' man."[96] These assertions were unsubstantiated but nonetheless were frequently repeated. The truth about Warfield's death is this: Although no autopsy was performed, the official cause of death was tuberculosis, which, according to his death certificate, he contracted while living in Baltimore. It is not unusual for a person who suffers from tuberculosis to die suddenly from a heart attack.[97] Warfield's body was shipped to Maryland where he was buried in the Mount Auburn Cemetery in Baltimore. Evidence of a headstone has yet to be documented. The Pilots sailed on without him for the remainder of the season and named Webster McDonald as the team's new manager. They finished near the bottom of the standings and disbanded by the end of the season along with the East-West League.

After Warfield's death, tributes poured in from sportswriters, players, and fans. W. Rollo Wilson, whose harsh opinions of Warfield had softened over the years, paid his respects. Five years before Warfield's death, Wilson wrote that he considered Warfield one of the greats, on par with Oscar Charleston and Biz Mackey, and lamented that integration in baseball would come too late for all three men.[98] Wilson was among the first to jump in to heap praise on the deceased. He noted, "It is significant that when news of [Warfield's] death was flashed here to Philly all white and colored teams halted their games to pay tribute to him."[99] Wilson added that the "steadying influence of the reliable Warfield at second base always had its effect on any infield in which he worked," and that "baseball men have paid tribute to his ability and to him as a man, and I would add my name to the list of those who saw in him as an upstanding sports figure and worthy model of our professional athlete."[100] Oscar Charleston remembered Warfield as "a gentleman first, and a ball player next," and Gus Greenlee agreed when he said that Warfield was the "finest and most gentlemanly players I have ever known."[101] Other tributes described Warfield as "quiet and modest" and noted that, at age 25, he had "surprised the old-timers by turning out a winning team."[102]

When Warfield died, his only immediate survivors were his father, Richard Warfield of Indianapolis, and his paternal aunt, Lucy Warfield Leavell, who lived near Pittsburgh. After Frank's death, his father moved to Pennsylvania to be closer to his sister and her family. Richard Warfield died of lobar pneumonia on February 14, 1938, in a hospital in Homestead. He was buried in the Oak Grove Cemetery in Beaver County, where his sister Lucy Warfield Leavell was buried later that year.

Frank Warfield's legacy as a player-manager is complicated. His life story has been muddled by journalistic bias, conflicts with players, repeated errors regarding his personal and professional life, and the passage of time. His lifetime batting average of .264 is not overly impressive, but in his time, he was acknowledged as one of the best second basemen in the Negro leagues and as a masterful player-manager.

Warfield showcased his brilliant baseball mind as the youngest player-manager in baseball history to win a "world series." He was small in stature and slender in build – he stood just 5-feet-7-inches tall and weighed 160 pounds.[103] But Warfield made the most of his physique as a tiny terror on the basepaths and was always a threat to stretch a single into extra bases, or to steal another base once he made it to the initial sack.

His extraordinary baserunning talents inspired his nickname, Weasel Warfield, but the use of this nickname by the press was extremely rare during his lifetime. It first appeared in print in 1930, just two years before his death, and in the context of the nose-biting incident between Warfield and Marcell. Later, one sportswriter correctly stated that Warfield's "pet name was 'the weasel' due to the fact that, like his namesake, he was cunning, brainy, and a strategist parexellence [sic]."[104] The "Weasel Warfield" nickname most often appeared in print after his death and took on a more negative connotation. This further shaped an increasingly unflattering perception of Warfield, especially when evaluating his worthiness for inclusion in the Hall of Fame. One writer claimed that Warfield rightfully earned the moniker by a reputation as a knife-wielding, overly competitive manager with a "mean streak" and a "vicious temper, who was universally reviled by his players."[105] But this does not tell the whole story. There is no doubt that Warfield was fiercely competitive and a disciplinarian – things he learned from his mentor, C.I. Taylor.[106] He very likely did carry a knife, as did many men of his era. It is also true that Warfield was involved in heated arguments with umpires and players – but that did not make him an outlier, particularly in the era in which he played and managed. In fact, poor umpiring was endemic during Warfield's career, especially during his tenure with Hilldale.[107] However, little evidence exists to suggest that it was always Warfield who threw the first punch.

Warfield's worthiness for the Hall of Fame is up for debate. Many of his teammates, some of whom he managed, are currently in the Hall of Fame. Warfield may never be enshrined at Cooperstown, but his mastery of second base and the basepaths, and his impressive record as one the youngest player-managers in all of baseball history to earn a pennant or world series flag for several different teams makes him worthy of reevaluation and recognition.

SOURCES

Unless otherwise indicated, all Negro League statistics and records were sourced from Seamheads.com.

Ancestry.com was used to access census, birth, death, marriage, military, immigration, and other genealogical and public records.

NOTES

1   Population of Kentucky by Counties and Minor Civil Divisions, December 29, 1900, *Census Bulletin No. 25*, Washington, D.C.: 15.

2   Jack S. Blocker Jr., "Black Migration to Muncie," *Indiana Magazine of History* 92 no. 4 (December 1996): 297-320.

3   "Notice," *Indianapolis Freeman*, August 3, 1889: 4.

4   Jack Glazier, *Been Coming Through Some Hard Times: Race, History, and Memory in Western Kentucky* (Knoxville: University of Tennessee Press, 2012).

5   "Short Work of Leavell," *Hopkinsville Kentuckian*, October 14, 1905: 1; "Gross Insult Avenged," *Kentuckian*, October 9, 1906: 1.

6   Leonard J. Moore, *Citizen Klansmen: The Ku Klux Klan in Indiana, 1921-1928* (Chapel Hill: University of North Carolina Press, 1997).

7   Kayla Dwyer, "Coalition Gathering Support to Rebuild 'Inner Loop,' This Time Underground," *Indianapolis Star*, August 24, 2021: A1.

8   "Chum Shot; Boy Runs Away," *Indianapolis Star*, June 29, 1910: 26.

9   "Chum Shot; Boy Runs Away"; "Colored Lad Wounded," *Indianapolis Sun*, June 30, 1910: 7; "Boy Shot in Shoulder," *Indianapolis News*, June 30, 1910: 20.

10 Billy Lewis, "Dennison [*sic*] Cubs Beat the Canleys [*sic*]," *Indianapolis Freeman*, June 28, 1913: 7; "Ellettsville Trims Gosport," *Bloomington* (Indiana) *Evening News*, May 18, 1914: 1.

11 Billy Lewis, "Dennison Cubs Beat the Canleys," *Indianapolis Freeman*, June 28, 1913: 7.

12 "The Denison Cubs Won the Game," *Martinsville* (Indiana) *Reporter-Times*, July 21, 1913: 2.

13 "Eastern Black Sox Slaughtered by A.B.C.'s," *Indianapolis Freeman*, September 13, 1913: 4.

14 "Look Who's Coming to Town Sunday," *Alexandria* (Indiana) *Times-Tribune*, August 15, 1914: 1.

15 J.H. Wright, "Indianapolis A.B.C. Defeats Louisville White Sox," *Indianapolis Freeman*, July 4, 1914: 4.

16 Wright.

17 Wright.

18 "Semi-Pro. News," *Indianapolis News*, June 21, 1915: 11.

19 "Young" Knox, "Gleanings Along the Firing Line," *Indianapolis Freeman*, July 10, 1915: 4.

20 "A.B.C.S [*sic*] Get Even with Louisville White Sox," *Indianapolis Star*, July 6, 1915: 9.

21 "A.B.C.S Get Even with Louisville White Sox."

22 "Johnson Shuts Out Sox," *Indianapolis Star*, July 7, 1915: 3.

23 "Taylor Also to Have Club in the Field," *Indianapolis Star*, March 20, 1916: 10.

24 Paul Debono, *The Chicago American Giants* (Jefferson, North Carolina, 2007), 67.

25 Debono, 77.

26 "Ninth Inning Rally Gives A.B.C.'s Game," *Evansville Courier and Press*, June 24, 1917: 8.

27 "Poor Support of Johnson Is Just One Cause," *Muncie* (Indiana) *Evening Press*, September 10, 1917: 8.

28 Debono, 69.

29 Debono, 79.

30 "A.'s [*sic*] Beat the Aviators in Close Scrap," *Indianapolis Star*, July 5, 1918: 10.

31 "Greys' 1918 Ball Season Probably Ended," *Muncie Evening News*, October 11, 1918: 2.

32 "Two Good Games Are Assured Fans," *Muncie Star Press*, August 16, 1918: 11.

33 "Soldier-Parcel Plans Advanced," *Indianapolis Star*, October 13, 1918: 52; "Red Cross Shipment," *Indianapolis News*, October 17, 1918: 12.

34 Debono, 82.

35 "American Giants Give Dayton Marcos Ball Lesson in 7 to 4 Game," *Chicago Whip*, September 20, 1919: 8.

36 "Detroit Stars Win in Detroit," *Chicago Whip*, April 24, 1920: 6; "Stars Galore with Detroit Colored Team," *Indianapolis Star*, July 3, 1920: 13.

37 "Marcos to Play Italians Today," *Dayton Daily News*, September 19, 1920: 13.

38 "Redding Misses No-Hit Game," *Brooklyn Times-Union*, October 18, 1920: 7.

39 "Baseball," *Palm Beach Post* (West Palm Beach, Florida), January 15, 1921: 4.

40 "The Big Teams in 1 to 1 Tie," *Chicago Whip*, March 19, 1921: 8.

41 "American Giants Play Local Team at Morris Brown," *Atlanta Journal*, March 28, 1921: 12; "Giants Defeat Martins," *Memphis Commercial Appeal*, April 11, 1921: 14.

42 "Detroit's Keystone King," *Chicago Whip*, April 9, 1921: 8.

43 "Frank Warfield," *Chicago Whip*, July 9, 1921: 8.

44 "Frank Warfield," *Chicago Whip*, October 22, 1921: 8.

45 "Sharing Honors with DeMoss," *Chicago Whip*, July 8, 1922: 8.

46 "Tigers Drop Two Games to St. Louis Stars," *Chicago Defender*, October 14, 1922.

47 "Tigers Drop Two Games to St. Louis Stars."

48 "Interrace Games Show Class of Race Players, Writer Says," *Chicago Defender*, September 23, 1933: 8.

49   "Warfield's Leaving Wrecked Detroit," *Baltimore Afro-American*, January 18, 1924: 14.

50   "Warfield's Leaving Wrecked Detroit."

51   "John Henry Lloyd Now Manager of Hillsdale [*sic*]," *New York Age*, January 27, 1923: 6.

52   "Hilldale President Suspends Manager John Henry Lloyd," *Pittsburgh Courier*, September 29, 1923: 6; W. Rollo Wilson, "Suspension of Lloyd Made Permanent by Darby Mogul," *Pittsburgh Courier*, October 6, 1923: 7.

53   "Suspension of Lloyd Made Permanent by Darby Mogul."

54   "Suspension of Lloyd Made Permanent by Darby Mogul."

55   "Suspension of Lloyd Made Permanent by Darby Mogul."

56   "Suspension of Lloyd Made Permanent by Darby Mogul."

57   Neil Lanctot, *Fair Dealing and Clean Playing: The Hilldale Club and the Development of Black Professional Baseball, 1910-1932* (Syracuse: Syracuse University Press, 2007), 102-103.

58   "Suspension of Lloyd Made Permanent by Darby Mogul."

59   W. Rollo Wilson, "Eastern Snapshots," *Pittsburgh Courier*, December 15, 1923: 7.

60   W. Rollo Wilson, "Through the Eyes," *Pittsburgh Courier*, July 11, 1958: 16.

61   Don Burley, "Confidentially Yours," *Little Rock Arkansas State Press,* March 30, 1951: 3.

62   "Close to 50,000 Fans Witnessed World Series Games," *Pittsburgh Courier*, November 1, 1924: 6.

63   "W. Rollo Wilson, "Eastern Snapshots," *Pittsburgh Courier*, February 7, 1925: 7.

64   W. Rollo Wilson, "Eastern Snapshots," *Pittsburgh Courier*, September 5, 1925: 13; W. Rollo Wilson, "Eastern Snapshots," *Pittsburgh Courier*, April 17, 1926: 14.

65   W.O. McGeehan, "Bodie Pilfers Put-Out from Peckinpaugh," *New York Tribune*, March 28, 1919: 19; W.O. McGeehan, "Down the Line," *Washington Evening Star,* July 6, 1929: 21.

66   Lanctot, 135.

67   Lanctot, 132-133.

68   John Holway, *The Complete Book of Baseball's Negro Leagues: The Other Half of Baseball History* (Fern Park, Florida, 2001), 205.

69   W. Rollo Wilson, "Eastern Snapshots," *Pittsburgh Courier*, April 17, 1926: 14.

70   Lanctot, 147.

71   "Otto Briggs Succeeds Warfield as Captain of Hilldale Club," *New York Age*, July 27, 1927: 6.

72   W. Rollo Wilson, "Sport Shots," *Pittsburgh Courier*, September 29, 1928: 18.

73   W. Rollo Wilson, "Sport Shots," *Pittsburgh Courier*, February 9, 1929: 12.

74   John Holway, "Baltimore's Great Black Ball Team," *Baltimore Sun*, August 28, 1977: K3; "Baltimore Gets Marcelle and Cason from Atlantic City for Three Players," *New York Age*, March 30, 1929: 6.

75   W. Rollo Wilson, "New American League Completes Schedule; All Loop Teams Impress," *Pittsburgh Courier*, September 28, 1929: 16.

76   W. Rollo Wilson, "New American League Completes Schedule; All Loop Teams Impress."

77   W. Rollo Wilson, "New American League Completes Schedule; All Loop Teams Impress."

78   "Black Sox Player Jailed Following Fight in Cuba," *Baltimore Afro-American*, February 8, 1930: 14.

79   "Black Sox Player Jailed Following Fight in Cuba."

80   "Black Sox Player Jailed Following Fight in Cuba." Oliver Marcell's surname was often misspelled as Marcelle.

81   "Black Sox Player Jailed Following Fight in Cuba."

82   Robert Peterson, *Only the Ball Was White: A History of Legendary Black Players and All-Black Professional Teams* (New York: Oxford University Press, 1982), 116.

83   Stephen R. Greenes, *Negro Leaguers and the Hall of Fame: The Case for Inducting 24 Overlooked Ballplayers* (Jefferson, North Carolina: McFarland, 2020), 87.

84   Bill Gibson, "Here Me Talkin' to Ya," *Baltimore Afro-American,* April 26, 1930: 14.

85   "Black Sox Relying on Suttles' Bat in Hilldale Contests," *Baltimore Evening Sun,* May 1, 1930: 37; "Black Sox to Face Only Team to Beath Them This Season," *Baltimore Evening Sun,* June 6, 1930: 45; "Black Sox Procure Three New Players to Fill Vacancies," *Baltimore Evening Sun,* June 8, 1930: 25; "Satchells [*sic*] Returns to Black Sox Fold for Hilldale Bill," *Baltimore Evening Sun,* July 31, 1930: 33.

86   "Colored Pro Baseball League to Meet Here," *Washington Post*, March 10, 1932: 12.

87   "Pilots Lose Loop Game," *Washington Evening Star*, May 20, 1932: 43.

88   "Here Me Talkin' to Ya," *Baltimore Afro-American*, June 25, 1932: 14.

89   "Here Me Talkin' To Ya."

90   "Wolves to Meet Revamped Pilots," *Detroit Free Press*, June 30, 1932: 17.

91   "Pilots to Be Strong Opponent," *Pittsburgh Courier*, July 3, 1932: 12; "Craws Await D.C.," *Pittsburgh Courier*, July 23, 1932: 15.

92   "Grays Cop Edge from Pilots," *Pittsburgh Courier*, July 9, 1932: 15.

93   "Crawfords Beat Pilots," *Pittsburgh Post-Gazette,* July 23, 1932: 16.

94   "Seventeen for Crawfords," *Pittsburgh Post-Gazette*, July 24, 1932: 13.

95   "Frank Warfield, Ball Player, Dies," *Chicago Defender*, July 30, 1932: 8.

96   James A. Riley, *The Biographical Encyclopedia of the Negro Baseball Leagues* (New York: Carroll & Graf Publishers, 1994), 817.

97   José Patricio López-López et al, "Tuberculosis and the Heart," *Journal of the American Heart Association*, March 18, 2021 Vol. 10 No. 7., https://doi.org/10.1161/JAHA.120.019435, accessed November 9, 2021.

98   W. Rollo Wilson, "Sport Shots," *Pittsburgh Courier*, January 15, 1927: 13.

99   W. Rollo Wilson, "Sport Shots," *Pittsburgh Courier*, August 6, 1932: 14.

100 W. Rollo Wilson, "Sport Shots," *Pittsburgh Courier*, August 6, 1932: 14.

101 "Baseball Notables Lament His Passing," *Pittsburgh Courier*, July 20, 1932: 15.

102 "Frank Warfield Dies Suddenly in Pittsburgh," *New York Age*, August 6, 1932: 6.

103 "Frank Warfield, Ball Player, Dies," *Chicago Defender*, July 30, 1932: 8.

104 Alvin Moses, "Beating the Gun," *Kansas City* (Kansas) *Plaindealer*, February 21, 1941: 3.

105 Dr. Layton Revel and Luis Munoz, "Frank Warfield," Center for Negro League Research, 2014, 1, 2; http://www.cnlbr.org/Portals/0/Hero/Frank-Warfield.pdf, accessed June 1, 2021; Stephen R. Greenes, *Negro Leaguers and the Hall of Fame: The Case for Inducting 24 Overlooked Ballplayers*, 87.

106 John Holway, "Indianapolis ABCs 1914," *Indianapolis Star*, August 25, 1973: 48, 50, 51.

107 Lanctot, 132-133.

FRANK WICKWARE

BY STEPHEN V. RICE

"Cannon Ball Redding and others of days gone by had plenty of speed, but Frank Wickware, speed ball artist from Coffeyville, Kan., was recognized as the king until LeRoy (Satchel) Paige arrived on the scene with his fast ball."

— *Chicago Defender*, 1930[1]

Frank Wickware was one of the premier Negro pitchers from 1910 to 1920. The tall right-hander with the fearsome fastball was among the preliminary candidates considered in 2006 for election to the National Baseball Hall of Fame by the Special Committee on the Negro Leagues.[2] Although he was not selected for induction, he did get inducted into the Kansas Baseball Hall of Fame in 2011.[3] Wickware lived a turbulent life, on and off the baseball diamond.

Born on March 18, 1888, in Girard, Kansas, Frank Ellis Wickware was the youngest child of Eldon and Mollie (Love) Wickware.[4] The family moved to Coffeyville about 1906.[5] On July 29, 1907, Frank threw a no-hitter for a Muskogee (Oklahoma) team against a Fort Worth squad.[6] He pitched for the Dallas Black Giants in 1908 and 1909, and was nicknamed "Zig Zag."[7]

Rube Foster, the great pitcher and manager, hired Wickware to pitch for the Chicago Leland Giants in 1910, and under Foster's tutelage he developed into a star. Wickware threw a two-hit shutout in Oklahoma

City on April 24.[8] In Chicago he hurled a no-hitter and struck out 14 Chicago Athletics on June 5, and he beat the Kansas City Giants with a three-hitter on June 26.[9] He defeated the Lancaster (Pennsylvania) Red

(Courtesy Noir-Tech Research, Inc.)

Frank Wickware was 5-3 with a 3.53 ERA for Chicago's 1920 championship team. He won 76 games over the course of a 12-year career.

Roses, a Class-B minor-league team, with a four-hit shutout on September 19 in Atlantic City.[10]

The 1910 Leland Giants featured future Hall of Famers Pete Hill in center field and John Henry Lloyd at shortstop. Bruce Petway, the team's backstop, was regarded as the best defensive catcher in Negro baseball. Unofficially, the team compiled an astounding 123-6 won-lost record, and Wickware posted an 18-1 record, through games of September.[11] Against tougher competition in Cuba (October to November) and in the California Winter League (November to February), the team won 15, lost 11, and tied 3.[12]

In 1911 Foster organized his own team called the Chicago American Giants. Wickware pitched for both the Leland Giants and the American Giants in 1911.[13] In early 1912 he pitched in Cuba for the Fe team[14] and rejoined the American Giants upon his return to the United States. On May 19 he shut out the Brooklyn Royal Giants in Chicago, and in August the Royal Giants "paid a large sum to Rube Foster" to acquire him.[15]

As a Royal Giant, Wickware faced Dick "Cannonball" Redding of the New York Lincoln Giants in both games of a doubleheader on August 25, 1912. Both pitchers threw two complete games that day; Wickware won the first game, 3-2, and Redding won the second, 3-0.[16] In a rematch two weeks later, Wickware outdueled Redding, 1-0.[17] That winter Wickware pitched for the Lincoln Giants in Cuba.[18]

After starting the 1913 season with the Royal Giants, Wickware jumped in May to the Schenectady (New York) Mohawk Giants, a Negro team assembled by Bill Wernecke, a White businessman.[19] The Mohawk Giants were well supported by Schenectady, a nearly all-White city. On May 25 a crowd of 3,500 turned out to see Wickware throw a five-hitter with 11 strikeouts against the visiting Smart Sets of Paterson, New Jersey.[20] On June 7, he lost a pitchers' duel, 2-1, to future Hall of Famer Cyclone Joe Williams and the Lincoln Giants.[21]

Wickware mixed a deceptive change-of-pace and sharp curveball with his dominating fastball, so that batters had no idea *what* was coming.[22] After receiving the ball, he might quick-pitch it or hold it a while before firing it with no windup, so that batters had no idea *when* it was coming.[23] He kept hitters off balance with these tricks he learned from Rube Foster.[24]

On Sunday, July 13, before nearly 6,000 fans in Schenectady, Wickware hurled a three-hit shutout in a 4-0 victory over the Troy Trojans of the Class-B New York State League.[25] "Wickware struck out eleven

players and called the fielders in after two were down in the ninth. He then struck out the last batter," a Black newspaper reported.[26] Wernecke profited financially when Wickware put on a show in front of a large Sunday crowd.

The Lincoln Giants and Foster's American Giants were scheduled to play a five-game championship series in New York City beginning July 17, 1913. Rod McMahon, owner of the Lincoln Giants, paid Wickware $100 in advance to pitch for his team in the series, but Wickware showed up to the first game in an American Giants uniform. Foster insisted that Wickware was pitching for him. The game was called off after McMahon and Foster argued for more than an hour.[27] Wickware would pitch for neither team in the series.

With Wickware AWOL and unavailable to pitch in Schenectady on Sunday, July 20, the irritated Wernecke went to the police with Henry Kearney, who swore out a warrant against Wickware for skipping out on a $10 board bill from Kearney's boarding house. Wickware, though, returned in time for the Sunday game. Despite the outstanding warrant for his arrest, he pitched against the Utica Utes of the New York State League, and his ninth-inning hit gave the Mohawk Giants a 4-3 victory before an enthusiastic crowd of 6,000. The next day he was arrested and pleaded guilty to the larceny charge, and his $25 fine was paid by one of his teammates.[28]

On August 3, 1913, Wickware spun a three-hit shutout in Schenectady with 15 strikeouts in a 5-0 triumph over the Albany Senators of the New York State League.[29] On August 12 the Brooklyn Royal Giants were aided by seven Mohawk Giants errors, including two by Wickware, and won, 11-7. Wickware vowed that he would beat the Royal Giants the next day, and he did exactly that by throwing a six-hitter in a 9-2 Mohawk Giants victory.[30]

Controversy swirled around Wickware, on and off the field:

- A White team from Rutland, Vermont, recruited Wickware to pitch for them in an exhibition game against the Chicago Cubs on August 24, but the Cubs refused to take the field against him. Although it was widely reported that "color prejudice" was the reason, the *New York Age* said: "The Cubs have seen Wickware pitch in Chicago and know that he is effective in the box. ... Chicago did not want to take a chance of having it advertised that [they were] defeated by a Negro."[31] Two days later, a White Northampton (Massachusetts) team forfeited a game rather than face Wickware pitching for a White

Bellows Falls (Vermont) team.[32]

- An August game between the Mohawk Giants and McMahon's Lincoln Giants was canceled by McMahon; "he would not play against Wickware, since Wickware had refused to play for him."[33]

- Wickware's wife, Dottie, was arrested in August for allegedly cutting the arm of May Bradley with a knife "during a quarrel between the women."[34] Bradley was the wife of Phil Bradley, the Mohawk Giants manager and center fielder.

Despite the distractions, Wickware pitched brilliantly. In Schenectady on September 14, he fanned 14 in a five-hit shutout of the Poughkeepsie Honey Bugs of the Class-D New York-New Jersey League. He and Phil Bradley slugged back-to-back home runs in the sixth inning; "so elated was one fan in the grand stand that he presented each player with a $5 bill."[35] Two weeks later, Wickware pitched shutouts in *both* games of a doubleheader versus the Cuban Giants of Buffalo.[36] His verified record for the 1913 Mohawk Giants was 24-5 with nine shutouts.[37] He was compared with the greatest White pitchers of the day, including Walter Johnson, Smoky Joe Wood, Christy Mathewson, and Grover Alexander.[38]

The most intriguing matchup of the season occurred on Sunday, October 5, in Schenectady. Wernecke had arranged a game between his Mohawk Giants and a barnstorming team known as Walter Johnson's All-Americans. Johnson, coming off a phenomenal 36-7 season with the Washington Senators, would face Wickware in "a test of the best white pitcher against the best colored twirler."[39] The game was to start at 3:00 P.M. but was delayed 75 minutes when Wickware and eight teammates stormed off the field before the first pitch, declaring they would not play unless Wernecke paid the $921 he owed them. This precipitated a "near riot" by the overflow crowd, as people swarmed to the ticket booth to demand refunds. According to the *Schenectady Union-Star*, "Wickware, in an ugly mood, used his tongue too freely as he strode about the crowd, swinging a bat dangerously near the spectators and muttering threats against Wernecke." A local businessman rushed $500 to the scene as partial settlement, and the players were persuaded to return to the field. The game lasted 5½ innings before it was called because of darkness. Johnson struck out 11 and gave up only two hits, but the Mohawk Giants prevailed, 1-0. Wickware had defeated the great Walter Johnson.[40]

The showdown with Johnson was supposed to be the final game of the Mohawk Giants' season, but after the game, Wickware and his teammates took the team uniforms and equipment and went to New York City, where they played as a team without Wernecke's consent. Wickware struck out 13 and allowed five hits on October 12, but the Mohawk Giants were edged 2-1 in 10 innings by the Royal Giants.[41]

Back home in Coffeyville, Wickware's father, Eldon, beamed with pride upon receiving a large poster advertising the game between the Mohawk Giants and Walter Johnson's All-Americans. Eldon worked as a janitor at the *Coffeyville Daily Journal*. "Young Wickware is regarded as the world's greatest colored pitcher," reported the *Journal*.[42]

From January to March 1914, two teams of Negro stars played a series of games in Palm Beach, Florida, to entertain guests of the Royal Poinciana and Breakers hotels. Pitching for Royal Poinciana, Wickware was defeated three times by Cyclone Joe Williams and the Breakers.[43]

Wickware returned to Schenectady in April to pitch for the Mohawk Giants under new management. He dominated the teams he faced: 15 strikeouts in a three-hit shutout of the Amsterdams on May 31; 18 K's in a four-hitter against a Schenectady team on June 14; and 17 strikeouts in a two-hit shutout of the Empires on July 9.[44] The Mohawk Giants failed financially and disbanded in July.[45] Rube Foster swept in and recruited Wickware to play for him.

Wickware was reunited with center fielder Pete Hill, shortstop John Henry Lloyd, and catcher Bruce Petway on the Chicago American Giants. On August 26 in Chicago, Wickware threw a no-hitter that was nearly a perfect game. George Shively of the Indianapolis ABCs led off the game by drawing a walk but was thrown out trying to steal second base. Wickware retired the next 26 batters in a row, as the American Giants nipped the ABCs, 1-0.[46] Four days later Wickware delivered a three-hit shutout and fanned 12 in a 3-0 victory over the Royal Giants.[47]

Sportswriter Frank G. Menke described Wickware's formidable curveball:

"Wickware has marvelous speed, a weird set of curves and wonderful control. And he has a trick that has made him feared among batters. He throws what seems to be a 'bean-ball,' but his control is so perfect that he never has hit a batter in the head. But when the batters see the ball, propelled with mighty force, come for their heads, they jump away – and the ball, taking its proper and well-timed curve, arches over the plate for a strike."[48]

On June 22, 1915, Wickware tossed a two-hitter in the American Giants' 6-1 victory over the Indianapolis ABCs. One of the hits was a single by 18-year-old Oscar Charleston, a future Hall of Famer.[49] Wickware pitched both games of a doubleheader against the New York Lincoln Stars on August 10, winning the first game, 2-1, in 12 innings, and losing the second game, 1-0.[50]

Wickware's nemesis in 1915 was a barnstorming team known as the Cuban Stars. Twenty-one-year-old Cristóbal Torriente, a future Hall of Famer, smacked two triples and a single off him in the Cubans' 6-1 triumph over the American Giants on the Fourth of July.[51] A week later Foster took Wickware out of the game after the Cubans scored five runs in the first inning.[52] On August 15 Foster left him in as the Cubans pounded him for 10 runs on 17 hits.[53]

The American Giants played in the California Winter League in November and December 1915. Presumably divorced from the knife-wielding Dottie, Wickware married Elizabeth McCann in Chicago on May 18, 1915, and his new wife accompanied him on the trip to California.[54] He posted a 6-1 record in the CWL, including a one-hit shutout on Thanksgiving Day against the San Diego Pantages, a team of top minor-league players, some with major-league experience.[55]

Wickware turned the tide against Cuban opponents in 1916. He and the American Giants defeated the Havana and Almendares teams in Cuba in March.[56] Pitching for the ABCs in Indianapolis on May 8, he overcame the Cuban Stars, 5-4, in 10 innings.[57] Back with the American Giants, he shut out the Cuban Stars in Chicago on July 7 and August 20.[58] He also hurled shutouts against the St. Louis Giants on July 11 and the Lincoln Stars on August 13; the latter was a 12-inning gem that the *Chicago Tribune* called "one of the best games" of Wickware's career.[59]

From April to July 1917, Wickware pitched for the Chicago Giants (not the American Giants) and Jewell's ABCs of Indianapolis, but he returned to the American Giants in August 1917 and remained with the team until his induction into the Army a year later.[60] He was stationed at Camp Grant in Rockford, Illinois, at the tail end of World War I.[61]

Wickware bounced from team to team. In May 1919 he hurled a three-hit shutout with 15 strikeouts for the Detroit Stars against the Hayes Wheel team of

(Courtesy Noir-Tech Research, Inc.)

Righthander Frank Wickware, picture here in a Schenectady Mohawk Giants uniform, was among the Negro Leaguers considered for the National Baseball Hall of Fame in 2006.

Jackson, Michigan.[62] He returned to the American Giants in July 1919, but in August he moved to the Bacharach Giants of Atlantic City.[63] He pitched for the Norfolk All-Stars in 1920 before rejoining the American Giants in July of that year.[64] From 1921 to 1923, Wickware pitched for the Chicago Giants, the Chicago Union Giants, and the Calgary Black Sox.[65]

Controversy was never far from Wickware. On June 11, 1924, he pitched the first inning of a game in Utica and "became dissatisfied with the ball being used and declined to continue in the box."[66] As a member of the Lincoln Giants in 1925, he was present when his teammate Dave Brown allegedly shot and killed a man on a Harlem street. Wickware was charged but later exonerated; Brown disappeared from the scene and was never located.[67]

Floyd "Jelly" Gardner, who was one of Wickware's teammates on the 1920 American Giants, said Wickware "was a dissipator but a good pitcher."[68] But Wickware's pitching skills declined rapidly as he entered his mid-30s and many felt alcohol was to blame. A 1926 editorial in the *Pittsburgh Courier* warned of "liquor, and its attendant evils," and stated that "Frank Wickware liquored himself out of big time baseball."[69]

At age 42, Wickware attempted a comeback as manager and pitcher of the Wickware Colored Giants of Bridgeport, Connecticut. On July 4, 1930, he threw a two-hitter but lost 1-0 to the Brooklyn Royal Giants.[70]

After his baseball career, Wickware settled in Schenectady, where he resided for the rest of his life. In 1939 he had a domestic dispute with his third wife, Sarah, and was charged with second-degree assault after he allegedly "struck his wife on the head with a six-foot stick," opening "a deep gash at the base of her skull."[71] In 1948 Wickware received a four-month sentence for his role in the theft of boots from the Army depot where he was employed.[72]

Wickware died on November 2, 1967, in Schenectady, at the age of 79. His obituary in the *Schenectady Gazette* recalled the glorious day in 1913 when he beat Walter Johnson, 1-0, and noted that "only the majors' color line ... prevented him from becoming a big league star."[73]

NOTES

1   *Chicago Defender*, August 30, 1930.

2   baseball-reference.com/bullpen/2006_Special_Committee_on_the_Negro_Leagues_Election.

3   wichitahof.com/kansas-baseball-hof-inductees.html.

4   1900 US Census; 1905 Kansas State Census; *Coffeyville* (Kansas) *Daily Journal*, May 16, 1910.

5   *Coffeyville Daily Journal*, April 7, 1919.

6   *Muskogee* (Oklahoma) *Times-Democrat*, August 1, 1907.

7   *San Antonio Express*, July 13 and August 10, 1908.

8   *Chicago Tribune*, April 25, 1910.

9   *Chicago Tribune*, June 6 and 27, 1910.

10   *Harrisburg* (Pennsylvania) *Daily Independent*, September 20, 1910.

11   Robert Charles Cottrell, *The Best Pitcher in Baseball: The Life of Rube Foster, Negro League Giant* (New York: New York University Press, 2001), 59.

12   William F. McNeil, *Black Baseball Out of Season: Pay for Play Outside of the Negro Leagues* (Jefferson, North Carolina: McFarland, 2007), 37; and *The California Winter League: America's First Integrated Professional Baseball League* (McFarland, 2002), 35-38.

13   *Chicago Tribune*, May 15 and 31; June 5 and 26; and July 6, 1911.

14   *Brooklyn Daily Eagle*, February 14 and March 6, 1912.

15   *Chicago Tribune*, May 20, 1912; *New York Age*, August 8, 1912.

16   *New York Age*, August 29, 1912.

17   *New York Age*, September 12, 1912.

18   *New York Age*, December 12, 1912.

19   *Schenectady* (New York) *Gazette*, May 21, 1913.

20   *Schenectady Gazette*, May 26, 1913.

21   *Schenectady Gazette*, June 9, 1913.

22   *Schenectady Gazette*, May 26 and August 14, 1913.

23   *Schenectady Gazette*, May 26, and July 7 and 14, 1913.

24   *Chicago Tribune*, December 10, 1911.

25   *Schenectady Gazette*, July 14, 1913.

26   *New York Age*, July 17, 1913.

27   *New York Age*, July 24, 1913.

28   *Schenectady Gazette*, July 21 and 22, 1913.

29   *Schenectady Gazette*, August 4, 1913.

30   *Schenectady Gazette*, August 13 and 14, 1913.

31   *New York Age*, August 28, 1913.

32   *Springfield* (Massachusetts) *Union*, August 27, 1913.

33   *Schenectady Gazette*, August 22, 1913.

34   *Schenectady Gazette*, August 26, 1913.

35   *Schenectady Gazette*, September 15, 1913.

36   *Schenectady Gazette*, September 29, 1913.

37   Frank M. Keetz, *The Mohawk Colored Giants of Schenectady* (Schenectady, New York: self-published, 1999), 7.

38   *Schenectady Gazette*, May 26 and September 5, 1913; *Coffeyville Daily Journal*, June 5, 1913; *Allentown* (Pennsylvania) *Democrat*, June 11, 1915.

39   *Schenectady Gazette*, October 1, 1913.

40   Keetz, 14–17.

41   Keetz, 17; *Brooklyn Daily Eagle*, October 13, 1913.

42   *Coffeyville Daily Journal*, November 22, 1913.

43   McNeil, *Black Baseball Out of Season*, 17-19.

44   *Schenectady Gazette*, June 1 and 15, 1914; *Amsterdam* (New York) *Evening Recorder*, July 10, 1914.

45   Keetz, 18-19.

46   *Chicago Tribune*, August 27, 1914.

47   *Chicago Defender*, September 5, 1914.

48   *Allentown* (Pennsylvania) *Democrat*, June 11, 1915.

49   *Chicago Tribune*, June 23, 1915.

50   *Chicago Tribune*, August 11, 1915.

51   *Chicago Defender*, July 10, 1915.

52   *Chicago Tribune*, July 12, 1915.

53   *Chicago Defender*, August 21, 1915.

54   Cook County, Illinois, Marriage Indexes, 1912-1942, at Ancestry.com; Paul Debono, *The Chicago American Giants* (Jefferson, North Carolina: McFarland, 2007), 58.

55   McNeil, *The California Winter League*, 51-55; *San Bernardino* (California) *News*, November 26, 1915.

56   *Chicago Defender*, March 11 and 18, and April 8, 1916.

57   *Indianapolis Star*, May 9, 1916.

58   *Chicago Tribune*, July 8 and August 21, 1916.

59   *Chicago Tribune*, July 12 and August 14, 1916.

60   *Chicago Tribune*, April 23, May 21, and July 24 and 28, 1917, and March 9 and May 28, 1918; *Chicago Defender*, August 18, 1917, and July 20 and 27, 1918.

61   *Chicago Defender*, August 17 and 24, 1918.

62   *Detroit Free Press*, May 26, 1919.

63   *Chicago Tribune*, July 3, 1919; *New York Age*, August 9, 1919.

64   *Chicago Defender*, June 12 and July 17, 1920.

65   *Chicago Defender*, May 14 and July 30, 1921; *Chicago Tribune*, June 22, 1921, and September 10, 1923.

66   *Schenectady Gazette*, June 12, 1924.

67   James E. Overmyer, *Black Ball and the Boardwalk: The Bacharach Giants of Atlantic City, 1916-1929* (Jefferson, North Carolina: McFarland, 2014), 132; *Chicago Defender*, May 23, 1925.

68   John B. Holway, *Blackball Tales* (Springfield, Virginia: Scorpio Books, 2008), 51.

69   *Pittsburgh Courier*, April 3, 1926.

70   *Schenectady Gazette*, July 22, 1930.

71   *Schenectady Gazette*, June 30, 1939.

72   *Schenectady Gazette*, March 24, 1948; *Schenectady Herald-Journal*, October 19, 1948.

73   *Schenectady Gazette*, November 6, 1967.

BOBBY WILLIAMS

BY SEAN KOLODZIEJ

It took a special type of athlete to play for Chicago American Giants manager Rube Foster. He liked to engage in small ball and built his teams around speed and bunting. He wanted only smart competitors on his team. Foster was known to say, "If you haven't got intelligence enough to fit into this play, you can't play here."[1] The ideal ballplayer for Foster was someone who was fast enough to steal a base, smart enough to know when to steal that base, and good enough with the bat to lay down a perfect bunt. Bobby Williams fit that role so well that he ended up playing for Foster for eight straight years.

Robert "Bobby" Lawns Williams was born on September 30, 1895, in New Orleans to George and Mary Williams. His father was a day laborer, who owned his own home in the Leonidas area of town. Bobby was the youngest of eight children. Nothing is known of his childhood, but one can imagine his family walking to nearby Lincoln Park to hear musicians like Buddy Bolden play music that eventually became known as jazz.

In the early 1910s, Bobby was a student at New Orleans University. This was a historically Black college that merged with Straight College in 1934 to form what is now known as Dillard University. During his time there, he played on the baseball team with Dave Malarcher, and "[b]etween 1913 and 1916 the baseball team lost not a single game. The success was due to two stars, David Malarcher and Robert Williams, who acted as coaches."[2] Williams eventually teamed up

again with Malarcher on the Chicago American Giants from 1920 to 1925.

Prior to each season, the American Giants made a "spring training" trip and played games in the South. While on this trip in 1916, Rube Foster signed Williams, who was then farmed out to the Dayton Giants.[3] This team was also nicknamed the Dayton Chappies after catcher-manager-co-owner George "Chappie" Johnson. Johnson was an ideal manager for the 21-year-old Williams. He was "quiet, calm, and dignified, and always showed class and maintained a gentlemanly demeanor, even in his protests with umpires."[4]

The American Giants played the Dayton Giants during the 1917 season, and it was then that Foster probably knew he was correct in signing Bobby Williams. A game in June between the two teams saw Williams make "a great one-hand stab of (John Henry "Pop") Lloyd's line drive."[5] Williams was a small man, even for the era in which he played, and his playing height was listed at 5-feet-5 and his weight as 145 pounds. It was his speed that likely drew the most attention from Foster

As the 1917 season neared its end, Foster was looking for a new shortstop. Pop Lloyd had been playing shortstop for Foster's American Giants since 1914. When the 1917 regular season ended, Foster decided to take his team to Palm Beach to play in the Florida Hotel League. However, Lloyd "had a job in the Army Quartermaster's depot in Chicago, and he decided to stay there instead of traveling to Florida."[6] Even though Lloyd was considered by many to be the best shortstop in all of baseball, his choice to stay behind in Chicago "displeased Foster, and by early spring the manager was singing the praises of a young shortstop named Bobby Williams."[7]

It did not take long for the Chicago newspapers to notice Williams. As early as March 2, 1918, the *Chicago Defender* wrote that Williams was a find and that "Rube Foster has a crack shortstop in Williams, the crack shortstop from New Orleans."[8] On March 30 the paper wrote that "Bobby cut a swath between second and third and the rich fans at the Royal Poinciana are still talking about him."[9]

The Royal Poinciana was a Palm Beach hotel that hired porters and waiters based on one qualification: that they played baseball well. Another hotel in the area, the Breakers, also had a baseball team, and the two teams played each other every January through March. Judy Johnson said about playing in Palm Beach: "The rivalry between the two teams was intense, but it was the money-making that lured many of the players down there. The pay and the tips were excellent."[10]

As the 1918 baseball season began, the Chicago fans took to Williams quickly. "Never has any player … taken with the fans on such a short stay as little Bobby Williams."[11] In a game against his old team, the Dayton Giants, he "went back near second, leaped in the air, stabbed [Samuel] DeWitt's Texas leaguer, turned a somersault and still held the ball in his gloved hand."[12] There was some drama on July 6, though. The *Chicago Defender* ran a story stating that Williams was missing and asked for the public's help in locating him. The paper feared he had "been kidnapped, lost, strayed or been stolen or perhaps he has fallen the victim of the Black Hand."[13] The Black Hand was a precursor to organized-crime syndicates that extorted its victims with threats of violence.

There is no record of exactly what happened to Williams that day. He must have been located quickly because a week later the news about Williams had shifted to his being drafted into the US Army. The United States had entered the World War in April of 1917 and, although Williams had registered for the draft in late May, he was still caught off guard by actually being called to duty. The *Chicago Defender* reported that "Bobby was last seen … sitting on the steps of Foster's home looking like a stray sheep waiting for a message from his draft board."[14]

Perhaps because of the uncertainty of war, Williams married Marie Skelton, a schoolteacher from Indianapolis. The marriage took place on August 27, 1918, in Winnebago, Illinois, a small town near Wisconsin. The couple's union did not last long; by the time the 1930 census was completed, Williams was listed as divorced.

As was the case on baseball teams, Williams spent his time in the Army as a member of a segregated unit. He served in the 803rd Pioneer Infantry Regiment's Company M, an African American outfit. By September the regiment was stationed at Camp Upton, New York. Williams was promoted to sergeant and then went overseas and served in Brest, France.

Pioneer infantry troops "did everything the infantry was too proud to do, and the engineers too lazy to do."[15] Their duties "were often summarized as building and repairing roads and buildings."[16] They usually provided manual labor to help the Regular Army troops and the engineers.

(Courtesy Noir-Tech Research, Inc.)

Bobby Williams, pictured here in a Pittsburgh Crawfords uniform, was the starting shortstop for the Chicago American Giants' first three NNL championship squads from 1920 to 1922.

The 803rd Pioneer Infantry Regiment did see combat in late October at the Toul Sector in France. It is not known how close to the lines they were. Although the 803rd had many casualties, only three members of Williams's company died. All three deaths were from the influenza epidemic that was spreading worldwide at the time.[17]

Williams returned home from France in February 1919 on the *USS President Grant*. This ship was for the "casual sick and wounded," although it is unknown what ailed Williams enough for him to be transported aboard this vessel. Williams's World War II draft registration card does mention that he had a scar on his right leg from a wound suffered in World War I. The *Chicago Defender* also mentioned "Bobby's overseas injury"[18] in reference to his being ready to start the 1920 season on time.

Whatever injury Williams sustained in the war; he was ready to play baseball again in 1919 and was welcomed back to the Chicago American Giants. The April 5 edition of the *Chicago Defender,* referring to the ballplayers returning from overseas, stated that "they were in good health and expect to be in the game for all it's worth."[19]

The 1919 season saw some significant changes in the American Giants lineup. Center fielder Pete Hill was replaced by Oscar Charleston, and Cristobal Torriente joined the team to play left field. Thus, Williams had the opportunity to learn from some of the best players the Negro Leagues ever saw.

In July of that year, interracial violence erupted in Chicago and "[r]oving gangs of white vigilantes ... pulled black commuters from trolleys and beat them, shot people from cars, looted black-owned businesses, and set fire to houses."[20] Eventually, the Illinois National Guard was called out and occupied Schorling Park, the American Giants' home ballpark which was right in the middle of the riot-torn area. Williams and the rest of the American Giants were in Detroit at the time of the riots, and they found themselves stranded. Rube Foster was forced to plan a trip that had his squad playing teams in the East. The team was not able to play another game at Schorling Park until August 31.

Available statistics indicate that Williams finished the 1919 season with just a .219 batting average. He had 16 RBIs in 42 league games, 12 walks and 5 sacrifice hits. These totals tell the story of how Rube Foster managed the American Giants. He "introduced the hit-and-run play, bunt-and-run, drag bunting, the double steals, the suicide squeeze play and tilting of the base

lines for bunt control."[21] Williams appeared to be a seamless fit for this style of play.

On February 13, 1920, the first Negro National League was formed in Kansas City, Missouri. At the center of it all was Foster. His Chicago American Giants joined seven other Midwestern teams to establish stability among Black baseball clubs.

Based on his play the previous year, Williams's place on the club for the 1920 season was secure. In late March, the *Chicago Defender* wrote that "the verdict of the fans is that Williams is here to stay and will prove a wonder this season."[22] Joining the American Giants as third baseman was Williams's old college teammate, David Malarcher. Together, they formed a solid left side of the infield for the next six years.

The Chicago American Giants took the NNL's inaugural pennant. Williams hit .212 with 26 RBIs in 60 league games. Collectively, the entire team hit for a .254 average, but their 92 sacrifice hits in 62 NNL games played tell the story of how this team won.

The Negro National League games ended in late September of 1920. Instead of playing more exhibition games with the American Giants, Williams joined the Dayton Marcos since that squad was in need of a shortstop. Dayton was in such dire straits that in the game before Williams joined the team, the Marcos had used a pitcher to play shortstop.[23] Little is known about Williams's time with Dayton, but he more than likely played with the team until its season ended in late October.

The year 1921 began with most of the American Giants going to Florida to play at the Poinciana Hotel again. Williams was among the team members who were getting ready for the coming season while also making extra money as porters. He rejoined the American Giants and they once more finished with the best record in the Negro National League. Williams put up average batting statistics, but he did end up with 17 sacrifice hits and 14 stolen bases in 84 league games. In an October 4 game against Hilldale, Williams stole second, third, and home in the same inning and finished with a total of four stolen bases that day.[24]

The 1922 season was similar to 1921. The American Giants again finished with the best record in the Negro National League. Williams's statistics were quite similar to what he put up in 1921: a .224 batting average to go with 15 sacrifice hits and 10 stolen bases in 74 league games.

As 1923 began, it was evident that Williams had become a fan favorite in Chicago. The *Chicago*

Defender wrote on January 13 that "in the number of answers we received from the fans that regularly attended the games of the Chicago club, Bobby's name continued to lead those named as shortstop, 10 to 1."[25] In 75 NNL games, Williams's batting average rose to a respectable .250, and his sacrifice hits again reached double digits with 12. Even though the American Giants fielded a similar team to the previous year's, they failed to capture the NNL pennant for the first time, finishing second to the Kansas City Monarchs, who were led by such stars as Bullet Rogan and Dobie Moore.

The American Giants finished second to the Kansas City Monarchs again in 1924. Williams may have had his best year as a hitter. He hit .273 with 50 RBIs in 75 league games. After the NNL season ended, Williams traveled to Cuba to play for the Leopardos de Santa Clara team. The *Chicago Defender* reported "with … our great little Bobby Williams … at short, the Santa Clara team in the Cuban league has jumped from the bottom to second place."[26] Led by the hitting of Alejandro Oms, Santa Clara finished in third place. Other players on the team included Oliver Marcell and future Hall of Famer Turkey Stearnes.

The Chicago American Giants returned for the 1925 season with pretty much the same lineup as the previous year's. Without any significant changes, the team fell to third place. The Monarchs once again took the pennant, while the St. Louis Stars finished in second place. Williams, playing in 85 NNL games, led the league with 25 sacrifice hits.

The 1926 season proved to be a tumultuous one for Williams. The Indianapolis ABCs, after seeing many of their star players leave for teams in the East, were in desperate need of players. Rube Foster agreed to have Bingo DeMoss leave the American Giants to manage the ABCs. DeMoss wanted to take Williams with him, but Williams did not want to leave Chicago. In late March, the Negro National League held a meeting of its board of directors. The *Chicago Defender* reported that DeMoss "may be detained here a few days longer dickering for the services of Bobby Williams."[27]

Williams reluctantly joined the Indianapolis club. However, by mid-May, he jumped his contract to play for the independent Homestead Grays, based in the Pittsburgh area. Frank "Fay" Young, sports editor of the *Defender,* did not take this news well. He wrote, "It looks bad for Bobby. Besides being outlawed by both league clubs, Bobby has begun to slip in his playing ability, according to those who follow the game day to day. Most of the Chicago fans were more than glad

to see him leave the line-up and Foster replace him, but they hoped the change would do the little fellow some good."[28]

If Young was correct about the Chicago fans' observations, Homestead fans nevertheless felt the exact opposite about Williams. The June 10 edition of the *New Castle News* (from New Castle, near Pittsburgh) reported that "the short-stopping position is in the hands of a star."[29] Williams must have loved switching teams, as the Homestead Grays won 43 straight games and finished with a record of 140-13-10.[30] The team was owned and managed by Cum Posey and was led by Hall of Fame pitcher Smokey Joe Williams.

Playing for the Grays had additional advantages. After the 1926 season ended, Bobby Williams traveled to Florida to play with Smokey Joe in the Florida Hotel League. Although information on these games is limited, it seems that he performed well and, at one point, may have managed the Breakers team.[31]

Williams remained with the Grays in 1927. By now, after playing with elite Negro baseball teams for 10 years, he was showing veteran leadership. None other than Cum Posey felt that Williams was shaping into a manager. Posey wrote, "(Sam) Streeter is no longer with the Grays but Bobby Williams has found his voice and is chief 'pusher.'"[32] The Grays once again played great baseball, but since most of their games were against other independent teams, semipro teams, and town teams, only limited statistics are available. After the Grays' 1927 season ended, Williams once again played for the Breakers Hotel in Florida.

After returning from Florida, Williams learned that he had been released by the Grays.[33] Posey believed he had found a shortstop "whom the management thought would fit into the Grays' style of play more aptly."[34] That shortstop was Charley Radcliffe, who was, at 21, a lot younger than Williams. According to the *Pittsburgh Courier,* "besides being a flash afield, he wields a wicked bat."[35] Williams did not waste any time finding new employment; he rejoined the Chicago American Giants to start the 1928 season. Perhaps because he was older, or perhaps because the Giants wanted catcher Pythias Russ to switch to shortstop, Williams found himself moved to third base. Before too long, it was evident that there was no spot on the field for him to play. In early July Williams was sent to the Cleveland Tigers.

The Tigers lost a lot of games during the first half of the 1928 season, and at the time Williams joined the team, owner M.C. Barkin fired manager Frank Duncan and released several players. The Tigers continued their losing ways and ended the season in seventh place. By August, Williams already had left the team to join the New York Lincoln Giants of the Eastern Colored League.

Williams spent the 1929 season playing for the Atlantic City Bacharach Giants of the American Negro League. He started out slowly, failed to hit, and was used mainly as a backup infielder. The team finished 21-50-2, in fifth place in the six-team league.

After retiring from baseball in 1930, Gus Greenlee asked Williams to manage his Pittsburgh Crawford Giants for the 1931 season. Greenlee, known for being a numbers runner and racketeer, had just purchased the baseball club and was determined to put together a great team. Williams gathered up exceptional players including Jimmie Crutchfield, Jasper "Jap" Washington, Sam "Lefty" Streeter, and Satchel Paige. As good as this team was, Greenlee was determined to make the next season's roster even better.

The Homestead Grays, the other Negro League team in Pittsburgh, had a great team in 1931. Greenlee decided to sign away all the Grays' best players for his Crawfords and accomplished his plan by offering far more money than Grays owner Cum Posey could afford. The first to sign was Oscar Charleston, who managed the Crawfords in 1932. Bobby Williams gave up his managing duties but stayed on the team as a backup infielder. Also joining the Crawfords were Ted "Double Duty" Radcliffe, Smokey Joe Williams, James "Cool Papa" Bell, Judy Johnson, and Josh Gibson. Williams played with seven future Hall of Famers that year. Greenlee Field, the new home of the Crawfords and one of the first Black-built and Black-owned ballparks, also opened that year.

The 1932 season turned out to be Williams's last year as a professional baseball player. By June the *Pittsburgh Courier* was reporting that "manager Oscar has been looking all around the country for a hale and hearty third baseman to help out Bobby Williams and his aging legs."[36] Williams finished the season batting only .140 with a .204 on-base percentage.

During the offseason, Greenlee sometimes hired his players for odd jobs. Ted Page, for instance, was hired as a lookout man at a numbers house. He was paid $15 a week to ring a bell if he saw anyone suspicious coming.[37] Although no evidence has been uncovered that shows Bobby Williams working a similar job, based on his future arrests, it seems that it was around this time that Williams was introduced to the illegal numbers lottery.

After taking a year off from the game, Williams was back in baseball in 1934. He now managed the Cleveland Red Sox of the Negro National League II. The *Pittsburgh Courier* felt that this was a good hire, describing Williams as "quiet, unassuming, but possessing a thorough knowledge of the game"[38] But the team played poorly and finished in last place with a 3-22 record. The team folded after the season ended.

On August 13, 1938, Williams played in the Homestead Grays' 25th anniversary baseball game. The team, made up of former Grays, played an all-White team of retired players at Pittsburgh's Forbes Field. Besides Williams, other former Grays who participated included Smokey Joe Williams, Jap Washington, and Sam Streeter, all of whom contributed to the Grays' victory that day.

In 1945 Williams took the job of managing the reconstituted Pittsburgh Crawfords of the newly formed United States League.[39] The league was the brainchild of Gus Greenlee and had the backing of Brooklyn Dodgers minority owner and general manager Branch Rickey, who ostensibly wanted to use the new circuit to scout Black players whom he might sign to break White baseball's color line. Other former players who managed teams in the league included Oscar Charleston, Dizzy Dismukes, Bingo DeMoss, and Webster McDonald. The league's games did not receive much press coverage, but the Crawfords were reported to have won the championship.[40] The USL did not last past the 1946 season.

Williams continued to live in Pittsburgh after his baseball career was over, but he did not find the same success that he had found on baseball diamonds. Between 1947 and 1961, he was arrested five times for running numbers.[41] He was essentially a bookie who took money for bets in an illegal lottery.

One bright spot in Williams's later years occurred when he was selected to vote in the 1952 *Pittsburgh Courier* Poll of Greatest Black Players. He was one of 31 experts, including 21 former players, who voted for the best Negro League players from 1910 to 1951. This poll is frequently referenced when baseball historians attempt to determine who the greatest players in the Negro Leagues were. Williams received one vote. It is not known if he voted for himself; there is only one known ballot, and it is not Williams's.[42]

Sometime between 1958 and 1963, Robert Williams married Helen Butler. Helen owned the home that Robert had lodged in since at least 1940. She was a widow whose first husband had died of tuberculosis in 1936. She had a daughter, Shirley, from that marriage.

Robert must have formed a close bond with Shirley because he is listed as her father in his obituary.

Robert Williams died on December 30, 1978, in Pittsburgh at the age of 83. He was buried in Allegheny Cemetery, where Josh Gibson, his former Hall of Fame teammate, also is buried.

ACKNOWLEDGMENTS

The author would like to thank fellow SABR members Bill Nowlin, Frederick C. Bush, and Thomas Kern, who took the time to answer emails about Bobby Williams's obituary. In addition, the author thanks Cassidy Lent, manager of reference services at the National Baseball Hall of Fame and Museum, who provided Williams's file and Hall of Fame questionnaire.

SOURCES

Ancestry.com was consulted for public records, including census information, birth, marriage, and death records, and military registration cards.

Unless otherwise indicated, all statistics and team records were taken from the Seamheads Negro League Database.

NOTES

1   John B. Holway, *Blackball Stars: Negro League Pioneers* (Westport, Connecticut: Meckler Books, 1988), 25.

2   John B. Holway, *Voices From the Great Black Baseball Leagues, Revised Edition* (Mineola, New York: Dover Publications, 2010), 45.

3   "Trio of American Giants," *Pittsburgh Courier*, March 14, 1925: 7.

4   Negro Leagues Baseball eMuseum: Personal Profiles: George "Chappie" Johnson https://nlbemuseum.com/history/players/johnsonch.html. Accessed December 15, 2021.

5   "American Giants Continue to Win," *Chicago Defender*, June 9, 1917: 8.

6   Robert Peterson, *Only the Ball Was White* (New York: Oxford University Press, 1992), 77.

7   Peterson, 77.

8   "Williams Is a Find," *Chicago Defender*, March 2, 1918: 7.

9   Mister Fan, "American Giants to Present New Line-up for This Season," *Chicago Defender*, March 30, 1918: 9.

10 William E. McNeil, *Black Baseball Out of Season* (Jefferson, North Carolina: McFarland & Company, 2015), 28.

11 "Williams Drafted: Mendez Shortstop," *Chicago Defender*, July 13, 1918: 9.

12 "Fosterites Win 2 from 'Chappies,'" *Chicago Defender*, June 22, 1918: 13.

13 "Twilight Game to American Giants in Eleventh," *Chicago Defender*, July 16, 1918: 9.

14 "Williams Drafted: Mendez Shortstop."

15 Margaret M. McMahon, *A Guide to the U.S. Pioneer Infantry Regiments in WWI* (Middletown, Delaware: Margaret M. McMahon Teaching & Training Company, 2018), 4.

16 McMahon, 37.

17 This information was obtained via the Fold3 Military Records website. See www.fold3.com.

18 "Nothing Lacking to Make Giants Great; 'Rube' Has Fine Team by All the Dope," *Chicago Defender*, April 10, 1920: 11.

19 "Giants' Recruits Work Hard," *Chicago Defender*, April 5, 1919: 11.

20 Gary Ashwill, "White Racial Violence and the Negro Leagues: The Chicago Riot of 1919," Agate Type, https://agatetype.typepad.com/agate_type/2020/06/white-racial-violence-the-negro-leagues-the-chicago-riot-of-1919.html, accessed December 15, 2021.

21 Larry Lester, *Rube Foster in His Time* (Jefferson, North Carolina: McFarland & Company, 2012), 102.

22 "Bobby Williams, Shortstop," *Chicago Defender*, March 27, 1920: 11.

23 "St, Louis 6, Dayton 0," *Dayton Herald*, September 18, 1920: 16.

24 John Holway, *The Complete Book of Baseball's Negro Leagues: The Other Half of Baseball History* (Fern Park, Florida: Hastings House, 2001), 161.

25 "Lyons, Torrienti, and Jim Brown Sign with A.M. Giants," *Chicago Defender*, January 13, 1923: 10.

26 "First Pictures of Cuban Baseball," *Chicago Defender*, November 29, 1924: 10. It should be noted that two books by Jorge Figueredo (*Cuban Baseball, A Statistical History, 1878-1961*, p. 160, and *Who's Who in Cuban Baseball, 1878-1961*, p. 361) that are often consulted for their reliability and thoroughness appear to be in error about the identity of the player named Williams who played for Santa Clara during the 1924-25 season. Figueredo identifies the player as Charles Williams in his *Statistical History* and as Charles A. Williams in *Who's Who*. According to the Seamheads Negro League database, there was only one Negro League player named Charles Williams, a second baseman who participated in five games with the Boston Resolutes in 1887. Seamheads lists no player named Charles A. Williams, but does list a Charley Raymore Williams, who was a second baseman with the Chicago American Giants from 1926-30. The common surname Williams and the fact that the two players both were members of the American Giants at times has likely led to the confusion. In addition to the *Chicago Defender* article of November 29, 1924, this author located a passenger list for the *S.S. Cuba*, leaving Havana on January 20, 1925, and arriving in Key West the same day. Bobby Williams was listed among the ship's passengers along with Oliver Marcell and Norman "Starmes," [*sic*] (Norman "Turkey" Stearnes; both men played on the Santa Clara team. The preponderance of the evidence points to the *Chicago Defender* article being correct in naming Bobby Williams as the player who was on the 1924-25 Santa Clara squad.

27 "Jim Taylor to Manage Cleveland: Move Comes as Big Surprise to St. Louis Ball Fans as Directors Meet," *Chicago Defender*, March 20, 1926: 11.

28 "Fay Says," *Chicago Defender*, May 15, 1926: 8.

29 "Grays to Play Ellwood Friday," *New Castle (Pennsylvania) News*, June 10, 1926: 21.

30 Cum Posey, "The Sportive Realm," *Pittsburgh Courier*, March 19, 1927: 17.

31 The Sportive Realm."

32 Cum Posey, "The Sportive Realm," *Pittsburgh Courier*, April 16, 1927: 16.

33 "New Shortstop to Appear in Lineup with Poseymen," *Pittsburgh Courier*, March 18, 1928: 30.

34 Posey, "The Sportive Realm," *Pittsburgh Courier*, March 24, 1928: 17.

35 "Charley Radcliffe and 'Bobo' Leonard New Acquisitions," *Pittsburgh Courier*, April 7, 1928: 17.

36 W. Rollo Wilson, "Philly Sees Some Western Ball," *Pittsburgh Courier*, June 11, 1932: 14.

37 Holway, *Voices From the Great Black Baseball Leagues*, 159.

38 "Bobby Williams to Manage Cleveland," *Pittsburgh Courier*, April 14, 1934: 13.

39 This Crawfords team was a completely new squad that had no relation to the previous iteration of the Crawfords. Greenlee had sold the original Crawfords franchise after the 1938 season, and the new owner moved the team first to Toledo and then to Indianapolis before it finally folded.

40   "United States League (1945-1946)," Center for Negro
      League Baseball Research, cnlbr.org.   http://www.cnlbr.org/
      Portals/0/Standings/United%20States%20League%20(1945-
      1946)%202019-10.pdf , accessed December 15, 2021.

41   For Williams's arrests, see the following: "Numbers Suspect Freed as His
      Pal 'Takes the Rap,'" *Pittsburgh Press*, November 25, 1947: 19; "Marauders
      Strike at Nine Places," *Pittsburgh Press,* June 1, 1948: 2; "Three Alleged

      Numbers Writers Held," *Pittsburgh Post-Gazette*, February 1, 1956: 16;
      "Hill Project Foils Raids on Numbers," *Pittsburgh Press*, January 14, 1957:
      2; "Dream Numbers Bad for Man," *Pittsburgh Press*, June 12, 1961: 2.

42   J. Fred Brillhart, "An Analysis of the 1952 Pittsburgh Courier Negro
      League Baseball Poll," The Donaldson Network, http://johndonald-
      son.bravehost.com/pdf/00237.pdf Accessed December 15, 2021.

TOM WILLIAMS

BY BILL JOHNSON

Thomas Williams's pitching career spanned only eight years, but in that time he proved to be an important member of Rube Foster's Chicago American Giants teams in the early years of the Negro National League.

Righthander Tom Williams had a 12-4 record and a 1.83 ERA for the American Giants' NNL-leading pitching staff. He had an outstanding 61-29 career record over the course of his nine-year career in the Negro Leagues.

(Courtesy Noir-Tech Research, Inc)

Although not much is documented about Williams's early life, he was born on September 28, 1896, in Charleston, South Carolina, to Andy Williams and Caroline Pryer.[1] By 1914, at the age of 18, he was enrolled at Morris Brown College, a historically Black institution, in Atlanta. Williams was a star pitcher on the school's baseball team and threw two no-hitters during the 1914 season alone, one against Alabama's Tuskegee University.[2] It is possible that, despite his young age, Williams was already a sophomore, as one article noted that Williams was "in midseason form," the comparison implying that this was not his first campaign.[3]

The press also dubbed the ace "Cyclone," likely as a homage to the brilliant Cyclone Joe Williams (perhaps better-known today as Smokey Joe), who had starred in Black baseball for nearly a decade. The moniker was an apt one, at least in the purview of his Southern Intercollegiate Athletic Conference (SIAC) competition.[4] In an early 1915 game against Morehouse, "Cyclone Williams was on the mound for the (Morris Brown) Giants and was almost invincible. ... Cyclone Williams whiffed sixteen of the Baptist boys."[5] In both 1915 and 1916, Morris Brown won the SIAC in their first two seasons of baseball competition, and in 1916 Morris Brown hosted Washington's Howard University for a national championship of sorts.[6] "In one of the greatest games that has ever been played in Atlanta, the fast Howard University aggregation met and defeated Morris Brown ... 4 to 1. ... 'Cyclone' Williams and [an otherwise unidentified catcher named] Addison formed the battery for the home team."[7]

Williams's baseball career took a turn in 1916 when he signed to play with the Bacharach City Giants, newly relocated from Jacksonville, Florida, to Atlantic City, New Jersey, while still enrolled at Morris Brown. His time there lasted only a few games. The next year he signed with Foster's American Giants, and he pitched well enough for the 1917 champions.[8] Williams was probably the number-two pitcher on the staff, behind Dick "Cannonball" Redding (another Morris Brown product), but this was a team that also had hurlers the caliber of Frank Wickware and Tom Johnson, the latter posting a 7-3 season record and a 2.57 ERA.[9]

Throwing almost exclusively to catcher George "Tubby" Dixon, and employing an arsenal of pitches that included "drop, spitter, fastball, and slow 'floater,'"[10] Williams is credited with 13 wins (against two losses) for the year. According to military draft registration records from 1917, he was married and lived at an address in south Chicago.[11] His wife's name is unknown, and by the time of the 1920 census, he was living alone in a boarding house in Philadelphia.[12] Regardless of marital status, Williams hit the road and joined a number of his American Giants teammates over the 1917-1918 winter by pitching for the Royal Poinciana Hotel team in the Florida Hotel League.

In early 1918, Williams arrived at the American Giants' train at the start of a road trip smelling of alcohol. Williams had a reputation for tippling, but manager Rube Foster had no patience for alcohol abuse.[13] Without work, Williams returned to Atlanta for a bit, even umpiring a game between Morehouse and Clarke Universities in early April.[14] Forced to find a job on the quick, the 21-year-old Williams spent 1918 and 1919 moving among John Henry "Pop" Lloyd's Brooklyn Royal Giants, Ed Bolden's Hilldale Daisies, and the Atlantic City Bacharach Giants.

In one particularly notable game, on September 14, 1918, Williams had the opportunity to test himself against the best players in the organized major leagues when he took the mound in a rare contest between Hilldale and the all-White World Series champion Boston Red Sox. The pitcher used his notorious pickoff move in the first inning to put Sherry Magee into a rundown between first base and second, but the Daisies failed to cover second, and Magee later scored on George Burns's single to center field. Williams gave up two more runs in the third, and the go-ahead run in the eighth to make the score 4-3, Boston. It was for naught, though, as a ninth-inning controversy resulted in a Boston forfeit and a 9-0 Hilldale win.[15]

All was forgiven, it seemed, when Williams rejoined the American Giants in the newly organized Negro National League in 1920. On a chilly April 11, he took the mound in the season opener against a White semipro team called the Rogers Parks. Although Chicago lost the game on a three-run fielding error, the 4,500 in attendance were privileged to watch the first foray of Rube Foster's new league.[16] On June 6 Williams tossed a six-hitter at the Magnets of Chicago, contributing to a 12-1 win at Schorling Park.[17] A week later, on June 13, he held the rival ABC's to five hits in a 9-1 American Giants victory.[18]

Over the following weeks, Williams enjoyed a run of success that led to wins over the Kansas City Monarchs, the St. Louis Giants, and the Dayton Marcos. Finally, on August 1, his luck gave out in a 5-4 extra-inning loss to Bullet Rogan and the Kansas City Monarchs, this time in the latter's home park.[19] For that inaugural season, Williams posted a 12-4 record and a 1.83 earned-run average in 157 innings, and logged 15 complete games. His ERA+ of 163 showed that he was well above league average in that department.[20] Interestingly, his 1.83 ERA was sandwiched between those of two teammates, with Dave Brown's 1.82 mark on one side, and Tom Johnson's 1.84 on the other.

Williams again pitched well in 1921, with a 14-8 record (2.87 ERA) in 163 innings pitched. In both years, 1920 and 1921, Chicago won the league title in convincing fashion. Despite the success, however, 1922 found Williams reunited with Dick Lundy with the independent Bacharach Giants in Delaware, and later in the year with the original Cyclone Joe Williams and his New York Lincoln Giants.

Back in Chicago as a reliever for the 1923 American Giants, Williams again had the chance to pitch against White major leaguers in a two-inning stint against the Detroit Tigers (with Heinie Manush, but without Ty Cobb). It was not a happy afternoon, as the pitcher yielded a bases-clearing triple in the ninth that contributed to a 7-1 drubbing by the Tigers.[21]

In 1924, despite waning skills, Williams still found ways to occasionally rekindle the magic. In May he tossed a two-hit complete-game against the Cleveland Browns, winning 5-1.[22] But in early August, in one of several examples of his lagging success, Williams appeared in relief against the Kansas City Monarchs and gave up four runs in a Chicago loss.[23]

In 1924, probably due to a NNL rule that teams could no longer indefinitely reserve an excessive inventory of players, Rube Foster released a number of veterans, including Williams.[24] Only 27 years old, the pitcher signed with his 1917 catcher, Bruce Petway, and the Detroit Stars.[25] Williams finished the 1924 season with Detroit, but no documentation has been found that he ever pitched again.

On January 30, 1937, a small notice headlined "Tom Williams, Ace Pitcher for Foster, Is Dead" appeared in the *Chicago Defender*. The obituary noted that Williams died in a Chicago area hospital after enduring an unspecified, lingering illness.[26] He had died at the age of 40 on January 19 in Bremen, Illinois, a Chicago suburb, and was buried in Restvale Cemetery in Alsip, Illinois. That site is also the final resting place for basketball star Nate "Sweetwater" Clifton as well as musical immortals Muddy Waters, Kansas Joe McCoy, and Luther Tucker.[27]

SOURCES

Statistical data is taken from the website www.seamheads.com, unless otherwise noted.

NOTES

1   Online: *Ancestry.com*. Illinois, U.S., Deaths and Stillbirths Index, 1916-1947 [database online]. Provo, Utah, USA: https://search.ancestry.com/cgi-bin/sse.dll?indiv=1&dbid=2542&h=2473529&tid=&pid=&queryId=770809537a699d7f9537074d50722728&usePUB=true&_phsrc=Xdq2&_phstart=successSource.

2   "Negro Twirler Hurls Fine No-Hit Game," *Atlanta Constitution*, April 5, 1914: 13.

3   "Negro Twirler Hurls Fine No-Hit Game."

4   Online: Southern Intercollegiate Athletic Conference - BR Bullpen (baseball-reference.com). Accessed June 3, 2021.

5   "Morris Brown 9, Morehouse 5," *Atlanta Constitution*, March 27, 1915: 6.

6   "Play for Championship," *Atlanta Constitution*, April 7, 1916: 10.

7   "Howard 4, Morris Brown 1," *Atlanta Constitution*, April 19, 1916: 8.

8   Online: 1917 Chicago American Giants – Seamheads Negro Leagues Database. Accessed June 3, 2021.

9   "Tom Johnson," Seamheads.com, https://www.seamheads.com/NegroLgs/player.php?playerID=johnso1tom.

10   James A. Riley, "Thomas Williams," *The Biographical Encyclopedia of the Negro Baseball Clubs* (New York: Carroll & Graf, 1994), 862.

11   Thomas Williams draft registration card, dated June 5, 1917. Online: 1917ThomasWilliamsWWIDraftRegistration (bravehost.com). Accessed June 4, 2021.

12   Fourteenth Census of the United States: 1920 – Population; Philadelphia Pennsylvania, Supervisor District 1, Enumeration District 1790, sheet 2B; January 3, 1920.

13   Paul DeBono, *The Chicago American Giants* (Jefferson, North Carolina: McFarland & Company, 2011), 66.

14   "Morehouse 19, Clarke 5," *Atlanta Constitution*, April 7, 1918: 7.

15   Bill Nowlin, "The One Time the 'Boston Red Sox' Played a Black Team," *Baseball Research Journal*, Society for American Baseball Research, Phoenix, Arizona, Spring 2021. Online: The One Time the 'Boston Red Sox' Played a Black Team – Society for American Baseball Research (sabr.org).

16   "Rogers Parks Start Semi-Pro Season by Downing Giants, 4-2," *Chicago Tribune*, April 12, 1920: 11. See also Dave Wyatt, "Foster's Crew Are Trounced," *Chicago Defender*, April 17, 1920: 9, and "Foster Raises the Lid," *Chicago Whip*, April 17, 1920: 5.

17   "Magnets Are Easy for Giants," *Chicago Defender*, June 12, 1920: 9.

18   "Amer. Giants, 9; A.B.C., 1," *Chicago Tribune*, June 4, 1920: 19. Both the *Defender* and *Tribune* box scores showed the pitcher as "B. Williams" though the *Defender* story specifically referred to the Williams in question as Tom Williams.

19   "Monarchs Won in 12 Innings," *Kansas City Times*, August 2, 1920: 8.

20   https://www.seamheads.com/NegroLgs/player.php?playerID=willio1tom.

21   "American Giants Bow, 7-1, Before Detroit Majors," *Chicago Tribune*, October 22, 1923: 26.

22   "American Giants Beat Cleveland," *Chicago Tribune*, May 13, 1924: 27.

23   "Monarchs and Am. Giants Split Four-Game Series," *Pittsburgh Courier*, August 9, 1924: 6.

24   "Monarchs and Sox in Big Trade," *Pittsburgh Courier*, March 14, 1925: 7.

25   "Daniels Seals Win Over Stars, 2-1," *Detroit Free Press*, September 8, 1924: 17.

26   "Tom Williams, Ace Pitcher for Foster, Is Dead," *Chicago Defender*, January 30, 1937: 17.

27   Find-a-Grave, online: Restvale Cemetery in Alsip, Illinois – Find A Grave Cemetery. Accessed June 4, 2021.

RUBE FOSTER

BY TIM ODZER

"If the talents of Christy Mathewson, John McGraw, Ban Johnson and Judge Kenesaw Mountain Landis were combined in a single body, and that body was enveloped in a black skin, the result would have to be named Andrew 'Rube' Foster. As an outstanding pitcher, a colorful and shrewd field manager, and the founder and stern administrator of the first viable Negro League, Foster was the most impressive figure in black baseball history."[1]

Jackie Robinson is considered by many to be the most famous Black baseball player. This opinion is understandable, for Robinson broke the color line and is well known in circles far removed from baseball. But perhaps the person with the greatest impact upon Black baseball is Andrew "Rube" Foster.[2] Not only was Foster one of the best pitchers and managers of the early twentieth century but he also was the architect of the Negro National League. Despite facing immense racial prejudice, Foster carried out three distinctive baseball positions during his lifetime and is often known as the "Father of Negro Baseball."

What was Foster like personally? He carried his religious heritage into adulthood. And he never indulged in intoxicants. He did tolerate drinking among his players, though if a player showed up to the ballpark hungover, Foster would tell him to go back to the hotel if he could not play.[3] Foster was respected by his players. Jelly Gardner, who played for Foster in the early 1920s, said "[Foster] was a nice manager, an even-tempered man. His dictums were not unreasonable, but if you broke one he'd clamp on you."[4] It is also known Foster was a hard worker. His son remembered that Foster would work from 8:30 at morning until nearly midnight during the time he was running

Hall of Famer Andrew Bishop "Rube" Foster, an early Blackball pitching star and owner of the Chicago American Giants, oversaw the founding of the first Negro National League in Kansas City, Missouri, in 1920.

both the American Giants and the Negro National League.[5]

Andrew Bishop Foster was born the son of Andrew and Evaline Foster on September 17, 1879, in Southeast Texas.[6] Foster's parents were born slaves and became sharecroppers. Most importantly for Foster's upbringing was his father's service as a Methodist preacher. Part of the first free Black generation, Foster grew up as the hope of Reconstruction gave way to the horror of Jim Crow. Although Foster was born the fourth of sixth children, only he and two of his siblings, Christiana (born 1877) and Johnson (born 1884), survived until adulthood. (A younger half-brother, William "Bill" Foster, followed in Rube's footsteps and was elected to the National Baseball Hall of Fame.) The lives of Foster's other siblings were taken by tuberculosis, a disease that undoubtedly affected young Andrew's interest in baseball. Foster himself said that "if it hadn't been for playing ball and living outdoors, I don't suppose I'd (be) here today."[7]

In 1897, one year after the US Supreme Court upheld the legality of "separate but equal" policies, Foster joined the Austin Reds of Tillotson College. The team was affiliated with a church where Foster's father was the presiding elder. In 1898 Foster joined the Waco Yellow Jackets. As he performed well, stories of his feats spread. For example, one tale had Foster pitching scoreless games every day for 11 days straight.[8]

In 1902, Frank Leland, a manager of the Chicago Unions, found Foster in Hot Springs, Arkansas. Foster worked in a local restaurant, and, it was said, spent his spare time pitching to Connie Mack's catchers. Leland persuaded Foster to join the Unions. Foster struggled with the Union Giants and opted to join an interracial semipro team in Otsego, Michigan.

When Otsego's season ended, Foster joined the Cuban X-Giants, one of the premier Black teams on the East Coast. According to the *New York Evening World,* owner E.B. Lamar said Foster was the greatest twirler he had ever seen. Not many box scores exist from Foster's 1903 campaign with the X-Giants, but he did throw a 3-0, five-hit shutout on July 16.[9] In September the X-Giants played the Philadelphia Giants. In the showdown, Foster starred, throwing four complete games as he helped the X-Giants to the title.

Around the time when the 5-foot-9, 230-pound Foster burst onto the baseball scene, a well-known legend first surfaced. Foster's success allegedly attracted the attention of John McGraw. As the story goes, feeling his talented young pitcher Christy Mathewson needed a teacher, McGraw allegedly asked Foster to tutor Mathewson. As such, Foster is credited by some with teaching Mathewson his famous fadeaway.

Lured by an increased salary, Foster jumped to the Philadelphia Giants in 1904. In the opening game of the Black season, Foster doubled as the starting left fielder for the Giants. Not only a pitcher, Foster was also a two-way player, spending time at first base, second base, catcher, and all the outfield positions.[10] The Philadelphia Giants played Foster's former employer, the Cuban X-Giants, in a best-of-three series for the city championship. Foster started the first game and won 8-4 with 18 strikeouts. The X-Giants won the second game, allowing Foster to pitch the third game. Foster won the city championship for his new team by allowing only three hits a 4-2 victory.

The Giants won 18 of 20 games to start 1905 behind Bill Monroe's .440 batting average and Grant "Home Run" Johnson's .405 average.[11] Hitting was contagious for the Giants in 1905, as Foster himself hit .289 with 114 hits and 3 home runs.[12] During the season the *Philadelphia Telegraph* lauded Foster as a pitcher, writing: "If Andrew Foster had not been born with a dark skin, the great pitcher would wear an American or National League uniform. ... Foster has never been equaled in a pitcher's box.[13]

In an interview a couple of years later, Foster said 1905 was when he became "Rube" Foster: "In 1905, I won 51 out of 55 games I pitched for that season. ... It was when we beat the Athletics, with Rube Waddell pitching, that they gave me the name of the colored Rube Waddell."[14] Modern research has cast doubt on this legend, with experts placing the date anywhere between 1902 and 1905.

The Philadelphia Giants finished the 1905 season playing a three-game series against the Brooklyn Royal Giants. Philadelphia swept the series, with Foster winning the second game. Foster played with the Philadelphia Giants again in 1906. In a September series against the Cuban X-Giants, Foster scattered 10 hits and struck out nine in a 3-2 win.[15] Around the same time, Foster wrote an essay for Sol White's book *History of Colored Base Ball* titled "How to Pitch." In closing his essay, Foster summarized his approach to pitching:

"The three great principles of pitching are good control, when to pitch certain balls, and where to pitch them. The longer you are in the game, the more you should gain by experience. Where inexperience will lose many games, nerve and experience will bring you out victor."[16]

As for his pitching repertoire, Foster threw a fastball, curveball, and screwball. Reflecting upon how Foster's stuff played, Dave Malarcher said:

"[Foster] had one of the most baffling curve balls I ever looked at. And he had a real good fast ball – real good fast ball – and he threw a curve ball that was more what people would call a fadeaway. It looked like that fast ball and it would get there and just flutter, like that, away from you."[17]

Seeking a bigger salary, Foster and several teammates left the Philadelphia Giants for the Leland Giants in Chicago. Foster was named player-manager. The 1907 Leland Giants posted a 110-10 record playing in the Chicago city circuit and in games against several top teams.[18] At the end of the season, the Leland Giants faced off against a major-league all-star team led by Mike Donlin. Foster started and won two of the three games. In recapping the series, the *Indianapolis Freeman* praised Foster's performance, writing: "Rube Foster is the pitcher of the Leland Giants, and he has all the speed of a Rusie, the tricks of a Radbourne, and the heady coolness and deliberation of a Cy Young. What does that make him? Why, the greatest baseball pitcher in the country: That is what the best ball players of white persuasion that have gone up against him say.[19]

Foster remained a top pitcher in 1908. A couple of superb games highlight his continued dominance. For instance, on July 20 Foster came into a game in the seventh inning, having started the game in right field. Foster went nine innings, giving only two hits with eight strikeouts and one walk. The Leland Giants won in 15 innings.[20] And on August 3, as part of a six-game series between the Philadelphia Giants and Leland Giants, Foster tossed a complete-game five-hitter as his Leland Giants won 11-1.

In 1909 Foster broke his leg in July after getting off to a strong start with 11 straight wins and four shutouts. He returned to pitch the second game of a three-game October series against the Chicago Cubs. Starting against a Cubs lineup that included future Hall of Fame shortstop Joe Tinker, Foster pitched eight strong innings, allowing only two runs. Leading 5-2 going into the ninth, Foster and the Leland Giants blew the game, allowing the Cubs to rally for four runs in the ninth and win 6-5.

To start 1910, Foster planned a barnstorming tour for the Leland Giants through several Southern states. In Palm Beach, Florida, they played the Brooklyn Royal Giants, who won the 1909 Eastern championship. Foster pitched two games against the Royal Giants. He threw a three-hitter in one and lost the other 1-0 even though he allowed only two hits.[21] During the regular season, Foster continued to pitch at a top level. On May 23, he matched up against José Méndez and emerged victorious, allowing only five hits and striking out four. And on September 9, Foster shut out the Oklahoma Giants. Featuring star players such as John Henry Lloyd, Pete Hill, and Home Run Johnson, the Leland Giants dominated their competition, winning 123 out of 129 games.

During the 1910 season, the White Sox moved to Comiskey Park and vacated South Side Park. Foster, seeing an opportunity, contacted John Schorling, White Sox owner Charles Comiskey's son-in-law, about the Leland Giants using South Side Park. Schorling and Foster became business partners. Foster gave Schorling half-ownership of the team; in exchange, Schorling constructed new bleacher seating fitting around 9,000 fans. With a new ballpark for his team, Foster rebranded his team as the Chicago American Giants.

The Chicago American Giants became Black baseball's preeminent squad and dominated their opposition. In 1911 the American Giants went 78-27 and claimed the first of four consecutive Western crowns. In 1912 the American Giants went 112-30. Though records are incomplete, the box scores that survive suggest that Foster remained a top-end pitcher, referred to by the *Chicago Defender* as the Marquard of Black baseball.[22] Foster called his team "the undisputed colored champions of the world" and brought his club to play in the California winter league.[23]

As the 1913 season commenced, the *Chicago Defender* lauded Foster for the success of the American Giants out west, saying that "much credit belongs to the greatest ball player and manager in the business, and one of the greatest and headiest men in the business, white or black."[24] In August 1913 Foster's team played a best-of-12 series against the Lincoln Giants, managed by John Henry Lloyd. The Lincoln Giants won the series. Still, it was another splendid campaign for the American Giants, as they played over 200 games.

The 1914 Chicago American Giants added Smokey Joe Williams and John Henry Lloyd to their team. The *Defender* suggested that Foster's squad was as good as several major-league teams and better than many others.[25] The American Giants amassed a 126-16 record in 1914. Foster continued pitching occasionally.

Against the Cuban Stars on May 26, he relieved Horace Jenkins in the eighth with two out and runners on second and third. Foster attempted to pick off the runner at second, but nobody was covering the bag. The ball sailed into center and allowed the Cubans to tie the game. In the bottom of the 10th, Foster gave up two runs and took the loss. But he bounced back in his next game against the Cuban Stars, facing only 28 batters in a one-hit shutout. In early September, Foster's squad played the Brooklyn Royal Giants for the "Colored World Series." Foster's team swept the four-game set behind the strong pitching of Frank Wickware, Lee Wade, and Horace Jenkins.

In White Organized Baseball, 1914 saw the Federal League challenge the National and American Leagues. At the outset of the season, Foster expressed optimism that the creation of the new league would force the baseball magnates to integrate their leagues. "[W]hen they let the black men in, just watch how many present-day stars lose their positions," he told the *Seattle Post-Intelligencer*.[26] The Federal League's challenge to Organized Baseball did not result in integration. Nor did Chicago's Federal League entry, the Whales, agree to a series against the American Giants, despite pleas from Foster.[27]

The American Giants started the 1915 season on a Western tour and went 20-6.[28] On March 27, 1915, the American Giants beat up on future Hall of Famer Stanley Coveleski and the Portland Beavers, 7-1. Foster continued to make occasional appearances as a player. On June 23 he held the Indianapolis ABCs to three hits in an 8-1 game.[29] But on July 5, Foster struggled, giving up three runs in the top of the eighth.[30]

In mid-July, the American Giants played the ABCs in what the *Chicago Defender* called "the battle royal of the season." On July 18 a massive fight broke out between the teams. As described by the *Chicago Defender*, after a discussion at home plate, "[b]oth teams grabbed bats, the umpire and Pete Hill had an argument and the umpire jerks out a gun and hits 'Pete' over the nose."[31] The umpire ordered a forfeit for the ABCs. The *Defender* complained about the incident, saying the fight threatened the future of Black baseball.[32] On August 7, 1915, Foster wrote an explanation to the baseball public in the *Indianapolis Freeman* seeking to apologize for the incident, calling it "the complete humiliation of a life's effort to advance and promote baseball among our people."[33] He also gave a candid glimpse into the racist invective he dealt with daily: "On Monday, July 18, I received the most complete humiliation. … I started out to the coaches box

and a police sergeant came upon the field and called me back, calling me the dirtiest names I had ever had said to me, first asking me who were it that started the argument at Sunday's game. I said I did not know, and he said to me: 'You black son-of-a-b … if you open your mouth, I will blow your brains out.'"[34]

ABCs manager C.I. Taylor was unsatisfied and entered into a back-and-forth with Foster in Black papers that marred the rest of the season. On a more positive front for Foster, it was announced on August 27 that John Henry Lloyd and Judy Gans were rejoining the American Giants. At the end of the season, Foster again challenged Joe Tinker's Chicago Whales to a postseason series. But Tinker, in the words of the *Defender*, was scared to accept the challenge.[35]

What was it about Foster's American Giants that scared White teams? Perhaps it was the style of play. They played a style of baseball termed inside baseball. As described by Willie Foster, inside baseball centered on bunting and stealing. According to Larry Lester, Foster introduced the hit-and-run play, bunt-and-run, drag batting, doubles, and the squeeze play to the national pastime.[36] A century before major-league teams shifted for every batter, Foster did so, routinely moving his infielders around the diamond.[37] Lester said Foster's style mirrored in the St. Louis Cardinals Gas House Gang of the 1930s, the Go-Go Chicago White Sox of the 1950s, and the Los Angeles Dodgers of the early 1960s.[38]

During the 1915-16 offseason, Foster scheduled games for the American Giants in Seattle, California, Havana, and Omaha. With Organized Baseball pursuing an antitrust lawsuit against the Federal League, Foster sought to purchase several Federal League ballparks; the *Indianapolis Freeman* said such a move would allow Blacks to "have a good sized major league [of] their own."[39]

At the start of the 1916 season, the *Chicago Defender* wrote that the American Giants "would make the White Sox look like a bunch of bush leaguers."[40] In August the American Giants defeated the New York Lincoln Giants in a best-of-seven series to win the "colored world championship." Later in October, the American Giants played the Indianapolis ABCs in another series designed to determine a black champion. Indianapolis won five of the games, but not without a forfeit by Chicago. The forfeit happened in the third game. In the middle of the game, Foster, while coaching at first base, put on a glove. The umpire asked Foster to take the glove off. In response, Foster asked what baseball rule he was violating by wearing the glove. The umpire said he did not know, and Foster refused to remove the glove. Eventually the umpire told Foster to either remove the glove or leave the field. Foster sent his players to the bench and the umpire declared it a forfeit in favor of the ABCs. The 1916 series prompted another back-and-forth in the Black papers between Taylor and Foster.

In 1917 the American Giants reigned supreme among Black baseball teams. Led by Leroy Grant, John Henry Lloyd, Pete Hill, and Cannonball Dick Redding, Foster's team easily took the season series from the ABCs. C.I. Taylor even wrote a letter to the *Indianapolis Freeman* in which he proclaimed, "Rube Foster has the greatest Colored aggregation in the business, and every true sport ought to give him the praise. ... Foster's club is truly the World's Colored Champion for 1917. ... All honor to him and his magnificent ball club."[41]

After the United States entered World War I, Foster lost several key players to the war effort.[42] But his team still excelled when it played, posting a record of 77 wins and 27 losses.[43] The *Chicago Defender* credited Foster for his team's success, writing: "The Giants were fortunate to have Foster, as he is without doubt one of the greatest leaders in baseball, and if he had twenty-five men, as the big leagues, all trained with experience before they come to him, there is no league pennant he would not have a monopoly on."[44]

With the war over, Foster anticipated a big 1919 season. He worked with John Schorling to add seating capacity to Schorling Park. Unfortunately for Foster, the American Giants spent most of the 1919 season on the road, as racial unrest occurred in Chicago. The turmoil started after a 17-year-old Black youth was killed after drifting into a White swimming area at a segregated beach.

After the 1919 season, Foster wrote a five-part series in the *Chicago Defender* titled the "Pitfalls of Baseball." Commenting on the challenges facing Black baseball and the need for an organized league, he wrote: "This will be the last time I will ever try and interest Colored club owners to get together on some working basis."[45]

On February 13, 1920, Foster organized a meeting at the Paseo YMCA in Kansas City. His agenda was simple: create a Negro baseball league that resembled the White-only major leagues. The owners of seven other Black baseball teams attended along with a few sportswriters and an attorney. Foster had long dreamed about creating a Black league and may have found the final impetus in the Chicago race riot of

1919. Over several days, eight teams – the Chicago American Giants, Detroit Stars, Cuban Stars, Kansas City Monarchs, St. Louis Giants, Indianapolis ABCs, Chicago Giants, and Dayton Marcos – agreed to a league constitution and bylaws, and appointed Foster president.[46] The league's motto was "We are the ship. All else is the sea."[47]

Foster believed in competitive balance. In his "Pitfalls of Baseball" series, he wrote that promoters did not realize that [having] the best ball club in the world and no one able to compete with it will lose more money on the season than those that are evenly matched."[48] To achieve that goal, he relinquished some of his top players, including allowing Oscar Charleston to re-sign with the ABCs. But even without the Hoosier Comet, Foster guided the 1920 Chicago American Giants to the first NNL pennant.

After the 1920 season, representatives of the National Association of Colored Professional Base Ball Clubs (who operated the Negro National League) re-elected Foster as league president and secretary.

As 1921 dawned, Foster added **Jimmie Lyons** to his outfield. His American Giants began the season in Palm Beach representing the Royal Poinciana Hotel.[49] During the NNL's second season, there was more competitive integrity. Behind Cristobal Torriente's impressive season, the American Giants still led the league, with a 44-22-2 record, but they were closely followed by the St. Louis Giants and the Kansas City Monarchs. It was a trying year for Foster personally. His 12-year-old daughter, Sarah, died. And Foster was accused of stealing from certain ballplayers. As he traveled through Atlanta in November, he was arrested and charged with stealing. Foster was released on bond and professed his innocence.[50]

The 1922 season was another strong season for the American Giants. Boosted by adding **John Beckwith** and the continued strong play of **Cristobal Torriente**, the Giants won their third straight NNL championship. But after the season, a newspaper column by Henry Brown criticized Foster's management of the league. Comparing Foster to a tyrant, Brown said, "Foster has dictated without a single reckoning and has backed up his 'take it or leave it' with a mailed fist."[51] Such criticism of Foster popped up sporadically during the 1920s. Foster responded in his state-of-the-league address, pointing out the increase in the number of teams and player salaries: "In the past three years branching out, creating an interest among the people introduced many new stars and raised the amount paid players from $50,000 yearly...[to] $500,000 the past three years."[52]

The 1923 American Giants did not repeat as champions, finishing in second place behind Kansas City.

Foster, as the league's president, congratulated Kansas City: "It is a pleasure to me to see the Kansas City Monarchs win the pennant in our league this year, despite the fact that my club finished behind; this in itself proves the sterling quality and ability of the team from the west."[53] Again in 1924, the American Giants finished behind Kansas City. During the 1924 season, more criticism of Foster surfaced. The *Kansas City Call* blasted Foster, saying he should not head the league because he "was for the American Giants, first, last, and always."[54] But contrary to the criticism, Foster pulled for the Kansas City Monarchs as they battled Hilldale in the first Colored World Series, supposedly signaling pitches to Monarchs pitcher José Méndez throughout the decisive game.[55] Foster oversaw the planning of the first Colored World Series in his capacity as president of the league. "He was very proud to have the responsibility and privilege and the honor … to be planning the big series. This really put him in the category of Ban Johnson and Judge Landis. He was very proud of the place he occupied," said Dave Malarcher years later.[56]

In early June of 1925, while in Indianapolis, Foster's players found him unconscious and lying against a gas heater at the Eubanks Boarding House, where he was staying. He had accidentally inhaled fumes from a leaking gas pipe. The inhalation caused Foster's mental health to deteriorate. In 1926 his erratic behavior spiraled to the point that he needed to be committed. Many stories about his antics during this time emerged. His wife, Sarah, said Foster heard voices telling him he was going to be called on to pitch in the World Series. American Giants pitcher Wee Willie Powell said Foster ran up and down the street in front of his house, while shortstop Bobby Williams spoke of how Foster bolted himself into his office and refused to leave until someone entered through the window and drew him out.[57] On September 8, 1926, the Associated Negro Press reported that Foster had been declared mentally irresponsible and was confined to an Illinois state institution.[58] Foster spent four years there before dying on December 9, 1930, at the age of 51. One of baseball's greatest-ever minds died in an insane asylum.

Without his leadership, the Negro National League Foster founded struggled to survive. Although it stayed intact until after his death, it was never really the same without Foster. With the impact of the Great Depression, the first Negro National League folded in 1931. However, the Negro Leagues would revive in the mid-1930s and continue through till 1960, and they

(Courtesy National Baseball Hall of Fame)

Foster was one of several 1920 American Giants personnel who came to a tragic end. Sadly, one of baseball's most brilliant minds, had to spend his final four years in an asylum in Kankakee, Illinois.

were the first professional league for major-league greats such as Jackie Robinson, Willie Mays, and Henry Aaron. Foster's vision of a sporting landscape that fostered and allowed Blacks to make a living was nevertheless achieved, as he raised the profile of baseball for his race throughout the nation. The Veterans Committee recognized Foster for his contributions to the game by electing him to the National Baseball Hall of Fame in 1981.

NOTES

1   Robert Peterson, *Only the Ball Was White* (New York: Oxford University Press, 1971), 103.

2   Another "Rube" Foster, born George Foster, pitched for the Boston Red Sox from 1913 to 1917, winning 58 games and two World Series championships with Boston.

3   Robert Charles Cottrell, *The Best Pitcher in Baseball* (New York: New York University Press, 2001), 125.

4   Cottrell, 125.

5   Robert Peterson, "Rube Foster: Player, Manager, Administrator," *Dayton Daily News*, June 17, 1970.

6   Some sources list Foster's birthplace as La Grange, Texas, while others list Calvert, Texas. Foster himself named La Grange as his birthplace in *The Negro in Chicago: A Study in Race Relations and a Race Riot* (Chicago: University of Chicago Press, 1922), 178. But his death certificate, along with Cottrell's biography, lists Calvert as his birthplace. For more information, see Gary Ashwill, "Where Was Rube Foster Really Born?", available at https://agatetype.typepad.com/agate_type/2008/08/where-was-rube.html#:~:text=Foster%20apparently%20named%20La%20Grange,perfectly%20reasonable%20alternative%20to%20Calvert.

7   Phil Dixon, *Andrew "Rube" Foster, A Harvest on Freedom's Fields* (Bloomington, Indiana: Xlibris, 2010), 55, quote attributed to Foster.

8   Cottrell, 9.

9   Cottrell, 11.

10   Cottrell, 15.

11   Larry Lester, *Rube Foster in His Time: On the Field and in the Papers with Black Baseball's Greatest Visionary* (Jefferson, North Carolina: McFarland & Company, Inc., Publishers, 2012), 21.

12   Lester, 21.

13   Lester, 24.

14   *Indianapolis Freeman*, September 14, 1907.

15   Lester, 25.

16   Andrew Foster, "How to Pitch," in Solomon White, ed., *History of Colored Base Ball* (Philadelphia: 1907). Republished as *Sol White's History of Colored Baseball with Other Documents on the Early Black Game, 1886-1936* (Lincoln, Nebraska: Bison Books, 1996), 100.

17   Cottrell, 86.

18   Cottrell, 35.

19   Cottrell, 37.

20   Cottrell, 43.

21   Cottrell, 54-55.

22   In 1912 Rube Marquard won 19 consecutive decisions en route to leading the National League with 26 wins.

23   Cottrell, 70.

24   Cottrell, 75

25   Cottrell, 78.

26   Cottrell, 79.

27   Handy Andy, "Foster Anxious to Tackle Tinx; American Giants' Manager Issues Challenge to Chicago Feds; Points to 1914 Record," *Chicago Tribune*, September 19, 1914.

28   Cottrell, 88.

29   Cottrell, 90.

30   Cottrell, 90.

31   "Fight Ends A.B.C. Game," *Chicago Defender*, July 31, 1915: 7.

32   Cottrell, 92.

33   "Rube Foster's Explanation to the Base Ball Public of the United States," *Indianapolis Freeman*, August 7, 1915.

34   Rube Foster's Explanation to the Base Ball Public of the United States."

35   "Rube Foster Challenges Tinker's Feds," *Chicago Defender*, October 9, 1915.

36   Lester, 103.

37   Lester, 104.

38   Lester, 105.

39   Cottrell, 100.

40   Cottrell, 102.

41   Cottrell, 110.

42   Cottrell, 114-115.

43   Lester, 106.

44   Cottrell, 119.

45   "Pitfalls of Baseball, Part V," *Chicago Defender*, December 27, 1919: 9.

46   Cottrell, 149-151.

47   Cottrell, 153.

48   "Pitfalls of Baseball, Part II," *Chicago Defender*, December 13, 1919: 11.

49   Cottrell, 158.

50   Cottrell, 160. It is unclear how the proceedings ended.

51   Henry Brown, "Foster and the League," *Chicago Whip*, October 28, 1922: 7.

52   "Negro National League Meets December 7 at Appomattox Club," *Chicago Whip*, November 18, 1922: 7.

53   Cottrell, 166.

54   Cottrell, 167.

55   Cottrell, 167.

56   Cottrell, 167.

57   Cottrell, 71.

58   Associated Negro Press, "'Rube' Foster Insane; In Chicago Hospital," *Pittsburgh Courier*, September 4, 1926: 1.

JOHN SCHORLING

BY KEN CARRANO

An examination of John Schorling's life yields more questions than answers. This is true of many individuals who lived in pre-internet times, especially those who were not famous or who had no offspring to further their story. It seems especially true for Schorling. How did he get involved with baseball? Was he ever a player or did he want to be a manager and booking agent? How did he come to be a business partner with Rube Foster? What was his relationship with Charles Comiskey? What did he do after he divested himself from the Chicago American Giants? Some of these questions can be answered, at least partially, but many mysteries remain.

Schorling was born on December 16, 1865, in Michigan City, Indiana,[1] to August (recorded as Angus in both the 1860 and 1880 censuses) and Sophia Schorling. The elder Schorling was a sash and blind maker in Michigan City, but the family relocated to Chicago after the Great Fire of 1871 and settled on the South Side near the intersection of 79th Street and Vincennes Avenue. They lived with Sophia's father, Charles Duensing, at the Ten Mile House, a tavern for travelers going to or from Chicago, and he soon took over as proprietor.[2] The elder Schorling purchased a large tract of land, presumably to develop into homes as Chicago recovered from the effects of the Fire, calling the subdivision Auburn.[3] It was here where a ballpark was built that became home to the Auburn Park team that the younger Schorling would manage. No records have been found to determine when the

ballpark was built, or if it was August or John who had the idea.

John Schorling was interested in baseball as many young men were in this age but managing a semipro team likely did not pay the bills, so other work was needed. In 1892 Schorling was identified as a coal dealer by the *Chicago Inter Ocean* in an article about the missing postmaster of the Auburn Park post office. Schorling and two others had posted the bond of postmaster John Hallenbeck, who left a note for his family in one of his shoes and disappeared. Schorling and the other bondsmen went to the post office and began sorting mail to get the office operational. Schorling had also helped to establish the Auburn Park Bank with Hallenbeck, who had a

(Chicago Chronicle, September 21, 1896)

AUBURN PARK CLUB, LEADERS IN THE AMATEUR BASEBALL LEAGUE.

John Schorling (center in suit and bow tie) was Rube Foster's business partner, and the American Giants' home field, Schorling Park, bore his name for several years.

mortgage there as well.[4] It was thought that because of overwork the postmaster may have committed suicide.[5]

Schorling continued his work as a coal dealer at the turn of the century, but this was to change. August Schorling had built a tavern at 79th & Vincennes called Schorling's Corner and, upon his death in 1904, John Schorling added the business to his duties with the Auburn Park team and ballpark.[6] The ballpark housed a number of other squads besides the Auburn Park team, notably as the occasional home of the Chicago Union Giants (1900-1904) and Leland Giants (1905-1909), prominent Negro teams that played in the Chicago semipro leagues as well as nationally against other Negro teams. Frank Leland, who managed the Union Giants and the renamed Leland Giants, recruited Foster in 1902 to pitch for his team.[7] After several years with the Philadelphia Giants, during which he led them to three consecutive championships.[8] Foster rejoined the Leland Giants in 1907 as a pitcher and manager.[9] Foster's relationship with Leland deteriorated over the next several years and, with Schorling continuing to book teams into the Auburn Park facility, a relationship was established. With Foster now controlling all aspects of the Giants' operations, he decided to break ties with Leland and partnered with Schorling to form one of the most important teams in Negro baseball history, the Chicago American Giants.

After the Chicago White Sox moved to the new "Baseball Palace of the World" at 35th and Shields, their original ballpark at 39th and Wentworth was vacant. Schorling leased the grounds and rebuilt the grandstand that Charles Comiskey had dismantled after he moved his franchise four blocks north.[10] "Schorling got hold of the South Side park, constructed a 'palatial plant,' and chose 'yours truly,' Foster noted, 'as the best available personage to organize and head a club.'"[11]

The relationship between Foster and Schorling, which began with only a handshake agreement, endured until Foster's untimely health issues began in 1926. In a January 1924 *Chicago Defender* article, Foster wrote:

> "Mr. Schorling is one of the best and most honorable men I have ever come in contact with. He made it possible for us to enjoy baseball in the city. The park was built exclusively for us, has been used the same way, and is an investment that runs into thousands of dollars. He has allowed to be paid through my hands

over $700,000 to Colored people alone. In our 12 years together, there has never been a difference of opinion. He has never asked me why I did anything or censured me for any steps taken. He has paid me more than any man before; he has given me many thousands of dollars that I knew did not come from the games, as it was just three years ago we were able to pay for the park.

> You can see or better judge the type of man he is when you take into consideration that every game, all contracts and permission for the use of the park, what anyone receives, all help and employees, rental of grounds have been trusted to me, and no one has been able to do any business with him until they came to me. This will give you better insight into how some men are made. When he wanted me he said, "I am fixing to invest lots of money in baseball. I want you with me. Name the terms." I told him. He said: "If that's what you want you must be worth it." That was our last business talk. This was 12 years ago."[12]

Others could see the strength of the relationship between the two as well. Dave Malarcher, an American Giants player who took over as the team's manager when Foster was stricken, said, "Both must have felt that they would live forever, and that they would need each other as long as they lived."[13] Others in the Negro baseball community were not as impressed with the relationship between the White tavern/ballpark owner and the Black manager. In a response to a dispute regarding gate receipts, Hilldale owner Edward Bolden asked the *Baltimore Afro-American* in 1923, "Why does Mr. Foster publish the fact that Schorling Park and the American Giants are the property of John Schorling, for whom the park is named, and Foster is but a chattel of his white boss?"[14]

The lack of a written contract came back to haunt the Foster family when, upon Foster's confinement to an insane asylum, Schorling took over total control of the American Giants.[15] While Schorling attended the Negro National League meetings in January of 1927 with Foster's wife, Sarah, he also attended a Whites-only dinner of NNL owners who had hoped to take more control of the league.[16] Sarah Foster tried to assert that Rube Foster was the team owner and that, as Rube's guardian, she should control the team. Schorling ignored Sarah's claim and acted as both owner and landlord of the American Giants until he sold the team to William Trimble in 1928.[17]

Once his financial interest in baseball had ended, Schorling turned to other ventures. The 1930 Census records his occupation as "real estate investment." After Schorling had taken over South Side Park when the White Sox vacated it in 1910 and rebuilt it as Schorling Park, he shut down his Auburn Park facility on 79th Street and began to subdivide the property his father had originally purchased. At this point in his life, John Schorling's trail grows cold. The only news about him to be found after 1930 is his obituary. Schorling died from pneumonia on March 23,1940, and was buried at Mt. Greenwood Cemetery in Chicago. He and his wife had no children, and Maud Payro Schorling died in 1950.

Schorling had married Maud Payro in 1898.[18] According to the 1900 Census, Payro's father was Canadian, and her mother was from Michigan. The 1900 Census also indicates that Charles Comiskey and his wife, Annie, had one child, 14-year-old Louis, who was their only living offspring. Several modern sources[19] state that Schorling was the son-in-law of Charles Comiskey, attempting to make a connection to Schorling's acquiring Comiskey's original ballpark. During the period of 1910-1911, no mention was found stating that it was Comiskey's son-in-law who took over his ballclub's former home. The fact that Comiskey removed sections of the grandstand makes it difficult to believe that there was anything but a business relationship involved here, especially considering that Comiskey's only offspring was his son when the Schorlings married. If there was any relationship between the two, it died when Schorling passed away.

NOTES

1   https://www.findagrave.com/memorial/53370878/john-m-schorling.

2   John Drury, "Old Chicago Houses," *Chicago Daily News,* April 19, 1940: 18.

3   John Drury, "Pioneer Inn Marked the Beginning of Auburn," *Chicago Daily News,* May 1, 1958: 2.

4   "Message in a Shoe," *Chicago Inter Ocean,* December 15, 1892: 1.

5   "Did Hollenbeck Kill Himself", *Chicago Tribune,* December 16, 1892: 5.

6   "Old Chicago Houses."

7   Robert Charles Cottrell, *The Best Pitcher in Baseball* (New York: New York University Press, 2004), 10.

8   Cottrell, 20-29. The term championship, especially in the days prior to the formation of the Negro National League in 1920, is always suspect. For example, the Philadelphia Giants won the "colored world's championship" in a series against the Atlantic City Royal Giants in 1905. In 1906, the Philadelphia Giants won the loosely formed "League of Independent Professional Ball Players."

9   Cottrell, 32.

10 "Fire Destroys American Giants Ball Park Seats," *Chicago Defender,* January 4, 1941: 24.

11 Cottrell, 66.

12 Andrew Rube Foster, "Rube Foster Has a Word to Say to the Baseball Fans," *Chicago Defender,* January 5, 1924: 8.

13 Cottrell, 121.

14 "Bolden Replies to Charges of Rube Foster," *Baltimore Afro-American,* January 26, 1923: 12.

15 Cottrell, 171.

16 Paul Debono, *The Chicago American Giants* (Jefferson, North Carolina: McFarland & Company, 2007), 115.

17 Debono, 116.

18 https://www.findagrave.com/memorial/53370878/john-m-schorling.

19 An incomplete listing of sources naming John Schorling as Charles Comiskey's son-in law includes these: Cottrell, 62; James A. Riley, *The Biographical Encyclopedia of the Negro Baseball Leagues* (New York: Carroll & Graf Publishers, Inc., 1994) as published at the Negro League Baseball Museum's eMuseum page https://nlbemuseum.com/history/players/fostera.html; Debono, 32; Rube Foster's page at the SABR BioProject: https://sabr.org/bioproj/person/andrew-rube-foster/; Rube Foster's page at the Baseball Hall of Fame: https://baseballhall.org/hall-of-famers/foster-rube.

SCHORLING PARK

BY KEN CARRANO

The ballpark on 39th Street in Chicago between Princeton and Wentworth Streets had as many names as any ballpark in the era before corporate sponsorship, when Parks can become Fields (Miller to American Family in Milwaukee) and poorly named Fields can become even more poorly named Fields (US Cellular to Guaranteed Rate in Chicago, a mere half-mile from the present subject). The ballpark in question here spent most of its life known as Schorling (or sometimes Schorling's) Park, but also spent its formative years as South Side Park, and was alternately known as White Sox Park, the 39th Street Grounds, Cole's Park, American Giants Park, Cole's American Giants Park, and an unnamed dog-racing track. Before its life ended in flames in 1940, the ballpark hosted numerous Hall of Famers, two of the most important baseball moguls in the sport's history, presidential candidates, community events, and possibly every other organized sport played on the South Side of Chicago. Its legacy exists in the assistance given to the formation of two major leagues. Schorling Park's life was a three-act play – the first almost entirely White, the second primarily Black with White accents, and the third a mixture of man, machine, and animals. The ballpark's story officially begins in 1900, but before that, attention must be turned to a cricket pitch.

PROLOGUE

The Wanderers Cricket Club was formed in April 1883 and started its life by playing at Lincoln Park, along the shore of Lake Michigan north of Chicago's

South Side Park (later known as Schorling Park), located on 39th Street between Princeton and Wentworth Streets, hosted its first game on April 21, 1900.

downtown.[1] By April 1884, however, because Lincoln Park, a public facility, was not always available, the cricket club had moved to a new ground on the South Side of Chicago at 37th Street and Indiana Avenue. By 1886, the Wanderers had branched into other sports, with reports in the local papers noting their games of rugby and soccer. In addition, a tennis club that had leased part of its grounds was absorbed by the Wanderers.[2] In 1887 baseball joined the party when some druggists and doctors who had been using the club grounds joined the club and formed the Wanderers Baseball Club.[3] The club, then hosting 145 male and 24 female members, planned to build a toboggan slide and flood the field for ice skating.

Gambling was in vogue at the Wanderers grounds. In September 1887, nearly 2,000 cranks paid 25 cents apiece to see a 100-yard race between two local athletes. When only one of them showed up for the race and ran, the stakeholders refused to pay the "winner," and management refused to refund the admission fee.[4] In 1890 the Wanderers expanded their mission to include track-and-field athletes, hosting these Olympic-type events at the 37th Street Grounds. After merging with another club in 1893, the Wanderers wandered a few blocks to the intersection of 39th Street and Wentworth Avenue, where its members had easier access to the streetcar line on Wentworth that traveled downtown. In early 1894, the Wanderers sponsored a concert to raise funds for new tennis courts and improvement of the facilities.[5] The larger physical plant at 39th and Wentworth allowed the Wanderers to host multiple events – on November 29, 1894, the grounds hosted an American football game at 9:30 A.M., a soccer match at 11 A.M., and a cricket match at 2:30 P.M.[6] In late 1894 the Wanderers built a shed large enough to host five curling rinks.[7] The club continued to add to its facilities and by January 1900 had built a hockey rink and was looking for opponents.[8] However, before the ice on the rink could melt, the club was on the move and a new tenant was moving in.

ACT ONE – A MOGUL COMES HOME

No matter where Charles Comiskey was playing or managing in baseball, he always knew that he would eventually come home. His father, Honest John Comiskey, came to Chicago in 1854 and settled into a life of public service, at various times holding the positions of clerk of the County Board of Commissioners, superintendent of the water meter department, and Chicago alderman.[9] Charles, born in 1859, had baseball, not public service, running through his veins. After a career as a first baseman and manager, including time with the Chicago entry in the Players' League (playing just a half-mile from the Wanderers Cricket Grounds at 35th and Wentworth), Comiskey became an owner as he took over the Sioux City, Iowa, franchise of the Western League and relocated it to St. Paul, Minnesota, in time for the 1895 season. Comiskey spent $4,000 to build a 1,500-seat ballpark in the Summit-University section of St. Paul, pulling his father out of retirement to act as construction supervisor.[10] But Comiskey and Western League Commissioner Ban Johnson had grander goals, and when the National League contracted four teams after the 1899 season, the men saw a "major" opportunity.

The Western League team owners met in Chicago in October 1899, renamed it the American League, and announced that teams might relocate to Cleveland, Buffalo, and Chicago.[11] Shortly, Comiskey said, "The American League will have a team in Chicago next year. It will be located on the South Side, and I will give Chicago a team of which it will be proud."[12]

Where exactly on the South Side still needed to be determined. At one point, Johnson asserted that Comiskey was planning to have a large raft anchored off the Lake Front (now Grant) Park to accommodate his patrons.[13] Finally, in March 1900, some news came on the name of the team and where it would play. Comiskey expressed his frustrations with finding a location, declaring, "I will either have a team in Chicago or else go on the police force."[14] The *Chicago Inter-Ocean* stated that Comiskey would name the club the White Stockings, the former name of the Chicago Orphans when Adrian "Cap" Anson ran the team. Comiskey met with the architect who had drawn up preliminary designs on a ballpark that Anson was considering building on the South Side earlier in the year. On March 6 Comiskey said he had secured the leases and would announce the location of the ballpark before the end of the week.[15] Two days later, the Wanderers Cricket Club announced that it was taking over the grounds of the former Chicago Cricket Club on 79th Street. It was rumored that their old plant on 39th Street would become the home of the White Stockings, but Johnson denied this.[16]

In addition to the issues of finding a home, there were issues with the other team in town. Orphans President James Hart was not fond of the idea of sharing the city with an American League team, although he did not express his concerns at first. "Our league was invited into Chicago last fall when Jim Hart told

President Johnson to go ahead and make arrangements for a Western League team in Chicago," Comiskey said. "We then changed the name of the organization from the Western League to the American League, and immediately began our preparation for the coming season. Then, and not until then, did Hart announce that under no circumstances would he consent to our entering Chicago."[17] The situation was resolved in late March when Hart, Johnson, and Comiskey worked out a compromise, and Comiskey finalized plans for the ballpark to be located at 39th and Wentworth.[18] Comiskey agreed to build his ballpark south of 35th Street, but it appears that he already had secured the Wanderers' old grounds.

Now that the ground had been secured, Comiskey had to go about the business of getting the ballpark built in time for the April start of the 1900 season. Honest John had died earlier in the year, so Comiskey decided to become his own general contractor. His first payday found him with cash in the bank but none in his pockets to pay his men, and as this payday was also Election Day in Chicago, the banks were closed. After getting a hotel to cash his $1,500 check into $100s and $50s, Comiskey still needed to break the bills further, sending his groundskeeper to every bar and grocery store in the area to get what he needed to pay the workers.[19] Work continued on the grandstands, and Comiskey announced that, in spite of the snowy April, his ballpark would open on Sunday, April 15, 1900, with a game against the Union Giants, "the crack colored team."[20] The weather would not cooperate as the grounds were too wet, and the game with the Unions was canceled. The ballpark's debut had to be delayed until April 21, the opening game for the new league in Chicago, against the Milwaukee Brewers. Some 5,200 hardy souls attended the opener, which the Brewers won, 5-4, including painters who continued to paint the fence while the game proceeded: "Two painters were just beginning work on the fence, and why they did not twist their necks off every time someone hit the ball it is impossible to say," the *Chicago Tribune* commented.[21]

Like many ballparks of this era, the outfield fences had to conform to the neighborhood surroundings, in this case the greenhouses of the J.F. Kidwell company. South Side Park had a spacious left field (398 feet to straightaway left), but the distance narrowed significantly as the fence moved to right, with the opening dimensions showing the right-field line a short 270 feet away. The park was oriented to the northeast, with the third-base line running parallel to Princeton Avenue and the first-base line running along 39th Street (Pershing Road). The tight location of the park caused Comiskey some issues early on, with the *Chicago Tribune* reporting on April 25 that "Comiskey's troubles commenced, for the greenhouse man just over right field fence is threatened with nervous prostration caused by the home runs which occasionally threaten his glass houses, and a factory across the road from the park has a claim for one plate glass window smashed by the unusually strong flight of a foul, which sailed across the grandstand and clear through Thirty-ninth

Game action at South Side Park (later Schorling Park) in 1907.

street through the window and into the factory."[22] Although the ballpark was operational, it clearly was not completed. The White Stockings left on April 27 for a road trip that would take them to every other American League city, and Comiskey used the time away to sod the diamond, add new entrances and exits, and paint the grandstand and bleachers.[23]

The White Stockings captured the inaugural American League pennant in 1900, and with the announcement that the American League now considered itself a major league, the stakes were raised. South Side Park was the host of the first game in the history of the now major AL on Wednesday, April 24, 1901, defeating the Cleveland Blues, 8-2. The Blues' Jack McCarthy had the honor of securing the first hit in AL history with a single in the first inning. Nine thousand was the listed attendance for the inaugural game, under the estimated capacity of 12,500. Four days later, on Sunday the 28th, 15,000 packed the park to see the White Stockings beat the Blues again, this time in a 13-1 rout. Comiskey took advantage of an 18-day road trip in early June to make further improvements to the grounds, adding box seats to the roof of the grandstand and extending the bleachers, thereby increasing the stated capacity of the park to 14,000.[24] Even with this additional capacity, Comiskey found he did not have enough seats for his patrons, with two September Sunday home dates drawing more than 18,000 fans to the South Side: "Comiskey may have had his first inkling that the 39th Street Grounds were wholly inadequate for professional baseball when 30,084[25] fans jammed the park on October 2, 1904, to cheer on Doc White as he attempted to extend his scoreless-inning streak past 45 (innings)."[26]

Even with the right-field wall extended out over time, South Side Park was a pitcher's paradise. In its 10-year existence as an American League home field, the ballpark on 39th Street hosted four of the first 11 no-hitters thrown in the AL. The first of the four, on September 20, 1902, was thought for years to be the first thrown in the American League, until further research by SABR member Gary Belleville determined that Pete Dowling threw a no-no in June 1901.[27] The highlight for White Sox fans during the team's tenure at South Side Park was the 1906 World Series against the crosstown rival Chicago Cubs. The games were alternated each day, with the Cubs' West Side Grounds hosting Games One, Three, and Five and South Side Park hosting games Two, Four, and Six. Surprisingly, the White Sox' Hitless Wonders won all three games played on the West Side, and won only Game Six at

their home ground. If the 1904 game that drew over 30,000 fans was not enough to convince Comiskey that his park was undersized, he had to look no further than the prior World Series, in which the New York Giants had attendance of 62,777 for their three home games vs. the 50,229 who attended games on the South Side.

Comiskey signed the death warrant for South Side Park in 1909 when he purchased a tract at 35th Street and Shields.[28] The area was familiar to him – this was the location of the Brotherhood Park that Comiskey managed in 1890. It would take many months before the Comiskey Park groundskeeper could rid the field of alfalfa that grew in what would be center field once the ballpark opened.[29] Even with the new ballpark coming, Comiskey was committed to his current location, touring South Side Park in February 1909 with an architect to make improvements to the grandstands and pavilions.[30] Comiskey also continued his habit of allowing others to use the ballpark. The Comiskey Cup was a lacrosse tournament held at the park for several years. Comiskey also agreed to allow an acetylene lighting system to be used in a running event on May 26, 1909, in which the competitors would circle the outfield at night. Comiskey was hesitant to allow the event during the day, because it would have been competition for the Cubs.[31]

Before the acetylene light could become a fire hazard, the park dodged a bullet when fire consumed the 50-cent stands in right field, about 40 feet from the main grandstand, on April 25, 1909. There was no clear indication of how the fire started, but it was suspected that a lighted cigar was dropped into the woodwork below the stands during the game with the St. Louis Browns that afternoon. The fire was discovered by a person who lived across the street from the ballpark and called the fire department. Firemen had to break into the grounds and, with the fire chief directing the operations from the middle of the diamond, were able to restrict the damage to the right-field pavilion. Comiskey estimated the damage at $5,000 and speculated that it would reduce the capacity of the park by 4,000. According to the *Chicago Tribune*, Comiskey was not all that concerned when he received a phone call alerting him to the fire, choosing instead to have a second helping of his wife's shortcake.[32] However, as soon as the fire was put out, workers started removing the still-hot beams and carpenters were secured to start rebuilding the grandstand. Cubs President Charles Murphy had offered the use of the West Side Grounds to Comiskey, but with the damage limited,

Comiskey declined the offer and the game scheduled for April 26 against the Browns went on as planned, a 1-0 White Sox victory. "I appreciate the offer of President Murphy to give us the use of the West Side grounds, when he understood we had been burned out, but I am glad we will not be compelled to accept his generosity," Comiskey said.[33]

The cornerstone of the Old Roman's new ballpark was laid on March 17, 1910, and South Side Park hosted its last American League game on June 27, 1910, a 6-2 loss to Cleveland. Even before the final game, Comiskey had found a new tenant for the park: "John Schorling has leased the old White Sox grounds for baseball purposes at 39th and Wentworth," a local publication wrote. "Johnny will make a success of it as he is an authority on these affairs, and is a popular manager. We hope he will put in a white team."[34] He did not.

ACT TWO – A NEW MOGUL ARISES

Frank Leland had a lot to do with the formation of the Chicago American Giants, but probably did not realize that he was doing this. Andrew "Rube" Foster was a pitcher and eventually manager for the very successful Leland Giants and was taking on more and more responsibility for team operations. Leland was a figurehead. "In reality, Leland had nothing to do with the success of the club. Fed up with the humiliation, Leland announced that he would form a new club known as 'Leland's Chicago Giants Baseball Club'"[35] Foster subsequently sued Leland for using the name, and won a court battle when a judge ruled that "hereafter no person or persons acting for the defendant [Frank Leland] shall in any fashion use the name 'Leland Giants' as the name of the defendant club or feature the name 'Leland' in connection ..."[36] This did not stop Leland from using his own name, and Chicago had two Leland Giants teams playing in the city.

Subsequently, "[i]n 1911[,] Foster entered into a partnership with a White businessman named John Schorling. Together they bought the ballpark that Charles Comiskey was vacating as he moved his White Sox into their sparkling new stadium, the current Comiskey Park, on 35th and Shields."[37] The original Leland Giants had played some of their games at Auburn Park, where Schorling, a tavern owner on the south side of the city, also managed a Chicago City League team and owned the ballpark at 79th and Wentworth. He was also a board member of the Leland Giants:

"Schorling had been the landlord for the Leland Giants at Auburn Park since 1905. Dealing directly with Schorling was a signal that he had cut ties with his business partners and would go it alone. The scheme Rube Foster hatched with Schorling was ambitious. He envisioned a repeat of the 1909 season with large crowds in attendance for games with top notch cross-town foes, East Coast teams, Cuban teams and culminating with an epic battle against either the National League Cubs or American League White Sox. Foster saw no reason why his team shouldn't play before large crowds every day – like Chicago's other major league teams."[38]

While Schorling had arranged his lease for South Side Park, he could not take possession immediately. The *Chicago Tribune* noted, "Schorling plans to open his new plant next spring, the present park remaining in the possession of the White Sox magnate until next November."[39] Work eventually started on the park in March 1911: "The process of converting the old White Sox grounds at Thirty-ninth Street and Wentworth Avenue into a semi-pro plant was started yesterday, when the first clods of earth were turned by workmen employed by John Schorling, lessee of the new way station on the Chicago Baseball League circuit.[40] The new ballpark was estimated to hold 4,500 and cost $15,000. Schorling had to have new stands built because the former owner, Comiskey, had taken out the existing stands: "Comiskey's excuse was that he did not want another club so close to the White Sox grounds."[41] Foster, for his part, was happy with his ground, averring, "Our park, on the South Side, is the finest semi-pro park in the world, reached by every streetcar in Chicago, right in the city."[42]

It did seem to Comiskey that Foster and Schorling were on the right track. There was one potential stumbling block, and "Comiskey, by all accounts, sought to convince [Schorling] and Foster that a new black baseball team in Chicago could not succeed if it scheduled games when the hometown White Sox were in town. Foster ignored Comiskey's advice, and the American Giants thrived. Ponying up 50 cents for admission entitled patrons to free ice water when they flocked to Schorling Park to watch black baseball's premier team."[43] Opening Day at Schorling Park for the American Giants was on May 13, 1911. "It was a momentous occasion, as the American Giants now had the keys to a major league park. There were locker rooms for home and visiting teams complete with hot showers."[44] The American Giants lost the inaugural game to the Spaldings (sponsored by Albert Spalding) in threatening weather in front of only 3,000 people.[45] The weather improved, and initially Schorling Park hosted many patrons: "One Sunday afternoon in 1911, an overflow crowd of 11,000 congregated to watch the American Giants; at nearby Comiskey Park, 9,000 had shown up to see the White Sox; across town, only 6,000 were attending a Cubs' game."[46] However, the crowds did not last as long as Foster had hoped. When the Chicago City League's best player, Jim Callahan. left his squad to join the White Sox, attendance at most City League games plummeted. The American Giants also were affected in that "[t]he loss of Callahan was a crushing blow to the City League as both the quantity and quality of play dropped off. Foster never intended to depend on the City League for his livelihood. He was more interested in competition on a national level, however finding worthy opponents and drawing crowds was tougher than expected."[47]

Schorling also knew that an idle ballpark would not ring the cash register. He was actively seeking partners in the ballpark's operation. A classified advertisement in the *Chicago Tribune* noted that concessions were for sale at "the best semi-pro ball park in the city."[48] In October 1911 Schorling Park hosted a professional wrestling match that featured Illa Vincent, "The Black Panther," who defeated Frank Ehrler, "The German Thunderbolt." It was noted that great credit was to be given to the promoters, as the match was "on the square."[49] Schorling Park hosted a great number of different events throughout its lifetime as a sporting venue. From 1914 through 1917, the Chicago Cornell-Hamburgs played many of their games at Schorling, drawing as many as 2,500 to watch the nascent pro football team.[50] The American Giants were not the only baseball team fighting for glory at Schorling Park. Numerous high-school and amateur games were played there. In 1913 Schorling donated the use of the park as a fundraiser for the South Side Old Folks Home.[51]

As the Federal League emerged, rumors circulated that the league had secured an option on Schorling Park for the Chicago entry to use. Schorling put these rumors to bed, stating, "No one holds an option on the American Giants Park at present. There was talk some time ago, but nothing came of it. Manager Rube Foster signed players for his 1914 American Giants club, and

we expect to have a colored team of the same caliber as he has played there in the past."[52] The Federal League's Chicago Whales eventually chose a location on the North Side of Chicago that most people now know as Wrigley Field, though its original name was Weeghman Park. In May 1914 Schorling told the *Chicago Broad Ax* what it took to have a successful ballpark, stating, "Was first to have a good team, secondly to have the arrangement of your seating capacity so as to give your patrons a good view, and third a good diamond. It takes a good deal of expense to keep a park in order and I want to say this that nowhere in the United States today, can you get the same amount of service as you get at the American Giants base ball park."[53]

That 1913 American Giants team had claimed the Western championship but lost four of five games to the New York Lincoln Giants in August of that year. The American Giants continued their winning ways during that decade, claiming championships in 1914, 1916, 1917, and 1918. The no-hitters that were prevalent when the White Sox occupied the 39th Street grounds did not disappear when the American Giants called the ballpark home. Frank Wickware faced the minimum 27 batters in his 1-0 no-hitter against the Indianapolis ABC's on August 26, 1914. Wickware walked George Shively to start the game. After Shively was thrown out stealing, Wickware retired the next 26 hitters to complete his gem. Dick Whitworth threw a 4-0 no-hitter against the American Giants on September 19, 1915, and the Giants' Tom Johnson threw a 7-3 no-hitter against the Detroit Stars on June 17, 1919. Six walks and three errors by Bobby Williams contributed to the odd scoreline.[54] Perhaps the best pitching matchup of the decade, at least for star power, occurred on June 8, 1914, when Rube Foster met Cy Young, pitching for Benton Harbor, at Schorling Park, with Foster prevailing, 5-4.[55]

Because of the Spanish flu[56] pandemic, the World Series was completed by early September in 1918, leaving the American Giants as the only game in town. They played four games over three weekends against a collection billed as the Major League All-Stars, including Hippo Vaughn and Red Faber. Foster's squad won three of the four contests.[57] Eventually, the Chicago health department shut down public gatherings, eliminating what would have been a lucrative exhibition between the American Giants and a barnstorming team led by Vaughn.[58]

The 1919 season was interrupted at Schorling Park as well, but not due to the pandemic. Schorling Park was located on the edge of the White working-class Bridgeport neighborhood. A block away sat the neighborhood now known as Bronzeville, an area settled by many African Americans who moved from the South during the Great Migration. Racial tensions boiled over that summer, and the American Giants were affected as well:

> "On July 27, 1919, a black youth swimming at near a "white" beach was attacked by a stone-throwing white male. The youth drowned, and when the police took no action against the white perpetrator, a riot broke out. After five days, the rioting and looting had claimed the lives of 23 blacks and 15 whites. The National Guard was called out and bivouacked at Schorling Park as order was restored. The American Giants canceled a number of games, playing many in Detroit. The American Giants did play a few games back at Schorling Park in September, but Foster used his time on the road to solidify the relationships that would help form the Negro National League (NNL) the next year."[59]

The NNL brought a level of organization to Black baseball that had been years in the making. However, the new league did come with increased operating expenses, and Schorling needed to increase gate receipts. The April 10, 1920, edition of the *Chicago Defender* announced that prices would rise for the 1920 season – bleacher seats would cost 30 cents, grandstand seats were now 50 cents, and box seats commanded 75 cents, all inclusive of the still-in-place war tax. It was noted that these prices were still much below the prices charged to see White big-league ball.[60] Foster's men did the former occupants of the ballpark one better by winning the NNL crown in 1920, 1921, and 1922. The success of the team brought big crowds to 39th and Wentworth, which sometimes caused trouble. The May 7, 1922, game between the American Giants and Kansas City Monarchs was ended after the eighth inning because of unruly fan behavior. An overflow crowd of 16,000 to 17,000 had begun to swarm the field. Efforts by Foster and other players to ask the fans to move back were futile. When the American Giants tied the game in the eighth, fans rushed the field. Seat cushions were thrown around, and soon soda bottles were thrown as well. Patrons had brought whiskey into the park and sold it in the rest rooms. (Prohibition had started in 1920.) The actions of some women in the ladies' restroom were deemed not fit to put into print. Schorling later asked federal agents to come to games to prevent future riots.[61]

Another incident occurred between the American Giants and Monarchs in 1923, but this time faulty construction was to blame. The popularity of the American Giants had caused Schorling to install temporary bleachers. A section of the bleachers collapsed in the seventh inning of a game on May 27, 1923, causing 1,500 patrons to tumble to the ground. Remarkably, only 28 people required trips to hospitals. Several hundred more were bruised but remained at the game. Once the injured were attended to, the game resumed, with the American Giants prevailing, 5-4.[62] Later that year, Schorling Park hosted many of the 30,000 Elks who paraded through the South Side, ending at the ballpark, where numerous events, including a ballgame and performances by drill squads, were held.[63]

The American Giants, like the White Sox before them, won the first several league pennants without the added benefit of participating in a World Series – because one did not exist. However, the Negro World Series came to Chicago without the American Giants in 1924 when Games Eight through Ten of the Negro League series between Hilldale and the Monarchs were played in Schorling Park. For an understanding of scale, the 1924 major-league World Series generated $1,098,104, while the Negro League Series generated $52,000. The winning share for the victorious Monarchs was $308 per player, while the Hilldale athletes received $193 each.[64] Schorling Park also hosted playoff games for the NNL pennant in 1925. In 1926 the American Giants won the second-half title in a tight race with the Monarchs, defeated the Monarchs in a playoff series to win the pennant, and triumphed over the Eastern Colored League's Atlantic City Bacharachs to win their first Negro World Series. The final five games of the series were played at Schorling Park, with the American Giants prevailing in the 11th and final game of the Series, 1-0, behind Rube Foster's brother Willie, who gave up 10 hits but escaped multiple jams before the American Giants plated the winning run in the bottom of the ninth inning. Fans carried their heroes off the field and celebrated on nearby State Street.[65]

ACT THREE – GONE TO THE DOGS

Tempering this celebration was the loss of Rube Foster. Earlier that year Foster had suffered what appeared to be a nervous breakdown, and had been committed to an asylum in Kankakee, Illinois. There was apparently no written contract between Schorling and Foster, and Schorling essentially took over the club, offering no compensation to the Foster family.[66] Sarah Foster, Rube's wife, offered some hope of Rube's comeback when she and Schorling attended a joint NNL/ECL meeting in January 1927, but league leaders were preparing to move on without Foster.[67] Schorling appointed Dave Malarcher as manager, but quietly sold the team to William Trimble, a White racetrack owner. The American Giants repeated as World Series champions, again defeating the Bacharachs, this time five games to four, with the first four games played at Schorling Park.[68]

The 1928 NNL season was not as successful as the previous two had been, with the American Giants losing the NNL playoff to the St. Louis Stars and then slipping to third place in 1929. Trimble seemed to take less of an interest in the team, preferring to stay in Florida rather than get the team ready for the season.[69] The American Giants' slide continued in 1930, but that year brought an innovation to Schorling Park – night baseball. The Monarchs brought their portable light system to Chicago for night games on June 21 and 22.[70] Seeing how popular the night games had been, Trimble put up lights at the ballpark less than six weeks later.[71] Another nine years passed before the Chicago White Sox installed lights, playing their first night game on August 14, 1939. Wrigley Field did not install lights until 1988.

In 1931 Monarchs owner John Wilkinson discussed his idea to move the Monarchs to Chicago. The ballpark had deteriorated, especially after Schorling sold the team. Wilkinson believed that the cost to renovate the facility would be several thousand dollars,[72] but he was still considering the move because "Chicago is the best baseball town in the country and I am sure a good team, proper accommodations and such would revive the sport to the level it once enjoyed."[73] In the end, Wilkinson decided that the cost would be too great to overcome and kept the Monarchs in Kansas City.[74] In addition to the possibility of the Monarchs moving to Chicago, there was interest in starting a professional Negro football league, with the presumed Chicago team playing at Schorling Park.[75] While the Monarchs' move was squashed, two other promoters, Abe Saperstein and Robert Cole, were interested in purchasing the team. Saperstein's idea was to take the American Giants on the road as a traveling attraction, and he hoped to team Willie Foster with Satchel Paige. The team he put together, called the Rube Foster Memorial Giants, fell apart quickly, but Cole was

able to put together a package to take control of the ballpark and reestablished the team. Cole immediately began improving what would now be known as Cole's American Giants Park, adding new bleachers and field boxes, and installing a loudspeaker system.[76]

Just as Cole and his team were making positive strides, it had to move. Cole had only a one-year lease on the ballpark, and it was not renewed. The ballpark was said to have been in "the hands of receivers for years," and it was leased to become a dog racing track.[77] Cole had the team play some games at Mills Park in Chicago, but the majority of his squad's "home" games took place in Indianapolis. The dog park never opened. Illinois Governor Henry Horner approved of dog racing, but only if there was no pari-mutuel betting. As a result, Cole was able to take over the ballpark again in 1934, after having the venue converted back into a baseball facility. The 1934 American Giants returned to respectability, and Cole's American Giants hosted several games of the playoff series with the Philadelphia Stars, which the Giants eventually lost.

Cole became less interested in running the team and sold the franchise to his assistant, Horace Hall, in the summer of 1935. As baseball moved slowly toward integration, more and more Black fans attended games at the various major-league ballparks that had been integrated. In fact, "[i]t was 'hip' among some Chicago blacks to check out the White Sox."[78] Attendance at American Giants Park suffered because of this, and no funds were available to keep the old wooden ballpark in shape. More and more nonbaseball attractions were brought in to keep the cash registers ringing. In July 1938 Olympic champion Jesse Owens appeared in exhibitions during a series between the American Giants and Birmingham Black Barons.[79] Boxing champion Joe Louis appeared in a horse show at the ballpark in September.[80] Louis also appeared in an all-star softball game a few days later. Chicago public high-school football games were held on those weekends when the American Giants were on the road. In September 1939, a midget-racing program for Black drivers was held on the field.[81] On September 13, 1940, presidential candidate Wendell Willkie campaigned on the south side of Chicago, holding a rally at American Giants Park that drew 15,000.

But the end was near. Vandals set fire to the ballpark on December 23, 1940, and the dilapidated structure burned quickly. The fire started in the third-base stands, and damage was estimated at between $2,000 and $8,000. Hall declared that the stands would be rebuilt immediately, but the second major fire at the ballpark was also its last.[82] "It was a historic landmark in the history of Negro League baseball. Yet, no one shed tears when (Schorling Park[83]) burned, as there was universal agreement that the old wooden ballpark had outlived its usefulness."[84]

EPILOGUE

The American Giants still had a team, but now had no ballpark for the 1941 season. Neither Hall nor the Negro American League seemed concerned about this problem, causing Fay Young of the *Chicago Defender* to write, "People cannot understand why, in a city like Chicago, that we have a ballpark which wouldn't be a credit to the Negros of Chittlin Switch, Mississippi. The money is here. The question is who will invest"[85] A group of investors did consider rebuilding the park, only to be scared off when they heard the American Giants owed $2,800 in back taxes on ticket sales.[86] Eventually what was left of the ballpark was razed. In 1945 Wentworth Gardens was built on the site to house war-industry workers. It is now a public housing project owned by the Chicago Housing Authority.[87] A marker stands at the northeast corner of 39th Street (Pershing Road) and Wentworth Avenue commemorating the life of Andrew "Rube" Foster, but there is no tribute to the ballpark that once stood on that site, where baseball immortals like Comiskey, Rube and Willie Foster, Young, Ed Walsh, Walter Johnson, Ty Cobb, John Henry Lloyd, Oscar Charleston, Paige, and Josh Gibson once played for their fans.

SOURCES

BOOKS

Axelson, G.W. *Commy – The Life Story of Charles A. Comiskey* (Jefferson, North Carolina: McFarland & Company, 2003)

Benson, Michael. *Ballparks of North America* (Jefferson, North Carolina: McFarland & Company, 1989)

Cottrell, Robert Charles. *The Best Pitcher in Baseball* (New York: New York University Press, 2004)

DeBono, Paul. *The Chicago American Giants* (Jefferson, North Carolina: McFarland & Company, 2007)

Holway, John. *The Complete Book of Baseball's Negro Leagues* (New York: Hastings House, 1990)

Lindberg, Richard C. *Stealing First in a Two-Team Town* (Champaign, Illinois: Sagamore Publishing, 1994)

Lowry, Philip J. *Green Cathedrals* (New York: Walker & Company, 2006)

NEWSPAPERS

Chicago Defender via ProQuest through the Carnegie Library of Pittsburgh

Chicago Broad Ax and *Chicago Daily News* through www.genealogybank.com

Chicago Inter-Ocean, *Chicago Tribune*, and *Southtown Economist* through www.newspapers.com

ONLINE SOURCES

www.baseball-reference.com

www.kalracing.com

www.profootballarchives.com

www.nonohitters.com

www.sabr.org

www.thecha.org

NOTES

1   "The City," *Chicago Tribune*, April 29, 1888: 20.

2   "The Wanderers Club," *Chicago Tribune*, October 2, 1887: 26.

3   "The Wanderers Club."

4   "Only One of Them Sprinted," *Chicago Tribune*, September 2, 1887: 9.

5   "Notes of Sport," *Chicago Tribune*, January 7, 1894: 7.

6   "Football Carnival Today," *Chicago Inter-Ocean*, November 29, 1884: 4.

7   "Curlers Get Busy," *Chicago Tribune*, December 12, 1894: 11.

8   "Wanderers Build a Hockey Rink," *Chicago Tribune*, January 2, 1900.

9   Richard C. Lindberg, *Stealing First in a Two-Team Town* (Champaign, Illinois: Sagamore Publishing, 1994), 13.

10 Lindberg, 35.

11 Lindberg, 40.

12 "Two Clubs in Chicago," *Chicago Tribune*, November 21, 1899: 4.

13 Untitled, *Chicago Tribune*, January 13, 1900: 6.

14 "Comiskey Issues an Ultimatum," *Chicago Tribune*, March 3, 1900: 6.

15 "He Names the Club," *Chicago Inter-Ocean*, March 7, 1900: 8.

16 "Wanderers Move to Parkside," *Chicago Tribune*, March 9, 1900: 9.

17 "Chicago's New Club," *Chicago Tribune*, February 25, 1900: 10.

18 "Left to the Lawyers," *Chicago Tribune*, March 20, 1900: 9.

19 Lindberg, 5-7; "Comiskey's Trials as Contractor," *Chicago Tribune*, April 4, 1900: 6.

20 "New Stands Are Ready," *Chicago Tribune*, April 12, 1900: 4.

21 "Brewers Win Opening Game," *Chicago Tribune*, April 22, 1900: 17.

22 "Target for Home Runs," *Chicago Tribune*, April 25, 1900: 6.

23 "Comiskey Signs Waler Brodie," *Chicago Inter-Ocean*, April 27, 1900: 8.

24 "Improves South Side Park," *Chicago Tribune*, June 27, 1901: 6.

25 The attendance total per Baseball-Reference.com was 30,098. https://www.baseball-reference.com/boxes/CHA/CHA190410021.shtml

26 Lindberg, 81.

27 No-hitters at South Side Park: September 20, 1902, Jim Callahan, Chicago White Sox; August 17, 1904, Jesse Tannehill, Boston

Americans; September 20, 1908, Frank Smith, Chicago White Sox; April 20, 1910, Addie Joss, Cleveland Naps.

28　"New Ball Park for $100,000," *Chicago Tribune,* January 20, 1909: 13.

29　Lindberg, 83.

30　"Plans Improvements at White Sox Park," *Chicago Inter-Ocean,* February 23, 1909: 9.

31　"Marathon Stars in Local Event," *Chicago Tribune,* April 14, 1909: 10.

32　"White Sox Park Scorched," *Chicago Tribune,* April 26, 1909: 1.

33　"White Sox Park Is Menaced by Fire," *Chicago Inter-Ocean,* April 26, 1909: 1-2.

34　Untitled, *Southtown Economist,* June 24, 1910: 4.

35　Paul DeBono, *The Chicago American Giants* (Jefferson, North Carolina: McFarland & Company, 2007), 32.

36　DeBono, 33.

37　Jerry Malloy, "Rube Foster and Black Baseball in Chicago," *Baseball in Chicago – 1986 SABR Convention Journal.*

38　DeBono, 36. Also Harold McGrath, "In the Field of Sport," *Indianapolis Freeman,* January 28, 1911.

39　"Semi-Pro Magnate Leases Sox Park for Next Season," *Chicago Tribune,* June 16, 1910: 10.

40　"Start Work on Old Sox Park," *Chicago Tribune,* March 11, 1911: 21.

41　"Fire Destroys American Giants Ball Park Seats," *Chicago Defender,* January 4, 1941: 24.

42　Andrew "Rube" Foster, "Negro Baseball," *Indianapolis Freeman,* December 23, 1911: 16.

43　Robert Charles Cottrell, *The Best Pitcher in Baseball* (New York: New York University Press, 2004), 63.

44　DeBono, 37.

45　DeBono, 37.

46　Cottrell, 63.

47　DeBono, 37.

48　Classified ad in *Chicago Tribune,* May 6, 1911: 15.

49　"Illa Vincent, The Black Panther, routed Frank Ehrler, The German Thunderbolt," *Chicago Broad Ax,* October 14, 1911: 2.

50　Pro Football Archives: https://www.profootballarchives.com/1916chich.html.

51　"Benefit for the Old Folks Home," *Chicago Defender,* August 16, 1913: 8.

52　"American Giants Hold Park," *Chicago Tribune,* December 31, 1913: 12.

53　"Banquet and Reception to Rube Foster and His American Giants at Odd Fellows Ball," *Chicago Broad Ax,* May 2, 1914: 2.

54　Nonohitters.com: https://www.nonohitters.com/negro-leagues-no-hitters/.

55　"American Giants Victors, 5-4," *Chicago Tribune,* June 8, 1914: 11.

56　It was called the Spanish flu but not because it was known to have originated in Spain. It was actually identified in America, Europe, and Asia at about the same time.

57　"All-Star Leaguers Will Compete Against American Giants," *Chicago Defender,* September 28, 1918: 9.

58　"Influenza Epidemic Closes Season for American Giants," *Chicago Defender,* November 2, 1918: 9.

59　DeBono, 71-72.

60　"Prices Up," *Chicago Defender,* April 10, 1920: 11.

61　"Near-Riot Stops Baseball Game," *Chicago Defender,* May 13, 1922: 1.

62　"1,500 Periled, 28 Hurt When Ball Stand Collapses," *Chicago Tribune,* May 28, 1923: 3.

63　"30.000 Colored Elks Hep-Hep to 25 Jazz Bands," *Chicago Tribune,* August 29, 1923: 9.

64　John Holway, *The Complete Book of Baseball's Negro Leagues* (New York: Hastings House, 1990), 195.

65　DeBono, 114.

66　Cottrell, 171.

67　DeBono, 115.

68　The White newspapers generally called the park American Giants Park or South Side Park after Schorling sold the team to Trimble.

69　DeBono, 122.

70　"Night Baseball," *Chicago Daily Times,* June 21, 1930: 24.

71　DeBono, 125.

72　"K.C. Boss Dickers for Chicago Park," *Chicago Defender,* August 8, 1931: 9.

73　"K.C. Boss Dickers for Chicago Park."

74　DeBono, 131.

75　"Professional Football to Hit Chicago," *Chicago Defender,* September 26, 1931: 8.

76　DeBono, 133; "Old Park Dresses Up," *Chicago Defender,* March 6, 1932: 22.

77　"Giants Lose Ball Grounds: Old Schorling Park Will Be Home of Dogs," *Chicago Defender,* May 6, 1933: 8.

78　DeBono, 145.

79　"Jesse Owens in Two Track Exhibitions," *Chicago Daily News,* July 1, 1938: 17.

80　Advertisement in the *Chicago Metropolitan Post,* September 10, 1938: 14.

81　http://www.kalracing.com/autoracing/Chicago_American_Giants_Main_Page.htm.

82　"Fire Destroys American Giants Baseball Seats."

83　The Black press, specifically the *Chicago Defender,* continued to call the ballpark Schorling Park, even after John Schorling died in early 1940.

84　DeBono, 154.

85　Fay Young, "The Stuff Is Here," *Chicago Defender,* May 17, 1941: 24.

86　DeBono, 155.

87　https://www.thecha.org/residents/public-housing/find-public-housing/wentworth-gardens. (Chicago Housing Authority).

1920 CHICAGO AMERICAN GIANTS TIMELINE

BY BILL NOWLIN

"There is every indication that next season baseball fans of America will have a circuit of western clubs." So began an article in the October 4 *Chicago Defender*.[1] As Rube Foster's American Giants prepared to wrap up their 1919 season with a game in Chicago on Sunday, October 5, against Whitman and Barnes, a team of White ballplayers, and then travel to Kansas City to play a "picked club of major leaguers" on October 11 and 12, Foster's real focus was on creating an eight-team league for 1920. The league was to include his Chicago team, and ones in Detroit (where two July games had drawn 19,000 fans), Dayton, Cleveland, Indianapolis, Kansas City, and St. Louis. The Cuban Stars would be a road team. Of Foster, the *Defender* wrote, "It has been his dream for years to see men of his Race have a circuit of their own."[2]

On November 29 the *Defender* published the first of six weekly articles on the "Pitfalls of Baseball" authored by Andrew "Rube" Foster. He provided a brief history of the business side of "Colored baseball," right down to detailing the salaries paid, noting that even the "smallest salary paid to the American Giants and Detroit equals the salary of any postoffice carrier, clerk or city schoolteacher in the United States."[3] This, despite having many fewer hours of actual work and not requiring literacy. It was particularly difficult for the organizers of any team to break even financially

without strong, capable leadership and a practiced eye for baseball talent.[4]

A meeting was called for February 13 and 14 at the Paseo YMCA in Kansas City to try to organize a league. Cary Lewis of the *Defender* was named secretary. Foster revealed that he had an incorporated charter for a Negro National Baseball League.[5] A constitution was written for a league to be started in 1921.[6] As it turns out, the league was launched in 1920.

On February 15, C.I. Taylor, owner of the Indianapolis ABCs, announced the formation of the National Negro Baseball Association, with Rube Foster as president. The league embraced eight ballclubs, three of which were named Giants: Chicago American Giants, Chicago Giants, Dayton Marcos, Detroit Stars, Indianapolis ABCs, Kansas City Monarchs, St. Louis Giants, and the Cuban Stars, "a traveling team."[7]

A March 20 article reported that Foster had assigned various players to different teams. Dick Whitworth and Oscar Charleston were said to be sent to Detroit and Indianapolis. Jose Mendez and John Donaldson were sent by Detroit Stars owner Tenny Blount to Kansas City. The goal was to have some parity and to increase competitiveness.[8]

Naturally, the success of the venture depended on the appeal to the fan base, as noted by Dave Wyatt in an April 3 article, "Success of the League Is Up to the Fans."[9]

Despite some of the players being sent elsewhere, the Chicago American Giants were seen, in effect, as the team to beat – "the club that National League clubs will have to beat this season to win championships." Fans were invited to watch them work out.[10]

Many of the Giants from the 1919 season were returning for the new season – the returnees included Charleston, DeMoss, Dixon, Gans, Grant, Tom Johnson, Wickware, and Bobby Williams. That many stars remained with the American Giants despite Rube Foster's attempt to move some players around to populate other teams in the new league to create more competitive teams. Parity was one thing, but the league was Foster's brainchild, and one can be pretty sure he did want a championship for his own team.

APRIL 11, 1920: ROGERS PARK 4, AMERICAN GIANTS 2, AT SCHORLING'S PARK, CHICAGO

The opening of the "semi-pro season" began with a defeat at the hands of the Rogers Parks, a White semipro team. Tom Williams and Jack Marshall pitched for the Giants. The Giants scored twice in the bottom of the first but were held scoreless from that point on. All the Rogers Park runs scored in the top of the fifth inning. With the bases loaded, a fly ball hit to John Reese in left field was so badly misjudged that not only did all three baserunners score but so did the unnamed batter.[11] Attendance was 4,500, on a very cold day, "which proved the public is hungry for baseball."[12]

A game had been planned against the Magnets of the Chicago League for the following day – April 18 – but it was rained out. An advertisement in the April 17 Defender listed the scheduled 3:00 P.M. Sunday games against the Magnets and on April 25 against Dodger Training A.C. of Intercity Assn. The ballpark name was advertised as American Giants Park, 39th St. and Wentworth Ave., though an accompanying news story was headlined "Magnets Play American Giants at Schorling Park Sunday."[13]

By May 15, the name of the park was listed as Schorling's Park in advertisements.

Note: Any time the text uses the word "Giants" without a modifying term, the reference is to Rube Foster's Chicago American Giants.

APRIL 25, 1920: DODGER TRAINING CLUB OF THE INTERCITY ASSOCIATION 9, CHICAGO AMERICAN GIANTS 6, AT SCHORLING'S PARK, CHICAGO

Hot prospect John "Big" Taylor pitched for the Giants in a 3:00 P.M. Sunday game and was tagged for five runs in the first inning. He was relieved by Marshall.[14] The Giants came back with two runs in the bottom of the first and two more in the second, only to see the Dodgers add three more in the fourth and put the game out of sight.[15] Taylor ended up pitching for the Chicago Giants during the 1920 season.

The official opening date of the new league's season was set for May 2.[16] Foster's team played its first league game on May 9. Dave Wyatt of the Chicago Defender felt there were many reasons for optimism as he didn't see any team poised to run away with it, although he did proceed to anoint the American Giants as preseason favorites. He wrote, "Foster is strong on pitchers and infielders, and his outfield looks good." His team was probably as good as any, and if it failed to prevail, Foster would be without an alibi. Wyatt noted overall that many of the players would be strangers to the fans of the "Western" clubs.[17]

The Defender let readers know that Malarcher had "ran afoul of a pair of mighty sharp spikes, sustaining a very severe wound in his hand."[18] Bill Riggins, whom the article called "a flashy youngster," was to play third base until Malarcher returned. Some early articles rendered his name as Wriggins.

MAY 2, 1920: CHICAGO AMERICAN GIANTS 7, ROMEOS 2, AT SCHORLING'S PARK

The Giants piled up all their runs in the first two innings, scoring five in the first and two more in the second. The Defender enthused, "Last Sunday the gang romped off with their first victory of the current season, and they did it in such a businesslike way that their admirers are once more rallying under their banner and proclaiming them to be all that advance notices have pictured them to be."[19] Jack Marshall started and Tom Johnson took over in the third. The Romeos were held scoreless until putting across two runs in the eighth.

MAY 9, 1920: CHICAGO AMERICAN GIANTS 8, CHICAGO GIANTS 3, AT SCHORLING'S PARK

This game appears to have been the first true league game. The *Defender's* ad for the game said the Chicago Giants were from the "Western Circuit, N.N.L." while the Dayton Marcos – advertised to play against the Chicago American Giants on May 16 – were simply listed as "of N.N.L."[20]

The two teams with practically identical names met up for their "annual scrap," wrote Captain James H. Smith in the *Defender* and, "as always, interest was at a fever heat. The largest crowd of this season turned out and the bantering was continuous throughout the contest."[21] Chicago Giants starter Walter Ball had a tough go. With one run in the first, four in the third inning, and two more in the fourth, the Chicago American Giants were well on their way to a win, with an 8-0 lead through six innings. Third baseman Dave Malarcher and second baseman Bingo DeMoss both had three hits for Foster's team, and left-hander Dave Brown pitched scoreless ball for the innings he pitched. After Tom Williams took over pitching, the Chicago Giants scored three. The *Chicago Whip* correspondent said the umpiring was execrable, to the detriment of the Chicago Giants, providing a couple of examples.[22]

MAY 16, 1920: DAYTON MARCOS 6, CHICAGO AMERICAN GIANTS 5, AT SCHORLING'S PARK

It was a game "of few hits but many bases on balls and errors."[23] The Marcos got to Marshall early, for two runs in the first and four in the third. Marshall himself had "an inability to locate the platter" but it was poor fielding by "a couple of inexperienced recruits who were being given a tryout" that proved particularly costly. In the first inning, catcher Buck Ewing tried to throw out a man stealing second and then, when getting him in a rundown between third and home, threw the ball so wildly into left field that two runs scored. Ewing committed three errors in the game. The Marcos scored their four runs in the third inning on one base hit, two walks, and three errors by the shortstop, Wiggins (or Wingfield).[24] Neither appear to have played in any other games for the Giants. It's also possible that "Wiggins" was Bill Riggins.

Cristobal Torriente led in base hits for Chicago, with two singles and a double that drove in their first run. He had been late in arriving due to an immigration holdup as he arrived in Tampa from Cuba. Dave Brown took over pitching in the fourth inning and struck out 10 of the Marcos while allowing just one hit.

MAY 22, 1920: CHICAGO AMERICAN GIANTS 6, DAYTON MARCOS 2, AT SCHORLING'S PARK

Willie Gray started for the Marcos and gave up four runs in the first inning before he was replaced by George Britt, who gave up a couple more runs in the third. The only two runs for Dayton came off Jack Marshall in the top of the second inning. Three of the four doubles in the game were by Giants – left fielder John Reese, second baseman Bingo DeMoss, and shortstop Bobby Williams. Chicago outhit Dayton, seven hits to six.[25]

MAY 23, 1920: CHICAGO AMERICAN GIANTS 6, KANSAS CITY MONARCHS 5 (11 INNINGS), AT SCHORLING'S PARK

The Giants scored three times in the first inning and added a fourth run in the second inning, but even staked to that lead, this time it was Brown who struggled. Kansas City came back with three runs in the second, and Johnson relieved him in the fifth when he walked two and hit a batter. The game drew 7,000.[26] Pitcher Tom Johnson won his own game in the bottom of the 11th, singling to drive in Eddie Boyd from second base on what was apparently a very close play: "Boyd was called safe, then out then safe again."[27] The *Chicago Tribune* explained that it was due to a "dropped throw at the plate."[28] The *Kansas City Sun* called it a "questionable decision."[29]

MAY 24, 1920: CHICAGO AMERICAN GIANTS 5, KANSAS CITY MONARCHS 0, AT SCHORLING'S PARK

Lieut. Tom Johnson[30] pitched a shutout for the Giants, beating the Monarchs' Sam Crawford. It was the second game of a five-game series.[31] Johnson "had the visitors at his mercy. He allowed but three scattered hits, a pinch hitter getting one of them in the ninth. A catch by Gans was the fielding feature."[32]

MAY 25, 1920: CHICAGO AMERICAN GIANTS 4, KANSAS CITY MONARCHS 1, AT SCHORLING'S PARK

The May 26 *Chicago Tribune* noted the game with a one-sentence "game story." It read: "American Giants scored still another victory over the Monarchs of Kansas City, 4 to 1, at Schorling Park yesterday."[33] Marshall would have had a shutout but for an error, reported the *Herald-Examiner*.[34]

MAY 26, 1920: CHICAGO AMERICAN GIANTS 3, KANSAS CITY MONARCHS 2, AT SCHORLING'S PARK

The fourth consecutive victory of the series saw the Giants score one in the fourth and two in the seventh, edging the Monarchs, who scored single runs in the fifth and eighth. Torriente and Dixon both doubled. Frank Wickware started but was relieved by Tom Williams at some point.

MAY 28, 1920: CHICAGO AMERICAN GIANTS 8, LOGAN SQUARES 3, AT LOGAN SQUARE, CHICAGO

Center fielder Bill Harley of the Logan Squares "was nearly the whole show in the game at Logan Square. ... Harley clouted a triple in the first with the sacks loaded. Gibby Nelson was hit hard."[35] The Giants outhit the Logan Squares 15-4. The Giants had scored four times in the top of the first, so even Harley's triple off Marshall couldn't sufficiently cut the deficit. The Logan Squares added one more in the fourth inning.

MAY 30, 1920: CHICAGO AMERICAN GIANTS 4, CUBAN STARS WEST 1, AT SCHORLING'S PARK

It was "the biggest crowd in the history of Schorling's park, estimated at 16,000."[36] They saw the hometown Giants beat the team without a home – the Cuban Stars, who were a yearlong traveling team without a home base. The score was 4-1, the Cubans scoring first off Tom Williams in the top of the third inning but then seeing the Chicagoans score twice in the fourth and twice in the sixth. Right-hander Cheo Hernandez pitched for the Cubans.

MAY 31, 1920: CHICAGO AMERICAN GIANTS 3, CUBAN STARS WEST 2, AT SCHORLING'S PARK

Lieut. Tom Johnson threw a three-hitter, reported the *Chicago Tribune*. Jose Leblanc pitched for the Cubans. Four Cubans committed errors in the game. The Giants got seven hits and won before "another record crowd."[37] The Giants scored one run in each of the first three innings. In all, they collected seven base hits, four of them by Torriente.[38]

JUNE 1, 1920: CHICAGO AMERICAN GIANTS 7, CUBAN STARS WEST 5, AT SCHORLING'S PARK

Dave Brown pitched against Faustino Valdez, as the Giants collected 15 hits off the Cuban pitcher. The opposition got to Brown for eight hits. The Cubans took a 2-0 lead in the top of the first, but the Giants immediately responded with three, adding a fourth run in the second and a fifth in the third. After the Cubans put two more runs across to lead off the fifth, the Giants responded in kind. The one run the Cubans got back in the eighth wasn't enough.[39]

JUNE 3, 1920: CHICAGO AMERICAN GIANTS 3, CUBAN STARS WEST 2 (13 INNINGS), AT SCHORLING'S PARK

Marshall allowed just six hits over 13 innings, going the distance while striking out 13. The Cuban Stars' pitchers, Martinez and Hernandez, allowed a dozen hits. Catcher George Dixon had three safeties and so did shortstop Bobby Williams, a double for Williams being the only extra-base hit. Each team committed four errors. There were two outs in the bottom of the 13th when the Giants scored the winning run on three errors committed by "the Islanders."[40] The *Chicago Tribune* reported this as the 12th consecutive win for the Giants.[41]

JUNE 4, 1920: CHICAGO AMERICAN GIANTS 8, LOGAN SQUARES 3, AT LOGAN SQUARE, CHICAGO

The *Defender* said that the American Giants had won six games in a row against three of their toughest foes. We count eight in a row before this nonleague game, but it's quite possible there were other games mixed in that did not turn up in our search of newspapers a century later. The *Defender* said, "The Foster team perhaps has the strongest pitching staff in the country today, and their infield has the edge on all so far seen."[42]

JUNE 5, 1920: CHICAGO AMERICAN GIANTS 7, DANVILLE 0, AT DANVILLE, ILLINOIS

Stopping over to play a Saturday game on their way to St. Louis, the Giants shut out a Danville nine, 7-0, Wickware pitching for the visitors and allowing only four hits to the Giants' 12. It was reported as their 13th consecutive win.[43]

JUNE 6, 1920: CHICAGO AMERICAN GIANTS 12, MAGNETS OF CHICAGO 1, AT SCHORLING'S PARK

Tom Williams threw a six-hitter in a game that reportedly drew 10,000.[44] The *Defender* said, "The Americans piled up enough stolen bases, pulled enough bunts and squeezed enough runs across the pan to last for a season."[45] Judy Gans had three base hits and Dave Malarcher had two. The Giants scored two runs in the second inning, three in the fifth, five in the seventh, and a final 12th run in the eighth. The *Whip* wrote, "The squeeze play was worked successfully six times for as many runs."[46] The team was reported to have left for St. Louis after the game.

JUNE 7, 1920: CHICAGO AMERICAN GIANTS 10, ST. LOUIS GIANTS 1, AT GIANTS PARK, ST. LOUIS

Tom Johnson allowed just five hits to St Louis while four St. Louis pitchers – Bill Drake, Jimmy Oldham, John Finner, and Wayne Carr – collectively gave up 12 hits and 10 runs. Drake pitched the first six innings and gave up nine hits and five runs. Oldham worked one-third of an inning and got his man out. Finner gave up two hits but four runs in 1⅔ innings. Carr apparently pitched the ninth. Meanwhile, Johnson walked three and struck out three, working a complete game for the American Giants. Four from Chicago got a pair of base hits apiece – Reese, DeMoss, Torriente, and Grant. There was only one extra-base hit in the game, a double by Malarcher. After three scoreless innings, Chicago scored three in the fourth, two in the fifth, four in the seventh, and one in the top of the ninth.[47]

JUNE 8, 1920: CHICAGO AMERICAN GIANTS 7, ST. LOUIS GIANTS 0, AT GIANTS PARK, ST. LOUIS

Dave "Lefty" Brown shut out St. Louis, allowing only three hits. Remarkably, all three were by center fielder Charlie Blackwell, who enjoyed a 3-for-4 day Two St. Louis batters walked, but Brown struck out six batters as well. Chicago scored two runs in the top of the first off left-hander Luther Farrell (who was identified as "Luther" and not "Farrell" in both the game story and box score.) The St. Louis pitcher – by either name – gave up only eight hits. The two runs in the first were enough for Chicago to win the game but the Giants added five more runs in the top of the seventh, just to make sure. Torriente had two base hits, one of them a double, and he stole three bases. Judy Gans hit a triple. St. Louis fielders committed four errors, which was said to have helped the visitors to all of their scores, three of the four errors aiding the scoring of runs.[48]

JUNE 9, 1920: CHICAGO AMERICAN GIANTS 6, ST. LOUIS GIANTS 0, AT GIANTS PARK, ST. LOUIS

As Brown had the day before, Jack Marshall held St. Louis to just three hits and shut them out again. The St. Louis team made three more errors. Wayne Carr was the losing pitcher. He gave up two runs in the first inning, one in the second, one in the third, and two in the fifth. Save for Reese, every batter in the Chicago lineup got exactly one base hit except for Torriente, who got two. Every one of the hits was a single, except for Torriente's – both of his were doubles. Marshall struck out 10.[49]

The *St. Louis Argus,* a weekly that catered to the Black community, was beyond unsparing in tearing apart the performance of the St. Louis Giants, saying such things as "pep on the playing field is an unknown commodity. The players go out to their positions with as much pep as a 99-year-old street-cleaner." The *Argus* even complained that they never even protested umpiring calls as vehemently as did visiting teams. The team acted as though "the Chicago team is the greatest and strongest team in the world, and it is impossible to beat them so why should we try."[50]

JUNE 10, 1920: ST. LOUIS GIANTS 3, CHICAGO AMERICAN GIANTS 2, AT GIANTS PARK, ST. LOUIS

The *Tribune* had a datelined June 10 article stating that the American Giants had lost to the St. Louis Giants on the 10th, 3-2, after their 17th consecutive win. Drake squared off against Chicago's Tom Williams and neither team scored a run for the first seven innings. St. Louis scored two runs in the bottom of the eighth, which Chicago matched in the top of the ninth. St. Louis won the game with a run in the ninth.[51] Drake had two base hits, "both of which counted in the runmaking."[52] The *Argus* acknowledged the win with a subhead "Giants Come to Earth and Win Thursday," referring to the St. Louis Giants.[53]

JUNE 11, 1920: CHICAGO AMERICAN GIANTS 6, ST. LOUIS GIANTS 3, AT GIANTS PARK, ST. LOUIS

The American Giants used three pitchers – Johnson, Wickware, and Marshall – each working three innings. They scored two runs in the top of the first off St. Louis pitchers Luther and Finner. St. Louis scored once in the fourth and once in the fifth, but then saw Chicago add three to its total in the sixth inning and a sixth run in the seventh. Gans and Malarcher both had triples.[54]

JUNE 12, 1920: MCCOY-NOLANS 6, CHICAGO AMERICAN GIANTS 4, AT MILWAUKEE

Overcoming a 4-0 deficit after the first 2½ innings, the McCoys scored four runs in the eighth. Pitching for the Giants was someone named Wichman (or in the box score, "Witch'n"). This was presumably Frank Wickware, who was relieved by Brown after 7⅔ innings.[55]

JUNE 13, 1920: CHICAGO AMERICAN GIANTS 9, INDIANAPOLIS ABCS 1, AT SCHORLING PARK

Tom Williams pitched a five-hitter.[56] The ABCs scored once in the top of the first but gave up three in the bottom of the first and another run in the second, two more each in the fifth and sixth, and a final one in the seventh. Malarcher hit a pair of doubles and Torriente hit a triple. His name was frequently spelled "Torrenti" and the *Defender* wrote of him in this game: "The feature of this context was the batting of Torrenti,

who released a fine exhibition of fielding, running and all-round play."[57] The paper credited Indianapolis third baseman Connie Day as playing a good game, but said that "for some unknown reason the old A. machine did not function up to the standard of former years."

JUNE 15, 1920: CHICAGO AMERICAN GIANTS 6, INDIANAPOLIS ABCS 2 (FIRST GAME OF DOUBLE-HEADER), AT SCHORLING PARK

JUNE 15, 1920: CHICAGO AMERICAN GIANTS 7, INDIANAPOLIS ABCS 0 (SECOND GAME OF DOUBLE-HEADER), AT SCHORLING PARK

The Monday, June 14, game was rained out, so the teams played two on Tuesday. Another one of those one-sentence articles in the June 16 *Chicago Tribune* provided the basics and no more.[58] The *Indianapolis Freeman* wasn't much more helpful, but it did offer three sentences: "The ABCs were defeated twice here this afternoon by the American Giants by the scores of 6 to 2 and 7 to 0. Dizzy Dismukes was wild in the first game and was succeeded by Dicta Johnson. Jim Jeffries went the route in the second game but lost because of poor support."[59]

JUNE 16, 1920: CHICAGO AMERICAN GIANTS 6, FORT SHERIDAN 2, AT FORT SHERIDAN, ILLINOIS

"More than 5,000 convalescent soldiers, officers, nurses, and medical corps men at Fort Sheridan watched the home team go down to defeat."[60] The Fort Sheridan team walked six and committed six errors. Marshall allowed four hits.[61]

JUNE 19, 1920: CHICAGO AMERICAN GIANTS 10, OAK PARKS 5, AT OAK PARK, CHICAGO

It's possible the Giants played two games on the 19th. The *Chicago Tribune* reported this game at Oak Park. The semipro team's pitcher, Beltz, was apparently belted for 12 hits and walked three. Oak Park had scored first, getting two runs off Tom Williams in the second inning. The Giants scored five times in the third, but Oak Park quickly came back with two more. Judy Gans hit a two-run homer in the fifth, as well as a double. At one point in the game, baserunner Tom

Williams was struck by a batted ball and thus out on the basepaths.[62]

JUNE 20, 1920: ROGERS PARK 1, CHICAGO AMERICAN GIANTS 0, AT SCHORLING PARK

"The American Giants entertained their old enemies, the Rogers Parks and believe me, it was some game. If you want to get your money's worth, just stage a battle between the Irish and Colored teams."[63] Sam Lafferty pitched shutout ball for the Rogers Parks and Tom Johnson nearly did the game for the American Giants, the lone run in the game scoring due to a second-inning error by DeMoss as he was attempting a double play.[64] Both pitchers threw four-hitters.

A lengthy article in the *Indianapolis Freeman* preceded the visit of Foster's Giants and provided some granular detail regarding a few of Foster's business successes.

"Foster's Club Biggest Drawing Card in Base Ball. – The American Giants, under Foster, have proven time and time again, that they are the best card in base ball, and when they appear here Sunday, he will be greeted by the largest attendance that have ever seen two clubs of color battle. People who never see games, always go when Rube comes to town. He has a following of ministers, doctors, lawyers, teachers and from every profession and all walks of life. He has the confidence of all that has [sic] ever met him. His friends are numbered by the millions. Fans here are waiting to see him again. Indianapolis opens her doors to him.

"Foster Biggest Speculator Ever in Game – All the big money deals engineered in colored base ball, he has been the guiding hand. Last season, he paid $1,750.00 for Navin Field two days, and made over $4,000.00 on the venture. He has refused $2,000.00 a Sunday to play his club East. C.I. Taylor offered Foster percentage on 12,000 paid admissions, rain or shine, to come to Indianapolis, yet Foster refused. Said he would gamble on his chances. The big fellow is lucky in his ventures, and always has proved his judgment once accepted was the best thing. – Colored Base Ball Lucky to Have Foster – All the managers through the Western circuit are praising Foster. They unanimously claim that his wonderful resources are unbelievable. May and June, considered bad baseball months before, Foster has manipulated the clubs that up to date, not one of the Western clubs has received less than $1,000

for each Sunday this season. Each city is drawing better than, at any other time in the history."[65]

JUNE 26, 1920: CHICAGO AMERICAN GIANTS 5, INDIANAPOLIS ABCS 4, AT NORTH WALNUT STREET PARK, MUNCIE, INDIANA

There was a big buildup locally for this Saturday 3:00 P.M. game in Muncie. A *Muncie Star Press* article earlier in the week announced the game, noting it as a "regularly scheduled league contest, transferred to this city from Indianapolis." The article added, "The colored men are noted for their faculty of pulling the unexpected at bat, on the bases and in the field and they often perform the most brilliant and sensational plays ever seen in baseball."[66]

Entering the game, wrote the *Star Press*, the Giants were in first place and C.I. Taylor's ABCs were in third. Frank Wickware started for the Chicago team and pitched the first seven innings. Left-hander Jim Jeffries pitched the whole game for Indianapolis; he'd been pitching for the team off and on since 1913. Both pitchers had one bad inning. The American Giants got to Jeffries for four runs in the top of the second inning. With one out, catcher Jim Brown walked. He reached second on a grounder by Judy Gans, who was safe on a low throw by shortstop Samuel DeWitt. Leroy Grant singled to left but Brown was held at third base. Jesse Williams doubled to left, driving in two runs. John Reese singled to center and drove in two more.

For Indianapolis, catcher Russell Powell singled and Connie Day walked. George Shively singled, loading the bases, and Morten Clark drove in two. Oscar Charleston singled to drive in Shively and Clark

(*Muncie Star-Press* (Muncie, Indiana), June 26, 1920)

but was thrown out trying to reach second base. It was tied, 4-4.

Both pitchers cracked down and only one more run scored in the game. Cristobal Torriente led off with a single. Jim Brown reached on another error by shortstop DeWitt. Gans grounded into an out, Torriente running to third base, whence he scored on a fly ball to left field. Dave Brown and Tom Williams both pitched in late-inning relief. The paper raved that "the game put up by both teams is easily the equal of that of the major league clubs."[67]

JUNE 27, 1920: INDIANAPOLIS ABCS 1, CHICAGO AMERICAN GIANTS 0 (10 INNINGS, FIRST GAME OF DOUBLEHEADER), AT WASHINGTON PARK, INDIANAPOLIS

JUNE 27, 1920: CHICAGO AMERICAN GIANTS 2, INDIANAPOLIS ABCS 2 (5 INNINGS, TIE GAME, SECOND GAME OF DOUBLEHEADER), AT WASHINGTON PARK, INDIANAPOLIS

Some 8,000 fans came out for this Sunday doubleheader and saw a scoreless nine-inning game pitched by both right-hander Big Ed Rile and by Dave Brown. It appears that Rile kept putting men on the bases, issuing walk after walk (13 in all, according to the box score) but allowed only four base hits. Brown allowed only two hits, one by Rile. An ABCs threat to score in the bottom of the ninth came to naught, but with nobody out in the 10th, Samuel Dewitt reached safely on a throwing error by second baseman Bingo DeMoss. Connie Day hit one back to Brown, but he also made a wild throw. Rile then hit a ball right at shortstop Bobby Williams but it "proved too hot for the little fellow."[68] It was another error, and the ballgame.

Rile pitched the second game, too. Chicago used both Jack Marshall and Tom Williams. The ABCs scored one in the first. After the Giants put up two runs in the top of the third, Indianapolis scored one more. It wasn't darkness but rather the Sunday Blue Laws that brought the game to a halt at 6:00 P.M.

STANDINGS

The *Chicago Defender* printed standings on page 9 of its July 3 issue, characterizing them as "Standing of the clubs of the western circuit of the proposed Negro National league … played up to week of June 27."

American Giants	18-2
Detroit	12-4
Indianapolis	15-11
Kansas City	11-14
Dayton	5-8
Cubans	6-12
Chicago Giants	1-8

The *Chicago Tribune* continued to include the American Giants in its list of "Semi-Pro Games" scheduled.[69]

JUNE 28, 1920: CHICAGO AMERICAN GIANTS 8, INDIANAPOLIS ABCS 8 (10 INNINGS, TIE GAME), AT WASHINGTON PARK, INDIANAPOLIS

Tom Williams went the full 10 innings for Chicago. It was a see-saw game, the Giants kicking things off with two runs in the top of the first and a third one in the third inning. The ABCs took the lead by scoring four in the bottom of the third. Chicago scored two runs in the fifth and bumped its lead to 6-4 with another run in the sixth. In the bottom of the seventh, Indianapolis scored three times to take a 7-6 lead. Chicago scored two in the eighth. Indianapolis scored one in the eighth. Neither team scored in the ninth or 10th.[70]

JUNE 29, 1920: INDIANAPOLIS ABCS 6, CHICAGO AMERICAN GIANTS 5, AT WASHINGTON PARK, INDIANAPOLIS

The ABCs built up a big lead. The Giants kept chipping away, but came up short. Marshall worked the game for Chicago, and he was tagged for two runs in the bottom of the fourth, then – after Chicago scored its first run in the top of the fifth – four more runs in the bottom of the inning. The Giants added a run in the sixth, another run in the seventh, and then two more runs in the eighth. Though Chicago had played error-free ball while Indianapolis committed three errors, the ABCs outhit the Giants 10 to 4.[71]

JUNE 30, 1920: CHICAGO AMERICAN GIANTS 6, INDIANAPOLIS ABCS 2, AT WASHINGTON PARK, INDIANAPOLIS

ABCs manager C.I. Taylor used Dizzy Dismukes and Jim Jeffries in an attempt to halt the Giants. The Giants used Tom Johnson. They were outhit by Indianapolis, nine hits to seven (three of the seven by Torriente, including the only extra-base hit, a double). Indianapolis scored the first run in the bottom of the first. Chicago matched that its next time up and added three more runs in the fourth inning. The Giants took a 5-1 lead in the fifth, gave one back in the sixth, and added another in the eighth inning for good measure.[72] The Giants "bunched" their hits, "and got all the 'breaks' in the contest," declared the *Indianapolis Star*.[73]

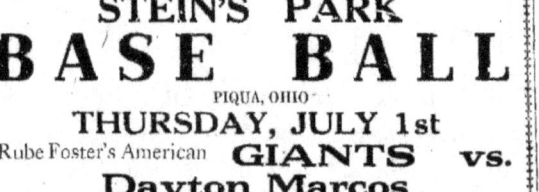

STEIN'S PARK
BASE BALL
PIQUA, OHIO
THURSDAY, JULY 1st
Rube Foster's American **GIANTS** vs.
Dayton Marcos

Friday and Saturday, July 2 and 3 at Westwood Field, Dayton, Ohio

The American Giants have lost but one series this season and the Marcos beat them. Rube Foster, the greatest pitcher of his day is managing them.

Games Called 3 P. M.

(Piqua Daily Call (Piqua, Ohio), June 30, 1920)

JULY 1, 1920: CHICAGO AMERICAN GIANTS 5, DAYTON MARCOS 0, AT WESTWOOD FIELD, DAYTON

Frank Wickware shut out the Marcos on six hits, striking out five. George Britt of Dayton struck out seven and allowed only one more hit than Wickware, but Chicago scored five runs and Dayton scored none. Each team made two errors. A pair of double plays helped the Giants. The game was scoreless through three innings, but the Giants scored three in the fourth. Britt gave up a pair of hits and then walked three batters in a row, followed by one more base hit, before recovering his control and striking out two while also picking a man off second. Jim Brown hit a home run in the eighth, but only because the ball was "lost in the high grass in right field."[74]

JULY 3, 1920: CHICAGO AMERICAN GIANTS 16, DAYTON MARCOS 4, AT WESTWOOD FIELD, DAYTON

This one was a lopsided win for the American Giants, who scored in every inning but the top of the first and the top of the eighth. The team's inning-by-inning scoring line was:

0 2 1 4 3 2 3 0 1

The Marcos took an early lead with one run in the bottom of the first. After the Giants scored twice in the top of the second, Dayton tied it, 2-2. From that point on, the game got away from the Marcos. They scored their other two runs in the bottom of the fourth, but then never had a runner cross home plate again. Dave Brown pitched for Chicago, with Tom Johnson taking over at some point. The Marcos pitchers victimized were Isaac Lane and George Britt.[75]

JULY 4, 1920: CHICAGO AMERICAN GIANTS 1, CUBAN STARS WEST 0, AT SCHORLING PARK

The only run of the game came in the first inning, when Dave Malarcher tripled off Cheo Hernandez, followed immediately by a "slashing single to center off Bingo DeMoss's bat."[76] Tom Williams shut out the Cuban Stars. Both teams had eight hits. The only other extra-base hits were a pair of doubles from the visitors.

JULY 5, 1920: CHICAGO AMERICAN GIANTS 4, NORMALS 3, AT NORMAL PARK, CHICAGO

There was a 10:30 A.M. game against the Normals at Normal Park, Marshall pitching. The park was on Racine Avenue between 61st and 62nd Streets. The Normals took a 2-0 lead in the fifth, but the Giants scored two in the top of the sixth and two more in the seventh for a 4-3 final win.[77] Bingo DeMoss hit a home run in the game, per the *Defender*.

JULY 5, 1920: KANSAS CITY MONARCHS 4, CHICAGO AMERICAN GIANTS 2, AT SCHORLING PARK

The July 6 *Tribune* ran a brief game story and box score on July 6, referring to this game as having occurred "yesterday."[78] Brown was tagged for three runs in the top of the first inning, while "Rugan" (Bullet Rogan of the Monarchs) threw a complete-game one-hitter in his first professional appearance as a pitcher.[79] The lone hit was a triple by DeMoss. Dave

Brown allowed only five hits. There were, however, five errors, all by the Giants. Rogan walked eight and balked twice, but he struck out 11. The *Defender* account rendered the name as Rogan as did the *Kansas City Sun*. A large crowd watched the game as Rogan "gave an exhibition of hurling that had 10,000 fans yelping and the American Giants standing on their heads."[80]

JULY 6, 1920: CHICAGO AMERICAN GIANTS 8, KANSAS CITY MONARCHS 6, AT SCHORLING PARK

The Monarchs outhit the Giants 16 to 9 (including all four extra-base hits in the game), but were outscored by two runs, 8-6. Bullet Rogan played right field and got a couple of base hits. The Monarchs committed a couple of errors. Tom Johnson, Jack Marshall, and Tom Williams all pitched for Chicago, while Sam Crawford and Jose Mendez worked for Kansas City.[81] Marshall got the win. The *Defender* wrote that the Giants "waited out Crawford's offerings, securing several bases on balls and they put the advantage to good use by stealing several bases, then by neatly executed maneuvering and a sprinkle of hits, they pulled up from behind and took the K.C. crowd into camp."[82]

JULY 7, 1920: CHICAGO AMERICAN GIANTS 2, KANSAS CITY MONARCHS 1 (12 INNINGS), AT SCHORLING PARK

Marshall pitched all 12 innings against the Monarchs, giving up 12 hits but striking out 7 Monarchs. Rube Curry worked the mound for the Monarchs, and he went the distance, too. He allowed only five hits in the game, though at least two of them came in the 12th, as Chicago prevailed. The *Chicago Tribune* said the Giants won by "bunching singles for the winning run."[83] The *Kansas City Sun* said that after Curry "walked the first man, a hit by Bingo DeMoss and Torriente's sacrifice fly won the game." The *Sun* added, "Jack Marshall was hit hard, but wonderful fielding by the Chicago club saved the game several times."[84]

JULY 8, 1920: CHICAGO AMERICAN GIANTS 6, KANSAS CITY MONARCHS 1, AT SCHORLING PARK

Tom Williams allowed the Monarchs only five hits and a lone run in the top of the sixth. The American Giants scored twice in the first inning. First baseman Leroy Grant added two more runs, hitting a rare home run in the third inning, scoring left fielder Judy Gans ahead of him.[85] The Giants scored single runs in the sixth and seventh.

JULY 11, 1920: CHICAGO AMERICAN GIANTS 5, ST. LOUIS GIANTS 2, AT SCHORLING PARK

The American Giants scored three in the bottom of the first and two more in the fifth. All five errors in the game were committed by St. Louis. Frank Wickware pitched for Chicago and gave up only one hit over the first eight innings. St. Louis bunched a walk and three hits in the top of the ninth, giving them their two runs.[86] Both pitchers – Wickware and St. Louis's Bill Drake – struck out six. The *Defender* claimed that 10,000 had watched the game.[87]

JULY 12, 1920: CHICAGO AMERICAN GIANTS 4, ST. LOUIS GIANTS 2, AT SCHORLING PARK

It was Tom Williams against St. Louis's John Finner. Torriente tripled twice in the game. The *Whip* called him "Torry."[88] Both Torriente and Dixon completed three-quarters of a cycle, each hitting a single, double, and triple.[89] Chicago scored once in the bottom of the first. St. Louis tied it in the second. Chicago got another run in the third, but St. Louis tied the score again in the top of the sixth. The Chicagoans loaded the bases in the bottom of the sixth and Leroy Grant hit a two-run single that gave them the edge and the final margin of victory.[90]

JULY 13, 1920: CHICAGO AMERICAN GIANTS 7, ST. LOUIS GIANTS 6, AT SCHORLING PARK

The *Tribune* attributed the win to "opportune hits by Torrienti and Grant."[91] Chicago scored four runs in the bottom of the first, gave one back in the second, but matched it with another of their own: 5-1, after two innings. St. Louis got two in the fourth and tied it with two more in the top of the seventh. Chicago made it 7-5 in the bottom of the seventh, gave up one run in the eighth, and held on to win.

The July 17 *Chicago Whip* offered something of a midseason look at the American Giants. "When the American Giants took the St. Louis Giants into camp last Sunday," the paper wrote, "they established a clear title to the honor of supremacy over all clubs that have shown here this season, and that goes for all clubs in the circuit, with the possible exception of the Detroit Stars; the two teams have not met as yet this season, but when they do, just lay your last Louie, there is going to be some real base ball gore spilled."[92] The article lauded the Stars, then continued. "One Hundred Thousand devotees of baseball have watched the efforts of the American Giants this season, they have witnessed the upset of opponent after opponent, and without much apparent effort."[93]

JULY 17, 1920: CHICAGO AMERICAN GIANTS 8, DAYTON MARCOS 2 (FIRST GAME); CHICAGO AMERICAN GIANTS 2, GARY WORKS 0, AT GLEASON PARK, GARY, INDIANA

The July 17 *Chicago Tribune* said the American Giants were to play the Marcos in Gary, Indiana, that day, with the winners of the game to play the Gary team. The *Gary Daily Tribune* provided a box score of the game that involved the local Gary Works team.

The scores of the game against the Marcos differ. The *Gary Daily Tribune* said the score was 8-2 in favor of Chicago and that an estimated 2,000 attended. There was nothing about the game itself – no narrative, not even a line score.[94] The July 19 *Gary Evening Tribune* reported the score at 7-3 and said it was "hard and stubbornly fought throughout."[95]

The game with Gary Works was well-played, too, Marshall pitching for the American Giants and shutting out Gary, 2-0, on five hits while striking out eight. A player named Gowlings was no slacker as a pitcher, either. He allowed but six hits and the two runs.

JULY 18, 1920: CHICAGO AMERICAN GIANTS 8, DAYTON MARCOS, 1, AT SCHORLING PARK

The American Giants scored two in the first inning and three in the second, adding three more in the later innings (two in the sixth and one in the eighth). An overflow crowd saw Tom Williams five-hit Dayton, which was down 7-0 until it scored its lone run in the top of the eighth. Catcher Jim Brown doubled for Chicago, the only one of the Giants' eight hits to go for extra bases.[96] The Marcos went through three pitchers. The number of walks is not indicated in the newspaper box scores we could access, but Dave Wyatt wrote in the *Defender* that "[t]he Marco pitchers failed to hurl

the ball so that it could be hit, so the Giants walked to first, then not a few of them stole near the whole route to the home base."[97] The game drew 15,000 spectators "who had paid hard cash to see a ball game, but were given an exhibition chess game."[98]

JULY 19, 1920: CHICAGO AMERICAN GIANTS 3, DAYTON MARCOS, 1, AT SCHORLING PARK

Frank Wickware held the Marcos to five hits for the second consecutive day. Wickware got one hit himself, and his teammates registered four more, one of them a double by Torriente. The same pitcher who had started for Dayton just the day before, left-hander Herlen Ragland (pulled early in that game), worked again.[99]

JULY 24, 1920: CHICAGO AMERICAN GIANTS 6, MELROSE PARK 0, AT SCHORLING PARK

The Melrose Parks were a White team shut out by Frank Wickware, who held them to three hits in this Saturday game at Schorling Park. Torriente played third base in lieu of Dave Malarcher, who was out with a "bum ankle." The third and final sentence of the *Defender*'s brief account reads: "Strunk, the visiting pitcher, was a trifle wild and errors aided the home club in getting some of their tallies."[100] Three errors were committed; the Giants had six base hits.

JULY 25, 1920: CHICAGO AMERICAN GIANTS 6, JOLIET 0, AT SCHORLING PARK

A very large crowd of 18,000 thronged the park. Mickey Ryan pitched for Joliet and Tom Williams for the Giants. Each team had five hits, with Fox's double for Joliet the only extra-base hit. Each team committed two errors. Neither team scored until the fourth. With one out, right fielder Jelly Gardner singled and was sacrificed to second by DeMoss. On a low roller to third base by Dave Brown, Gardner ran to third and then continued for home. Caught in a rundown, he was blocked by the catcher and ruled safe at home due to interference. Third baseman Aaron of Joliet nearly got into a fistfight with the umpire at one point, perhaps at this stage in the game. Or perhaps he was one of the four (!) Joliet players Williams picked off during the game. Even some of the Joliet fans started pulling for Williams, "getting disgusted with the actions of their own team."[101] There were a number of heated disputes and at one point Joliet even threatened to leave the field.

After the game, the American Giants "boarded a rattler" – taking the train to St. Louis for a scheduled five games. It was to be a "crucial test" for the team, wrote the *Defender*, though acknowledging that with all the games they'd own, they'd pretty much left the other teams in the dust. As the paper put it, they "have shown such a clean pair of heels to all circuit competitors that the dust had long since ceased to obstruct the vision of the unfortunates."[102]

STANDINGS

At this point in the season, the *Chicago Whip* printed standings showing the teams thus, through July 22:

As of Friday morning, July 23, 1920

American Giants =.865 (a record of 32-5)
Detroit Stars = .562
ABCs = .545
K.C. Monarchs = .520
Cubans = .457
Marcos = .286
Chicago Giants = .135

Against each of the teams in question, the Chicago American Giants had records of:

Detroit Stars   0-0
(the two teams had not played each other yet)
ABCs   5-2
KC   8-1
Cubans   5-0
St. Louis Giants   7-1
Marcos   6-1
Chicago Giants   1-0

JULY 26, 1920: CHICAGO AMERICAN GIANTS 6, ST. LOUIS GIANTS 4, AT GIANTS PARK, ST. LOUIS

In the first of five Giants vs. Giants games at Giants Park, the Chicago American Giants came out on top. Starting for St. Louis was their winningest pitcher, right-hander Bill "Plunk" Drake. He retired the side in the top of the first inning and saw his team take a quick 1-0 lead. Chicago tied it in the second, to which St. Louis responded with two more runs off Chicago starter Tom Johnson, another right-hander. Three Chicago runs in the top of the third gave them a 4-3 lead and the score held through the seventh inning. In the eighth, both teams scored again. Chicago scored

twice, giving it a 6-3 lead, and St. Louis got back one. With neither putting a run across in the ninth, the final stood at 6-4. The *St. Louis Globe-Democrat* declared that the "fielding of [St. Louis second baseman Lee] Hill and [Cristobal] Torriente was the outstanding feature of the game."[103] There was only one error charged to each team. Who drove in the runs is unclear, but the available box score shows that Torriente scored twice. Chicago scored its fourth run in the fifth. DeMoss had three hits for Chicago and left fielder Doc Dudley had three for St. Louis.

JULY 27, 1920: CHICAGO AMERICAN GIANTS 4, ST. LOUIS GIANTS 1, AT GIANTS PARK, ST. LOUIS

The two pitchers for the second game of this series were Wayne Carr for the St. Louis Giants and left-hander Dave Brown for Chicago. Carr held Chicago to five hits (Torriente had two, as did catcher Jim Brown) while Dave Brown gave up six. A cluster of three runs in the top of the second inning made the difference in the game. It included a walk, a hit batsman, and two base hits, not necessarily in that order. St. Louis scored its lone run in the bottom of the ninth inning.[104]

JULY 28, 1920: ST. LOUIS GIANTS 5, CHICAGO AMERICAN GIANTS 0, AT GIANTS PARK, ST. LOUIS

John Finner threw a shutout in the Wednesday afternoon game, allowing the visitors just five scattered hits (no more than one in any inning), which included two by left fielder Jelly Gardner. The only extra-base hit was by George Dixon, a double. Listed as pitcher for Chicago was "S. W'ams" – presumably Tom Williams.[105] Finner was boosted by St. Louis scoring four runs in the bottom of the first inning, three of them on a bases-clearing hit by third baseman Dick Wallace. The fifth run was scored in the third inning. Finner walked no one and struck out four. Catcher Dave Kennard had a 3-for-3 game for St. Louis. The *Argus*, which had been so tough on the hometown team in July, acknowledged Finner's work as "masterly."[106]

JULY 29, 1920: ST. LOUIS GIANTS 8, CHICAGO AMERICAN GIANTS 4, AT GIANTS PARK, ST. LOUIS

St. Louis evened the series at two wins apiece with an 8-4 win over Chicago. It was Drake again for St. Louis. Pitching for the Chicagoans was Jack Marshall.

The first run scored was by Chicago, in the top of the first. St. Louis responded with three runs in the fourth inning. Chicago tied the game, scoring twice more in the top of the fifth inning, but St. Louis put the game away with five runs in the bottom of the sixth. Two players had three hits apiece – St. Louis short-stop Eddie Holtz and Chicago center fielder Torriente, whose three hits were a double, triple, and home run in a 3-for-4 game.[107]

JULY 30, 1920: CHICAGO AMERICAN GIANTS 9, ST. LOUIS GIANTS 2, AT GIANTS PARK, ST. LOUIS

Dave Brown pitched again for Chicago and won again, this time allowing only two hits – a single by right fielder Sidney Brooks and a double by center fielder Charlie Blackwell. Wayne Carr started for St. Louis. He gave up one run in the top of the third inning but was hammered for five more runs in the fourth and was relieved by Finner. Before the inning was over, Chicago had scored eight runs. Jelly Gardner had three hits, as did third baseman Dave Malarcher.[108]

JULY 31, 1920: CHICAGO AMERICAN GIANTS 9, KANSAS CITY MONARCHS 7, AT AMERICAN ASSOCIATION PARK, KANSAS CITY

The Giants scored a couple of runs in the top of the first (Torriente tripled), and it didn't take long for the game to get heated when Monarchs center fielder John Donaldson "slid viciously into [Leroy] Grant at first and collided with the Chicago first sacker." A fistfight broke out. "Police rushed on the field and quiet was restored."[109] Tom Johnson and Tom Williams pitched for Chicago, Johnson reportedly pitching well but vic-timized by multiple errors behind him on the field. The Monarchs scored three runs in the first, adding single runs in the second (on a home run by first baseman George Carr), another in the fifth, and two more in the sixth. The Monarchs led, 7-2, through the first seven innings, Rube Curry holding the Giants to just three hits. They broke through with five runs in the top of the eighth and two more in the ninth.

AUGUST 1, 1920: KANSAS CITY MONARCHS 5, CHICAGO AMERICAN GIANTS 4 (12 INNINGS), AT AMERICAN ASSOCIATION PARK, KANSAS CITY

This Sunday game drew 15,000, which the *Kansas City Times* called the largest crowd of the year at Association Park.[110] Once again the Giants had to come from behind. They faced a formidable foe in Bullet Rogan, who "was master of the situation at all stages of the contest, hurling and batting in fiendish fashion."[111] Rogan was 4-for-5 with a double and a triple, and he held the Giants to just four hits while striking out 13. In the meantime, "Tom Williams did not loom up as the Tom of former days." Catcher Jim Brown "did emergency duty at first base." One of the four hits came from pinch-hitter John Reese, batting for Williams in the ninth. The game was settled by back-to-back hits by Donaldson and Rogan himself (a double) in the bottom of the 12th.

AUGUST 2, 1920: KANSAS CITY MONARCHS 5, CHICAGO AMERICAN GIANTS 4, AT AMERICAN ASSOCIATION PARK, KANSAS CITY

The score was the same as the day before, but this one was a nine-inning game. It was Sam Crawford for the Monarchs against Jack Marshall. The Giants scored twice in the first inning and twice more in the second but then were shut down the rest of the way. The Monarchs got one run in the second, added two in the first, tied it with one in the sixth, and took the lead with one more in the seventh.[112]

AUGUST 3, 1920: KANSAS CITY MONARCHS 6, CHICAGO AMERICAN GIANTS 5, AT AMERICAN ASSOCIATION PARK, KANSAS CITY

It was Williams and Wickware against Currie and Crawford. The five-run bottom of the third by the Monarchs might have discouraged the Giants but they battled back with three runs in the top of the fifth and tied the game with two more in the seventh. That's when Crawford entered the game and struck out Torriente ("the Black Babe Ruth," per the *Kansas City Sun*) with the bases loaded. Kansas City's Dobie Moore hit a solo home run in the Monarchs' half of the seventh, giving them the 6-5 lead that they held onto for the victory.[113]

AUGUST 4, 1920: CHICAGO AMERICAN GIANTS 4, KANSAS CITY MONARCHS 2, AT AMERICAN ASSOCIATION PARK, KANSAS CITY

Dave Brown threw a four-hitter, holding the Monarchs to two fourth-inning runs. Bullet Rogan was touched up for 10 hits, including a triple by Dixon. Chicago scored once in the fourth (on four hits) and plated three more runs in the top of the eighth. The loss was reported to be the first of the season for Bullet Rogan.[114]

AUGUST 5, 1920: KANSAS CITY MONARCHS 4, CHICAGO AMERICAN GIANTS 0, AT AMERICAN ASSOCIATION PARK, KANSAS CITY

The visit to Kansas City presented the season's roughest stretch for the Chicago American Giants, as they lost four out of six games. They were shut out in this one, 4-0, behind the seven-hit pitching of Sam Crawford. Each of the hits was a single, one each by seven of the Giants. (Malarcher and first baseman Jim Brown were hitless.) Cristobal Torriente pitched for the Giants, and batted cleanup. He allowed only five hits, three of them (including a triple) by George Carr.

Confusingly, given the six games we are able to track more than 100 years later, the *Defender* said the "Giants returned home Friday after a strenuous trip in Kansas City where they won two and lost two, the fifth game being thrown out because the umpire allowed two runs to score on a ball that had hit him."[115] The paper then noted the score of the August 7 game in Gary.

This is an odd discrepancy, since there were six games played against the Monarchs, not five or four.

AUGUST 7, 1920: BACHARACH GIANTS 11, CHICAGO AMERICAN GIANTS 4 (FIRST GAME), AT GLEASON PARK, GARY, INDIANA

Atlantic City's Bacharach Giants played a game against the Chicago American Giants and dominated. Torriente homered in the game, but Chicago came up seven runs short.[116] Right-hander Harold Treadwell pitched a complete game for the Bacharachs, a four-hitter. and it was close for the first four innings, tied 3-3 at that point. The Bacharachs scored three in the fifth and five in the eighth. Jack Marshall and Frank

Wickware (from the fifth inning on) were the pitchers for Chicago.[117] The *Gary Evening Post* laid blame for the loss on the "loose playing" of Torriente.[118] His play was deemed "the main cause of Rube's downfall when the big fielder let a single go through his legs in the first inning with a man on second, both men scoring on the play and then again, later in the game, the big fellow missed on [sic] easy chance with two out, after which the gang from the east ran up a total of five scores." Torriente did, however, have the game's only home run. Both Cago and Marcell were acclaimed, and shortstop London's fielding was "phenomenal." London was actually Dick Lundy. Oliver Marcell played third base. We don't know who "Cago" was – the catcher apparently, but the name doesn't appear similar to any known to be playing for the Bacharachs. He was listed as both "Rogo" and "Togo" in the *Gary Daily Tribune* box score.[119] The *Post* offered, "These men are really stars, their color alone keeping them out of the big show."[120]

Because the Bacharachs had won the first game, it was they who played the Gary Works team in the second. The Gary team beat an "evidently tired" Bacharachs team, 7-4, in a seven-inning game. Lundy committed four errors.[121]

AUGUST 8, 1920: CHICAGO AMERICAN GIANTS 7, BACHARACH GIANTS 3, AT SCHORLING PARK

Tom Williams held the Bacharachs to two runs in the first and one in the seventh, while his teammates matched the two runs in the bottom of the first, adding single runs in the third and fifth and then three insurance runs in the seventh. Williams had two of Chicago's 11 hits (the only extra-base hit a double by Torriente), while holding the New York team to seven.[122] It was, wrote the *Freeman*, "the largest crowd that ever attended a ballgame at Schorling Park."[123] The *Defender* mentioned this game in a column entitled "Rough Stuff!" arguing that "no matter how hard the game or how hotly contested, the fact that a team is in the rear should be no excuse for the ill mannerism of some of the players." The article mentioned the Bacharach Giants' Oliver Marcell as having to be restrained early in the game for approaching the mound after a wild pitch came too close to him. The *Defender* thought he should have been ejected. When he came to bat again in the third inning, there was a lot of hissing from the stands and he "proceeded to make immoral movements with part of his body that would resemble a hoochy-coochy dancer." The paper noted that "many of Chicago's best ladies" were in the box seats and argued that either the player or the team should be barred from playing in Chicago.[124]

AUGUST 9, 1920: CHICAGO AMERICAN GIANTS 3, BACHARACH GIANTS 2 (10 INNINGS), AT SCHORLING PARK

A well-fought battle saw the Bacharach Giants score once in the first and once in the second off starter Tom Johnson. The host team evened it up with two runs in the bottom of the sixth. Having entered the game at some point, Tom Williams got the win when Jelly Gardner singled in the bottom of the 10th and Dave Malarcher's drive to right field sent him home.[125]

AUGUST 10, 1920: CHICAGO AMERICAN GIANTS 5, BACHARACH GIANTS 1, AT SCHORLING PARK

The Tuesday game gave Chicago its third straight win against the visiting Bacharachs. Wickware and Dave Brown pitched for Chicago, with Treadwell and Ryan working for the Bacharachs. The New Yorkers scored once in the first, but the American Giants scored twice and added three more in the fourth. The Chicagoans outhit the visitors, 7-5.[126]

AUGUST 11, 1920: CHICAGO AMERICAN GIANTS 5, BACHARACH GIANTS 4, AT SCHORLING PARK,

A two-sentence capsule in the *Atlantic City Press* shows that the Bacharachs outhit the Chicago team, 12 hits to 6, but came up one run short. Chicago scored twice in the bottom of the second and twice in the third. The visitors scored once in the top of the third, added two more in the fifth and tied the game in the top of the eighth. Chicago scored its fifth run in the bottom of the eighth. No players for either team are named – neither pitchers nor batters – but there were nine errors in the game, six by the Bacharachs and three by Chicago, and one of the two sentences says, "Costly errors by Smith resulted in the defeat of the invaders."[127]

AUGUST 12, 1920: BACHARACH AMERICAN GIANTS 8, CHICAGO AMERICAN GIANTS 1, AT SCHORLING PARK

The *Indiana Daily Times* (later the *Indianapolis Times*) confirmed the loss, but provided no other information – not even the score. Fortunately, Gary Ashwill had located a box score from the *Chicago Herald-Examiner.* It shows Jack Marshall pitching for Chicago, but getting lit up for 13 base hits, allowing three runs in the fourth inning, one in the seventh, and four more in the eighth. Jesse Barber both doubled and tripled, while Dick Lundy, Johnny Pugh, and Julio Rojo all had doubles. The only extra-base hit for Chicago was a double by DeMoss. The Chicago-based Giants scored their one run in the first inning, and then never another. Andrew "String Bean" Williams pitched for the Bacharachs, allowing seven hits, two of them by Marshall.[128]

AUGUST 14, 1920: CHICAGO AMERICAN GIANTS VS. CUBAN STARS WEST, AT GARY, INDIANA – SCORE AND DETAIL UNCERTAIN

There was also to have been a rematch of the Gary Works team against Foster's team in the day's second game, per the *Gary Daily Tribune*.[129] Whether it occurred or not, we have been unable to determine, despite the diligent digging of David S. Hess, librarian of the Indiana Room of the Gary Public Library and Cultural Center. Larry Lester's records (compiled by others working with him) show the game as a 3-0 win for the Giants. This appears to be one game – if it even occurred – that remains a mystery.

AUGUST 15, 1920: CUBAN STARS WEST 8, CHICAGO AMERICAN GIANTS 5, AT SCHORLING PARK

The *Indianapolis Freeman* presented a box score of the "opening of the series" between these two teams.[130] The *Defender,* titling its story the same, offered more narrative, saying the game was "full of hitting and weird playing."[131] Dave Brown was hit hard for four singles and three runs in the top of the first. His teammates got back two right away off Cheo Hernandez, thanks to a two-out single by Mothell. They tied it with one more run in the bottom of the second. The Cubans responded with three in the top of the third, when catcher Eufemio Abreu came to bat with the bases loaded and hit a long drive to left-center. Left fielder Gans and center fielder Torriente both ran for it. Torriente, "failing to hear Judy Gans yelling that he had it, made a desperate leap. The ball hit his gloved hand, but he failed to hold it, the impact with the flying Judy Gans sending both to the ground." The visitors added single runs in the fourth and fifth. Foster's crew put a fourth run on the board in the bottom of the third and a fifth and final run in the bottom of the ninth. Both pitchers walked four and struck out four. Jesse Williams doubled but committed two errors.

AUGUST 16, 1920: CHICAGO AMERICAN GIANTS 9, CUBAN STARS WEST 2, AT SCHORLING PARK

Tom Johnson allowed the traveling Cubans nine hits but just two runs.[132] Chicago accumulated 12 hits, one of them "with the hassocks crowded," a fifth-inning grand slam over the right-field wall by Cristobal Torriente, one of his three hits.[133]

AUGUST 17, 1920: CHICAGO AMERICAN GIANTS 6, LOGAN SQUARES 1, AT SUTTON PARK, MINONK, ILLINOIS

This exhibition game drew a crowd around 3,000. Four of the Giants' six runs came in via errors by the Logan Squares, managed by former Chicago White Sox player Jimmy Callahan, though the Giants outhit their opponents, nine hits to five. Gardner had three hits, and Dixon and Reese each had two.[134]

AUGUST 19, 1920: CHICAGO AMERICAN GIANTS 5, LOGAN SQUARES 1, AT SUTTON PARK, MINONK, ILLINOIS

Marshall pitched for the American Giants. Both teams tallied eight hits, but the Giants "bunched" theirs. The lone run for the Logan Squares came on a sixth-inning home run by their right fielder named Ginger. DeMoss and Torriente each had two hits. Malarcher tripled.[135]

AUGUST 22, 1920: CHICAGO AMERICAN GIANTS 5, KANSAS CITY MONARCHS 1, AT SCHORLING PARK

The Giants bunched three infield hits in the bottom of the first inning, giving them their first run. They got two more in the third (or fourth) inning when

Torriente led off with a triple.[136] Jim Brown walked, and then stole second base. Judy Gans hit a roller to third base and Torriente scored, while Brown ran to third. He scored when Leroy Grant grounded into an out on another slow-rolling ball. The Monarchs got one in the seventh when Rogan singled, stole second base, and then – with two outs – scored when catcher Vicente Rodriguez hit a ball that left fielder Gans misjudged in the sun. The Giants got only five hits off Sam Crawford, two of them by DeMoss. In the eighth, DeMoss stole second and then stole third. Apparently two other stolen bases, a single, an infield hit, and a fielder's choice somehow combined to produce two more runs. Dave Brown pitched for the American Giants and allowed the Monarchs only five base hits.

AUGUST 27, 1920: CHICAGO AMERICAN GIANTS 14, FORT WAYNE COLORED GIANTS 3, AT LEAGUE PARK, FORT WAYNE, INDIANA

There was a buildup for this game, but not because it was expected to be a close one: It was to see the Chicago American Giants in action. The *Fort Wayne Sentinel* noted that they typically drew between 10,000 and 15,000 to Sunday games in Chicago. The *Sentinel* added, "The visitors will arrive at noon, Friday, coming direct from Chicago. The club travels in big league style and carries sixteen players. They will be met by a committee of colored citizens, and will be entertained while in the city."[137]

Even though the Fort Wayne team had "bolstered their line-up for the occasion," they were outscored, 14-3, and outhit, 18-3. Torriente tripled twice, and three Chicago players doubled (Bobby Williams, Grant, and DeMoss). Three pitchers got in some work for Foster's team, each one working three innings: Frank Wickware, Dave Brown, and Tom Williams. "The home club never had a chance," reported the *Fort Wayne Sentinel*. Indeed, the game account suggested that at least one of the base hits (by shortstop Golden) was due to "liberal scoring." Center fielder Cooper got the other two hits.

Chicago scored three times in the first inning. Torriente's bases-loaded triple gave them three more in the second. They had two other three-run innings, the sixth and the eighth, with single runs in the seventh and ninth. They might have kept on scoring but for what was said to be a triple play that Fort Wayne pulled off. Grant was already on base. The game account reads as though it was a triple play that registered the second, third, and fourth outs of the top of the ninth: "[Bobby] Williams flew out to Barker but his brother [Tom Williams] smacked one for a single sending Grant to counting territory. Gardner also singled and it looked like several more runs were due but [right fielder] Wells caught Malarcher's offering and quickly doubled Gardner off first and [first baseman] Riddles whipped the ball across to Suggs, who tagged Williams before he could get back to second, completing a triple play retiring the side."[138]

Lefty Tossler pitched the whole game for Fort Wayne.[139]

STANDINGS

Standings were published in the August 28 *Defender* and the September 4 *Freeman*. The *Defender* said they were "for the week of Aug. 15."[140]

	W	L	Pct.
American Giants	42	12	.777
Detroit Stars	23	17	.575
K.C. Monarchs	34	30	.531
Ind'pls. ABCs	33	30	.52
Cuban Stars	24	27	.470
Dayton Marcos	15	32	.319
Chicago Giants	7	28	.200

The *Freeman* noted that "The American Giants have pounced upon the underdogs 32 times and have won 15 of the 21 games played against their nearest rivals, the Kansas City Monarchs." It declared that the "American Giants have a comfortable lead and it will probably endure until the close of the season. The Western Circuit leader recently won four games out of six over the Bacharach Giants, the Eastern Circuit representative, so the showing up to date gives the Western Circuit Runner, an edge as to who is who in championship flag fight for the season, 1920."[141]

AUGUST 28, 1920: CHICAGO AMERICAN GIANTS 8, LINCOLN LIFERS 1, AT LEAGUE PARK, FORT WAYNE, INDIANA

Tickets cost $1.00 for men and 50 cents for women or children. Clergymen were admitted free of charge. The Chicago American Giants faced off against the Lincoln Lifers, a team sponsored by the Lincoln National Life Insurance Company, headquartered in Fort Wayne. Jack Marshall pitched for Chicago, and he was masterful, striking out 17 (including striking out the side twice) and allowing just one base hit, a single over second base in the second inning. Only two balls were hit out of the infield against him, and the Lincoln team's only run scored on a throwing error by DeMoss in the fourth. Chicago got 13 hits, the biggest one a seventh-inning two-run homer by "Torrentti" which was reported as the first home run of the year at the ballpark.[142] Five runs on five hits in the second inning sealed the game.

AUGUST 29, 1920: CHICAGO AMERICAN GIANTS 5, ROGERS PARK 1, AT SCHORLING PARK

The White semipro team outhit the Giants, six to five, but Tom Williams held them to one run, striking out 11, while Rogers Park's Tom Lafferty gave up a two-run homer to right-center by Cristobal Torriente and a two-run triple to Bobby Williams in the second inning. Williams then stole home for another run. The victory, said the *Chicago Whip*, "went to the dark boys."[143] The Giants scored a total of three in the second and two in the third, after which Lafferty settled back down and held them hitless for the rest of the game. Rogers Park got its lone run in the top of the ninth, due to errors by Grant at first base and Bobby Williams at shortstop.[144]

SEPTEMBER 4, 1920: CHICAGO AMERICAN GIANTS 8, DETROIT STARS 3, AT NAVIN FIELD, DETROIT

Several days apparently passed before the team played another game. Dave Brown allowed the Stars just four hits, two apiece by Jimmie Lyons and Frank Warfield. Meanwhile Judy Gans was 4-for-4 (with two triples) and Bingo DeMoss was 3-for-3 (with two doubles), as the Giants collected 12 hits and 19 total bases. Gifford McDonald started for Detroit but was relieved by Andy Cooper in the second inning.[145] Cooper went the rest of the way. There might have been even more extra-base hits, but "Torriente and Lyons robbed each other of sure triples by sensational catches."[146]

The next day's Sunday game was rained out. A doubleheader was scheduled at Navin Field for Monday, which was Labor Day.

SEPTEMBER 6, 1920: DETROIT STARS 4, CHICAGO AMERICAN GIANTS 1 (FIRST GAME OF DOUBLEHEADER), AT NAVIN FIELD, DETROIT

Right-hander Bill Gatewood held the Giants scoreless on five hits through the first eight innings. In the top of the ninth inning, three singles garnered the Giants one run. Detroit had scored one run in the first inning and three more in the fifth on two singles and a three-run homer from second baseman Frank Warfield.[147]

Warfield left the Stars and joined the Giants later in the season, and is listed as playing in four games for them.

SEPTEMBER 6, 1920: CHICAGO AMERICAN GIANTS 5, DETROIT STARS 4 (SECOND GAME OF DOUBLEHEADER), AT NAVIN FIELD, DETROIT

Bill Holland, pitching the second game for the Stars, "allowed but five hits, but errors by his teammates accounted for the five runs."[148] The line score in the *Chicago Whip* showed six base hits by the Giants, while the Stars had seven (and benefited from two Giants errors). Marshall started for Chicago and was relieved by Williams.[149]

SEPTEMBER 7, 1920: CHICAGO AMERICAN GIANTS 6, DETROIT STARS 3, AT MACK PARK, DETROIT

Jimmie Lyons, more typically used in center field by the Stars, pitched in five known games in 1920. This was one of his two starts, and he did exceptionally well for the first eight innings, allowing just four hits and one third-inning run. That gave the Giants the lead, but the Stars got two runs in the fourth and one in the sixth off Johnson and (at some point) Brown. In the top of the ninth, it all fell apart for Detroit as Chicago scored five runs. Holland had come in to pitch at some point in the ninth. Chicago got a man on first, thanks to a hit-by-pitch. Another batter walked. Riggins committed an error and a couple of singles in the mix gave the Giants a 6-3 lead and the game.[150]

SEPTEMBER 8, 1920: DETROIT STARS 5, CHICAGO AMERICAN GIANTS 3, AT MACK PARK, DETROIT

After just one day of rest, Bill Gatewood took the mound again and won another game for the Detroit Stars. Frank Wickware was the losing pitcher for Chicago. He gave up 10 hits to the six Gatewood granted. Two of Detroit's hits were home runs, one by Jimmie Lyons and the other by Chick Harper. Lyons had two more hits, both singles. Riggins hit a double and two singles, together with Lyons accounting for six of the Stars' 10 hits. The two were also said to have each made a "sensational catch."[151]

Detroit scored first, with two runs in the bottom of the third. Chicago took a lead with all three of their runs in the fourth. The Stars added two in the sixth and one in the eighth.

Another game that never was? The September 3 issue of the *Bloomington* (Illinois) *Pantagraph* said there was to have been a September 10 game in Bloomington (or Minonk, some 35 miles from Bloomington) between Joe Green's Chicago Giants and Rube Foster's Chicago American Giants. Were there games in Detroit on both September 8 and 11, this would have required Foster's Giants to travel from Detroit to Bloomington and back, a round trip of nearly 800 miles.

SEPTEMBER 11, 1920: CHICAGO AMERICAN GIANTS 11, DETROIT STARS 2, AT MACK PARK, DETROIT

We were unable to learn more about this game.[152] SABR member Gary Gillette suggested, "This is one of those unlucky Saturday games that didn't get covered by the weekly African American newspapers because the game was a week old when the next issue was published."

SEPTEMBER 12, 1920: CHICAGO AMERICAN GIANTS 5, DETROIT STARS 2 (FIRST GAME); DETROIT STARS 2, CHICAGO AMERICAN GIANTS 1 (SECOND GAME), AT SCHORLING PARK

Tom Williams pitched the first game and Frank Wickware the second, opposed by Detroit's Bill Holland and Bill Gatewood. The Stars played error-free ball; the Giants committed one in each game.[153] Torriente doubled and tripled in the first game, a win in which he was 4-for-4. Bobby Williams also tripled.[154]

In the first game, Stars catcher Bruce Petway was said to have thrown out six Chicago runners trying to steal second base, though the accompanying box score shows him with only four assists.[155] Though Negro League doubleheaders often were scheduled for seven innings, the second game went a full nine innings, the Stars scoring one in the first and one in the fourth. The Giants got their lone run in the third.

SEPTEMBER 14, 1920: CHICAGO AMERICAN GIANTS 3, BLOOMINGTON 1, AT FLANAGAN, ILLINOIS

The battery of Brown and Brown (Dave and Jim) worked together to beat the 1919 Three-I League champion Bloomington Bloomers, 3-1. Bloomington had easily won the 1919 pennant, finishing 12½ games ahead of second-place Peoria. The Giants scored once in the first and twice in the top of the sixth. The lone run the Bloomers got was in the bottom of the fourth inning. "Moose" Romine pitched for the Bloomers and the game attracted a crowd of 1,500.[156]

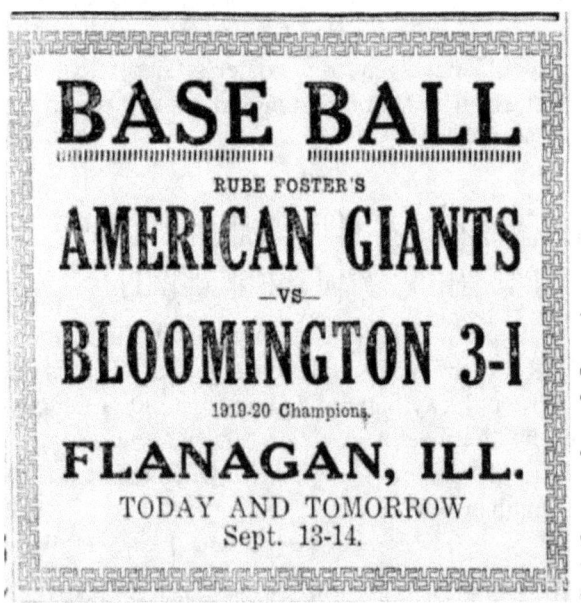

(Pantagraph, September 13, 1920)

SEPTEMBER 19, 1920: CHICAGO AMERICAN GIANTS 8, INDIANAPOLIS ABCS 2, AT SCHORLING PARK

Dave Brown faced off against ABCs pitcher Dicta Johnson and held the visitors to five base hits and two third-inning runs. Chicago had scored three runs in the bottom of the first inning and never gave up their advantage. They added a pair of runs in the fourth and three more in the bottom of the seventh. Gardner and DeMoss both had three-hit days, Gardner's double being the only extra-base hit of the game. It was a rough day for Indy shortstop Morten Clark, who committed three errors, though he did get two of his team's five hits.[157]

Of Brown, the *Whip* wrote, "He is truly the most effective pitcher on the circuit, having downed all the strong circuit clubs, with more to spare than any other hurler."[158]

The American Giants had drawn more than 200,000 to Schorling Park. They were said to have drawn the largest crowd ever at Association Park in Kansas City, set a weekday record in St. Louis, "filled the Indianapolis park to capacity" and "jammed Navin Field" in Detroit.[159]

On this date (September 19), the *Dayton Daily News* reported that shortstop Bobby Williams had been signed by the Marcos and would play that afternoon against the All-Italians.[160]

"AMERICAN GIANTS ARE CHAMPIONS"[161]

In a story datelined Chicago on September 22, the *Omaha Monitor* looked back on the league season and declared, "The American Giants, considered the weak sister of the league, after disposing of [Dick] Whitworth, leading pitcher of the world, Francis Star, 3rd baseman, [Jesse] Barber, crack outfielder, [Oscar] Charleston, greatest outfielder in the world, their chances did not even look encouraging, but when the Gong sounded, Foster surprised the base ball world, with a machine that has never been surpassed in Chicago, by any of the great clubs he has handled."[162] The *article* outlined their dominance, saying the American Giants had "defeated every club in the league, winning 4 of 7 from Detroit, 9 out of 12 from St. Louis Giants, 9 out of 10 from Cuban Stars, 11 out of 15 from Kansas City, 8 out of 9 from Dayton, even Chicago Giants have not beaten them one game. So no one can say it was a flash in the pan, but the best club in circuit."[163]

SEPTEMBER 20, 1920 ?

There was to be a 3:30 game played in Nashville, against the Nashville White Sox at the Sulphur Dell ballpark. It was previewed on page 16 of the September 19 issue of the *Tennessean* and then advertised on page 8 of the September 20 paper. But was it ever played? We can find no indication that it was, nor that it was canceled. Weather was not an issue.[164]

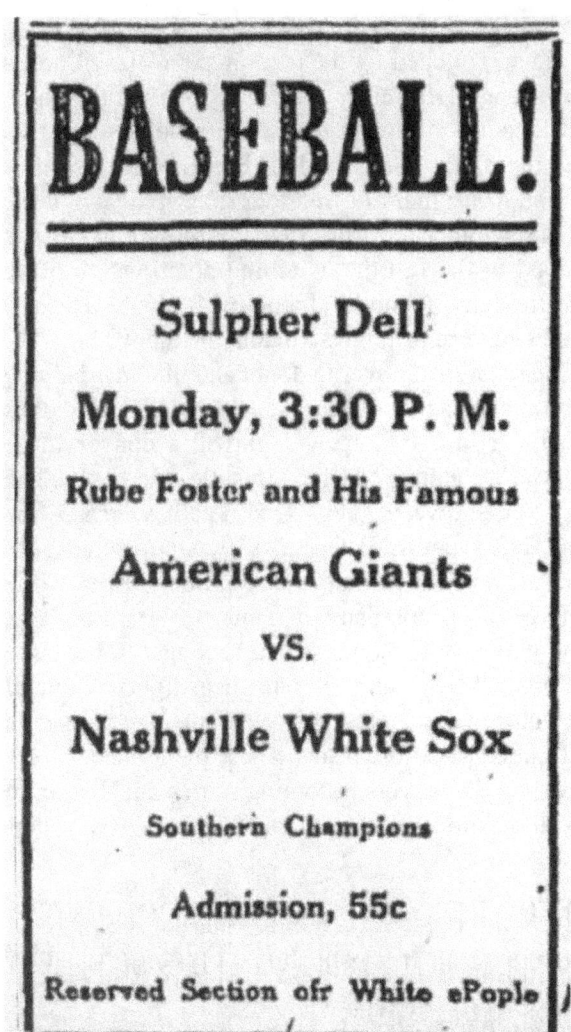

BASEBALL!

Sulpher Dell

Monday, 3:30 P. M.

Rube Foster and His Famous

American Giants

vs.

Nashville White Sox

Southern Champions

Admission, 55c

Reserved Section ofr White ePople

(Tennessean (Nashville), September 20, 1920)

and Malarcher doubled. The *News* praised the work of Knoxville's Maddox, the "one-armed wonder" who "made a pretty catch in left, bagged one of the hits and swiped a base. Despite the handicap of one arm, Maddox manages to do what any other fielder can do. He is a Houdini when it comes to catching a ball and making his glove disappear."[165]

SEPTEMBER 22, 1920: CHICAGO AMERICAN GIANTS 5, KNOXVILLE GIANTS 3, AT RICKWOOD FIELD, BIRMINGHAM, ALABAMA

It was Williams vs. Williams. Tom Williams pitched a solid game for Chicago, and even drove in two runs for his team in a 2-for-4 day at the plate. Lennie Williams pitched for Knoxville, "colored champions of the South." One might expect Chicago to have scored more than they did. Not only did they collect 12 base hits, but they were aided by seven Knoxville errors. Chicago scored once in the first, once in the third, twice in the fifth, and once more in the eighth. Both Malarcher and Torriente doubled, and catcher Jim Brown tripled. Tom Williams allowed just five hits and held Knoxville scoreless until the bottom of the ninth inning, when they hit safely three more times and benefited from an "inexcusable miscue" that allowed them to score three times. Once more, Maddox impressed; he "accepted several difficult chances and handled himself as well as any of his teammates."[166]

SEPTEMBER 21, 1920: CHICAGO AMERICAN GIANTS 10, KNOXVILLE GIANTS 0, AT RICKWOOD FIELD, BIRMINGHAM, ALABAMA

Foster's Chicago American Giants scored early and late – three runs in the top of the first inning and seven more runs in the top of the ninth. They didn't score at all in between, and the Knoxville Giants never scored. Jack Marshall pitched a four-hit shutout, the first of the four scattered hits coming in the fourth inning. Pitching for Knoxville was "Steel Arm" Dickey, who was victimized by errors in the first inning, all three runs apparently scoring as a result. Knoxville committed six errors in the course of the game. The *Birmingham News* said that Dickey had come into the game riding a streak of 25 consecutive victories. Errors aside (one of them was his), he only walked one and pitched well until the ninth when Chicago collected seven base hits for the seven runs. DeMoss tripled

SEPTEMBER 23, 1920: CHICAGO AMERICAN GIANTS 7, KNOXVILLE GIANTS 2, AT RICKWOOD FIELD, BIRMINGHAM, ALABAMA

"Knoxville No Match for Chicago Giants" – so read the headline in the next day's *Birmingham News*. It was another loss for the team from Tennessee. The *News* appears to have mixed up its Browns, writing that Dave Brown pitched for Chicago. Fore was the pitcher for Knoxville. Brown allowed six base hits and Fore double that number – an even dozen. There were errors by both teams, four by Chicago and five by Knoxville. The catchers (Mothell and Sanders) were singled out for "erratic throwing." (The *News* rendered Mothell as "Marthel." For the third game in a row, Maddox was 2-for-4 and the "bright shining star" with a triple to deep left field to go with "two pretty catches in center."[167]

SEPTEMBER 25, 1920: CHICAGO AMERICAN GIANTS 6, MONTGOMERY GREY SOX 4, AT BALLPARK ON SOUTH HOLT STREET, MONTGOMERY, ALABAMA

The Saturday afternoon game attracted "one of the largest crowds of the season." The Montgomery team built up an early lead off Chicago starter Jack Marshall with two runs in the first inning, and additional single runs in both the second and third. Chicago got back three runs in the top of the fourth off 19-year-old left-hander Sam Streeter (who joined Foster's American Giants the following year). With the Grey Sox still holding a 4-3 lead in the fifth, the Giants loaded the bases. A "low drive" was hit to Jimmy Moss, the Montgomery right fielder. He failed to catch it and it got by him, with all three baserunners scoring on the error. Chicago held a 6-4 lead. Montgomery didn't score in the bottom of the fifth, nor did Chicago in the top of the sixth. With the Grey Sox batting in the bottom of the sixth, they began to mount a rally, but rain arrived and the game was called, the 6-4 score after five serving as the final tally.[168]

SEPTEMBER 26, 1920: CHICAGO AMERICAN GIANTS 6, MONTGOMERY GREY SOX 5, AT BALLPARK ON SOUTH HOLT STREET, MONTGOMERY, ALABAMA

Jack Marshall started for Chicago but was pounced on by the Grey Sox in the first inning and got hammered for four runs. He settled down after the initial inning and only allowed one more run – in the fifth – the rest of the way. Chicago scored its first two runs in the top of the fifth, making it 4-2 until that Grey Sox run bumped the Montgomery lead to 5-2. The American Giants tied the score with three runs off Montgomery's Mason in the top of the seventh, two of the runs on a bases-loaded pinch-hit triple by Jelly Gardner. They took the edge the next inning, adding a sixth run in the eighth.[169]

SEPTEMBER 27, 1920: CHICAGO AMERICAN GIANTS 10, BIRMINGHAM BLACK BARONS 2, AT RICKWOOD FIELD, BIRMINGHAM, ALABAMA

The Chicago American Giants continued to rack up the wins in Alabama. A recent arrival from Cuba, listed as "Roderiz" (almost certainly Conrado "Red" Rodriguez) pitched for the Birmingham Black Barons and Chicago left fielder Judy Gans pitched the game for Chicago – allowing just seven base hits and two first-inning runs. Gans held the Barons scoreless after the first. Rodriguez allowed four runs in the top of the first and another four runs in the third inning. He was relieved in the fourth, switching positions with the right fielder, Juennello (Juanelo Mirabal). Chicago added single runs in the sixth and the eighth.

The game was never in doubt and the *Birmingham News* declared that Chicago could "easily have doubled the count if they had played a conservative and waiting game."[170] Chicago stole five bases. The box score showed George Dixon as having a 3-for-3 day, but it contradicted itself by stating that both Torriente and Dixon made outs on third strikes while bunting. The accompanying game story said it was a game played with some strong feelings: "The game was marred by wrangling and 'near fights.' Several times during the contest police and plain clothes men were called to restore peace. These disturbances were caused by the players becoming somewhat 'rough' in making a putout or stealing bases."

SEPTEMBER 28, 1920: CHICAGO AMERICAN GIANTS 6, BIRMINGHAM BLACK BARONS 4, AT RICKWOOD FIELD, BIRMINGHAM, ALABAMA

The Black Barons outhit the Giants, 10 hits to 5, but came up short in the runs column. Torriente had two of Chicago's five hits, one of them a home run. Gardner had two hits, too, and a player named Taylor (perhaps a borrowed player) had the other hit. Zeigler pitched for Birmingham; at the plate, he was 2-for-4 with aa double. He struck out seven. Chicago scored three times in the top of the first, added a run in the second, and added two more in the fourth.

It's not clear who pitched for Chicago; it was probably Dave Brown, though the box score shows "M. Brown."[171] He pitched first and collected three at-bats as a batter, while striking out four and walking two. Williams relieved later in the game and was tagged with three runs in the bottom of the ninth on three hits combined with an error.

SEPTEMBER 29, 1920: CHICAGO AMERICAN GIANTS 8, BIRMINGHAM BLACK BARONS 3, AT RICKWOOD FIELD, BIRMINGHAM, ALABAMA

The final game of the series against the Black Barons received less attention. A brief story in the *Birmingham News* concluded "The Giants have met and humiliated every club in the Southern circuit with comparative ease. Foster has a perfect working machine when it comes to playing the national pastime and it is worth the time and trouble for every fan in Birmingham to watch them in action."[172]

Dickey, who had pitched for Knoxville eight days earlier, now took the ball for Birmingham. Frank Wickware started for Chicago. The Giants scored in five different innings: one in the first, two in the fourth, one in the sixth, one in the eighth, and finally three runs in the top of the ninth. Wickware held the Black Barons scoreless in the innings he pitched. At some point, Marshall took over. For the second game in a row, Birmingham scored three runs in the bottom of the ninth. And, for the second game in a row, that wasn't enough to catch up with the lead Chicago had established.

Each box score in Birmingham and Montgomery referred to the visitors as the Chicago Giants, apparently not mindful that there was another team by that name and that Foster's team was named the Chicago American Giants.

SEPTEMBER 30, 1920: CHICAGO AMERICAN GIANTS 5, KNOXVILLE GIANTS 3, AT RICKWOOD FIELD, BIRMINGHAM, ALABAMA

The Giants played another game against the Knoxville Giants, and won, 5-3, completing their nine games in Alabama with nine victories. No accounts of this game have yet been found.

OCTOBER 2, 1920: CHICAGO AMERICAN GIANTS 2, KNOXVILLE GIANTS 1, AT BOOKER T. WASHINGTON PARK, KNOXVILLE, TENNESSEE

The win was described as Chicago's 14th in a row.[173] Dave Brown was pitching for Chicago, with Dink Mothell, who had broken in with the Kansas City Monarchs in 1920, as his catcher. Neither team scored for seven innings. Knoxville got one run in the bottom

of the eighth. Chicago scored two runs in the top of the ninth. The *Journal and Tribune* from Knoxville declared, "Dickey pitched good ball for Knoxville, but the local negroes were outclassed."[174]

There had been an October 3 game scheduled for Chattanooga but it apparently did not occur. There was confusion in the press at this point, The October 9 *New York Tribune* wrote that Rube Foster's team had "won the Western semi-pro championship last Sunday when they defeated the Detroit Giants in Chicago before a crowd of 22,000 fans." The "last Sunday" would have been October 3. The newspaper may not have been the most accurate in that it was foreshadowing the October 10 doubleheader as between "Rube Foster's famous Bacharach Giants, of Chicago" taking on "the Bacharach Giants, of Atlantic City." It appeared to have Giants on the mind as well, with the reference to the Detroit Giants, perhaps a reference to the Detroit Stars – though so far as we know Foster's Giants hadn't played them since September 12.[175]

On the morning of October 3, the *Chattanooga Daily Times* said that "Rube Foster's Chicago American Giants will meet the Knoxville Giants, winner of the negro southern league pennant," and called it a "world's series." The paper said the game at Andrews Field would be called at 3:30 and informed readers: "The third base grandstand will be reserved for white people."[176]

A diligent search of both Chattanooga and Knoxville papers does not show any game in either city, despite its having been advertised. The weather was fair and clear. If there were White people sitting in their reserved section, they were likely disappointed not to see baseball.

OCTOBER 4, 1920: CHICAGO AMERICAN GIANTS 12, ATLANTA BLACK CRACKERS 0 (FIRST GAME OF DOUBLEHEADER), AT PONCE DE LEON PARK, ATLANTA

Six errors proved very costly as the Atlanta Black Crackers were "swamped" in the first game of a 2:00 P.M. doubleheader, 12-0. Tom Williams allowed seven hits, but his opponent Harris allowed only two more. Six errors, every one of them committed by Atlanta, were major factors in the large winning margin.[177]

OCTOBER 4, 1920: ATLANTA BLACK CRACKERS 3, CHICAGO AMERICAN GIANTS 2 (SIX INNINGS,

SECOND GAME OF DOUBLEHEADER), AT PONCE DE LEON PARK, ATLANTA

Atlanta righted itself and played error-free ball in the second game. Chicago scored first, with two runs in the top of the first inning. Atlanta scored three runs off Frank Wickware in the bottom of the second inning, the third (and go-ahead) run coming in when, with runners on first and second base, Wickware threw wildly to first base. It was the only error of the game for either club. The next four innings preceding sunset were scoreless, and the Black Crackers won. This was said to be "the first time Foster's aggregation has ever been defeated by a southern club."[178] It was the first time the Chicago team had lost a game to anyone since September 12.

OCTOBER 6, 1920: CHICAGO AMERICAN GIANTS 11, BACHARACH GIANTS 10 (SIX INNINGS), AT SHIBE PARK, PHILADELPHIA

After what the *Atlantic City Press* called "six long drawn-out innings," the game was called on account of darkness.[179] Daylight hours were shorter, in October, and 21 runs had scored. The batteries were Williams pitching to Julio Rojo for the Bacharachs and Brown pitching to Brown (Dave to Jim) for Chicago. The Chicagoans scored six runs in the top of the first; Atlantic City came back with three. Chicago added one in the second and four more in the top of the fifth. With an 11-1 lead, things were looking good for the Giants from Chicago. But then the Bacharachs Giants scored one in the bottom of the fifth and pulled within a run, scoring five times in the bottom of the sixth. They had the momentum going their way and Dave Brown seems to have lost his effectiveness, Had the game been able to continue, it's possible that Atlantic City would have come out on top. Williams was likely Andrew "String Bean" Williams.

OCTOBER 7, 1920: CHICAGO AMERICAN GIANTS 13, BACHARACH GIANTS 1 (EIGHT INNINGS), AT SHIBE PARK, PHILADELPHIA

The battery for the Giants was Tom Johnson and Jim Brown, and Johnson threw a one-hitter. The Bacharachs started Red Ryan, but before the game was over, he'd been relieved in turn by pitchers named Winter and Pierce. Chicago scored four in the first inning, three more in the fourth inning, and added five in the sixth inning. The Bacharachs got their lone run in the seventh, according to the *Chicago Tribune*, after which Chicago put up one final run in the eighth inning. The Atlantic City team committed three errors.[180] The *Atlantic City Press* agreed on the number of errors and that the starters were Ryan and Johnson, and the innings in which Chicago scored, but had the Bacharachs getting their one run in the first inning, not the seventh.[181]

OCTOBER 8, 1920: BACHARACH GIANTS 7, CHICAGO AMERICAN GIANTS 0, AT SHIBE PARK, PHILADELPHIA

In the third game of the series, Cannonball Redding held Chicago to just two hits, striking out six, and shutting them out, 7-0. Frank Wickware pitched for Chicago, yielding 10 hits, the Bacharachs scoring three runs in the first, two in the third, and one each in the eighth and ninth.[182]

OCTOBER 9, 1920: CHICAGO AMERICAN GIANTS 8, BACHARACH GIANTS 5, AT FEDERAL LEAGUE PARK, HARRISON, NEW JERSEY

Little could be found about this game except for a line score in the *Defender,* which reported that 14,000 fans packed the park for the game.[183] Seamheads also lacks information about this game.

OCTOBER 10, 1920: BACHARACH GIANTS 5, CHICAGO AMERICAN GIANTS 3 (FIRST GAME OF DOUBLEHEADER), AT EBBETS FIELD, BROOKLYN

In what was billed as the "Colored World Series," the Bacharach Giants swept the doubleheader. Dick "Cannonball" Redding held Chicago to three runs on seven hits and struck out eight. Tom Williams pitched for Chicago, allowing eight hits and striking out two. The batting standout for Chicago was "Torriende" with a double and a triple in four at-bats. Jesse Barber, Dick Lundy, and Redding all tripled for the Bacharachs.[184]

OCTOBER 10, 1920: BACHARACH GIANTS 7, CHICAGO AMERICAN GIANTS 3 (SECOND GAME OF DOUBLEHEADER, SEVEN INNINGS), AT EBBETS FIELD, BROOKLYN

The Bacharachs scored five times off Frank Wickware in the bottom of the second inning. He was relieved after three innings and Marshall threw the final four innings. The Bacharachs outhit the American Giants, eight to six, but the Giants committed five errors to just two by the Bacharachs. Dick Lundy homered for the victors, George Shively tripled, and Bill Handy doubled. Joe Ryan pitched for the Bacharachs. The only extra-base hit for Chicago was a triple by Frank Warfield.[185]

OCTOBER 13, 1920: CHICAGO AMERICAN GIANTS 5, BACHARACH GIANTS 0, AT BLACK SOX BALL PARK, WESTPORT, MARYLAND

The available line score shows an eight-inning game in which the Chicagoans scored two runs in the first, two in the third, and a fifth run in the eighth. There were a couple of fielding gems that were featured, particularly one by outfielder Jelly Gardner who "ran back nearly to the fence in the last inning to get Barber's apparent hit in his bare hand[,]" pulling off "a play that shook the overcrowded stands." The account in the *Afro American* said, "Fans were treated to the sight of a colored umpire behind the plate and there was no kicking on his decisions."[186]

OCTOBER 14, 1920: CHICAGO AMERICAN GIANTS 2, BACHARACH GIANTS 2 (TIE), AT AMERICAN LEAGUE PARK, WASHINGTON

The October 12 *Washington Herald* announced games for the 14th and 15th: "The Bacharach Giants of Atlantic City, champions of the East, are to play Andrew 'Rube' Foster's American Giants of Chicago, Thursday and Friday afternoons at American League Park. The American Giants have defeated every colored aggregation west of Pittsburg, and the Bacharachs have cleaned up all the crack colored teams East of that point. It will be the champions of the West versus the champions of the East."[187] The day after the first game the *Herald* reported a tie game, with the Bacharachs having scored twice in the second inning and Foster's team having scored two in the fourth. It was a pitchers' duel between Cannonball Redding of the Bacharachs and Slim Sykes of the Chicago team. Rick Bush suggests this may have been Doc Sykes who lived in Baltimore and appeared in a couple of games for the Baltimore Black Sox in 1920. Someone seems to have spared the American Giants from a difficult situation as the game was called due to darkness in the ninth inning "when the Bacharachs had the bases full with no outs."[188]

OCTOBER 15 ?

We could not find any trace of an October 15 game, though the October 13 *Washington Evening Star* also said a game was scheduled, saying, "Twelve games in all for the world colored championship will be played in various cities by the nines."[189] The *Evening Star* of October 16 includes scores from many other sporting events, but not this one.

OCTOBER 17, 1920: CHICAGO AMERICAN GIANTS 2, BACHARACH GIANTS 0 (FIRST GAME OF DOUBLE-HEADER), AT EBBETS FIELD, BROOKLYN

"Redding Misses No-Hit Game" – so read the headline in the *Brooklyn Times-Union*.[190] He had two outs and two strikes in the ninth inning, and then lost a no-hitter – and the ballgame. Fourteen thousand fans turned out and saw two low-scoring games. The *Brooklyn Daily Eagle* reported a much smaller crowd and reported different totals for each game – 3,000 for the first game and 2,000 for the second game.[191] Chicago shut out the Bacharachs in both games. "Johnson" (likely Tom Johnson) pitched the first game for the Giants against Cannonball Redding, who almost no-hit the Giants. Johnson allowed just five base hits, but Redding allowed two. Neither team scored for the first eight innings and, reported the *Times-Union*, Redding entered the ninth inning without surrendering a hit. He had benefited from exceptional defense, with third baseman Oliver Marcell cited for three "brilliant" ones, including a catch of a liner from catcher Jim Brown a foot off the ground while stretched out flat on his stomach. The Bacharachs pitcher "disposed of the first two batters … on easy chances, but then momentarily lost control, passing DeMoss after he had two strikes on him. Torriende [*sic*] shattered his no-hit dreams by slashing safely through the box. Dickson [*sic* – George Dixon, batting for Jim Brown) was here inserted as a pinch-hitter and made good by bouncing the ball off the right field wall for three bases, chasing both the men on the bases home."[192] Johnson allowed just five base hits, benefiting from three double plays. Redding allowed just the two that did him in. Redding walked four men in all, and Johnson walked three.

OCTOBER 17, 1920: CHICAGO AMERICAN GIANTS 1, BACHARACH GIANTS 0 (SIX INNINGS, SECOND GAME OF DOUBLEHEADER), AT EBBETS FIELD, BROOKLYN

Merven "Red" Ryan pitched the second game for the Bacharachs. The *Defender* account didn't say who pitched for Chicago, but the *Daily Eagle* and *Times-Union* both say it was Tom Williams.[193] This game had fewer hits – four for the Bacharachs and only two for the Chicagoans, one of them a triple by DeMoss. Both pitchers struck out six. The lone run scored in the top of the fourth inning. DeMoss drew a base on balls – the only walk issued by either side. He stole second,

and then took third as Torriente hit into an infield out. Shortstop Frank Warfield – who had played during the regular season for the Detroit Stars, only joining the Giants for postseason games – hit a fly ball to George Shively in left field. DeMoss tagged and scored on the sacrifice, the winning run of the game.[194]

OCTOBER 31, 1920: NORMALS 4, CHICAGO AMERICAN GIANTS 2, AT SCHORLING PARK

The final game of the season was to have been on October 24, but heavy rain prevented play, so the game was postponed until the following Sunday, October 31. Jack Quinn, pitcher for the New York Yankees, pitched for the Normals, striking out 12 and allowing four hits. Quinn had been 18-10 for the Yankees with a 3.20 earned-run average. Dave Brown pitched for Rube Foster's team and was tagged for four runs in the top of the third inning.[195]

SOURCES

Thanks to Larry Lester for providing the initial listing of Chicago American Giants games for 1920, and additional newspaper accounts. Thanks to Rich Bogovich and Rick Bush for a lot of information, as well to the following SABR members and others who helped supply game stories, box scores, or other information: Mark Aubrey, Paul Debono, Jeff Findlay, Peggy Gripshover, Leslie Heaphy, Tom Hufford, Linda Jones of the Gary Public Library, Alan Morris, Skip Nipper, Bill Plott, Tim Tassler, and Steve Turpin, and, from Ball State University, Lindsay Vesperry, Sarah Allison, Sara McKinley, and Jim Connolly.

Thanks to Carl Riechers for laboring through fact-checking and Len Levin for copyediting this lengthy timeline.

For a complete history of the Chicago American Giants, see Paul Debono, *The Chicago American Giants* (Jefferson, North Carolina: McFarland, 2007).

As with the other articles in SABR's book on the 1920 team, Seamheads is the source for statistics.

NOTES

1   Cary B. Lewis, "Baseball Circuit for Next Season," *Chicago Defender*, October 4, 1919: 11.

2   Lewis.

3   Andrew "Rube" Foster, "Pitfalls of Baseball," *Chicago Defender*, December 13, 1919: 11. The American Giants salary was $450 a week in 1919.

4   In a January column, Foster wrote, "The money will naturally come from the whites." Andrew "Rube" Foster, "Pitfalls of Baseball," *Chicago Defender*, January 3, 1920: 9. He restated this in the following week's column as a matter of fact, though adding, "I have fought against delivering Colored baseball into the control of whites, thinking that with a show of patronage from the fans we would get together. The get-together effort has been a failure." Andrew "Rube" Foster, "Pitfalls of Baseball," *Chicago Defender*, January 10, 1920: 9.

5   Cary B. Lewis, "Baseball Magnates Hold Conference," *Chicago Defender*, February 14, 1920: 11.

6   "Baseball Men Write League Constitution,"
Chicago Defender, February 21, 1920: 9.

7   "Eight Clubs to Make Up Negro Baseball League,"
Chicago Defender, February 16, 1920: 13.

8   "'Rube' Assigns Players to Giants," *Chicago Defender*, March 20, 1920: 9.

9   Dave Wyatt, "Success of the League Is Up to the
Fans," *Chicago Defender*, April 3, 1920: 9.

10   "Giants Mobilizing," *Chicago Defender*, April 3, 1920: 9.

11   "Rogers Parks Start Semi-Pro Season by Downing Giants, 4-2,"
Chicago Tribune, April 12, 1920: 11. See also Dave Wyatt, "Foster's
Crew Are Trounced," *Chicago Defender*, April 17, 1920: 9.

12   "Foster Raises the Lid," *Chicago Whip*, April 17, 1920: 5.

13   Both the story and the advertisement appear
on page 9 of the April 17 *Defender*.

14   "Leaguers Rout the Giants," *Chicago Defender*, May 1, 1920: 9.

15   The *Chicago Tribune* often provided brief lines scores or box scores,
with perhaps a line or two of text. Information that is otherwise unat-
tributed comes from such brief bits of information in the *Tribune*.

16   An advertisement in the April 24 *Defender* said the Giants would
play a May 2 game against the Romeos of Chicago League.

17   Dave Wyatt, "Teams Are Well Framed," *Chicago Defender*, April 24, 1920: 9.

18   "'Round the Baselines," *Chicago Defender*, April 24, 1920: 9.

19   Clarence Freeman, "American Giants Pull a Win,"
Chicago Defender, May 8, 1920: 16.

20   Advertisement in *Chicago Defender*, May 8, 1920: 16.

21   Captain James H. Smith, "Foster's Crew Puts Kibosh on
Chicago Giants," *Chicago Defender*, May 15, 1920: 9.

22   "American Giants Win from Chicago Giants, *Chicago Whip*, May 15, 1920: 5.

23   "Marcos 6; Am. Giants 5," *Chicago Tribune*, May 17, 1920: 19.

24   The game story says the shortstop committed three errors; the box score
says two. The story named him Wingfield; the box score called him
Wiggins. See Captain James H. Smith, "American Giants Walloped
by the Dayton Marcos," *Chicago Defender*, May 22, 1920: 9.

25   "Amer. Giants, 6; Marcos, 4," *Chicago Tribune*, May
23, 1920: A2. Despite the headline, the box score and
game story both clearly show the score as 6-2.

26   Dave Wyatt, "American Giants Win in 11th,"
Chicago Defender, May 29, 1920: 9.

27   "Giants Take Two Falls from K.C. Monarchs,"
Chicago Whip, May 29, 1920: 5.

28   "Fosters Score Win in Eleventh," *Chicago Tribune*, May 24, 1920: 18.

29   *Kansas City Sun*, May 29, 1920: 8.

30   Johnson had been drafted into the US Army in World War I. Because
he had attended college, he received an officer's commission.

31   "Monarchs Lose Second," *Chicago Defender*, May 29, 1920: 9.

32   "American Giants Beat Kansas City Monarchs,"
Chicago Herald-Examiner, May 25, 1920: 7.

33   "American Giants Slip Monarchs Another Defeat,"
Chicago Tribune, May 26, 1920: 14.

34   "Giants Score Another Victory Over Monarchs,"
Chicago Herald-Examiner, May 26, 1920: 10.

35   "Logan Squares Beaten by American Giants," *Chicago
Herald-Examiner*, May 29, 1920: 10.

36   "16,000 Fans See Fosters Win, 4-1," *Chicago Tribune*, May 31, 1920: 21.

37   "Amer. Giants 3, Cubans 2," *Chicago Tribune*, June 1, 1920: 23.

38   "American Giants Win Another from Cubans,"
Chicago Herald-Examiner, June 1, 1920: 9.

39   "Amer. Giants 7, Cubans 5," *Chicago Tribune*, June 2, 1920: 15.

40   "American Giants on Top; Beat Cubans in 13th,
3-2," *Chicago Tribune*, June 4, 1920: 15.

41   "American Giants on Top." It may have been league win number 11.

42   "American Giants on a Rampage," *Chicago Defender*, June 5, 1920: 9.

43   "Am. Giants, 7; Danville, 0," *Chicago Tribune*, June 6, 1920: A2.

44   "Sports Briefs," *Chicago Whip*, June 12, 1920. That said,
the game was so lopsided that by the last three half-innings
"the umpires and players were all who were present."

45   "Magnets Are Easy for Giants," *Chicago Defender*, June 12, 1920: 9.

46   "Sports Briefs," *Chicago Whip*, June 12, 1920. The paper
disparaged the Magnets, saying they "looked good in practice, but that was all," then adding, "The Magnets should be
named the 'Maggots,' they crawl around so much."

47   "Johnson's Pitching Defeats Giants, 10-1," *St. Louis
Globe-Democrat*, June 8, 1920: 16.

48   "Chicago Giants Win from St. Louis Team," *St.
Louis Globe-Democrat*, June 9, 1920: 16.

49   "St. Louis Giants Lose Third Straight, 6-0," *St.
Louis Globe-Democrat*, June 10, 1920: 19.

50   "Giants Charter Airship for the Chicago Series,"
St. Louis Argus, June 11, 1920: 5.

51   "St. Louis Giants, 3; Am. Giants, 2," *Chicago Tribune*, June 11, 1920: 17.

52   "St. Louis Giants Win from Chicago Team, 3-2," *St. Louis Globe-
Democrat*, June 11, 1920: 18. In each of the three successive editions
of the *Globe-Democrat*, the newspaper errantly referred to the visitors
as the "Chicago Giants" rather than the Chicago American Giants.

53   "Giants Charter Airship for the Chicago Series,"
St. Louis Argus, June 11, 1920: 5.

54   "St. Louis Giants Drop Final to Chicago, 6-3," *St.
Louis Globe-Democrat*, June 12, 1920: 11.

55   "M'Coys 6, Amer. Giants 4," *Chicago Tribune*, June 13, 1920: A2.

56   "Amer. Giants, 9; ABC, 1," *Chicago Tribune*, June 4, 1920: 19. Both the
Defender and *Tribune* box scores showed the pitcher as "B. Williams"
though the *Defender* story specifically referred to the Williams in question
as Tom Williams. "Giants Victorious," *Chicago Defender*, June 19, 1920: 20.

57   "Giants Victorious."

58   "American Giants Take Twin Bill," *Chicago Tribune*, June 16, 1920: 14.

59   "A.'s Lose 2 Games," *Indianapolis Freeman*, June 19, 1920: 4.

60   "American Giants Victors over Fort Sheridan, 6-2,"
Chicago Tribune, June 17, 1920: 13.

61   "Rogers Parks Blank Giants," *Chicago Whip*, June 26, 1920: 5.

62   "Oak Parks Lose, 10-5," *Chicago Tribune*, June 20, 1920: 17.

63   *Chicago Whip*, June 26, 1920: 5.

64   Rogers Pk., 1; Am. Giants, 0," *Chicago Tribune*, June 21, 1920: 19.

65   "Rube Foster, Bull of Basham," *Indianapolis Freeman*, June 26, 1920: 5.

66   "ABCs and Giants Play Here Saturday," *Muncie
(Indiana) Star Press*, June 22, 1920: 11.

67   "A.B.C.'s Defeated by Giants, 5 to 4," *Muncie Star Press*, June 27, 1920: 14.

68   "Foster's Crew Blanked by ABCs," *Chicago Defender*, July 3, 1920: 9.

69   See, for instance, "Semi-Pro Games Today," *Chicago Tribune*, July 5, 1920: 18.

70   "Giants and ABCs Tie," *Indianapolis News*, June 29, 1920: 20.

71   "ABCs Win Again," *Indianapolis News*, June 30, 1920: 20.

72   "American Giants Cop the Final Game from A.'s 6 to 2," *Indianapolis Freeman*, July 3, 1920: 3.

73   "American Giants Cop Final Game from A's, 6 to 2," *Indianapolis Star*, July 1, 1920: 18.

74   "Colored Teams Battle Bravely for Piqua Fans," *Piqua* (Ohio) *Daily Call*, July 2, 1920: 8.

75   "American Giants Defeat Marcos," *Dayton Daily News*, July 4, 1920: 35.

76   "K.C's Down Ruben in First; Americans Beat Cubans 1-0," *Indianapolis Freeman*, July 10, 1920: 3.

77   "Buckeye of Normals Pitches 5th Shutout as Team Splits Even," *Chicago Tribune*, July 6, 1920: 23.

78   "Monarchs Hold Fosters to 1 Hit for 4-2 Triumph," *Chicago Tribune*, July 6, 1920: 23.

79   Phil S. Dixon, *Wilber "Bullet" Rogan and the Kansas City Monarchs* (Jefferson, North Carolina: McFarland, 2010), 133.

80   Dave Wyatt, "Rogan Stops the American Giants," *Chicago Defender*, July 10, 1920: 9.

81   "Kansas City Monarchs Lose, 8-6, to Amer. Giants," *Chicago Tribune*, July 7, 1920: 15.

82   "Foster's Giants Win from K.C. Monarchs," *Chicago Defender*, July 10, 1920: 9.

83   "American Giants Win in 12th Round, 2-1," *Chicago Tribune*, July 8, 1920: 15.

84   *Kansas City Sun*, July 10. 1920: 8.

85   As of January 2022, the Seamheads database reflects only four home runs for the entire 1920 league season for the American Giants.

86   "Fosters Upset St. Louis Giants," *Chicago Tribune*, July 12, 1920: 15.

87   "Fosters Trounce St. Louisans," *Chicago Defender*, July 17, 1920: 9.

88   "Chicagoans Win from St. Louis," *Chicago Whip*, July 17, 1920: 5.

89   "Giants Annex Another," *Chicago Defender*, July 17, 1920: 9.

90   "Foster's Giants Win Again, 4-2," *Chicago Tribune*, July 13, 1920: 13.

91   "Fosters, 7; St. Louis, 6," *Chicago Tribune*, July 14, 1920: 10.

92   "American Giants Display Class," *Chicago Whip*, July 17, 1920: 5.

93   "American Giants Display Class."

94   "Giants Win Pair," *Gary Daily Tribune*, July 19, 1920: 4.

95   *Gary Evening Post*, July 19: 1920: 4.

96   "Giants 8; Dayton 1," *Chicago Tribune*, July 19, 1920: 11.

97   Dave Wyatt, "Marcos Lose to the Giants," *Chicago Defender*, July 24, 1920: 9. See also, "Marcos Are Trounced by Giants," *Chicago Whip*, July 24, 1920: 5.

98   Julius Culpepper, "Written on the Cuff," *Chicago Whip*, July 24, 1920: 5.

99   "American Giants Trim Dayton Nine Again, 3-1," *Chicago Tribune*, July 20, 1920: 14.

100   "Wickware Holds Melrose Parks as Giants Win," *Chicago Defender*, July 31, 1920: 9.

101   Mister Fan, "American Giants Trounce Joliet, 6-0," *Chicago Defender*, July 31, 1920: 9.

102   "American Giants Face Crucial Test," *Chicago Defender*, July 24, 1920: 9.

103   "Chicago Giants Win from St. Louis Team," *St. Louis Globe-Democrat*, July 27, 1920: 10. The *Globe-Democrat* provided box scores and a few sentences about each of the five games in the series but presented the visitors throughout as the "Chicago Giants" and not the "Chicago American Giants."

104   Game details are from "Chicago Victor Over St. Louis Giants, 4-1," *St. Louis Globe-Democrat*, July 28, 1920: 8.

105   "Finner Pitches Local Giants to Victory, 5-0," *St. Louis Globe-Democrat*, July 29, 1920: 9.

106   "Giants Hault [*sic*] Rube," *St. Louis Argus*, July 30, 1920: 5.

107   "St. Louis Giants Win from Chicago, 8 to 4," *St. Louis Globe-Democrat*, July 30, 1920: 9.

108   "Chicago Giants Win Final from St. Louis," *St. Louis Globe-Democrat*, July 31, 1920: 7.

109   "Fist Fight Livens Kansas City Game," *Chicago Defender*, August 7, 1920: 6.

110   "Monarchs Won in 12 Innings," *Kansas City Times*, August 2, 1920: 8.

111   "Foster Loses in the 12th," *Chicago Defender*, August 7, 1920: 6.

112   "Third Game to Monarchs," *Kansas City Times*, August 3, 1920: 8.

113   Chas. A. Starks, "Monarchs Swamp the Mighty Rube," *Kansas City Sun*, July 7, 1920: 8.

114   "First Defeat for Rogan," *Kansas City Times*, August 5, 1920: 9.

115   "Food for Fans," *Chicago Defender*, August 14, 1920: 6.

116   "Food for Fans."

117   "Giants Lose at Gary," *Chicago Whip*, August 21, 1920: 5.

118   "Rube's Giants Lose to Stars," *Gary Evening Post*, August 9, 1920: 3. The newspaper spelled it "lose playing."

119   "Gary Workers Win in Second Diamond Bill," *Gary Daily Tribune*, August 9, 1920: 4. "Rogo" was almost certainly catcher Julio Rojo.

120   "Rube's Giants Lose to Stars."

121   "Gary Workers Win in Second Diamond Bill."

122   "Am. Giants, 7; Bacharachs, 3," *Chicago Tribune*, August 9, 1920: 15.

123   "Rube Fosters's American Giants Beat Bacharachs by Score [of] 7 to 3," *Indianapolis Freeman*, August 14, 1920: 4.

124   "Rough Stuff!," *Chicago Defender*, August 14, 1920: 6.

125   "Bacharachs Lose in Tenth," *Chicago Defender*, August 14, 1920: 6.

126   "American Giants, 5; Bacharachs, 1," *Chicago Defender*, August 14, 1920: 15.

127   "Bacharach's [*sic*] Lose," *Atlantic City Press*, August 12, 1920, page number unknown.

128   "Bacharachs Down Fosters," *Chicago Herald and Examiner*, date uncertain.

129   "Fosters in Last Scrap Here Sun.," *Gary Daily Tribune*, August 12, 1920: 4.

130   "Cubans Beat American Giants," *Indianapolis Freeman*, August 21, 1920: 5.

131   "Cubans Beat American Giants," *Chicago Defender*, August 28, 1920: 6.

132   "American Giants Cop, 9-2," *Chicago Tribune*, August 17, 1920: 15.

133   "Giants Down Cubans Monday," *Chicago Whip*, August 21, 1920: 5.

134   "Great Crowd Sees Game at Minonk," *Bloomington* (Illinois) *Pantagraph*, August 19, 1920: 9. The name of the park was provided by David Uphoff, thanks to SABR member Jeff Findlay.

135   "Bloomers May Play American Giants in Exhibit Win Again," *Bloomington Pantagraph*, August 20, 1920: 10. The box score is internally inconsistent, suggesting in one place that Malarcher tripled twice.

136 The game story said it was in the third inning; the accompanying box score shows it in the fourth. See "American Giants Take Kansas City's Measure," *Chicago Defender*, August 29, 1920: 6.

137 "American Giants' Line-up Shows All-Star Players," *Fort Wayne Sentinel*, August 25, 1920: 14.

138 "Easily Down Local Colored Club; Face Hard Battle This Afternoon," *Fort Wayne Sentinel*, August 28, 1920: 8.

139 Tossler – the original family spelling – was a great-grand-uncle of SABR member Tim Tassler. The Fort Wayne's team battery this day – Tossler and Bade – were White ballplayers on an integrated team.

140 "League Standings," *Chicago Defender*, August 28, 1920: 6.

141 "American Giants Leading League," *Indianapolis Freeman*, September 4, 1920: 7.

142 "American Giants Are Victors over Lifers," *Fort Wayne Sentinel*, August 29, 1920: 9.

143 "Am. Giants Down Chi-Leaguers," *Chicago Whip*, September 5, 1920: 5.

144 Mister Fan, "American Giants Win from Rogers Parks," *Chicago Defender*, September 4, 1920: 6; "Fosters Thump Rogers Park, 5-1," *Chicago Tribune*, August 30, 1920: 13.

145 "Stars Are Losers in First Battle," *Detroit Free Press*, September 5, 1920: 13.

146 "American Giants Pound Detroit Hurlers, Winning 8 to 3," *Chicago Defender*, September 11, 1920: 6.

147 "Stars Split with American Giants," *Detroit Free Press*, September 7, 1920: 16.

148 "Stars Split with American Giants."

149 "Giants Win One, Lose One," *Chicago Whip*, September 11, 1920: 5.

150 "American Giants Beat Stars, 6 -3," *Detroit Free Press*, September 8, 1950: 15.

151 "Gatewood Again Stops the Giants," *Detroit Free Press*, September 9, 1950: 15.

152 The score and venue information was supplied by Larry Lester.

153 "American Giants Divide Bill with Detroit Stars," *Chicago Tribune*, September 13, 1920: 15.

154 "Giants and Stars Split Even," *Chicago Defender*, September 18, 1920: 6.

155 "Stars and Giants Divide Bill," *Chicago Whip*, September 18, 1920: 5.

156 "Contest at Flanagan," *Bloomington Pantagraph*, September 15, 1920: 10.

157 *Chicago Defender*, September 25, 1920: 6.

158 "ABC Flayed," *Chicago Whip*, September 25, 1920: 5.

159 Dave Wyatt, "Foster Team Ends Chicago Season," *Chicago Whip*, September 25, 1920: 5.

160 "Marcos to Play 'Italians' Today; Title Series On," *Dayton Daily News*, September 19, 1920: 13.

161 "American Giants Are Champions," *Savannah Gazette*, September 25, 1920: 14.

162 Associated Negro Press, "American Giants Winners Negro League Race," *Omaha Monitor*, September 23, 1920: 2. One suspects a misprint that should have read "Bill Francis, star third baseman."

163 "American Giants Winners Negro League Race." One wonders why the wire service writer had thought the American Giants were foreseen as a "weak sister."

164 Thanks to Skip Nipper for providing the information, and to Mark Aubrey for also trying to help track down the possibility of this still-elusive game.

165 "American Giants Beat Knoxville," *Birmingham News*, September 22, 1920: 15. The *Birmingham Reporter* showed the American

166 "Windy City Club Wins from Giants," *Birmingham News*, September 23, 1920: 14.

167 "Knoxville No Match for Chicago Giants," *Birmingham News*, September 24, 1920: 17. As the *St. Louis Globe-Democrat* repeatedly had, the *News* referred to the team as the "Chicago Giants" rather than the Chicago American Giants.

168 "Chicago Giants Defeat Grey Sox," *Montgomery Advertiser*, September 26, 1920: 9.

169 "Chicago Giants Win Hard-Fought Battle," *Montgomery Advertiser*, September 27, 1920: 2.

170 "Black Barons Go Down to Defeat," *Birmingham News*, September 2, 1920: 15.

171 "Windy City Nine Win Second Game," *Birmingham News*, September 29, 1920: 15.

172 "Chicago Giants Are to Meet Montgomery Sox," *Birmingham News*, September 29, 1920: 23.

173 "American Giants, 2; Knoxville, 1," *Chicago Defender*, October 9, 1920: 6.

174 "Giants Lose Second to Chicago by 2-1 Score," *Knoxville Journal and Tribune*, October 3, 1920: 4.

175 "Bacharachs to Play Here," *New York Tribune*, October 9, 1920: 12.

176 "Negro Champion Teams to Play Here Today," *Chattanooga Daily Times*, October 3, 1920: 18.

177 "Black Crackers and American Giants Divide," *Atlanta Constitution*, October 5, 1920: 12.

178 "Black Crackers and American Giants Divide."

179 "Americans Beat Bacharach Giants," *Atlantic City Press*, October 7, 1920.

180 "American Giants Cop, 13-1," *Chicago Tribune*, October 8, 1902: 21. Rick Bush suggests that this was probably Nip Winters (who joined Atlantic City full-time in 1921) and perhaps Nat Pierce (who played for the Philadelphia Royal Stars in 1922).

181 "American Giants Rout Local Bacharach Giants," *Atlantic City Press*, October 8, 1920.

182 "Bacharachs Turn Tables on Giants," *Atlantic City Press*, October 9, 1920.

183 "Rube Wins in Jersey," *Chicago Defender*, October 16, 1920: 6.

184 "Bacharachs Twice Beat American Giants," *Brooklyn Daily Eagle*, October 11, 1920: 22.

185 "Bacharachs Twice Beat American Giants."

186 "Chicago Shuts Out Bacharachs," *Afro-American* (Baltimore), October 15, 1920: 7.

187 "Crack Colored Team to Play Series Here," *Washington Herald*, October 12, 1920: 9.

188 "American Giants Tie Bacharachs," *Washington Herald*, October 15, 1920: 12.

189 "Star Series Tomorrow," *Washington Evening Star*, October 13, 1920: 26.

190 "Redding Misses No-Hit Game," *Brooklyn Times-Union*, October 18, 1920: 7.

191 "Bacharachs Beaten Twice by American Giants," *Brooklyn Daily Eagle*, October 18, 1920: 18. The *Daily Eagle* box score contradicts itself, in one place showing DeMoss with a base hit, but does not offer the narrative provided by the *Times-Union*.

192 "Redding Misses No-Hit Game."

193 "Rube Defeats Bacharachs Twice," *Chicago Defender*, October 23, 1920: 6. See also "Bacharachs Beaten Twice by American Giants."

194 "Redding Misses No-Hit Game."

195 "Foster's Men Lose Final," *Chicago Defender*, November 6, 1920: 9.

Giants scoring seven runs in the top of the ninth for a final of 10-0. See box score on page 1 of the September 25, 1920 edition.

AMERICAN GIANTS BARELY AVOID NO-HITTER AND WIN A "WORLD SERIES"

OCTOBER 17, 1920: CHICAGO AMERICAN GIANTS 2, BACHARACH GIANTS 0, FIRST GAME OF DOUBLEHEADER CHICAGO AMERICAN GIANTS 1, BACHARACH GIANTS 0 (SIX INNINGS), SECOND GAME OF DOUBLEHEADER AT EBBETS FIELD, BROOKLYN

BY RICHARD BOGOVICH

One of the doubleheader's several previews in the *New York Tribune* said the games were part of the "Little World Series." Interestingly, the two paragraphs did not mention the race of Rube Foster's Chicago American Giants and the Atlantic City Bacharach Giants, much less note that the Chicago club was the champion of the Negro National League in that circuit's first season of existence. In fact, the *Tribune* implied that the series was to determine the nation's "semi-pro" championship. A *New York Times Evening Telegram* preview of the prior Sunday's doubleheader between the two teams at the same park stated explicitly, while also omitting any mention of race, "The world series in point will be for the semiprofessional title of the United States. ..." Conversely, the *Brooklyn Daily Times*, for one, did characterize the

doubleheader correctly: "The games are advertised for the championship of the colored teams of the country."[1] Regardless of the extent to which the *Tribune* and *Telegram* sports departments misunderstood the significance of the games, the players involved might have welcomed the free publicity.

Less than a week earlier, Brooklyn had been abuzz with baseball fever. Alas, on October 12, their Brooklyn Robins (later the Dodgers) had lost the World Series to the Cleveland Indians, five games to two. The most recent game of that series at Ebbets Field had been played on October 7. Though the off-season had begun, baseball remained big news, including in Brooklyn because of the Robins' owner, Charles Ebbets. On the day of this doubleheader between the American Giants and the Bacharachs, the *Brooklyn*

Daily Eagle announced on its front page that Ebbets had been asked by Assistant State's Attorney Hartley L. Replogle of Cook County, Illinois, to appear before a grand jury that was investigating corruption in the major leagues.[2] The focus was the infamous 1919 World Series between the Cincinnati Reds and the Chicago White Sox.

Beginning on August 7, the two teams played six games in Chicago, and the American Giants won four from the visitors.[3] The Bacharach Giants never appeared in the NNL's standings but the club had affiliated with the league in May and was considered an "associate member."[4] The Bacharach Giants had the second-best winning percentage among the East's major independent teams, finishing behind the Brooklyn Royal Giants. Brooklyn's record of 13-7-2 equaled a winning percentage of .650 while the Bacharachs' record of 22-16-2 yielded a winning percentage of .579.[5] Apparently, however, the Bacharachs and the Royal Giants did not play each other during the 1920 season.[6]

Just before the Bacharach Giants began the series with their Chicago counterparts, they had defeated Babe Ruth's All-Stars at Philadelphia's Shibe Park, home of the AL's Athletics, on October 4 by a score of 9-4. In addition to Ruth, who started at first base but later pitched, among the four other major leaguers on the All-Stars was starting pitcher Carl Mays.[7] On October 4 the American Giants finished a postseason tour of Southern cities by splitting a doubleheader with the Atlanta Black Crackers. The American Giants had played their last regular-season game not quite three weeks into September and had clinched the pennant comfortably long before then.[8]

The entire series between Atlantic City and Chicago received much more advance publicity than reporting of outcomes. Sometimes newspapers were inconsistent about the number of games to be played in their city, and it remains unknown whether certain announced games were actually played, such as one scheduled to take place in Wilmington, Delaware.[9] Similarly, as the series progressed, papers did not always agree on how many games had been played already.[10] Nevertheless, sufficient evidence exists that the first game of the series took place on October 6 in Shibe Park, and by the time of the doubleheader the series was tied (possibly with three wins each).[11]

A Sunday, October 10, doubleheader had drawn "some 12,000 enthusiasts," according to the *Brooklyn Daily Times*. For the October 17 doubleheader rematch, the *Chicago Defender* gave the attendance as 14,000. In stark contrast, the bottom of the *Brooklyn Daily Eagle*'s first box score reported the attendance at just 3,000, while the end of its second box score put that figure even lower, at 2,000.[12] In part because the weather was so pleasant on October 17, a turnout of 14,000 seems much more likely than just 3,000.

Most of this twin bill's previews did not mention the first game's starting time, but on the day before, the *Brooklyn Daily Times* had specified 2:00 P.M. As far as is known, none of the previews said anything about the price of tickets, not even the large ad in the *New York Age* (a prominent African American weekly) that had promoted the prior Sunday's doubleheader between the same two teams.[13] The temperature on the 17th peaked at 4:30 (likely just after the first game concluded), when thermometers reached 68 degrees.[14] There was a pair of umpires for the doubleheader a week earlier, apparently a duo with whom the Bacharach Giants were familiar, but the twin bill on October 17 was called by just one ump, named Jones.[15] Whoever he was, that's the authority figure who presumably got the game going by yelling, "Play ball!"

In many ways, the teams were evenly matched. Each lineup was missing only one of its regular-season members. For Chicago, 21-year-old Frank Warfield was at shortstop instead of Bobby Williams. For Atlantic City, 27-year-old George Shively patrolled left field and frequent center fielder Lico Mederos was absent. The teams had the same average age, 27, and almost all of the players spent more than a decade with top African American clubs of that era. One difference was time spent with their respective teams. All the American Giants except Warfield played multiple years with that club, while only shortstop Dick Lundy spent a tenure of any great length with the Bacharachs; he played off and on for the team from 1916 to 1927.[16]

The American Giants batted first against Atlantic City's player-manager, Dick "Cannonball" Redding. He had an uneventful first inning, and then Chicago's pitcher took the hill. He was listed as "Johnston" in two box scores the next day but as "Johnson" in the *Times*; thus, he was presumably Tom Johnson, whose record for Chicago was 11-0 in 1920. Johnson likewise faced no threat in his first inning of work, and he ultimately pitched a complete game in which he scattered five singles. Only George Shively managed two hits off Johnson. One of the Bacharachs reached on an error, and the box scores disagreed on whether Johnson walked three or two hitters. However, the Bacharachs left only two runners on base during the entire game, due in part to three double plays behind Johnson.[17]

Redding, who also pitched the entire contest, fared better overall across the first eight innings. He helped his own cause considerably by striking out seven American Giants (while Johnson fanned nobody). Offsetting those strikeouts to an extent were four walks and a hit batsman. Redding did not benefit from any double plays, but the fielding behind him drew considerable the praise from one Brooklyn daily: "Left fielder Shively roamed all over the outfield and pulled down several flies that were labelled for extra bases," the *Times* enthused. The paper also heaped praise on teammate Oliver Marcell:

> "Third sacker Marcelles [*sic*] was particularly brilliant. He cut off at least three safeties by making great stops and catches of difficult chances. One catch, while lying flat on his stomach, was the fielding feature. With two out in the seventh Catcher Brown, of the Westerners, hit a liner toward third that did not rise more than a foot from the ground. Marcelles fell flat, and with a desperate effort, grabbed the scorcher with his gloved hand."[18]

Such stellar defensive play helped to keep Chicago off the scoreboard, but Johnson was also hurling a shutout. The American Giants failed to mount a threat against Redding in the top of the eighth inning, and the game had become a "thriller," as the *Brooklyn Citizen* commented, because he took a no-hitter into the ninth.

The *Times* provided details of that dramatic inning, though something in its account fails to add up after looking at the three box scores. "Redding disposed of the first two batters in this frame on easy chances, but then momentarily lost control, passing Demoss [*sic*] after he had two strikes on him," the *Times* wrote. Therefore, not only was Redding merely one out from nine complete innings of no-hit pitching, but he was also one strike away. However, there may have been only one out before Bingo DeMoss walked. In any case, future Hall of Famer Cristóbal Torriente batted next against Redding. "Torriende [*sic*] shattered his no-hit dreams by slashing safely through the box," the *Times* continued. "Dickson [*sic*] was here inserted as a pinch hitter and made good by bouncing the ball off the right field wall for three bases, chasing both the men on the bases home."[19]

The complicating factor is that the trio of box scores all agree that Warfield was in the batting order right behind Torriente, yet George Dixon, a catcher, batted for starting catcher Jim Brown (who had lined out so powerfully to Marcell to end the seventh inning). The box scores also agree that Dixon remained in the game to catch the bottom of the ninth inning for Johnson. If Dixon batted for the newcomer Warfield rather than Brown, then the box scores all omitted Warfield's replacement at shortstop (who would have been inserted in Brown's spot in the batting order). On the other hand, the two box scores that recorded at-bats implied that Brown did indeed bat in the ninth inning as well (in which case he very likely made the third out).[20] If Brown did not bat right after Dixon's triple because he was removed, then Warfield must have made the second out – which would mean DeMoss walked after the first out rather than after two men were out.

Whatever the correct personnel and batting order may have been, the American Giants suddenly had a two-run lead. There is no indication that the Bacharachs managed any sort of rally in the bottom half of the frame, and Johnson had a shutout. If the American Giants could claim a second victory that afternoon, they would claim the crown in this "World Series."

Therefore, the second game started after 4:00.[21] Box scores show that, other than using different starting pitchers, the two teams used lineups that were almost identical to those of the first game. The lone exception was that the pinch-hitting hero of the first game, George Dixon, was behind the plate for Chicago rather than sitting on the bench and hoping to enter as a substitute.[22] The two starting pitchers for the second game were 22-year-old Red Ryan for the Bacharachs and 23-year-old Tom Williams for the American Giants, each of whom was eight years younger than his respective first-game counterpart.[23]

Once again, the American Giants played the role of the visiting team and batted first. Box scores in three Brooklyn dailies agree that there was no scoring in the first three innings. In the top of the fourth inning, Chicago played what today is often called "small ball," which was wise given how many scoreless innings the two teams had already played that afternoon. Bingo DeMoss led off the fourth with a walk – the only free pass issued by either moundsman – and stole second while Torriente followed at bat. DeMoss went to third as Torriente made an infield out. That brought up Frank Warfield with one out, and the newcomer lifted a fly to left field on which DeMoss scored.[24]

DeMoss also hit a triple in either the first or sixth inning, but Chicago had only one other hit in the second game, a single by Warfield. The Bacharachs had but one extra-base hit among their four safeties, a double by Bill Handy. Ryan tried to help his own cause on offense with one of his team's few hits and the game's only other stolen base, but his efforts went for naught. Redding, his manager, batted for him in the bottom of the game's sixth and final inning.[25]

Each pitcher struck out six opponents, and as additional evidence of just how closely matched the teams were that afternoon, the game ended with Chicago winning, 1-0. There was disagreement among three box scores about the number of innings the two teams actually played. The *Citizen*'s line score showed nine innings and stated that "Redding batted for Redding [*sic*; Ryan] in the ninth." The *Eagle*'s box score similarly noted that Redding pinch-hit "for Ryan in 9th inning," yet its line score beneath that note showed only six innings. The *Times* also printed a six-inning line score. The two box scores that reported the duration of the game agreed that it took one hour to complete. Additionally, those two box scores showed Chicago with 19 at-bats and Atlantic City with 21, totals befitting a six-inning game and not one lasting a full nine.[26]

Though the *Times* had the most detailed coverage of the doubleheader after the fact, it fell to a Brooklyn newspaper to indicate the significance of the outcome. "The American Giants have won five of the eight games played between the teams," the *Citizen* noted.[27] Still, in their coverage none of the three papers connected the games to a championship of any sort as had been done beforehand. Nevertheless, by sweeping this doubleheader, Rube Foster capped an incredibly important and successful year, which began with the launch of a successful league, included winning that circuit's first pennant the previous month, and ended with the conquest of the Bacharachs in the East.

SOURCES

The Seamheads.com Negro Leagues Database was consulted for all statistics.

NOTES

1   "'Little World Series' Set for Ebbets Field," *New York Tribune*, October 13, 1920: 14. "Championship at Stake in Ebbets Field Games," *New York Evening Telegram*, October 9, 1920: 6. "Redding and Ryan Pitchers for the Bacharach Giants," *Brooklyn Daily Times*, October 15, 1920: 14. Interestingly, the *Tribune*'s announcement originated in Lexington, Kentucky, and not Chicago or Atlantic City.

2   "Ebbets and Frazee Invited to Appear Before Grand Jury," *Brooklyn Daily Eagle*, October 17, 1920: 1.

3   "Rube's Giants Lose to Stars," *Gary* (Indiana) *Evening Post*, August 9, 1920: 3. "American Giants Leading League," *Freeman* (Indianapolis), September 4, 1920: 7.

4   "Seen and Heard," *New York Age*, May 22, 1920: 7. Center for Negro League Baseball Research, "Formation of the Negro National League, http://www.cnlbr.org/Portals/0/FL/ Formation%20of%20Negro%20National%20League.pdf.

5   For the records of NNL and Eastern independent teams in 1920, see https:// www.seamheads.com/NegroLgs/year.php?yearID=1920. See also Center for Negro League Baseball Research, "'Colored Championship' Series," http:// www.cnlbr.org/Portals/0/RL/Colored%20Championship%20Series%20 (1920-1931).pdf.Though the Hilldale club of Philadelphia was a distant third among top Eastern teams with a record of 9-9-2, it played Brooklyn in a four-game series during the first half of October to name the "Colored Champion of the East" for 1920. "It is important not to confuse a 'Colored Championship' with a Negro League World Series Champion," the Center for Negro League Baseball Research cautioned. "Many if not most 'Colored Championship' series were played between two self-appointed teams, while the Negro League World Series was played [between] the champions from two different formalized leagues." (The Center for Negro League Baseball Research said Hilldale won the final game and thus the series, contrary to "Series Ends in Tie," *Philadelphia Inquirer*, October 16, 1920: 14.) The overlapping series between Chicago and Atlantic City was much more similar to the first official Negro League World Series in 1924.

6   See daily reports for the Bacharach Giants compiled by Peter W. Gorton at http://negroleagues.bravehost.com/aaj.html, where there are also links to the same for many other 1920 clubs.

7   "Babe Ruth's Nine Beaten by Bacharach Giants," *Philadelphia Inquirer*, October 5, 1920: 18. Besides Ruth and Mays, the others identified by the *Inquirer* as major leaguers were center fielder Wally Schang, right fielder Lefty O'Doul, and a catcher named Hoffman, but the latter surname doesn't obviously correspond to any contemporary minor-league catcher of some accomplishment, much less any major leaguer around then.

8   "Black Crackers and American Giants Divide," *Atlanta Constitution*, October 5, 1920: 12. Dave Wyatt, "Foster Team Ends Chicago Season," *Chicago Whip*, September 25, 1920: 5.

9   "Colored Championship," *Wilmington* (Delaware) *Evening Journal*, October 9, 1920: 5. "Bacharach Giants and Americans Clash Today," *Wilmington Morning News*, October 11, 1920: 12.

10   Each team won two games in Philadelphia, according to "American Giants Play Bacharachs Today," *New York Evening Telegram*, October 10, 1920: 8. However, coverage has been found for only three games. Through October 13, the clubs had met reportedly met nine times and each won four, according to "Chicargo [*sic*] Shuts Out Bacharachs," *Baltimore Afro-American*, October 15, 1929: 7. Yet when this October 17 doubleheader was previewed, each team reportedly had won only three games, according to "Colored Teams Contest for the Championship," *Brooklyn Daily Times*, October 16, 1920: 8.

11   "Game at Shibe Park," *Philadelphia Evening Public Ledger*, October 6, 1920: 21. On the previous page was an ad for the game, promoting the "World's Col. Championship." Agreeing with the *Brooklyn Daily Times* that the series was tied at three wins each by the October 17 doubleheader was "Foster's Semi-Pro Nine Meets Bacharachs Today," *New York Tribune*, October 17, 1920: 22. See also Bill Nowlin, "1920 Chicago American Giants Timeline," elsewhere in this publication. It's possible a game was played that month which the teams agreed would not "count" and was merely an exhibition. That was true of the nightcap following the third game of the 1942 Negro League World Series, according to "Monarchs Trounce Grays for 3-0 Edge in Series," *Baltimore Afro-American*, September 15, 1942: 19.

12   "Bacharachs Win Double Header," *Brooklyn Daily Times*, October 11, 1920: 8. "Rube Defeats Bacharachs Twice," *Chicago Defender*, October 23, 1920: 6. "Bacharachs Beaten Twice by Chicago Giants," *Brooklyn Daily Eagle*, October 18, 1920: section 2, 2.

13   "Colored Teams Contest for the Championship," *Brooklyn Daily Times*, October 16, 1920: 8. See also the ad in the *New York Age*, October 9, 1920: 6. In addition to the first doubleheader at Ebbets Field on Sunday the 10th,

this ad promoted two other games as well, both in nearby Harrison, New Jersey, at 3:30. The same two teams played there on the 9th, while on the 11th the Bacharach Giants were to play "John J. McGraw's N.Y. Giants."

14 "The Weather," *Brooklyn Standard Union,* October 18, 1920: 2.

15 "Bacharachs Twice Beat American Giants," *Brooklyn Daily Eagle,* October 11, 1920: section 2, 4. "Bacharachs Beaten Twice by Chicago Giants." Based on searches of four Brooklyn newspapers, Jones may not have umpired any other games in Brooklyn that entire year. The umpires for the October 10 doubleheader were named "Jamieson" and Smith. Frequent Bacharachs umpire C.J. Jamison was African American but the race of umpire W.T. Smith wasn't made clear in "Baseball Dope," *Chicago Defender,* October 23, 1920: 6.

16 Based on calculated ages as well as other player data accessible via https://www.seamheads.com/NegroLgs/year.php?yearID=1920.

17 "Redding and Ryan Beaten in Twin Bill," *Brooklyn Citizen,* October 18, 1920: 5. "Redding Misses No-Hit Game," *Brooklyn Daily Times,* October 18, 1920: 7. "Bacharachs Beaten Twice by Chicago Giants."

18 "Redding Misses No-Hit Game."

19 "Redding Misses No-Hit Game."

20 "Redding Misses No-Hit Game." Oddly, the *Citizen* and *Eagle* box scores showed DeMoss with a hit in addition to Torriente and Dixon, yet also showed Chicago's total hits as just two, about which the *Times* was adamant.

21 "Colored Teams Contest for the Championship," *Brooklyn Daily Times,* October 16, 1920: 8. The first game lasted two hours, according to "Redding Misses No-Hit Game." However, the first game's duration was reported at 2 hours and 10 minutes in "Bacharachs Beaten Twice by Chicago Giants."

22 "Redding and Ryan Beaten in Twin Bill." "Redding Misses No-Hit Game." "Bacharachs Beaten Twice by Chicago Giants." The *Citizen*'s box score for the first game lists the same Bacharachs as in the other two papers' batting orders except in a somewhat different sequence, but the *Citizen*'s box score for the second game showed the batting orders exactly the same as the other two papers' box scores.

23 Based on calculated ages, accessible via https://www.seamheads.com/NegroLgs/year.php?yearID=1920.

24 "Redding Misses No-Hit Game." The details about the fourth inning were provided only by the *Times.*

25 "Redding Misses No-Hit Game."

26 "Redding Misses No-Hit Game." The *Times* came close to getting Ryan's actual first name correct. It called him "Mervin" while Seamheads shows his first name as "Merven," at https://www.seamheads.com/NegroLgs/player.php?playerID=ryan-01red.

27 "Redding and Ryan Beaten in Twin Bill."

AMERICAN GIANTS END HISTORIC SEASON WITH LOSS TO JACK QUINN-LED NORMALS

OCTOBER 31, 1920: NORMALS 4, CHICAGO AMERICAN GIANTS 2, AT SCHORLING PARK, CHICAGO

BY JOAL RYAN

It was almost November, but Rube Foster's 1920 Chicago American Giants were still at it, and taking on Jack Quinn, the spitballing 18-game winner for that season's New York Yankees. The owner-manager's team and, indeed, Foster's league, the Negro National League of Colored Base Ball Professionals (NNL), did not survive and thrive by avoiding challenges.

Foster rang in 1920 by proposing the formation of what would become the NNL. By February, the league was a reality, and by September, his American Giants were pennant-winners. Foster's achievement went beyond the standings: His league had lasted the season, a first for a Negro Leagues organization.[1] After wrapping up NNL action, the American Giants hit the road. Their postseason barnstorming tour took them first to the South and then to the East Coast, where they closed out their run by sweeping a doubleheader at Ebbets Field from the Atlantic City Bacharach Giants, an independent Negro Leagues team.[2] Then

Foster's squad returned to Chicago to play one final game. Their opponents: Jack Quinn and the Normals.

A White semipro team that played its home games at Normal Park, then the football home to the Chicago Cardinals,[3] the 1920 Normals were managed by Charley Giesman[4] and featured ever-evolving lineups that occasionally spotlighted players in between big-league stints. On October 9, 1920, for instance, Charlie Deal, the veteran third baseman for the Chicago Cubs, popped up in the Normals' starting nine just six days after playing in his National League squad's season finale.[5] The same game was to have seen the Normals give the ball to right-hander Jack Quinn, two weeks past his own final major-league start of the year.[6] (A *Chicago Tribune* box score from the Normals' October 9 game, however, shows that Normals regular Paul "Shorty" Des Jardien, not Quinn, took the mound in the game.)[7]

While the Normals primarily competed against other White semipro teams that belonged to what was known as the Chicago League,[8] they also participated in interracial exhibition games. The same was true of the American Giants. In 1920, even while playing the inaugural NNL schedule, Foster's team made time for side action with White teams from Chicago, including the Normals. That year, the Normals and American Giants first met on July 5 at Normal Park.[9] With Shorty Des Jardien on the mound for the semipros, the American Giants were held scoreless through five innings, and the Normals went up 2-0. Then, powered in part by a home run from second baseman Bingo DeMoss, the American Giants battled back with two runs each in the sixth and seventh innings, and won the game, 4-3.[10]

By the time the teams planned to meet again in the fall at the American Giants' Schorling Park, their matchup was called a "championship."[11] And while the *Chicago Tribune* used purple prose to describe the exhibition, the game was indeed to be a meeting of winners. While Foster's team had claimed the NNL pennant, the Normals, as of the October 17 results of the "three cornered series" involving the Normals, Pyotts, and Logan Squares, were Chicago's interpark champs.[12] The October 22 edition of the *Chicago Tribune* noted that the Normals "disbanded after last Sunday's game," presumably the interpark tournament finale.[13] But the paper also reported that Charley Giesman had "gathered the men together again," including Jack Quinn, for an October 24 matchup against the American Giants.[14] After rain washed out the date, the October 26 *Tribune* reported, Giesman and Rube Foster "got together ... and decided to try again Sunday."[15] The new date was October 31. Quinn remained available to the Normals, and was scheduled to start the contest at Schorling. In addition to the Yankees star, the *Tribune* promised that the Normals "will have one or two additional topnotchers."[16]

True to the reporting, the Normals' Halloween lineup bore little resemblance to the one the team had used as recently as October 9. Charlie Deal and Shorty Des Jardien were absent from the box scores, as was every other starter save catcher Leo Dixon, who had spent the bulk of 1920 with the Rock Island Islanders of the Illinois-Indiana-Iowa League, better known as the Three-I or Three-Eye League. Showing up in the batting order instead were names like Wickland, Mostil, and Pechous – presumably Al Wickland, Johnny Mostil, and Charlie Pechous, all minor-league all-stars that year with the Midwest-centric American Association.[17] Rounding out the Normals' starting lineup were Quinn, the pitcher; Leo

Dixon, the catcher; a second baseman noted only as Winkler; a left fielder listed as Schick (possibly Morrie Schick, an outfielder who was a Chicago product but who had spent the 1920 regular season on the West Coast with the Pacific Coast League's San Francisco Seals); first baseman Beale (possibly the same Beale who'd handled the position that year for the Chicago League's Samson Tractors);[18] and shortstop Daubert (presumably *not* the star big-league first baseman Jake Daubert, though possibly his cousin Harry Daubert, who had been noted as playing shortstop in 1920 for the Toledo Rail Lights, an Ohio semipro team.)[19]

Foster, meanwhile, came to play with an American Giants lineup that needed little tinkering. It included Jelly Gardner in the leadoff spot and playing right; third baseman (and future Negro Leagues manager) Dave Malarcher; second baseman Bingo DeMoss; and Robert Edward "Judy" Gans in left. Six-foot-tall "Long Tom" Johnson,[20] who was a primary right-handed weapon on Foster's roster, was the starter. Johnson's batterymate was listed in the box scores from both the *Chicago Tribune* and *Chicago Whip* as "B. Dixon" (though George Dixon was one of the American Giants' catchers in 1920). Foster's lineup card was missing two usual names: Bobby Williams, the starting shortstop; and, most notably, the team's top hitter, Cristóbal Torriente, the future Baseball Hall of Famer. (Torriente possibly was in, or en route, to his native Cuba, where days after the Normals-American Giants game, the slugger made headlines for outshining Babe Ruth in barnstorming action there.[21]) In Williams's place was a player listed alternately as "B'kwith" and "Beck'h," possibly John Beckwith, a versatile infielder from the NNL's Chicago Giants, or his brother, Stanley Beckwith, a former shortstop with the Chicago Giants. In center field in place of Torriente, and batting cleanup, was a player listed only as Hill, possibly Pete Hill, the strong-hitting outfielder of the NNL's Detroit Stars (and an American Giants alumnus).

Game day in Chicago was unseasonably warm, with an afternoon high of 60 degrees. *Chicago Whip* sportswriter Julius Culpepper described the turnout as consisting of a "very large crowd of dyed in the wool fans."[22] But it turned out to be a trying day for the Schorling Park faithful. Jack Quinn was on, striking out 12; and Tom Johnson was not, "pitching a bum of a game," as Culpepper wrote. Johnson walked four in an outing that saw him relieved in the third by right-hander Tom Williams, owner of one of the stingiest ERAs in 1920 NNL play (1.83). Inheriting a mess,

Williams gave up a two-run triple to his first batter, the Normals' Schick, but then settled in and painted "a beauty" of a game, Culpepper reported. In all, the Normals posted four runs in the third – the only scoring they needed. Quinn gave up just four hits and held Foster's crew to two runs, both of which came in the sixth inning due to what the *Chicago Tribune* called "[w]abbly [*sic*] fielding."[23] (The box scores in the local Chicago papers show errors were charged to the Normals' Schick and Daubert; Judy Gans was assessed the American Giants' lone error.) The Normals won the game, 4-2 – a close outcome that the *Tribune* nonetheless described as a "trounc[ing]."[24] The Black press was not much more forgiving. Culpepper described the American Giants' loss as a "disastrous defeat."[25] Ultimately, though, the *Whip* writer noted that there was no shame in how things played out. "The fact that the Fosterites were beaten," Culpepper wrote, "does not say they were outclassed. ..."[26] Rube Foster's Chicago American Giants lost their last game, but by surviving and thriving in a history-making season, they still had won the first war.

SOURCES

In addition to the sources cited in the notes below, the author consulted Baseball-Reference.com, Seamheads.com, Bravehost (negroleagues.bravehost.com/aab.html), and The Encyclopedia of Chicago (online) at www.encyclopedia.chicagohistory.org/pages/114.html.

NOTES

1 For more on Foster, see Larry Lester, "Andrew (Rube) Foster: Gem of a Man," in *From Rube to Robinson: SABR's Best Articles on Black Baseball* (2020): 30.

2 "Rube Defeats Bacharachs Twice," *Chicago Defender*, October 23, 1920: 6.

3 Normal Park History, Pro-Football-Reference.com, https://www.pro-football-reference.com/stadiums/CHI94.htm. Accessed on January 7, 2022.

4 "Star Girl Nines Clash Today at Pyott Diamond," *Chicago Tribune*, August 28, 1920: 9.

5 "Star Girl Nines Clash Today at Pyott Diamond."

6 "Semi-Pros Stage Big Games Today," *Chicago Tribune*, October 9, 1920: 15.

7 "Two Hits Off Des Jardien; Normals Win Game, 6 to 0," *Chicago Tribune*, October 10, 1920: 18.

8 "Semipros Book 18 Sunday Tilts," *Munster* (Indiana) *Times*, May 11, 1920: 9.

9 "Buckeye of Normals Pitches 5th Shutout as Team Splits Even," *Chicago Tribune*, July 6, 1920: 23.

10 Dave Wyatt, "Rogan Stops the American Giants," *Chicago Defender*, July 10, 1920: 9.

11 "Rebook Baseball Game," *Chicago Tribune*, October 26, 1920: 20.

12 "Squares Defeat Pyotts 7-3: Give Normals Title," *Chicago Tribune*, October 18, 1920: 18.

13 "Jack Quinn to Hurl for Normals Against Giants," *Chicago Tribune*, October 22, 1920: 18.

14 "Jack Quinn to Hurl for Normals Against Giants."

15 "Jack Quinn to Hurl for Normals Against Giants."

16 "Jack Quinn to Hurl for Normals Against Giants."

17 "Semi-Pros Stage Big Games Today," *Chicago Tribune*, October 9, 1920: 15.

18 "Kipps Beaten 12 to 0 in Final Tilt with Samons; Lose on Saturday 12 to 4," *Capital Times* (Madison, Wisconsin), September 13, 1920: 6.

19 Untitled item, *Neodesha* (Kansas) *Register*, July 29, 1920: 6. (A more direct link between Harry Daubert and the Chicago semipro baseball scene of 1920 might be found in a *Chicago Tribune* item of August 7, 1920, "Niesen Signs Rail Lights Shortstop for Samson Game" [page 7]. The brief notes that "Jake Daubert," described as the "star shortstop of the Toledo Rail Lights, and also a cousin of the champion Reds' first sacker," was bound for the Pyotts, a Chicago rival of the Normals. That information, save for the name, jibes with the *Neodesha Register* item, and it would seem that the *Tribune* confused Jake Daubert for Harry Daubert.)

20 Julius Culpepper, "Normals Defeat Giants," *Chicago Whip*, November 6, 1920: 5.

21 Alex Coffey, "Cristóbal Torriente Bests the Bambino," National Baseball Hall of Fame, last accessed on January 7, 2022: https://baseballhall.org/discover-more/stories/going-deep/cristobal-torriente-bests-the-bambino.

22 "Normals Defeat Giants."

23 "Jack Quinn Too Much and Normals Win, 4-2 for American Giants," *Chicago Tribune*, November 1, 1920: 18.

24 "Jack Quinn Too Much and Normals Win, 4-2 for American Giants."

25 "Normals Defeat Giants."

26 "Normals Defeat Giants."

"WE ARE THE SHIP, ALL ELSE THE SEA": THE FOUNDING OF THE NEGRO NATIONAL LEAGUE

BY JOHN BAUER

As witnessed during commemorations in 2020 celebrating a century of Negro League baseball, the foundation of the Negro National League in 1920 provides a generally accepted starting point for Black baseball's league era. Black baseball, through the experience of Black ballplayers and the establishment of clubs that became institutions, already had a history that stretched decades back into the nineteenth century. Also, while 1920 may have been the watershed year in the establishment of a league of Black ballclubs, the idea of creating such a league among top Black clubs was not new; and those efforts also formed part of the prehistory of Negro League baseball.

There had been an effort as early as 1886 to organize the Southern League of Colored Base Ballists, which was followed up by an 1887 attempt to organize the League of Colored Base Ball Clubs among teams in the East and Midwest.[1] Neither effort gained much traction. The top Black clubs of the time, such as the Cuban Giants, may have found barnstorming to be more profitable. The next serious effort to organize a league was almost two decades later. An Eastern circuit of six clubs dubbed the International League of Colored Baseball Clubs in America and Cuba (ILBCAC), led by Walter Schlichter and his then-dominant Philadelphia Giants, materialized in early 1906. That effort morphed into another effort by Schlichter and other power brokers (many of whom, like Schlichter, were White) in Eastern Black baseball to form a league in October of that year. Schlichter and promoters John Connor and Nat Strong backed plans to form the National Association of Colored Baseball Clubs of the United States and Cuba (NACBC) on a model similar to the American and National Leagues.[2] The NACBC, however, would come to operate very differently, acting more like as a booking agent for Eastern and Midwestern clubs than as a traditional baseball league.[3]

Chicago's Frank Leland, owner of the Midwestern powerhouse Leland Giants, was part of an effort in 1907 to create a professional league among interested Midwestern cities. The National Colored Baseball League was the product of a meeting in Indianapolis in December 1907; however, the league quickly fell apart and never played a game. Recognizing the counterproductive effects of player raiding and contract jumping, attorney Beauregard Mosely of the Leland Giants led an effort in 1910 to bring together the leading clubs of the Midwest and South. Mosely published a 17-point manifesto that addressed governance, admission prices, transportation costs, and player salaries, among many topics.[4] Eight clubs were represented at an

Hall of Famer Rube Foster, portrayed here in a Chicago American Giants uniform, was renowned for his pitching ability before becoming a legend as the founder of the first Negro National League in 1920.

organizational meeting in Chicago in December 1910, but only a few had credible financial backing.[5] The product of that meeting, the Negro National Baseball League of America, also collapsed as quickly as it formed; travel costs were deemed too great to permit the clubs to be profitable.[6]

Led by Rube Foster, the Chicago American Giants were born from a split with the Leland Giants to become the elite club of the 1910s. The American Giants profited from a combination of barnstorming through the West and South, while arranging "championship" series against the leading clubs of the East and Midwest. Foster became a powerful voice for organizing Black baseball similarly to the major leagues throughout the decade. Penning articles in Black newspapers including the *Chicago Defender* and *Indianapolis Freeman*, Foster pressed the case that better organization would improve the legitimacy and public perception of Black baseball.

In January 1917, player-turned-sportswriter Sol White joined with others in announcing intentions to form a Negro Baseball League; that effort also failed,

primarily through the disruptions caused by World War I. The war was perhaps an unlikely contributor to the eventual formation of the Negro National League. Factories in Northern cities required labor to build the machines that would propel America and her allies to victory. The Great Migration witnessed the emigration of millions of Southern Blacks to the cities of the Northeast and Midwest. In Chicago, the Black population more than doubled between 1910 and 1920, growing from 44,000 to 110,000.[7] The Black populations of other Northern cities also swelled, increasing the potential audience for Black ballclubs. Sol White would again be active after the war, outlining plans for an effective and compact circuit comprising established teams with home ballparks and traveling teams that would float among stadiums.

Following on White's work, momentum increased for an organized Black league in late 1919. With the war over and clubs such as the American Giants coming off financially successful seasons, the timing seemed right. Sports journalist Carey B. Lewis, writing in the *Chicago Defender*, predicted a Midwestern league run by Black entrepreneurs for the 1920 season. Foster, who was never shy about expressing his views on the state of Black baseball and the need to organize, offered detailed opinions in a series of articles that appeared in the *Chicago Defender* between November 1919 and January 1920. Foster focused on the "Pitfalls of Baseball," many of which were exacerbated by the lack of organization within the Black game. Foster commented on scheduling, leadership, business judgment, player defections, and stadium availability. He urged other Black baseball magnates to set aside past differences and create an effective structure. "We cannot get along without an organization," Foster wrote.[8] In his final article, he proposed a national association of Western and Eastern circuits culminating in the championship series, but noted the previous failure of such expansive efforts.[9] Nonetheless, Foster announced a meeting to be held in Kansas City in February 1920 with the goal of organizing a league that proved predominantly Midwestern.

Foster's proposal received "cautious support" from Indianapolis ABCs manager C.I. Taylor and sportswriter Dave Wyatt in subsequent issues of *The Competitor*.[10] As Taylor stated, "We have the goods, but we haven't the organization to deliver them."[11] Foster and Taylor had feuded during an intense rivalry between their clubs in the mid-1910s as Taylor claimed Foster rebuffed his earlier suggestions to organize a league.[12] Now, the two rivals appeared to share the same vision. Wyatt expressed concerns that demand for talent outweighed the supply, and it would be challenging to maintain competitive balance within an eight-team league.[13] Foster worked to set the foundation for a successful meeting in Kansas City, traveling to recruit principally the owners of Midwestern clubs in an effort to complete a circuit. In the specific case of Kansas City, Foster sided with White promoter J.L. Wilkinson over local Black businessmen as Wilkinson converted his All Nations team into the Kansas City Monarchs. Wilkinson crucially had access to the ballpark where the American Association Blues played their games. Foster also courted Eastern clubs, including Ed Bolden and the Hilldale club outside of Philadelphia, but those efforts did not reap immediate dividends.[14]

Indeed, an organizational meeting of Midwestern teams was held at the Paseo YMCA and Street's Hotel in Kansas City on February 13 and 14, 1920. The clubs and representatives in attendance were: Chicago American Giants, Rube Foster; Chicago Giants, Joe Green; Detroit Stars, Tenny Blount; Indianapolis ABCs, C.I. Taylor; Kansas City Monarchs, J.L.

Courtesy Noir-Tech Research, Inc.)

Second baseman Bingo DeMoss spent 11 of his 21 seasons in the Negro Leagues with the Chicago American Giants and was a member of the franchise's first three NNL championship squads from 1920 to 1922.

Wilkinson; and St. Louis Giants, Lorenzo Cobb. Although not present, the Cuban Stars and Dayton Marcos rounded out the league. Cuban Stars owner Abe Molina voiced support for the effort and gave Foster his proxy for the meeting.[15] Dayton Marcos owner John Matthews is listed as an attendee in some reports but it appears that the flu kept him in Ohio. Foster came prepared to the meeting, and he created a mild surprise when he presented the delegates with drafts of the corporate charter and articles of incorporation for the new league. Versions of the latter had already been filed in several states where the league would operate and several where it would not.[16]

In addition to the clubs represented at the meeting, several sportswriters were present, not just to report on the events but to play an active role in the league's proceedings. In fact, Lewis, Elwood Knox of the *Indianapolis Freeman*, and Charles Marshall and Dave Wyatt of the *Indianapolis Ledger* were joined by attorney Elisha Scott, from nearby Topeka, Kansas, in drafting the league's constitution. Scott served as the lead drafter for the governing documents. In the constitution, the league was officially known as the National Association of Colored Professional Base Ball Clubs, but Negro National League became the standard reference to the new circuit. To sign on formally, the clubs agreed to pay a $500 deposit, respect contracts, and play a schedule of league matches.

In order to facilitate competitive balance, some players were transferred between clubs. This process was overseen by the sportswriters, and several impact players changed hands. Oscar Charleston, who joined Chicago in 1919, returned to Indianapolis, where he played previously from 1915 to 1918. Sam Crawford, who spent most of his career in Chicago but played for Detroit in 1919, was sent to Kansas City, along with former All-Nations players and fellow pitchers Jose Mendez and John Donaldson. Pitcher-outfielder Jimmie Lyons transferred from St. Louis to Detroit, although he would land in Chicago the following season.

Foster was named league president and secretary, a role that set up potential conflicts of interest between his league office and his roles of owner and manager of a member club. St. Louis club official W.E. Ferance pointed out the absurdity of complaints about Foster the manager, being sent to Foster the secretary, to be ruled on by Foster the president. Another source of criticism concerned the provision that Foster's booking agency received a fee for all games. Clubs were committed to the 5 percent assessment, which meant

Foster pocketed 10 percent of every gate; owners grumbled about this throughout Foster's presidency. The league treasury also received 10 percent of all receipts, which, when combined with rental fees and visiting club guarantees, took a significant bite into profitability in this and future seasons. Foster would also receive criticism for engineering the league schedule to ensure that a greater proportion of lucrative weekend games were played at Schorling Park.

The NNL initially intended to commence operations in 1921 in order to allow clubs enough time to secure playing facilities. Only a handful of clubs, including Chicago, Indianapolis, and Kansas City, had stable ballpark arrangements. Nonetheless, adapting a quote from Frederick Douglass, the league embraced the motto, "We Are the Ship, All Else the Sea," and announced in late February its intent to start play in 1920. Ballpark availability indeed had an effect on scheduling arrangements, particularly with the Chicago Giants and Cuban Stars operating exclusively as traveling teams. As a result, the NNL had an unbalanced scheduling format and also permitted the scheduling of games against nonleague competition to boost gate receipts.

The first recognized NNL game was played on May 2, 1920 with the Chicago Giants visiting the ABCs at Indianapolis's Washington Park. Behind Ed "Huck" Rile's pitching, the ABCs claimed a 4-2 victory before 8,000 fans. The ABCs appeared likely to be one of the contending teams for the NNL pennant. Not only was Oscar Charleston back in town, the team had maintained key pieces from a roster that challenged the American Giants for championships in the mid-1910s. First baseman Ben Taylor (one of several brothers whom C.I. Taylor would manage) and left fielder George Shively provided punch to a formidable lineup. In addition to Rile, Dizzy Dizmukes and Dicta Johnson remained pitching holdovers from prior championship teams. Dismukes and Johnson would make up the innings lost when Rile jumped his contract in midseason for the Eastern Lincoln Giants.

The formation of the NNL did not resolve all of the issues that impeded league formation in the past, and challenges remained apparent throughout the season. Despite efforts at player redistribution, competitive balance proved to be an issue. The Chicago Giants suffered from their status as a traveling team; records credit the team with only five league wins out of 36 games; the Giants logged only about half as many league games as other NNL clubs. The offense ranked near the bottom of the league although veteran

Outfielder/Pitcher Cristóbal Torriente, a member of both the National Baseball Hall of Fame and Cuban Baseball Hall of Fame, was also a member of the American Giants' first three NNL championship teams.

outfielders Frank Duncan and Horace Jenkins (formerly of the American Giants) and third baseman Willie Green led the lineup. Nineteen-year-old catcher (also named) Frank Duncan and 20-year-old shortstop John Beckwith were at the beginning of what proved to be long Negro League careers, but neither could help the Giants avoid the cellar. The pitching was the league's worst by most measures, with John Taylor throwing generally solid innings for which his won-lost record did him no justice; the rest of the staff was subpar, including a now-fading Walter Ball, who was winless in his NNL starts. Along with the Giants, the Dayton Marcos were also overmatched. Candy Jim Taylor was near the start of a managerial career that featured three Black baseball championships, but his Marcos were a seventh-place team. Though 36 years old, Taylor also served as the regular third baseman and still had enough spring in his step to steal a fair number of bases. Left fielder Koke Alexander was the only regular who produced offensively on a consistent basis. Similar to Taylor in Chicago, George Britt proved an effective starter among a staff otherwise lacking; his career would see better days in coming years with the Homestead Grays.

The Cuban Stars featured a lineup of four future Cuban Hall of Fame inductees, including manager Tinti Molina. Outfielders Valentin Dreke and Bernardo Baro, also future inductees, supplied the most significant contributions from an otherwise weak-hitting squad. Pitchers Jose Leblanc, Cheo Hernandez, and Faustino Valdes threw all but a handful of innings; their collective effectiveness ranked near of the top of the NNL and helped the club eke out a winning record at 35-34, which was good enough for fifth place.

The American Giants raced out to a commanding position, winning 32 of their first 37 games.[17] This achievement may not have been apparent to fans, as the NNL failed to produce standings, box scores, or batting and pitching statistics that might have enhanced interest. Foster's team had been expected to be challenged by the aforementioned Indianapolis ABCs as well as St. Louis, Detroit, and Kansas City. The St. Louis Giants, however, struggled during the campaign. Young pitchers Bill Drake and Wayne Carr joined veteran John Finner in throwing most of the innings, but their production was average at best. Deprived of Lyons through the preseason player reshuffling, the offense proved similarly average. While they lacked pop, these Giants definitely had speed with second baseman Lee Hill and outfielder Charlie Blackwell among the most active NNL players on the basepaths. Ultimately, player-manager Dick Wallace led St. Louis to a 32-40 record and a sixth-place finish.

Indianapolis joined Kansas City and Detroit among the chasing pack after the American Giants stormed through the first half of the league schedule. The ABCs wound up in fourth with a record of 44-38-4. Wilkinson built a formidable challenger from the remnants of the All Nations team. The acquisitions Crawford, Mendez, and Donaldson hurled key innings for the Monarchs, especially when combined with innings-leader Rube Curry and future Hall of Famer Bullet Rogan; Rogan was just getting started in dominating the mound through the 1920s. Rogan, Donaldson, and Mendez also contributed beyond the mound. Mendez served as player-manager and the "player" part of that title included part-time shortstop despite a weak bat. Rogan and Donaldson manned the outfield most days when they were not pitching, both batting near .300 and swiping several bases for good measure. George Carr, Bartolo Portuondo, and Hurley McNair exemplified the Monarchs' potent combination of hitting for average and stealing bases

once they got on base. The rise of the Detroit Stars as a creditable challenger to the American Giants in 1919 carried over to the 1920 season. American Giants alumnus Pete Hill managed the Stars while also taking regular assignments in the outfield. Hill was joined by former Chicago teammates catcher Bruce Petway and pitcher Bill Gatewood. The addition of Lyons, with his impressive combination of slugging and speed, added to the sense of expectation. On the mound, Bill Holland worked alongside Gatewood in providing as daunting a one-two punch as any club.

Ultimately, as happened throughout the prior decade of independent play, the American Giants proved too strong for the competition. Chicago won the inaugural NNL pennant with a .717 winning percentage (43-17-2), besting nearest challengers Kansas City (44-33-2, .571, 7½ games behind) and Detroit (37-27, .578, 8 games behind) by a comfortable margin. Outfielder Cristobal Torriente and second baseman Bingo DeMoss paced an offense that possessed neither overwhelming power nor speed, but had a knack for getting on base long before the value of walks became appreciated. Backstop Jim Brown minimized any sense of loss by Petway's departure to Detroit in 1919. Former Star Dave Malarcher commenced a long association with the American Giants, as third baseman and later as Foster's managerial successor. Foster's days on the mound were over, but the pitching was in capable hands. Tom Williams, recruited from Hilldale, joined Dave Brown and Tom Johnson in anchoring the NNL's most imposing group of pitchers. The American Giants were effectively wire-to-wire champions notwithstanding the absence of daily standings and box scores to mark the accomplishment.

While managing his club to the title, Foster also wore his league-president "hat" in continuing to promote the idea of a truly national association of Black clubs. His efforts led to the Atlantic City Bacharach Giants accepting associate membership status during the campaign. The NNL had agreed not to raid the roster of an associate member. In return for not having their players poached, the Bacharach Giants agreed to travel west to play against NNL clubs. With Cannonball Dick Redding pitching, NNL teams did not mind the attendance boost that usually accompanied a Bacharach Giants visit. After the season, the newly minted champion American Giants traveled east to return the favor, meeting the Bacharach Giants at major-league venues Ebbets Field and Shibe Park. In that series of games, Foster saw the potential for a

Black World Series that would match the best of East and West.[18]

The December league meeting in Indianapolis provided the capstone to a successful NNL season. It was claimed that one million fans had patronized NNL games; other sources peg the figure at closer to 600,000.[19] Whatever the exact figure, the league appeared to have been a financial success, with Foster proclaiming all clubs profitable; and the meeting featured constitutional changes to secure those gains. To maintain respectability with the public, the owners approved changes to fine or punish inappropriate conduct by owners and players and prohibited managers from yanking their teams off the field as acts of protest. To bind the clubs even more closely to the association, the deposit was also increased to $1,000. With Foster continuing to think nationally, Eastern power Hilldale joined Atlantic City as an associate member, and their deposit would be the subject of a dispute when the Pennsylvania club joined the Eastern Colored League in 1923. There were changes for the NNL's Ohio contingent, as the Dayton Marcos moved to Columbus for 1921 with Sol White managing the re-christened Buckeyes; meanwhile, the Cuban Stars secured Redland Field in Cincinnati as a home base. The "ship" had proved seaworthy, so to speak, and the NNL was poised to continue an upward trajectory in building off the successes of the 1920 season.

SOURCES

In addition to the sources cited in the Notes, the author consulted the following:

baseball-reference.com

seamheads.com (statistical references and roster information are generally to this website.)

Graf, John, ed. *From Rube to Robinson: SABR's Best Articles on Black Baseball* (Phoenix: Society for American Baseball Research, 2020).

Holway, John B. *Blackball Stars: Negro League Pioneers* (Westport, Connecticut: Meckler Books, 1988).

Peterson, Robert. *Only the Ball Was White* (New York: Oxford University Press, 1970).

Riley, James A. *The Biographical Encyclopedia of the Negro Baseball Leagues* (New York: Carroll & Graf Publishers, 1994).

NOTES

1   Neil Lanctot, *Fair Dealing & Clean Playing: The Hilldale Club and the Development of Black Professional Baseball, 1910-1932* (Syracuse, New York: Syracuse University Press, 1994), 79.

2   Michael E. Lomax, *Black Baseball Entrepreneurs, 1902-1931: The Negro National and Eastern Colored Leagues* (Syracuse, New York: Syracuse University Press, 2014), 39.

3   Lomax, 57.

4   Mark Ribowsky, *A Complete History of the Negro Leagues: 1884 to 1955* (Toronto: Citadel Press, 1995), 123.

5   Lomax, 101.

6   Paul Debono, *The Chicago American Giants* (Jefferson, North Carolina: McFarland & Co., Inc., 2007), 36.

7   Lanctot, *Fair Dealing*, 72.

8   Larry Lester, *Rube Foster in His Time: On the Field and in the Papers with Black Baseball's Greatest Visionary* (Jefferson, North Carolina: McFarland & Co., Inc., 2012), 113.

9   Lomax, 247.

10 Lanctot, 82.

11 Lester, 116.

12 Lanctot, 82.

13 Lanctot, 83.

14 Ribowsky, *A Complete History of the Negro Leagues*, 103.

15 Lomax, 250.

16 Debono, 75.

17 Lanctot, 84.

18 Debono, 80.

19 Debono 82; Lomax, 39.

THE CHICAGO AMERICAN GIANTS: A HISTORY

BY JOHN BAUER

The arc of the history of the Chicago American Giants follows closely with the arc of Black and Negro League baseball in the United States. The story of one cannot be told without the other. The American Giants were born from the baseball genius and business acumen of Rube Foster, a titanic figure without whom any history of the Negro Leagues would also be incomplete. While the name "Chicago American Giants" might be time-stamped with 1911, their history effectively stretches backward an approximate quarter-century to the Chicago Unions from the early years of Black baseball in the Windy City.

The Unions emerged as the city's top Black team around 1886, and the club soon came under the sponsorship of Frank Leland and other Black businessmen, including W.S. Peters.[1] Leland became an influential figure in the establishment of baseball as an institution in Chicago's Black community. By 1896, the Unions had become a professional club, and Leland's connections helped to secure playing fields in Chicago at a time when grounds could not be taken for granted. The Unions soon had company when the Page Fence Giants, one of the early powers of Black baseball, moved from Michigan to Chicago in 1899 and adopted the name Columbia Giants. The Unions and Columbia Giants both enjoyed success and competed in championship series with top Black clubs from New York. By 1901, the Union club split apart with Frank Leland consolidating his faction with the financially tottering Columbia Giants to form the Chicago Union Giants. The following year, a young Texas pitcher already in possession of an outsized reputation joined the Union Giants: Rube Foster. Though Foster joined the Philadelphia Giants in 1904, he returned within a few seasons. Meanwhile, Leland's team adopted the name Leland Giants in 1905 and, through formation of the Leland Giants Baseball and Amusement Company, secured the financial backing that stabilized the ballclub and positioned Leland as the top Black baseball owner in the Midwest.[2]

Leland recruited Foster back to Chicago in 1907, and Foster brought several Philadelphia Stars teammates with him, including outfielder Pete Hill and catcher Pete Booker. The American Giants began playing games at South Side Park, attracting good crowds at the home of Charles Comiskey's White Sox. As Leland became more active in Chicago politics and dealt with health issues, Foster consolidated his position over on-field and off-field affairs. As manager, Foster swapped out players originally brought in by Leland with his own men, an effort that resulted in the 1909 Chicago City League championship. While learning the business and collecting fees as a booking agent, Foster also aligned himself with Beauregard Mosely, the lead lawyer for the Leland Giants Baseball and Amusement Company, and Major R.R. Jackson, a previous financial backer of Leland. Tensions between Leland and Foster festered and by 1910 the Foster-Mosely-Jackson combination forced Leland out of his own company. Leland announced his plans to form a new baseball club but shockingly lost a lawsuit over the use of the Leland Giants name. Foster and Mosely maintained control over the Leland Giants while Leland formed the Chicago Giants. The 1910 Leland Giants may have been the finest team Foster assembled for a baseball season, with second baseman Grant Johnson, shortstop John Henry Lloyd, pitcher Frank Wickware, and catcher Bruce Petway supplementing an already strong team. Foster claimed the Black world championship for the Leland Giants with 123 wins against a mere six losses.[3]

By the following season, 1911, Foster had left the Leland Giants and launched the Chicago American Giants. After barnstorming in the spring, the American Giants played their home opener on May 13 at South Side Park, by now the former home of the White Sox. Foster secured the grounds through a partnership with John Schorling, who had control of the site through his connections to Comiskey. He renamed the field Schorling Park, which was appropriate considering his layout of $10,000 on renovations[4] that included a new 9,000-seat grandstand. Mosely and the Leland Giants gradually withdrew into local baseball, and Leland himself took more interest in politics before his death in 1914. The field was effectively cleared in Chicago for Foster and the American Giants, and Schorling Park became the stage for their ambitions.

Foster signed pitcher Bill Gatewood and third baseman Candy Jim Taylor for the 1912 season, one in which Foster claimed 112 wins from 132 games as well as the "colored" championship. Foster took the American Giants to the West Coast for the 1912-13 winter season, and the team won the California Winter League championship. That became the pattern for much of the decade: The American Giants combined winter barnstorming through the West and South with summer series against the leading clubs of the East and Midwest for unofficial championships of Black baseball. For the 1913 season, the American Giants returned an almost intact roster except for Wickware. Foster agreed to a championship series with the Lincoln Giants of New York. The teams battled in a tightly contested series in Chicago over a three-week period with outfielder-pitcher Judy Gans outdueling Gatewood in the deciding match to secure a 4-1 victory and the "World's Colored Championship" for the Lincoln Giants.

Foster soon had competition in his Midwestern backyard as the Indianapolis ABCs emerged as a credible rival. Managed by C.I. Taylor, the club aggressively recruited talent in the face of local competition from the Federal League's Indianapolis Hoosiers. With a lineup that included C.I.'s brothers Candy Jim, Steel Arm, and Ben, as well as George Shively, the ABCs challenged the American Giants to a championship series. Chicago won seven of 11 games against Indianapolis in 1914 and then claimed another "Colored Championship" after sweeping four games from the Brooklyn Royal Giants. In response, Taylor added Oscar Charleston, Bingo DeMoss, and Dizzy Dismukes in preparation for a 1915 rematch. After the American Giants won three of five games at Schorling Park in June, the series shifted to Indianapolis in July. The Indianapolis leg was characterized by chippy play on the field and heated rhetoric between Foster and Taylor. The first game was forfeited to the ABCs by the umpires due to alleged stalling by Foster, the specific events of which were hotly disputed. The next day, police intervened twice in an ABCs victory. After Chicago dropped two more games and thus the series, a war of words in the Black press erupted between Foster and Taylor. Despite the results, Foster tried to claim the championship of Black baseball.

Foster set about improving the American Giants ahead of a 1915-16 winter barnstorming tour, adding first baseman (and ex-American Giant) Leroy Grant.

Published on the eve of Opening Day of the Negro National League, the Chicago Defender *ran a schedule showing the array of games planned for the day.*

The ABCs remained the primary thorn in Foster's side in 1916, and a series of games in Indianapolis in October and November ended again in controversy. Foster removed his team from the field in one game after an argument with an umpire about whether he could wear a glove in the coaching box. The question of the championship remained the subject of recriminations between the two managers, with the budding rivalry providing mixed publicity for Black baseball. Before the 1917 season, Foster signed second baseman Bingo DeMoss and pitcher Cannonball Dick Redding. The American Giants seemed poised for success, but World War I affected baseball as players were drafted into the armed forces and reductions in playing schedules were necessitated. Nonetheless, between the American Giants and his fledgling booking agency, Foster squeezed in enough baseball to keep the turnstiles moving at Schorling Park. To assist with the war effort, the American Giants and ABCs barnstormed through major-league ballparks, with Chicago taking 15 of 19 games.[5]

Lloyd and Wickware moved east with the Brooklyn Royal Giants, furthering weakening the team, although former foe Judy Gans was now in the fold. Chicago scheduled games in the East to take on emerging powers in Hilldale and the Bacharach Giants, but the depleted American Giants were swept for their troubles. Foster added outfielders Oscar Charleston and Cristobal Torriente for the 1919 season, but by this time, a new Midwestern rival was emerging. With several former American Giants in the fold, including player-manager Pete Hill, the Detroit Stars became the next contender for the throne. In a series between the clubs, the American Giants claimed five wins in the first six games before the Stars stormed back with five straight wins. After a delay of a few weeks because of race riots in Chicago, the American Giants won the final two games, 2-1 and 5-3, to take the series in Detroit. The American Giants headed farther east, swinging through New York and Pennsylvania for games against leading Eastern clubs. The successful tours generated a profit of $15,000 for the 1919 season,[6] putting the American Giants on solid financial footing.

In the offseason, Foster penned a series of articles in the *Chicago Defender* on the state of Black baseball. The "Pitfalls of Baseball" became a launching point for another attempt at forming a Black baseball league. This time the efforts proved successful. After a series of meetings in Kansas City in February 1920 for a league to start play in 1921, the Negro National League brought forward its plans by a year and started play in May 1920. As part of the effort to achieve competitive balance, players were moved across teams. That effort required Chicago to sacrifice Charleston, who returned to Indianapolis. The American Giants assembled a formidable squad. Dave Malarcher emerged as the regular third baseman, Torriente returned to play center field, and Tom Williams, Dave Brown, and Tom Johnson anchored a solid pitching staff. Chicago won the inaugural NNL pennant with a .717 winning percentage (43-17-2), besting nearest challenger, Kansas City (44-33-2, .571, 7½ games behind) and Detroit (37-27, .578, 8 games behind) by a comfortable margin. After the season, Chicago traveled east to play the Atlantic City Bacharach Giants in a precursor to a Black World Series that matched the top teams from the East and West, with the two clubs staging a series of games at Ebbets Field and Shibe Park.

Heading into 1921, Gans left Chicago to become manager of the Lincoln Giants and was replaced in the outfield by Jimmie Lyons from Detroit. Chicago claimed another NNL pennant but this time with a smaller margin over the St. Louis Stars. For 1922, Foster revamped his pitching staff with Ed "Huck" Rile signing from Columbus, former American Giant Dick Whitworth rejoining from Hilldale, and Cuban pitcher Juan Luis Padron landing in Chicago. The purchase of infielder John Beckwith from the Chicago Giants bolstered the lineup for a competitive pennant race. The American Giants narrowly won their third straight pennant on a percentage points basis ahead of Indianapolis, Kansas City, and Detroit.

With the founding of the Eastern Colored League for the 1923 season, the NNL had competition for players, and the American Giants were no exception. Rile and Brown defected to ECL clubs, leaving Chicago without a pitching ace. Rile returned in response to Foster's edict banning ECL defectors who did not return to their NNL clubs, and led the club with 15 wins. The NNL remained generally stable in the face of ECL competition, with Chicago, Detroit, Indianapolis, Kansas City, and St. Louis on decent footing. To shore up the circuit, Foster recruited the Memphis Red Sox and Birmingham Black Barons as associate members, and he acquired his half-brother, pitcher Willie Foster, from Memphis in the process. In the end, the Monarchs claimed their first pennant, just ahead of the second-place American Giants. An anonymous letter was published in Black newspapers purportedly written by American Giants players, stating that they did not play hard because Foster did not pay well; Foster disputed the letter's contents.[7]

The NNL and the American Giants continued to suffer ECL defections before the 1924 season. Oscar Charleston left Indianapolis for Harrisburg, Pennsylvania, and the ABCs folded in midseason. To prevent similar actions, Foster used the relative financial largess of the American Giants to keep other clubs afloat.[8] The American Giants were not immune to losses to ECL clubs, as Beckwith and Lyons joined the Baltimore Black Sox and Washington Potomacs, respectively, and Chicago again finished runner-up to the pennant-winning Monarchs. It was unclear how long the NNL-ECL war could continue, and a compromise seemed necessary. Indeed, the two leagues agreed to cease player raiding and to compensate for past contract-jumping, accommodations that made possible a Colored World Series between the two league champions. Kansas City defeated Hilldale in a 10-game Series that was staged in multiple cities before disappointing crowds.

The NNL adopted a split-season format for 1925, in which the winners of each 50-game half were to meet in a championship series. Huck Rile was shipped to the revived Indianapolis ABCs to assist with roster balance, but Padron led the staff and even won the Schorling Park home opener with a shutout against Kansas City. The American Giants took three of five against the defending NNL champs, but the auspicious start did not last. During a road trip to Indianapolis in May, Foster was found on the floor of a boarding house bathroom after he had apparently been overcome by natural gas. Neither Foster nor the American Giants seemed to recover as Chicago finished both halves of the NNL season in third place. Kansas City defeated St. Louis for the NNL title, but Hilldale avenged the prior season's loss in the World Series.

After the season, Foster conducted a makeover of the American Giants. Torriente, DeMoss, and Williams, who had been lineup fixtures since the pre-NNL days, were traded. The Torriente trade yielded George Sweatt from Kansas City; DeMoss and Williams were traded to the ABCs, where the latter was to become player-manager but kept heading east to join Homestead. Padron also departed for Indianapolis, clearing the way for Willie Foster to assume the role of staff ace. When Memphis and Birmingham left the NNL for the Negro Southern League – a circuit not included in the NNL-ECL detente – Foster poached second baseman Charley Williams and third baseman Sanford Jackson from the Memphis Red Sox and outfielder Sandy Thompson from the Birmingham Black Barons, moves that contributed directly to another championship in 1926.

The American Giants had a promising start, but the Monarchs dominated in head-to-head games, leading to a fourth-place finish in the first half of Chicago's 1926 season. More disconcerting, Foster's increasingly erratic behavior necessitated his taking a sabbatical to start the second half. Malarcher assumed the managerial duties, the first American Giants skipper other than Foster, and led Chicago to a second-half championship and a date against Kansas City for the NNL title. After falling behind four games to one, the American Giants won the next two to set up a decisive doubleheader on September 29. Willie Foster and Bullet Rogan threw shutout baseball through eight innings before Jackson's winning run in the ninth leveled the series for Chicago. With darkness approaching, the teams agreed to play five innings to decide the NNL title. Foster and Rogan again took to the mound, with Foster tossing zeros in a championship-clinching 5-0 win. The American Giants next faced the ECL champion Bacharach Giants in an 11-game Colored World Series. The first six games were played in Atlantic City, Baltimore, and Philadelphia, with the Bacharach Giants achieving a 3-1 advantage (with two tied) before the series moved to Chicago. The American Giants won three of the next four to set up a decisive Game Eleven. With Willie Foster on the mound, the game was decided in the ninth inning when Thompson's liner scored Jelly Gardner for the series-winning run. It is not clear to what extent Rube Foster enjoyed the American Giants' World Series triumph; he had been committed to an institution and spent his remaining years in care until his death in 1930. Without Foster's leadership, Black baseball lost an anchor in the face of coming challenges that led to the collapse of both leagues.

Schorling and Foster's wife, Sarah, jointly represented the American Giants at the combined NNL-ECL winter meetings in advance of the 1927 season, but Schorling began to assert the dominant hand over club matters. Although Thompson and Gardner departed (they returned the following season), Malarcher guided the American Giants to a first-half victory and then an NNL series win over second-half victor Birmingham. The Bacharach Giants again provided the opposition in the 1927 World Series. The best-of-nine series opened in Chicago, and the American Giants swept the first four games before the series headed east. The Bacharach Giants won three of the next four, with the other game ending in a tie. Chicago claimed the ninth and final game to secure another Black baseball championship, but this series was to be the last of its kind. The ECL was on the brink of collapse as economic conditions were declining, a circumstance that had particularly adverse effects for African Americans. With fewer patrons buying tickets, the ECL's finances suffered, and the league folded in the middle of the 1928 season.

Concerned about making ends meet and fearing that other owners were trying to freeze out his ballpark from staging games,[9] Schorling sold out to William Trimble, a White racetrack owner and florist. As Black baseball's belts tightened in response to challenging economic conditions, the NNL followed suit. Rosters were reduced to 14 players across the league and Trimble closely watched expenses. The club lost Gardner to the Homestead Grays and Sweatt to the US Postal Service; the latter chose steady civil-service work over the low wages offered by Trimble.[10] Malarcher departed in midseason because of his own salary dispute. Under outfielder-manager George Harney, Chicago secured the second-half title to force a championship playoff with St. Louis. The Stars edged the American Giants five games to four for the NNL pennant.

Trimble exhibited an increasingly distant style of ownership,[11] a notable change from the hands-on approach of Rube Foster. Additional players left for better-paying Postal Service jobs, playing only on weekends, if at all.[12] Harney was among the postal workers moonlighting on ball fields, and catcher-first baseman Jim Brown took over in the dugout. Brown could not steer the American Giants back to the postseason as the Monarchs claimed both halves of the 1929 NNL season to obviate the need for a championship playoff. Amid declining attendance, the American Giants scheduled postseason series to make up the shortfall. Strengthened by players from other NNL clubs, the American Giants swept the Homestead Grays in a six-game series at Schorling Park in October and then took four of six against an aggregation of White major-league players.

As the Depression gripped the country, baseball everywhere experimented with lighting systems to stimulate night-game attendance. After the Monarchs brought their portable lighting system to Schorling Park to favorable reviews, Trimble installed his own system.[13] The American Giants finished fourth overall in 1930, just above .500 in NNL play. The mediocrity was not inspiring admissions at Schorling Park, and the club again turned to barnstorming as night baseball

proved underwhelming. With new owner Charles Bidwill signing the checks, a veritable all-star team in American Giants flannels won three of four games against White major leaguers.

The American Giants were in a state of chaos ahead of the 1931 season. Bidwill seemed unsure what to do with his new asset, and several players, including Willie Foster, left the club. A group of former American Giants emerged under Malarcher's leadership as the Columbia American Giants, but this club dropped out of the NNL for independent status midway through the season. In fact, there appears to have been little roster consistency across the two seasons, and there are only 24 recorded NNL games for 1931 against 102 league games for 1930.

After the completion of the 1931 season, the NNL collapsed. The Malarcher-led team wound up in the Negro Southern League for the 1932 season, eschewing the East-West League organized by Homestead Grays owner Cum Posey. Robert Cole, a Black businessman who made his money in funeral burial insurance, acquired the lease on Schorling Park. Cole provided a home for the Malarcher club, which was identified as Cole's American Giants and then as the Chicago American Giants. Willie Foster rejoined the team and Turkey Stearnes was signed to play center field. By whatever prefix, the American Giants rode a first-half championship into a playoff against the Nashville Elite Giants. With a 4-3 series win, the American Giants claimed what was to be their final league championship.

The remaining two decades of American Giants did not come close to replicating the success of the 1910s and 1920s. Schorling Park had provided the American Giants with a benefit enjoyed by few Black ballclubs: an established and permanent home in proximity to where many Black patrons resided. That changed when Cole gave up the lease, which was assumed by White promoters who converted the venue into a dog track. Cole moved the *Chicago* American Giants to Indianapolis for the 1933 season (and the ABCs were shipped to Detroit). The club joined the revived Negro National League, which included many teams from the short-lived East-West League. Cole signed catcher Larry Brown, first baseman Mule Suttles, shortstop Willie Wells, and pitcher Willie "Sug" Cornelius, and kept the American Giants among the contenders for a while longer. The American Giants and Pittsburgh Crawfords battled each other for the pennant, easily outclassing the rest of the league. In a show of their hegemony for the 1933 season, the teams also dominated the West and East rosters for the inaugural All-Star Game at Comiskey Park on September 10; Willie Foster pitched a complete game in the West's 11-7 win. The pennant, however, went east as the Crawfords topped the American Giants.

The American Giants returned to Schorling Park in 1934. The dog-track venture had failed when the Illinois legislature had refused to legalize such racing,[14] and the ground had been reconverted for baseball. After two seasons with the Chicago Cardinals, Joe Lillard played a more prominent role with the American Giants as the NFL's own color barrier took hold. Lillard became the regular left fielder and Ted Trent led the pitching staff. The NNL opted for a split season and a season-ending championship series. The American Giants won the first-half title, and again supplied most of the players for the West's All-Star Game roster; Foster lost this time, dropping a 1-0 decision to the East's Satchel Paige. The NNL championship series with the Philadelphia Stars was not without problems, however. There was a lengthy delay between the fourth and fifth games and the sixth was marred by a controversy because Stars slugger Jud Wilson was allowed to remain in the game after hitting umpire Bert Gholston. Although Gholston argued initially that he did not see who struck him, Malarcher protested the decision; however, the league caved in even after the assault was verified and Wilson kept playing. After splitting the first six games, Game Seven ended with a 4-4 score because of a local curfew. One more game was played to decide the championship, and Stars ace Slim Jones capped his stellar season by outdueling Sug Cornelius, 2-0.

Malarcher left the manager's spot after four seasons in his second stint, and catcher Larry Brown took over as player-manager in 1935. The American Giants once again returned a settled core, although Lillard departed the club. Suttles may have provided the season's highlight with his walk-off home run that decided the All-Star Game. Otherwise, Chicago sank to sixth place in league play. Cole had been losing interest in the American Giants in deference to other business interests, which became an issue with other owners such as Greenlee.[15] The American Giants had been losing fans, which made road treks by Eastern clubs much less lucrative than they had been in the Rube Foster days. Cole stepped away from team affairs, and his associate, Horace Hull, assumed control. Citing travel costs, Hull withdrew the American Giants from the NNL before the 1936 season in hopes of anchoring a new alliance of Midwestern clubs.[16]

That effort failed to materialize, and a mere 18 games are formally recorded for that year as an independent club. Moreover, without league protection, Chicago was raided by NNL teams, with Suttles, Stearnes, Foster, and Alex Radcliffe among those American Giants who found new homes in the East.

Something closer to the normality of a league reason returned with the formation of the Negro American League in 1937. Hull served as chair of the NAL, which occupied a similar footprint as the original NNL. Hull hired Candy Jim Taylor to manage the American Giants, but the Negro Leagues now faced competition from the Dominican Republic in recruiting players. Herman Dunlap and newly returned Alex Radcliffe provided what passed for offense on this weak-hitting team while Cornelius, Trent, and Foster provided consistent pitching. It was enough for the American Giants to qualify for a championship playoff in the NAL's split-season format, but the Kansas City Monarchs took five out of seven games from Chicago to earn their first of many NAL crowns.

Taylor managed the keep the American Giants competitive over the next two seasons, with first-division finishes among a revolving door of teams in the NAL. Kansas City's supremacy remained a constant, however. Cornelius and Trent continued to supply innings and Dunlap, Radcliffe, and Wilson Redus led the offense. Pepper Basset joined the American Giants for 1939 after the Crawfords folded in Pittsburgh. Basset, Cornelius, and Radcliffe left after the season, as did Taylor. Redus then replaced Taylor as manager for the 1940 season, but he lasted only one season. The emergence of Donald Reeves as a power-hitting right fielder and Lefty Bowe as a potential ace could not stop the American Giants from settling into mediocrity. In fact, Bowe left during the season to join the traveling Ethiopian Clowns exhibition club. New competition from the Mexican League placed greater pressure on Negro League owners to maintain talent at reasonable wages. The year ended with a Christmas Eve arson that destroyed Schorling Park. The ballpark had been deteriorating for years, emblematic of the debt and decline that had overtaken the once great club.

Memphis native J.B. Martin, who had been active with his hometown Red Sox and eventually assumed the NAL presidency, joined a consortium that invested in the American Giants as a prelude to an eventual takeover. Martin rented Comiskey Park as a replacement for Schorling Park; however, rental costs limited the American Giants to a mere four home games in 1941.[17] Martin rejected offers from businessmen to build a new ballpark in Chicago, and the club continued to founder as Martin evinced a greater interest in Chicago politics than in the American Giants. Taylor returned as manager, and he was joined by other recent players such as Basset, Cornelius, and Radcliffe in a partial reunion of the 1939 team. Right fielder and former Crawford Jimmie Crutchfield also was added to the fold. Despite an otherwise creditable roster, the American Giants managed only a fifth-place finish in a six-team league. Taylor recruited Cool Papa Bell, returning from a stint in the Mexican League, for the 1942 season, but the team sank further as a 7-29 record marked the first time the team had finished in last place in the league era of Black baseball.

Taylor left Chicago again to become manager of the Homestead Grays, where he was joined by Bell. Center fielder Lloyd Davenport came west in the Bell trade, and 41-year-old Ted "Double Duty" Radcliffe, Alex's brother, signed from Memphis as catcher-manager. Double Duty stabilized the team in 1943 and even claimed a first-half championship. Davenport emerged as a top offensive contributor along with Alex Radcliffe (still going at 37) and left fielder John Bissant. Twenty-year-old Art Pennington started to emerge as a key player, and Gentry Jessup assumed the role of ace that he occupied for several seasons. With Birmingham claiming the second-half title, Kansas City's four-season reign atop the NAL ended; however, the NAL crown was claimed by the Birmingham Black Barons in a five-game series win over Chicago.

Martin's takeover was complete by the 1944 season, but the club could not build on the success of the prior season. Double Duty departed for Birmingham, with DeMoss returning as manager in his stead. The American Giants slumped in a season of managerial merry-go-round as DeMoss was fired in June and replaced by Davenport. Davenport attempted to join the new iteration of the Pittsburgh Crawfords but ended up being traded to Cleveland as Bissant guided the club through the remainder of a sixth-place season. Martin lured Taylor back as skipper for 1945. With Gentry Jessup, Walter McCoy, and Gready McKinnis leading the staff, and Pennington leading the offense, Chicago improved to fourth place.

The Negro Leagues were turned upside down when the Brooklyn Dodgers signed Jackie Robinson before the 1946 season. As is well known, Robinson spent the year in Montreal and made his major-league debut in 1947. As was the case with other Negro League owners, Martin became focused on protecting the Negro Leagues from encroachments by White major-league clubs.[18] Foreign leagues also remained a threat, as was evidenced by the American Giants losing second baseman Jesse Douglass, McKinnis, and Pennington to Mexico. Jessup and third baseman Clyde Nelson represented Chicago in the All-Star Game, providing the "highlight" to a last-place finish. After another last-place finish in 1947, Taylor was released from managerial duties. John Ritchey won the NAL batting crown but was poached by the Pacific Coast League's San Diego Padres without compensation after Martin forgot to offer the young backstop a contract. Though Ritchey never made it to the major leagues, he broke the PCL's color barrier in 1948. Former American Giant and catcher Quincey Trouppe was acquired from the Cleveland Buckeyes to serve as player-manager for the 1948 campaign. Chicago signed four players from Puerto Rico, including pitcher Roberto Vargas and right fielder Bienvenido Rodriguez. Another newcomer, shortstop Jim Pendleton, provided some offensive spark for the offense, but the American Giants once again finished last.

After Pendleton (to the Dodgers organization) and Pennington (to PCL Portland) departed for potential major-league opportunities, Trouppe and Vargas left due to pay disputes with Martin. Trouppe tired of Martin's parsimony, especially when the manager's plan to acquire a young Willie Mays was scrapped by Martin's refusal to pay $300 in advance money. Trouppe was replaced by Winfield Welch, who had guided Birmingham to NAL pennants in 1944 and 1945. Alvin Gipson emerged to complement Jessup's pitching as the American Giants contended in the revamped 1949 NAL. Several NNL clubs had joined the NAL after the former circuit's collapse. One of those clubs, the Baltimore Elite Giants, bested Chicago for the league championship, for which the American Giants had qualified after the Monarchs ceded the spot rather than pay the rent for the ballpark.

Double Duty Radcliffe succeeded Welch for the 1950 season, one in which the American Giants integrated. Chicago signed four White players, including two from the Chicago Industrial League, but none of them saw significant action. The anticipated attendance boost lasted exactly one game, as the American Giants drew their largest crowd of the season (8,579) on July 9 before the gate returned to its usual dismal figures the following week. Jessup's long tenure as the American Giants pitcher of the 1940s did not extend into the 1950s; the longtime rotation fixture left for

Manitoba and the ManDak League. In his place, Othello Strong led the hurlers while Douglass had an MVP season, according to the *Chicago Defender*.[19] Despite a strong season, the American Giants were denied an opportunity at the pennant because game reports had not been sent to the NAL office; instead, Kansas City was awarded the title.

Welch returned in 1951, but his title expanded beyond manager. Martin sold the club to Welch for $50,000,[20] but Welch fronted for Harlem Globetrotters promoter Abe Saperstein. Saperstein's motive was to position the American Giants to acquire Black players for the St. Louis Browns, who had been recently acquired by Bill Veeck.[21] Paige joined the American Giants for a spell before joining the Browns in July.[22] By 1952, the NAL was reduced to a six-team circuit and profits from player sales to major-league teams resulted in increasingly modest dividends. The American Giants primarily barnstormed that season, and manager Paul Hardy guided the team to a second-place finish in a four-team tournament that also included Indianapolis, Kansas City, and Philadelphia. That tournament represented the last time the American Giants competed for honors. By April 1953, the American Giants dropped out of the NAL, and the franchise folded shortly thereafter. The Negro American League hung on through 1962, but it did so without the once-proud Chicago American Giants, one of the original great clubs of Black baseball.

SOURCES

In addition to the sources cited in the Notes, the author consulted the following sources:

baseball-reference.com

seamheads.com

Graf, John, ed. *From Rube to Robinson: SABR's Best Articles on Black Baseball* (Phoenix: SABR, 2020).

Holway, John B. *Blackball Stars: Negro League Pioneers* (Westport, Connecticut: Meckler Books, 1988).

Peterson, Robert. *Only the Ball Was White* (New York: Oxford University Press, 1970).

Riley, James A. *The Biographical Encyclopedia of the Negro Baseball Leagues* (New York: Carroll & Graf Publishers, 1994).

NOTES

1   Mark Ribowsky, *A Complete History of the Negro Leagues: 1884 to 1955* (Toronto: Citadel Press, 1995), 42.

2   Michael E. Lomax, *Black Baseball Entrepreneurs, 1902-1931: The Negro National and Eastern Colored Leagues* (Syracuse, New York: Syracuse University Press, 2014), 4; Neil Lanctot, *Fair Dealing & Clean Playing: The Hilldale Club and the Development of Black Professional Baseball, 1910-1932*, (Syracuse, New York: Syracuse University Press, 1994), 32.

3   Larry Lester, *Rube Foster in His Time: On the Field and in the Papers with Black Baseball's Greatest Visionary* (Jefferson, North Carolina: McFarland & Co., Inc., 2012), 48.

4   Paul Debono, *The Chicago American Giants* (Jefferson, North Carolina: McFarland & Co., Inc., 2007), 37.

5   Debono, 64.

6   Lanctot, *Fair Dealing & Clean Playing*, 78.

7   Debono, 95-96.

8   Lester, 58.

9   Lomax, 389.

10   Debono, 120.

11   Debono, 121.

12   Lomax: 399.

13   Debono, 125.

14   Neil Lanctot, *Negro League Baseball: The Rise and Ruin of a Black Institution* (Philadelphia: University of Pennsylvania Press, 2004), 26.

15   Lanctot, *Negro League Baseball*, 46.

16   Lanctot, *Negro League Baseball*, 50.

17   Debono, 155.

18   Debono, 170.

19   Debono, 182.

20   Debono, 193.

21   Debono, 93,

22   Debono, 185, 209; Bob Towner, "Hittable but Magical, That's Satchel Paige," *South Bend Tribune*, July 7, 1951, accessed at: https://michianamemory.sjcpl.org/digital/collection/p16827coll14/id/152/.

CONTRIBUTORS

John Bauer resides with his wife and two children in Bedford, New Hampshire. By day, he is an attorney specializing in insurance regulatory law and corporate law. By night, he spends many spring and summer evenings cheering for the San Francisco Giants, and many fall and winter evenings reading history. He is a past and ongoing contributor to other SABR and baseball history projects.

Peter C. Bjarkman, the author of more than three dozen books on sport, was the recipient of SABR's Henry Chadwick Award in 2017, the Society's highest award for baseball research. His most prominent work was on Cuban baseball. He was a frequent contributor to LaVidaBaseball.com and the US-based internet website BaseballdeCuba.com, and appeared frequently on radio and television sports talk shows. He was author of *A History of Cuban Baseball 1864-2006* and (with Mark Rucker) *Smoke: The Romance and Lore of Cuban Baseball*. He was co-editor of the 2016 SABR book *Baseball's Alternative Universe: Cuban Baseball Legends*. He died in Havana in October 2018.

Richard Bogovich's new book in 2022 is *Frank Grant: The Life of a Black Baseball Pioneer*. For McFarland & Co. he'd previously written *Kid Nichols: A Biography of the Hall of Fame Pitcher* and *The Who: A Who's Who*. He has contributed to such SABR books as *When the Monarchs Reigned: Kansas City's 1942 Negro League Champions* and *The Newark Eagles Take Flight: The Story of the 1946 Negro League Champions*. He works for the Wendland Utz law firm in Rochester, Minnesota.

Frederick C. "Rick" Bush joined SABR in March 2014. Since that time, he has written articles for numerous SABR books as well as the Biography and Games Project websites. The current volume about the 1920 Chicago American Giants is the fifth in a series of SABR books about notable Negro League teams that he has co-edited with Bill Nowlin. Previous volumes include *Bittersweet Goodbye: The Black Barons, the Grays, and the 1948 Negro League World Series* (2017); *The Newark Eagles Take Flight: The Story of the 1946 Negro League Champions* (2019); *Pride of Smoketown: The 1935 Pittsburgh Crawfords* (2020); and *When the Monarchs Reigned: Kansas City's 1942 Negro League Champions* (2021). A sixth book about the 1934 Philadelphia Stars is already in progress. Rick lives with his wife, Michelle, their three sons, Michael, Andrew, and Daniel, and their border collie, Bailey, in the greater Houston area. He teaches English at Wharton County Junior College's satellite campus in Sugar Land, the home of the Astros' Triple-A affiliate.

A lifelong White Sox fan surrounded by Cubs fans in the northern suburbs of Chicago, **Ken Carrano** works as chief financial officer for a large landscaping firm and as a soccer referee. He has been a SABR member since 1992, and has contributed to several SABR publications and the SABR Games Project. Ken and his Brewers' fan wife, Ann, share two children, two golden retrievers, and a mutual distain for the blue side of Chicago.

Margaret M. "Peggy" Gripshover is a professor of geography at Western Kentucky University. She earned her Ph.D. in Geography at the University of Tennessee and her M.S. and B.S. degrees in Geography from Marshall University. She has been a SABR member since 2006 and combines her love of baseball with her geographic research on race, ethnicity, urbanization, horse racing, and cultural landscapes. Peggy has published articles in the *Baseball Research Journal*, contributed a chapter to *Northsiders: Essays on the History and Culture of the Chicago Cubs*, edited by Gerald R. Wood and Andy Hazucha (McFarland, 2008). She also wrote chapters for *Bittersweet Goodbye: The Black Barons, the Grays, and the 1948 Negro League World Series* (SABR 2017); *The Newark Eagles Take Flight: The Story of the 1946 Negro League Champions* (SABR 2019); *Pride of Smoketown: The 1935 Pittsburgh Crawfords* (SABR 2020); and *When the Monarchs Reigned: Kansas City's 1942 Negro League Champions* (SABR 2021), all edited by Frederick C. Bush and Bill Nowlin. She is a native of Cincinnati and a lifelong Reds fan. She lives in Bowling Green, Kentucky, with her husband, Thomas L. Bell, and their Australian shepherd, Bella.

Chris Hicks began watching baseball with his grandfather as a child, which led to a lifelong passion for the game and his local Kansas City Royals. A wheelchair user since childhood, Chris became interested in the history of the game and the baseball card collecting hobby. His uncle took him to a Monarchs reunion in the early 1990s. This began years of learning independently about the history of the game. He joined SABR in 2020.

Bill Johnson is a longtime SABR member and has contributed biographies to several SABR BioProject books, including *The Pride of Smoketown* and *That's Joy in Braveland*. He and his wife live in Hinesville, Georgia.

Thomas E. Kern was born and raised in Southwest Pennsylvania. Listening to the mellifluous voices of Bob Prince and Jim Woods in his youth, how could one not become a lifelong Pirates fan? He now lives in Silver Spring, Maryland, and sees the Nationals and Orioles as often as possible. He is a SABR member dating back to the mid-1980s. With a love and appreciation for Negro League Baseball, he has written SABR bios for Leon Day, John Henry Lloyd, Willie Foster, Judy Johnson, Turkey Stearnes, Hilton Smith, Louis Santop, and Buck Ewing. Tom's day job is in the field of transportation technology.

Sean Kolodziej, a SABR member since 2018, is a lifelong Cubs fan. He was born, raised, and still lives in Joliet, Illinois, with his wife, Amy. His greatest moment at Wrigley Field was watching Glenallen Hill hit a home run onto the rooftop of a building on Waveland Avenue.

For over 20 years, **Kevin Larkin** patrolled the highways and byways of the roads in his home town of Great Barrington, Massachusetts. When not at work keeping the citizens of his hometown safe, inevitably Larkin was listening to a baseball game on the radio. He has been going to baseball games since he was 5 years old. His baseball life is the only thing he loves more than his children and grandchildren. One day while he was browsing in a local bookstore, the owner asked him if he was interested in writing a book about baseball. Larkin's first effort was *Baseball in the Bay State: A History of Baseball in Massachusetts*. He then took quite an interest in the history of the game, authoring a book on one of his heroes, Lou Gehrig, called *Gehrig: Game by Game*, a look at every game the Iron Horse played during his major-league career. He has since written three more books on the sport and had two more due out in the summer of 2022. He writes and fact-checks for SABR, an experience he considers the best decision he has ever made. He also hosts a baseball history show on a local radio station. According to Larkin, writing about baseball is a great way to keep the memory of the sport alive and he will continue to delve into sports history with more to come.

Len Levin is a longtime newspaper editor in New England, now retired. He lives in Providence with his wife, Linda, and an overachieving orange cat. He now (Len, not the cat) is the grammarian for the Rhode Island Supreme Court and edits its decisions. He also copyedits many SABR books, including this one. He is just down the interstate from Fenway Park, where he has spent many happy hours.

Robert Nash is a retired special collections librarian and professor emeritus at the University of Nebraska at Omaha. A SABR member since 1992, he previously contributed to SABR's *Kansas City Royals: A Royal Tradition* and *Jackie: Perspectives on 42*. His research on baseball has also been published in McFarland's *Rosenblatt Stadium: Essays and Memories of Omaha's Historic Ballpark, 1948-2012* and *The African American Baseball Experience in Nebraska*.

Bill Nowlin was born in Boston, and grew up in Lexington, Massachusetts ("The Birthplace of American Liberty"), where he guided tourists around the Battle Green for summers all through high school and college. The same month he began teaching political science at university in 1970, he founded the Rounder Records label with two friends. Retired and living in Cambridge, Massachusetts, he has enjoyed writing for SABR publications and helping edit books for SABR as well. His father sold hot dogs at Fenway Park in the 1930s; he has eaten many hot dogs there in later decades.

Tim Odzer has been a SABR member since 2011. Passionate about baseball from an early age, Tim contributes to both the BioProject and the Games Project. A 2019 graduate of the University of Chicago Law School, Tim practices as an attorney in Miami. When not working, he often is at a Marlins game.

Richard J. Puerzer is an associate professor and chairperson of the Department of Engineering at Hofstra University. He has contributed to several SABR Books, including, *Bittersweet Goodbye: The Black Barons, The Grays, and the 1948 Negro League World Series* (2017), *Moments of Joy and Heartbreak: 66 Significant Episodes in the History of the Pittsburgh Pirates* (2018), *The Newark Eagles Take Flight: The Story of the 1946 Negro League Champions* (2019), and *Pride of Smoketown: The 1935 Pittsburgh Crawfords* (2020). His writings on baseball have also appeared in *Nine: A Journal of Baseball History and Culture; Black Ball; The National Pastime; The Cooperstown Symposium on Baseball and American Culture proceedings; Zisk;* and *Spitball.*

Stephen V. Rice, Ph.D., hails from Detroit and lives in Collierville, Tennessee. He has authored 150 articles for the SABR BioProject and Games Project. In his day job, he is a software architect in the Computational Biology department at St. Jude Children's Research Hospital in Memphis.

Carl Riechers retired from United Parcel Service in 2012 after 35 years of service. With more free time, he became a SABR member that same year. Born and raised in the suburbs of St. Louis, he became a big fan of the Cardinals. He and his wife, Janet, have three children and he is the proud grandpa of two.

Joal Ryan is a Los Angeles-based journalist. She's penned a Motherlode piece for the *New York Times* about coaching her son's rec baseball teams, and has contributed to the *Los Angeles Times*, 247Sports, CNET, Yahoo!, and more. She joined SABR in 2021.

Jeb Stewart is a lawyer in Birmingham, Alabama, who enjoys taking his sons, Nolan and Ryan, and his wife, Stephanie, to the Rickwood Classic each year. He has been a SABR member since 2012 and is co-president of the Rickwood Field SABR Chapter. He is an executive committee member on the Board of the Friends of Rickwood Field and is a regular contributor to the *Rickwood Times*. He also edits the Friends' quarterly newsletter, "Rickwood Tales." He has written several biographies for SABR's Baseball Biography Project.

Dave Wilkie is an elementary teacher at Central Montessori School in Richmond, Virginia, where he lives with his wife and son. He grew up in Western Canada idolizing Willie McCovey and the San Francisco Giants. His obsession with Negro League baseball can be traced to a 1983 mail-order purchase of the book *The All-Time All-Stars of Black Baseball*, by SABR member James A. Riley. He has written SABR biographies on Negro League greats Sam Bankhead, Johnny Davis, Chester Williams, Cool Papa Bell, and Frank Duncan. He plans to continue writing biographies on these forgotten legends with the hopes of publishing his own book some day.

SABR Books on the Negro Leagues and Black Baseball

From Rube to Robinson: SABR's Best Articles on Black Baseball

From Rube to Robinson brings together the best Negro League baseball scholarship that the Society of American Baseball Research (SABR) has ever produced, culled from its journals, Biography Project, and award-winning essays. The book includes a star-studded list of scholars and historians, from the late Jerry Malloy and Jules Tygiel, to award winners Larry Lester, Geri Strecker, and Jeremy Beer, and a host of other talented writers. The essays cover topics ranging over nearly a century, from 1866 and the earliest known Black baseball championship, to 1962 and the end of the Negro American League.

Edited by John Graf; Associate Editors Duke Goldman and Larry Lester
$24.95 paperback (ISBN 978-1-970159-41-7)
$9.99 ebook (ISBN 978-1-970159-40-0)
8.5"X11", 220 pages

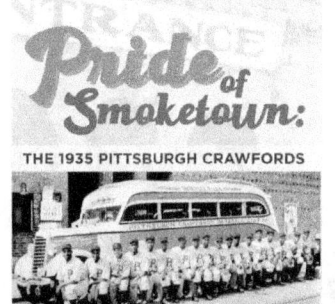

Pride of Smoketown: The 1935 Pittsburgh Crawfords

The 1935 Pittsburgh Crawfords team, one of the dominant teams in Negro League history, is often compared to the legendary 1927 "Murderer's Row" New York Yankees. The squad from "Smoketown"—a nickname that the *Pittsburgh Courier* often applied to the metropolis better-known as "Steel City"—boasted four Hall-of-Fame players in outfielder James "Cool Papa" Bell, first baseman/manager Oscar Charleston, catcher Josh Gibson, and third baseman William "Judy" Johnson. This volume contains exhaustively-researched articles about the players, front office personnel, Greenlee Field, and the exciting games and history of the team that were written and edited by 25 SABR members. The inclusion of historical photos about every subject in the book helps to shine a spotlight on the 1935 Pittsburgh Crawfords, who truly were the Pride of Smoketown.

Edited by Frederick C. Bush and Bill Nowlin
$29.95 paperback (ISBN 978-1-970159-25-7)
$9.99 ebook (ISBN 978-1-970159-24-0)
8.5"X11", 340 pages, over 60 photos

The Newark Eagles Take Flight: The Story of the 1946 Negro League Champions

The Newark Eagles won only one Negro National League pennant during the franchise's 15-year tenure in the Garden State, but the 1946 squad that ran away with the NNL and then triumphed over the Kansas City Monarchs in a seven-game World Series was a team for the ages. The returning WWII veterans composed a veritable "Who's Who in the Negro Leagues" and included Leon Day, Larry Doby, Monte Irvin, and Max Manning, as well as numerous role players. Four of the Eagles' stars—Day, Doby, Irvin, and player/manager Raleigh "Biz" Mackey, as well as co-owner Effa Manley—have been enshrined in the National Baseball Hall of Fame in Cooperstown. In addition to biographies of the players, co-owners, and P.A. announcer, there are also articles about Newark's Ruppert Stadium, Leon Day's Opening Day no-hitter, a sensational midseason game, the season's two East-West All-Star Games, and the 1946 Negro League World Series between the Eagles and the renowned Kansas City Monarchs.

Edited by Frederick C. Bush and Bill Nowlin
$24.95 paperback (ISBN 978-1-970159-07-3)
$9.99 ebook (ISBN 978-1-970159-06-6)
8.5"X11", 228 pages, over 60 photos

Bittersweet Goodbye: The Black Barons, The Grays, and the 1948 Negro League World Series

This book was inspired by the last Negro League World Series ever played and presents biographies of the players on the two contending teams in 1948—the Birmingham Black Barons and the Homestead Grays—as well as the managers, the owners, and articles on the ballparks the teams called home. Also included are articles that recap the season's two East-West All-Star Games, the Negro National League and Negro American League playoff series, and the World Series itself. Additional context is provided in essays about the effects of baseball's integration on the Negro Leagues, the exodus of Negro League players to Canada, and the signing away of top Negro League players, specifically Willie Mays. Many of the players' lives and careers have been presented to a much greater extent than previously possible.

Edited by Frederick C. Bush and Bill Nowlin
$21.95 paperback (ISBN 978-1-943816-55-2)
$9.99 ebook (ISBN 978-1-943816-54-5)
8.5"X11", 442 pages, over 100 photos and images

Friends of SABR

You can become a Friend of SABR by giving as little as $10 per month or by making a one-time gift of $1,000 or more. When you do so, you will be inducted into a community of passionate baseball fans dedicated to supporting SABR's work.

Friends of SABR receive the following benefits:
- ✓ Annual Friends of SABR Commemorative Lapel Pin
- ✓ Recognition in This Week in SABR, SABR.org, and the SABR Annual Report
- ✓ Access to the SABR Annual Convention VIP donor event
- ✓ Invitations to exclusive Friends of SABR events

SABR On-Deck Circle - $10/month, $30/month, $50/month
Get in the SABR On-Deck Circle, and help SABR become the essential community for the world of baseball. Your support will build capacity around all things SABR, including publications, website content, podcast development, and community growth.

A monthly gift is deducted from your bank account or charged to a credit card until you tell us to stop. No more email, mail, or phone reminders.

  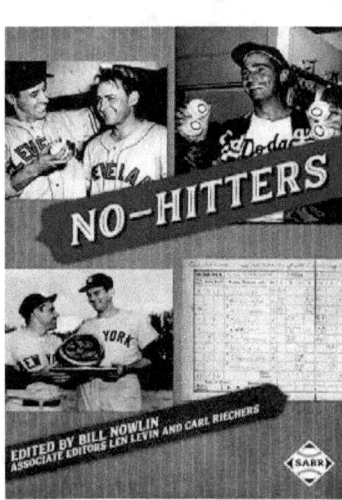

Join the SABR On-Deck Circle

Payment Info: _____Visa _____Mastercard

Name on Card: _____

Card #: _____

Exp. Date: _____ Security Code: _____

Signature: _____

- ○ $10/month
- ○ $30/month
- ○ $50/month
- ○ Other amount _____

Go to sabr.org/donate to make your gift online

Society for American Baseball Research

Cronkite School at ASU
555 N. Central Ave. #416, Phoenix, AZ 85004
602.496.1460 (phone)
SABR.org

Become a SABR member today!

If you're interested in baseball — writing about it, reading about it, talking about it — there's a place for you in the Society for American Baseball Research.

SABR memberships are available on annual, multi-year, or monthly subscription basis. Annual and monthly subscription memberships auto-renew for your convenience. Young Professional memberships are for ages 30 and under. Senior memberships are for ages 65 and older. Student memberships are available to currently enrolled middle/high school or full-time college/university students. Monthly subscription members receive SABR publications electronically and are eligible for SABR event discounts after 12 months.

Here's a list of some of the key benefits you'll receive as a SABR member:

- Receive two editions (spring and fall) of the *Baseball Research Journal*, our flagship publication
- Receive expanded e-book edition of *The National Pastime*, our annual convention journal
- 8-10 new e-books published by the SABR Digital Library, all FREE to members
- "This Week in SABR" e-newsletter, sent to members every Friday
- Join dozens of research committees, from Statistical Analysis to Women in Baseball.
- Join one of 70+ regional chapters in the U.S., Canada, Latin America, and abroad
- Participate in online discussion groups
- Ask and answer baseball research questions on the SABR-L e-mail listserv
- Complete archives of *The Sporting News* dating back to 1886 and other research resources
- Promote your research in "This Week in SABR"
- Diamond Dollars Case Competition
- Yoseloff Scholarships

- Discounts on SABR national conferences, including the SABR National Convention, the SABR Analytics Conference, Jerry Malloy Negro League Conference, Frederick Ivor-Campbell 19th Century Conference, and the Arizona Fall League Experience
- Publish your research in peer-reviewed SABR journals
- Collaborate with SABR researchers and experts
- Contribute to Baseball Biography Project or the SABR Games Project
- List your new book in the SABR Bookshelf
- Lead a SABR research committee or chapter
- Networking opportunities at SABR Analytics Conference
- Meet baseball authors and historians at SABR events and chapter meetings
- 50% discounts on paperback versions of SABR e-books
- Discounts with other partners in the baseball community
- SABR research awards

We hope you'll join the most passionate international community of baseball fans at SABR! Check us out online at SABR.org/join.

SABR MEMBERSHIP FORM

	Standard	Senior	Young Pro.	Student
Annual:	❑ $65	❑ $45	❑ $45	❑ $25
3 Year:	❑ $175	❑ $129	❑ $129	
5 Year:	❑ $249			
Monthly:	❑ $6.95	❑ $4.95	❑ $4.95	

(International members wishing to be mailed the Baseball Research Journal should add $10/yr for Canada/Mexico or $19/yr for overseas locations.)

Participate in Our Donor Program!

Support the preservation of baseball research. Designate your gift toward:
❑ General Fund ❑ Endowment Fund ❑ Research Resources ❑_____
❑ I want to maximize the impact of my gift; do not send any donor premiums
❑ I would like this gift to remain anonymous.

Note: Any donation not designated will be placed in the General Fund.
SABR is a 501 (c) (3) not-for-profit organization & donations are tax-deductible to the extent allowed by law.

Name _____

E-mail* _____

Address _____

City _____ ST_____ ZIP_____

Phone _____ Birthday _____

* Your e-mail address on file ensures you will receive the most recent SABR news.

Dues $_____

Donation $_____

Amount Enclosed $_____

Do you work for a matching grant corporation? Call (602) 496-1460 for details.

If you wish to pay by credit card, please contact the SABR office at (602) 496-1460 or sign up securely online at SABR.org/join. We accept Visa, Mastercard & Discover.

Do you wish to receive the *Baseball Research Journal* electronically? ❑ Yes ❑ No
Our e-books are available in PDF, Kindle, or EPUB (iBooks, iPad, Nook) formats.

Mail to: SABR, Cronkite School at ASU, 555 N. Central Ave. #416, Phoenix, AZ 85004

10/19

www.ingramcontent.com/pod-product-compliance
Lightning Source LLC
Chambersburg PA
CBHW080955120626
46546CB00010B/2898